Ideology in Language Use

The relationship between language and ideology has long been central to research in discourse analysis, pragmatics, sociolinguistics, and linguistic anthropology, and has also informed other fields such as sociology and literary criticism. This book, by one of the world's leading pragmaticists, introduces a new framework for the study of ideology in written language, using the tools, methods, and theories of pragmatics and discourse analysis. Illustrations are drawn systematically from a coherent corpus of excerpts from late nineteenth- and early twentieth-century history textbooks dealing with episodes of colonial history, and in particular the 1857 'Indian Mutiny.' It includes the complete corpus of excerpts, allowing researchers and students to evaluate all illustrations; at the same time, this provides useful practice and training materials. The book is intended not only as a teaching tool in language-, discourse-, and communication-oriented programs, but also for historians and social and political scientists.

JEF VERSCHUEREN is a professor in the Department of Linguistics at the University of Antwerp.

Ideology in Language Use

Pragmatic Guidelines for Empirical Research

JEF VERSCHUEREN

IPrA Research Center, University of Antwerp
and
Monash University, Melbourne / EHESS-Maison des Sciences de l'Homme, Paris

CAMBRIDGE
UNIVERSITY PRESS

CAMBRIDGE UNIVERSITY PRESS
Cambridge, New York, Melbourne, Madrid, Cape Town,
Singapore, São Paulo, Delhi, Mexico City

Cambridge University Press
The Edinburgh Building, Cambridge CB2 8RU, UK

Published in the United States of America by Cambridge University Press, New York

www.cambridge.org
Information on this title: www.cambridge.org/9781107695900

First published 2012
First paperback edition 2013

A catalogue record for this publication is available from the British Library

Library of Congress Cataloguing in Publication Data
Verschueren, Jef.
  Ideology in language use : pragmatic guidelines for empirical research / Jef Verschueren.
    p.   cm.
  Includes bibliographical references and index.
  ISBN 978-1-107-00652-2
  1. Language and culture.   2. Ideology.   3. Discourse analysis–Social aspects.
  4. Pragmatics.   I. Title.
  P35.V527 2011
  306.44–dc23
  2011041575

ISBN 978-1-107-00652-2 Hardback
ISBN 978-1-107-69590-0 Paperback

To the memory of Tim McDaniel:
True scholar, great friend

Contents

Figures

Tables

Preface

The public sphere is an arena with never-ending struggles over meaning. Situations may 'arise' but, more often than not, human agents are involved whose decisions and actions are based on assessments of and disputes over a present or prior context as well as hopes for the future. Decisions have to be argued for in advance. Actions may require subsequent legitimation. The idea that an issue – any issue – could be settled once and for all is an illusion. Not so long ago, for instance, some of us were convinced that Europeans' views of their past as colonizers had finally matured, a strongly critical stance being allowed to come to the foreground. As in other areas of debate, however, the pendulum kept swinging. A social and political dynamics trying to cope with more recent questions concerning diversity and patterns of dominance, and the possible conclusions one might have to draw on the basis of an admission of past errors, led, in France, to the adoption of law 2005-158 (23 February 2005), "portant reconnaissance de la Nation et contribution nationale en faveur des Français rapatriés."[1] Article 1 says,

> La Nation exprime sa reconnaissance aux femmes et aux hommes qui ont participé à l'oeuvre accomplie par la France dans les anciens départements français d'Algérie, au Maroc, en Tunisie et en Indochine ainsi que dans les territoires placés antérieurement sous la souveraineté française.[2]

With this opening article, as well as with the title, this law casts itself as a means of protecting French citizens who served in former French colonies against undue personal disregard and disapprobation. This is fully compatible with the many practical measures specified in the law to the benefit of those citizens, or with an article explicitly prohibiting attacks on anyone identifiable as or supposed to have been an *harki*, an Algerian soldier loyal to the French during the Algerian War of Independence. This noble goal of protecting individuals who can barely be held responsible *as* individuals for policies of the state is used in passing,

---

[1] See Claude Liauzu (2005); "bearing on recognition of the Nation and the national contribution in favor of the repatriated French." Note that, throughout this book, all translations from French sources are my own.

[2] "The Nation expresses its recognition of the women and men who have participated in the work accomplished by France in the former French departments in Algeria, Morocco, Tunisia, and Indochina as well as in the territories placed earlier under French sovereignty."

however, as a frame of legitimation for measures with clear *ideological signifi-cance*. Thus Article 4 says,

> Les programmes de recherche universitaire accordent à l'histoire de la présence française outre-mer, notamment en Afrique du Nord, la place qu'elle mérite.

> Les programmes scolaires reconnaissent en particulier le rôle positif de la présence française outre-mer, notamment en Afrique du Nord, et accordent à l'histoire et aux sacrifices des combattants de l'armée française issus de ces territoires la place éminente à laquelle ils ont droit.[3]

This is a straightforward instruction for history writing and history teaching. The heart of the matter is a definition of events, discursively generated meaning, which enters the cycle of assessments, arguments, decisions, actions, legitimations.

The purpose of this book is to provide a research tool, methodological build-ing blocks, for the investigation of such processes. Its background is linguistic pragmatics, the interdisciplinary science of *language use*. But the target audience includes students in all fields of inquiry to which the societal construction of frames of reference or ways of viewing actions and events, as mediated through discourse, is relevant: historians, sociologists, anthropologists, and political sci-entists, to name just a few broad categories.

The book has been specifically designed for training purposes. That is why there is an extensive appendix (Appendix 2) with the texts I use for purposes of illustration – all taken from history textbooks published during the transition years from the nineteenth to the twentieth century and bearing on colonial his-tory. No full-scale analysis is provided. Rather, issues for analytical attention are defined and illustrated. Appendix 2 is sufficiently rich to allow further prac-tice of all angles of approach reviewed in this book without a student having to go through the process of looking for appropriate materials which require their own contextual specifications before matters of detail can be addressed. These extracts are also available online at www.cambridge.org/verschueren

Unoriginal as it may sound, this book has been much too long in the mak-ing. A skeletal picture was presented as early as 1996 at the 5th International Pragmatics Conference in Mexico City. First it had to wait for two other book projects to be completed, then an eight-year spell as dean of my faculty at the University of Antwerp took my mind and time in other directions.

During that latter period, fortunately, I enjoyed a three-month research stay at Monash University (June–September 2004), during which the first half of this book was written. I will be forever grateful to Keith Allan for inviting me and providing a stimulating environment for research, which has led to other

---

[3] "University research programs give the history of French overseas presence, specifically in North Africa, the place it deserves.

Educational programs recognize in particular the positive role of the French overseas presence, specifically in North Africa, and grant the history and the sacrifices of the soldiers in the French army coming from these territories the eminent place to which they are entitled."

fruitful forms of collaboration as well (most recently, the organization of the 11th International Pragmatics Conference, July 2009, in Melbourne); to Marko Pavlyshyn and Brian Nelson, heads – before and after my arrival, respectively – of my host institution, the School of Languages, Cultures and Linguistics; to Irene Romanowski and Lona Gottschalk, for their logistical support; to Brian Gerrard and Richard Overell of the Rare Books section of Monash's Sir Louis Matheson Library, who were helpful beyond the call of duty while I was collecting most of the sources I am now using as illustrative data; and to many Melbourne colleagues, including Kate Burridge, Michael Clyne, Marisa Cordella, Ana Deumert, and Anna Margetts, for useful discussions.

After Monash, the half-finished manuscript entered a dormant state again, to the great frustration of a number of doctoral students who could have used better-developed methodological advice in their language-and-ideology-related endeavors, until I emerged from the deanship at the end of September 2009. I completed this book while enjoying the hospitality of the École des hautes études en sciences sociales (ÉHESS) and the Maison des sciences de l'homme (MSH) in Paris. I owe a serious debt of gratitude to Michel de Fornel (Centre linguistique anthropologique et sociolinguistique), and Louis Quéré (Centre d'études des mouvements sociaux) for their kind invitations to ÉHESS, Institut Marcel Mauss; to Michel Wieviorka, Director of the Fondation MSH, and Jean-Luc Lory, Director of the Maison Suger (Fondation MSH), for providing the unparalleled hospitality at 16–18 rue Suger; to the entire staff of the Maison Suger for making life so easy. I also thank FWO-Vlaanderen for financially supporting the sabbatical year I was enjoying, the University of Antwerp for granting me a leave of absence, and Bruno Tritsmans, my successor as dean of the Faculty of Arts, for systematically not bothering me with all the unfinished business I left behind.

In the course of the past fifteen years, roughly, I have been able to benefit from working with many students and close colleagues, traces of whose contributions are no doubt to be found in the following pages. A minimal list includes Kaspar Beelen, Jan Blommaert, Frank Brisard, Chris Bulcaen, Eric Caers, Jonathan Clifton, Roel Coesemans, Pol Cuvelier, Helge Daniëls, Walter De Mulder, Patrick Dendale, Sigurd D'hondt, Gino Eelen, Isabel Gomez Diez, Geert Jacobs, Jürgen Jaspers, Lut Lams, Gilberte Lenaerts, Katrijn Maryns, Michael Meeuwis, Liesbeth Michiels, Eva Palmans, Stefanie Peeters, Kim Sleurs, Dorien Van de Mieroop, Sarah Van Hoof, Tom Van Hout, Eline Versluys, Matylda Weidner, and Jan Zienkowski. Outside this immediate past and present circle, in order not to forget too many colleagues whose ideas have had an impact on my own thinking, I must restrict myself to a few of the guests received at the IPrA Research Center (ipra.ua.ac.be) over the years: Monica Aznárez, Teresa Carbó, Paul Chilton, Jenny Cook-Gumperz, Carmen Curcó, Baudouin Dupret, Irene Fonte, John Gumperz, 'Daisy' Jiang Hui, Monika Kopytowska, Rūta Marčinkevicienė, Luisa Martín Rojo, Inés Olza, Rod Watson, Igor Žagar, and, last but not least, Jan-Ola Östman, who is probably my steadiest fellow traveler in academia. I would like to reserve a special mention for three historians. Steven Epstein strengthened my belief in the potential relevance of a pragmatics-based approach to historical data during the discussions we had while we were co-residents at the Bellagio Study and Conference Center (February–March 1997) and by demonstrating it in his *Speaking of Slavery* (2001). At the University of Antwerp, interesting collaboration on historical data is being developed with Henk de Smaele and Marnix Beyen; Marnix also undertook a thorough critical reading of the post-Melbourne half of the manuscript, saving me from some important errors. Finally, this book benefits from a last-minute reading by Johannes Angermüller, and from extensive comments by Rod Watson and two anonymous reviewers as well as a dedicated editor, Helen Barton, production editor Elizabeth Davey, and copy-editor Karen Anderson Howes at Cambridge University Press. All remaining mistakes are of course my own responsibility.

Acknowledgements are not complete without thanking Ann Verhaert (some 13,000+ times) for sharing work and life.

Every effort has been made to secure necessary permissions to reproduce copyright material in this work, though in some cases it has proved impossible to trace copyright holders. If any omissions are brought to our notice, we will be happy to include appropriate acknowledgements in any subsequent edition.

Introduction

Consider a few simple anecdotes that may clarify the topic of this book and hint at its basic tenets.

The first one relates to an old friend who once said, when our conversation turned to a war that was front-page news at the time, "Let ideologies die, let people live." A lifetime of experience lay behind this recipe. Born a Bolivian German, he received his education in Germany in the 1930s. Imbued with Nazi propaganda, he enlisted, was sent to the eastern front, and survived a dangerous head injury, but would have gone back to fight if he had been strong enough after his recovery. His beliefs were not shaken until most of the cruel and criminal realities of the Nazi regime had been fully exposed, forcing the viewpoint of the victims upon anyone who did not refuse to see. During the days when we were neighbors in his new home country, the USA, he used to frown a bit sadly whenever his president explained why another war needed to be fought. *Déjà vu.* And he understood why the rhetoric worked.

In a different context, I listened to Regina Schwartz's story of how she used to teach about the Bible with great enthusiasm. She viewed the Exodus as the central event of the narrative, a myth of liberation directly relevant to cries for freedom and emancipation movements of the day. Until a student asked, "What about the Canaanites?" This embarrassing shift of perspective, focusing on the conquest and exile of the 'Others', led to her book-length answer to the student's question, *The Curse of Cain* (Schwartz 1997), in which she unveils the other side of the Bible as a story of collective identity construction (one God, one land, one people, one nation) which may lend itself – and often did – to endless legitimations of violence and injustice.

The third anecdote bears on personal experience as a seventeen-year-old Flemish student in the late 1960s, when I participated in a demonstration demanding separation between the Francophone and the Flemish parts of the University of Leuven, and the removal of the Francophone section from the Flemish city of Leuven altogether. Riding the waves of the international student movement of those days, we were led to believe that we were fighting for democracy by returning to Francophone Belgium their own university (which would make it less 'elitist') while safeguarding Flanders from another 'oil slick' such as the bilingual (but French-dominated) Brussels spreading in the middle of Flemish territory.[1] Years later, as a graduate student in Berkeley, a Jewish-American fellow student asked me during a dinner party to explain why the University of Leuven had to be split in two. It struck me that I had never really questioned the measures that were taken, even though in the process an entire new city was created, Louvain-la-Neuve. I did not get beyond the reproduction of commonplaces such as "Otherwise Leuven would have become another Brussels." "What is so terrible about Brussels?" my interrogator continued. I parroted some more platitudes until the crossexamination culminated in a verdict: "Look, Nazi prosecution of German Jews did not start with concentration camps – it started with relocations!" It did not take me too much longer, fortunately, to understand that the 'Belgian model' for dealing with diversity, which I had never questioned (imagine, an aspiring linguist not questioning the institutionalization of a language border, nor the equation – even if metaphorical – of the spread of a language with environmental pollution!), was in fact a peaceful version of what would, years later, be called 'ethnic cleansing.'

These are just three anecdotes, but each of them illustrates the strength of what is commonly referred to as *ideology*. Once ways of thinking about relations between groups of people are felt to be 'normal', they may become powerful tools for legitimating attitudes, behavior, and policies, whatever the frequently negative consequences in terms of discrimination, patterns of dominance, and even violence. Each of the anecdotes also shows, however, that changes of perspective are possible. Such shifts usually require critical incidents, but since ideological struggle (and, by extension, most social struggle) centers around *meaning*, simple acts of *questioning* may be enough. Its power and its change-ability[2] turn ideology into a necessary object of systematic scrutiny in the social sciences. Research may not only help us to gain a better understanding of some of the processes of meaning generation that affect everyone's life, but it may also provoke the kind of questioning needed to pave the way for attempts at improving the fate of the less powerful. This expression of hope is purposefully naïve, aware of the limited contribution a researcher can make, but refusing to

---

[1] Note the subtly aberrant use of "returning." The Francophone section of the University of Leuven had never been anywhere outside Leuven, where French and later (Flemish) Dutch became the languages of teaching after Latin had been abandoned. For those too young to remember, or too far removed: The establishment of a language border in 1963 created two officially monolingual territories in Belgium, the outcome of what started as an emancipatory struggle ending the *de facto* dominance of French in public institutional life in spite of the numerical majority of Flemish speakers. It left only Brussels as a bilingual island in otherwise Flemish territory. In that context, the presence of a partly Francophone institution in the Flemish city of Leuven was felt to be an 'undemocratic' anomaly by many Flemish politicians and activists.

[2] Changeability takes different forms. It may also mean, for instance, that perspectives are not necessarily applied logically in the same way to the same types of phenomena at different times or in different contexts. I will come back to this property of ideologies later. But it may be useful to point to an example here: The old friend from the first anecdote suddenly showed fewer objections when the bombing of Yugoslavia started under the Clinton administration. Yugoslavia was at the time the only remaining European communist country; though he had obviously shed the old Nazi ideology, it may simply have been harder to get rid of the corresponding (but easily detachable) anti-communism.

be immobilized by such awareness. The limitations are serious indeed. In order to have any impact, changes of perspective should extend beyond the individual. Some of the more effective instruments to bring this about are education and the mass media; though both are indeed instruments of change, they are also entangled in the structures of power that will resist change.[3] Moreover, any new perspective is susceptible to unpredictable transformations and applications. A permanent monitoring of ideological processes, therefore, is imperative.

In other words, I fully side with Eagleton's (2007, p. xxiii) observation that "it is because people do not cease to desire, struggle and imagine, even in the most apparently unpropitious of conditions, that the practice of political emancipation is a genuine possibility." However constraining frames of thought may be, people do not just passively absorb them; the importance – and potential – of agency should never be ignored.

There has been a lot of theorizing about ideology. It would take us too far – and within the scope of one small book certainly not far enough – to give an overview. For a history of the concept and an overview of its various manifestations, I would refer the reader to McLellan (1995), Heywood (2007), and Billig (1982), depending on whether one wants a brief introduction, a focus on political issues, or an emphasis on social-psychological implications, respectively. An interesting selection of readings, some more basic than others, is to be found in Žižek (ed.) (1994). Theoretically coherent treatments of the topic, from an angle that is closely related to my own, are developed by Thompson (1984, 1990, 1995) and – possibly with the closest affinity to the tenets of this book – by Eagleton (2007). Also relevant is the tradition of the sociology of knowledge (Mannheim 1936, Berger and Luckmann 1966), which often deals with ideological issues without using that term, as well as the microsociological, praxis-oriented, often ethnomethodological studies of the situated production of knowledge (e.g., Garfinkel 1967, Goffman 1981). For a critical elaboration of some of the fundamental issues involved in the connections between discourse and power or between discourse and knowledge, in relation to which ideology can be defined, the reader may turn, for instance, to Bourdieu (1991), Foucault (1972), or the Frankfurt School of Critical Theory (e.g., Habermas 1979). My own theoretical starting point is summarized as briefly as possible in Chapter 1 of this book.[4]

What must be kept in mind from the outset is that my use of the term 'ideology' bears on much more mundane and everyday processes than the grand political

---

[3] On a similar note, Hobsbawm (1997, p. 363) says, "The third limitation on the historian's function as mythslayer is even more obvious. In the short run they are impotent against those who choose to believe historical myth, especially if they hold political power, which, in many countries, and especially the numerous new states, entails control over what is still the most important channel of imparting historical information, the schools." He adds: "These limitations do not diminish the public responsibility of the historian."

[4] Further reading: Ball and Dagger (2001, 2004), Baradat (1999), Barth (1961), Bell (1960), Boudon (1986), Decker (2004), Eagleton (ed.) (1994), Hawkes (2003), Larrain (1994), Meyer *et al.* (eds.) (2009), Smith (2001), Susser (1988), Talshir, Humphrey and Freeden (eds.) (2006), Taylor (2010), Žižek (ed.) (1989, 2005).

strands of thought it is usually associated with (such as liberalism, conservatism, socialism, Marxism, nationalism, anarchism, fascism, fundamentalism, and the like). This is true even if my opening anecdotes touch upon ways of thinking that are not unrelated to what goes under such 'isms.' Moreover, I explicitly distance myself from a reification of ideology that would posit it as an autonomous reality in the world of thought in contrast with discourse, or with history, in such a way as to talk of dominance and hegemony as facts rather than processes. In other words, praxis and processes are the real focus.

In contrast to the abundance of theories, there is a true scarcity of methodological reflections and in particular of research guidelines. When guidelines are formulated, either they tend to remain vague or they give the impression that simple steps can lead from observations to interpretations. A lack of procedural openness often leads to conclusions with insufficiently explained foundations, while a lack of procedural systematicity may produce results that make it hard to distinguish between preconceived ideas, research findings, and mere speculation.[5] The main purpose of this book, then, is to reflect on methodological requirements for empirical ideology research, and in particular to offer procedures for engaging with ideology in practice.[6] Without, at this stage, going into the details of what 'ideology' may mean precisely, it should be clear that here the term is not used unless social phenomena, processes, and relations are at stake. The study of ideology, therefore, is not a gratuitous endeavor. It always touches upon issues of great consequence. Its findings may also have consequences, or efforts may be made to use or abuse them in the pursuit of specific goals affecting the lives of real people. As a result, a serious degree of responsibility is involved and the need for methodical analysis, controllability, and accuracy can hardly be overestimated. I hope to bring research practice closer to those ideals with the proposals that make up the substance of this book. Hence the desire to formulate guidelines for research that is truly 'empirical' – not to be confused with 'empiricist.' A side effect may be that the guidelines themselves, though inspired by a theoretical position on the notion of ideology, may turn ideology into a more 'operational' notion, thus eliminating some of the fuzziness in which it tends to be couched.

The venture is 'reflexive' in a literal sense. The need for it developed in the course of research into a societal debate surrounding the presence of 'migrants' in Belgium and in particular in Flanders.[7] This research was not originally

---

[5] See, for instance, my (Verschueren 2001) critique of a type of critical discourse analysis, as represented by Norman Fairclough (1992), as well as my more general warnings (in Verschueren 1999c) related to the risk of ideologized research in the wider domain of linguistic pragmatics (i.e., the science of language use). Helpful examples or overviews of methods of discourse and text analysis, many of them relevant for ideology research, can be found in Cap (2002), Jalbert (ed.) (1999), Mann and Thompson (1992), Renkema (ed.) (2009), Titscher *et al.* (1998), and Wodak and Meyer (eds.) (2009).

[6] Two highly recommended recent books with goals close to my own, but different in approach and with a different scope, are Chilton (2004) and Scollon (2008).

[7] The research in question has been reported in numerous publications, including Blommaert and Verschueren (1991b, 1993, 1994, and in particular 1998); the scope of the same line of research

defined as ideology research at all, and there was no definition of ideology at its source. Rather, it was a spinoff of an earlier interest in problems of intercultural and international communication.[8] In a heterogeneous social world – i.e., in *any* social world – questions about communication beyond the level of the purely individual (and sometimes even at that level) are inseparable from ideas about group identities and intergroup relations. Similarly, questions related to the discourse on 'migrant problems' turned out to be inseparable from ideas about what a society should look like. Hence our shorthand description of the minority–majority debate, as conducted in this case primarily by members of the majority, as *a debate on diversity*. For reasons that will become clear in Chapter 1, this overarching issue can only be described as ideological. Hence the redefinition of an investigation into a specific intercultural communication topic as a type of ideology research. It is this investigation that, retroactively, will serve as a first systematic point of reference for the more general theoretical and methodological reflections in this book (mainly in Chapters 1 and 2). For the sake of brevity, it will be referred to, whenever necessary, as our 'migrant research'.

One other type of data source, of a strictly historical nature, will be used equally systematically but much more extensively, starting with the general theoretical and methodological principles (in Chapters 1 and 2) all the way through the details of research guidelines and procedures (in Chapter 3). It consists in late nineteenth- and early twentieth-century discourse on (parts of) the colonial world and colonization in French and British history textbooks, starting in particular from Lavisse (1902) and narrowing the topic to accounts of the 1857 'Indian Mutiny' in a wide range of British counterparts. In contrast to the migrant research, which can be looked back upon to be evaluated in terms of the principles put forward in this book (though the materials are too elaborate for them to be a usefully coherent point of reference when we come to detailed guidelines and procedures), the history book materials have not yet been the subject of a full analysis and are adduced for the purposes of illustrating actual research processes, showing how the relevant questions can be asked and the appropriate steps can be taken in conducting an ideology-oriented investigation; needless to say, the 'reflection' involved here is of a different nature.

The temptation to supplement systematic reference to the 'debating diversity' or 'migrant' research (in Chapters 1 and 2) and these historical textbook writings bearing on aspects of colonization (in Chapters 1, 2 and 3) with more sporadic examples (which could be amply provided by accounts of events in the world today) will be resisted. For different types of examples, the reader may consult

was extended beyond Belgium into the realm of European nationalist tendencies in Blommaert and Verschueren (1992, 1996), Meeuwis (1993), and D'hondt, Blommaert and Verschueren (1995). Earlier attempts at deriving methodological guidelines and procedures are reflected in Verschueren (1995, 1996) and in chapter 8 of Verschueren (1999b).
[8] This earlier interest is reflected in Verschueren (1984, 1985a, 1989) as well as in Blommaert and Verschueren (eds.) (1991a).

earlier work leading up to this book,[9] while it should be clear that the recommendations in the following pages are intended to be relevant for any topically selected discourse-based study of ideological patterns and processes.[10]

The theoretical Chapter 1 will be followed by 'rules of engagement' (Chapter 2), the most general preliminary guidelines for engaging with ideology. Chapter 3, the bulkiest part of this book, will go into the more practical guidelines and procedural details specifying how to investigate ideology empirically. This enterprise goes against the grain of a widespread anti-methodological stance, as embodied in the suggestion "that more understanding is to be gained by using the traditional, ill-defined skills of scholarship than by following a rigorous, up-to-date methodology" (Billig 1988, p. 199). The main challenge will be to avoid a situation in which "The reliance upon a single methodology would inevitably dull the critical edge" (Billig 1991, p. 22), while at the same time being precise enough to make the guidelines operational. This may amount to showing that a clear set of guidelines and procedures, based on equally clear general principles, formulated in such a way that it is adequate for the empirical study of ideology, should never be describable as 'a single methodology' and does not fit the caricature of methodology as an impersonal set of rules that will inevitably lead two researchers to identical results.[11] A methodologically adequate approach should enable two researchers to sensibly compare and evaluate their results beyond the mere voicing of contrasting opinions.

[9] In particular, D'hondt, Blommaert and Verschueren (1995), Meeuwis (1993), Verschueren (1996, 1999b, 2001). The growing literature on language ideologies provides another 'case' with systematic alternative sets of examples; see, e.g., Bauman and Briggs (2003), Blommaert (ed.) (1999b), Gal and Woolard (eds.) (2001); for an overview, Kroskrity (2010).

[10] See, e.g., Verschueren, Östman and Meeuwis (2002) for a specific field of investigation defined as the monitoring of international communication, which can easily be seen as an endeavor that would benefit from an application of the methods advocated in this book.

[11] The wording of this sentence was inspired by the fact that Billig's (1988) plea for "traditional scholarship" as opposed to "a rigorous, up-to-date methodology" adduces only an example of quantitative content analysis to illustrate the inadequacy of "methodology" to achieve an understanding of ideology. That is what I am alluding to as a caricature of methodology.

1 Language use and ideology

Though the concept started its career that way, 'ideology' is no longer seen as the systematic analysis of sensations and ideas which should provide the basis for all scientific knowledge.[1] Ideology is no longer an academic discipline, but rather an object of investigation. It is related to *ideas, beliefs*, and *opinions*, but this relationship is not a straightforward one. Ideas, beliefs, and opinions, as such, do not make ideology. Simplifying a bit, they are merely 'contents of thinking,' whereas *ideology* is associated with *underlying patterns of meaning, frames of interpretation, world views*, or *forms of everyday thinking and explanation*. Thus the ways in which beliefs, ideas, or opinions are discursively used, i.e. their *forms of expression* as well as the *rhetorical purposes* they serve, are just as important for ideology as the contents of thinking for which these three terms serve as labels.[2]

Let me illustrate this first point by asking whether there is anything ideological about an utterance such as the final one in the introduction to this book:

> A methodologically adequate approach should enable two researchers to sensibly compare and evaluate their results beyond the mere voicing of contrasting opinions.

This utterance certainly expresses an idea or opinion and – unless it is insincere – a belief. In order to identify ideological content, however, a deeper level of meaning would have to be found that we may expect to serve as a wider frame of interpretation or as a pattern of explanation that can be directed at multiple targets, thus with the potential of transcending the *ad hoc* character of the example under consideration. One such meaningful element, reflected in but not recoverable with certainty from the quoted utterance, could be the general way of thinking about language (i.e., possibly a 'language ideology') that enables the author to refer to "the mere voicing of contrasting opinions." Implicitly, this phrase presents language ("voicing") as a potentially straightforward ("mere") vehicle

---

[1] I am referring to the French philosopher Antoine Destutt de Tracy who launched this endeavor in 1796 in order to spread the ideas of the Enlightenment. The scholars who worked with him in the pursuit of this goal are generally known as *les idéologues*. See Destutt de Tracy (1803).

[2] When we talk about ideas, beliefs, and opinions, we generally think of highly differentiated mental phenomena (measurable, for instance, by means of opinion polls, designed to identify types and degrees of variability). One could be tempted, therefore, to regard them as the volatile and variable counterparts to supposedly stable patterns and frames that would constitute ideology. However, it would be misleading to ignore the dynamics and variability characterizing ideology itself, as will be shown later.

for the expression of ideational contents ("opinions") which may be identifiably separable ("contrasting") entities. Let us call this perspective on language, for the time being, the 'vehicle view of language.'[3] Whether the present author actually subscribes to that view is irrelevant at this point but will have to be addressed later.

A second aspect of a first approximation of the concept of ideology can also be discussed in relation to the closing utterance in my introduction. In addition to expressing an idea, that utterance is also a *maxim*, a succinctly formulated basic principle or rule of conduct. It expresses a (research) *attitude*, adherence to certain *values*, and even a (research) *mentality*. This observation, in its own right, is not enough to qualify the utterance unequivocally as an ideological claim. Ideological patterns of meaning are rarely so plainly prescriptive. Typically, *ideology* – and hence its discursive manifestation – *balances description and prescription* (both of which can be explicit and implicit to varying degrees). In other words, it involves theories of how things are in combination with theories of how things should be. An explicit rule of conduct, as in the utterance under discussion, by no means guarantees the presence of a general underlying pattern of meaning and interpretation that would deserve the label ideology. The prescriptiveness of ideology consists mainly in a form of *normativity* that is akin to *commonsensicality*. The products of common-sense reflections (mainly descriptive) are turned into norms (both in the sense of what is seen as normal, and in the regulative and prescriptive sense). Furthermore, the common sense in question is not the invention of individuals, but common sense with a history, common sense that members of a wider community appeal to in order to be persuasive. Hence, nothing can be said on this score about the ideological caliber of the utterance without a further exploration of the wider discourse it fits into, much of which is still to be produced/interpreted at the time this sentence is written/read.[4]

Before moving on, I should not leave any doubt about the fact that ideology is a fully integrated *sociocultural-cognitive phenomenon*.[5] As the notion of

---

[3] Linguists will recognize this 'vehicle view of language' as an instance of what Reddy (1979) called the "conduit metaphor" describing an everyday pattern of talk about talk according to which thoughts are wrapped in a linguistic form which then serves as a conduit before the thoughts are unwrapped in the interpretation process.

[4] An interesting connection should be pointed out between what I have said so far and the notion of *permissible statements* or *utterances*. When statements or utterances are felt *not* to be 'permissible,' this is usually related to what common sense dictates as a norm within a given community, and hence to ideology.

[5] A strong argument for not forgetting the cognitive dimension is made by Chilton (2005). Note that neither cognition nor society/culture can be seen as taking precedence over the other. In theories of ideology, the focus may shift from one to the other. Thus Eagleton (2007, p. 19) describes Althusser's view of ideology as a shift "from a *cognitive* to an *affective* theory of ideology," adding:

> – which is not necessarily to deny that ideology contains certain cognitive elements, or to reduce it to the merely 'subjective'. It is certainly subjective in the sense of being subject-centred: its utterances are to be deciphered as expressive of a speaker's attitudes or lived relations to the world.

'common' sense implies, cognition is not seen as a purely individual property of human beings, even though each individual carries a unique apparatus in which the processing takes place – Vygotsky's (1978) "mind in society."[6] What makes ideology special as a cognitive phenomenon, while it shares social situatedness with most other higher forms of cognitive processing, is that it also has aspects of society as its object (the next point to be clarified) and that its social situatedness involves a specific form of intersubjectivity or sharing (to be explained later), as well as affect and stance.[7]

A third general property of ideology, then, already hinted at in the Introduction and further underscored in the previous paragraph, is that the normative or commonsensical frames of interpretation which the term refers to bear on aspects of *social reality*. This is meant in a wide sense, including sociohistorical, sociopolitical, sociocultural, and similar aspects. But, for instance, ideas about the shape of the earth are not ideological under this definition, even though changes in such beliefs may be induced or hampered by ideological processes. Within the realm of social reality, of particular importance are *social relations in the sphere of publicness*, i.e., the public positioning of people in relation to each other, usually involving the level of (perceived) groups.[8] More often than not, *relations of power and dominance* are involved. That is why Thompson's (1990, pp. 7, 56) definition of ideology as "*meaning in the service of power*," and his view of ideology research as the study of "*the ways in which meaning serves to establish and sustain relations of domination*" touches the very core of what we should be interested in.

Yet, there are good reasons not to restrict social relations in the public sphere *a priori* to relations of domination for the purposes of ideology research. For one thing, at the theoretical level, powerless and dominated groups may – and usually do – have their ideologies too. Moreover, there is a good methodological reason. Whether patterns of meaning bear on social issues or on social relations is a matter of relatively straightforward analytical observation. But what functions are served by that meaning in relation to social patterns – the establishment and sustenance of domination being one such function – is an entirely empirical issue

Note also that the debate over cognitivism in the social sciences is very much alive, and that there are good reasons to argue against purely cognitivist interpretations in favor of giving center stage to constitutive practices (see, e.g., Dupret 2011, Watson and Coulter 2008).

[6] This entire book is formulated against the background of a theory of linguistic pragmatics (as presented in Verschueren 1999b) to which the notion of 'mind in society' is very important. Central to the theory is the notion of adaptability (see Verschueren and Brisard 2002) which allows us, amongst other things, to talk systematically about processes of language use in terms of their status *vis-à-vis* the medium of adaptability which is the human mind, seen as the seat of cognitive abilities that have an essential link with the intersubjective level of society.

[7] In Eagleton's (2007, p. 20) words: "Ideological statements, then, would seem to be subjective but not private [...] On the one hand, ideology is no mere set of doctrines but the stuff which makes up uniquely what we are, constitutive of our very identities; on the other hand it presents itself as an 'Everybody knows that,' a kind of anonymous universal truth."

[8] I realize that the term 'public' evokes its opposite 'private,' that the distinction is not always so clear, and that it may even be related to aspects of language ideology (see Gal 2005). It is used here in an untheorized everyday sense.

that can, at best, be decided only upon completion of the analysis. Taking the final utterance of the introduction as our example again, if it can be established that the utterance is the expression of a vehicle view of language, it may also be the case that it represents a type of language ideology that allows institutions of various types (e.g., academia) to establish and maintain an in-group's domination by imposing certain communicative norms on others whose conceptualization and handling of language may not fit the same paradigm. Clearly a whole lot of analytical work would have to be done to establish the plausibility of such an interpretation, and a domination perspective cannot be taken as the starting point for the analysis. Even if simply differing views of language were involved that affect aspects of social interaction and relationships, of which none could be said to be dominant, that would not make the patterns of meaning that are at issue any less 'ideological.'

The strong focus on processes of domination in which meaning plays a role, even if it results from analyses, rather than antedating them, is the reason why ideology research is predominantly a critical enterprise, even if we do not follow Engels in his characterization of ideology as 'false consciousness.'[9] The relation of all this to politics should be clear, where struggle is central and takes the form of *struggles over meaning* (categorization, highlighting, and perception – all to be discussed later) and *struggles over norms*. Thus typical 'ideological themes' can be seen to emerge, such as *identity*, which invoke further themes such as *prejudice* and *stereotyping*.[10]

On the basis of these elementary observations, I can try to present a preliminary definition of ideology in the form of the following thesis:

> **Thesis 1: We can define as ideological any basic pattern of meaning or frame of interpretation bearing on or involved in (an) aspect(s) of social 'reality' (in particular in the realm of social relations in the public sphere), felt to be commonsensical, and often functioning in a normative way.**

Note the single quotation marks enclosing 'reality,' warding off suspicions that ontological claims are involved concerning a reality outside the meaning in

---

[9] The study of ideology as a critical enterprise goes back to Karl Marx (see, e.g., 1977), whose position it was that what makes ideas into ideology is their connection with the conflictual nature of social and economic relationships. We also find this view very strongly in Althusser (see, e.g., 1971a, 1971b), who sees ideology in capitalist society as the cement that fixes a system of class domination. Such a critical angle, which was totally absent from the work of the French *idéologues*, was also suspended in the writings of Lenin (see, e.g., 1969) and Lukács (see, e.g., 1971), and in much of the work of Mannheim (see, e.g., 1936). These authors viewed ideology less negatively, either as a function of the political goal of promoting a proletarian ideology as a positive social force (as in the case of Lenin), or in order to objectify the study of ideology in such a way that the same type of analysis could be used for systems of thought that one wanted to criticize and for one's own thought (as in the case of Mannheim). For an extensive discussion of the false consciousness view of ideology (recently resurrected by Bénabou 2008), see Rosen (1996).

[10] For a classic treatment of prejudice, see Allport (1979).

question. Note also that, for basically the same reason, the patterns of meaning or frames of interpretation that are defined as ideological may either 'bear on' or 'be involved in' aspects of social reality, or both. Any form of social action is, as eloquently explained by Winch (1958), 'meaningful' in the sense that it is interpreted by the actors engaged in it. Hence practices are inseparable from the concepts in terms of which they are interpreted. Therefore, ideology is rarely outside the social reality it bears on and tends to be partly constitutive of that reality.

A few additional points have to be made to clarify the nature of the common sense involved. First of all, how do we decide whether an aspect of meaning functions commonsensically? The meaning in question should clearly be taken for granted or, more negatively, should not be questioned. This means that individuals would assume that they *share* this meaning with other individuals. Thus (an assumption of) *intersubjectivity* or *common ground* is involved. In that sense, ideologies are comparable to what are known as *paradigms* in the philosophy of science: specific ways of looking, based on taken-for-granted premises (even if they were formulated explicitly at a certain time) that are shared within a community or generation of scientists. Like paradigms, ideologies (if we can use the plural at all[11]) are *community-based*. Their relevance, while going beyond the individual, does not extend beyond a given society or community, even if they induce forms of behavior that clearly affect members of other societies or communities, and even if the formulation risks circularity given the fact that shared patterns of interpretation are at least partly constitutive of what passes as a community. Moreover, their traces may be restricted to forms of expression (say 'language use' or 'discourse' – see pp. 17–19) directly bearing on or involved in the aspect(s) of social 'reality' in question. In other words, frames of interpretation may vary across different realms of social action. Thus, returning once more to the final utterance of the introduction, a vehicle view of language could dictate the interpretation of what goes on in a specific institutional setting (say, academia), while being at odds with the way in which everyday interaction is conceived. But if discourses pertaining to aspects of 'reality' within the same realm of social action come in different genres,[12] the unquestioned nature of the ideological meaning in question may remain constant across those genres. Thus our hypothetical vehicle view of language as used in an institutional setting could be expected to manifest itself (in its common-sense, taken-for-granted,

---

[11] Like most comparisons, this one also has its dangers. Paradigms in scientific work (see Kuhn 1962) are usually relatively clearly delineated. This is not generally the case with ideology (except in its reasoned and purposefully constructed manifestations – e.g., some of the great political ideologies such as communism or liberalism – which are of less interest to us here). Hence it is safer to speak of ideology and ideological meaning rather than to run the risk of reification by using the plural 'ideologies' or the countable singular 'an ideology.'

[12] The term 'genre' is used here to refer to relatively stable discourse types associated with different spheres of human activity (see Verschueren 1999b, pp. 151–156). Its origins go back to Bakhtin (1986). For a good example of its current use, see Bauman and Briggs (1992) or Muntigl and Gruber (eds.) (2005), and for a recent overview Solin (2009).

unquestioned form) in, among other things, guidelines for, reports on, and discussions about, the relevant institutional proceedings.

I can summarize the above in the form of the following subthesis:

Thesis 1.1: *The common-sense (basic/normative) nature of ideological meaning is manifested in the fact that it is rarely questioned, in a given society or community, in discourse related to the 'reality' in question, possibly across various discourse genres.*

Briefly, when one is inclined to say "But that is normal," there is a good chance that ideology is at work.[13] Its not being recognized as ideological, its coincidence with normalcy, is what makes ideology powerful. In Eagleton's (2007, p. xvii) words, "Ideology [...] is always most effective when invisible."

The intersubjectivity of aspects of ideological meaning should not lead us to the conclusion that what we are dealing with is stable. *Ideology evolves.* Its dynamics may result from occasional explicit questioning, from forms of interaction between different frames of interpretation, but also from changing circumstances that induce adaptations in ways of thinking.

Without an appeal to dynamics, in combination with reference to the society or community basis of ideology, it would be hard to make sense of the issue of *hegemony*.[14] Whereas the term originally refers to the influence of one state over another, in this context it bears on relations of dominance and power between different strata of a society. In the context of discussing ideology, its use is based on the observation that dominant classes may be able to avoid coercion by obtaining the consent of the oppressed, i.e., by successfully making certain patterns of meaning or frames of interpretation (e.g., pertaining to the unequal structuring of society) seem natural, by turning them into common sense. Hegemony in this sense involves the internalization of the authority one may be subjected to. Hegemony and ideology do not coincide. Consent may also be obtained by non-ideological means; e.g., feeding people well may keep them from (even considering) acts of resistance. And, though the establishment of hegemony is often an ideological process in the sense that the consent-based maintenance of the power and dominance that it involves is usually supported by meaning, it is not a necessary property of all ideology (unless one wants to restrict ideology exclusively to meaning in the service of power, which, as argued before, I am not inclined to

[13] Van Dijk (2001, p. 15) distinguishes the 'group knowledge' that is ideology-based from what he calls 'common ground.' In contrast to the ideological group knowledge, common ground would be non-ideological cultural knowledge shared by all culturally competent members of a society across groups (i.e., "the sociocognitive basis of our common sense," as presupposed in all public discourse). Though it is of course the case that aspects of meaning are shared across groups, there is no sound basis for defining these *a priori* as non-ideological.

[14] The notion of hegemony was developed in particular by Gramsci (see, e.g., 1971, 1985), who inherited it from Lenin and Lukács. For an extensive explanation and interesting use of the concept, see Laclau and Mouffe (2001).

do). The hegemonic potential of ideology is clearly related to its spread, though spread does not have to imply hegemony. This is expressed briefly, and hesitantly, in the following thesis:

Thesis 1.1.1: *The wider the society or community, and the wider the range of discourse genres in which a given pattern of meaning or frame of interpretation escapes questioning, the more 'hegemonic' it may be.*

Though 'ideology' is not necessarily, but just *may* be hegemonic, this should not lead us to believe that it would make sense even to speak of ideology in relation to the world view of an individual. That would contradict what I have said about intersubjectivity, sharedness, the community-based character of ideology and its relation to common sense, normality, and the public sphere.[15] The structure and size of the community, however, are unimportant: An ideological study of the world view of smaller communities and non-dominant classes is perfectly feasible.[16]

Questions of hegemony go beyond what this methodological treatise on ideology research aims at. The notion bears less on patterns of ideological meaning (the core topic I want to be able to investigate) than on mechanisms by which such patterns may get established and the consequences they may have for the life of a society. Introducing the notion, however, underscores the fact that practices are involved and not just ideas, the dynamics of ideology, and the agency (even if submissive) that is involved on the part of those acquiring or acquiescing to certain frames of interpretation.

The common-sense nature of ideology, whether or not hegemonic, has direct consequences for its forms of expression, described as follows:

Thesis 1.2: *Its not being questioned means that the meaning concerned is often (though not always and not exclusively) carried along implicitly rather than being formulated explicitly.*

This, in turn, has immediate implications for the methodology of empirical ideology research, as spelled out later (especially in Chapter 3).

Thesis 1 and its subtheses focus on inherent properties of ideology. More needs to be said about the relation between ideological meaning and the experiences of community members (Thesis 2), ideology and its manifestations (Thesis 3,

---

[15] It may be useful to distinguish between 'ideology' and 'world view' by saying that an ideology is always a world view, but that a world view does not have to be an ideology: A world view may pertain to non-social as well as social phenomena, and it may be held privately by an individual – both aspects being incompatible with our notion of ideology.
[16] Ginzburg (1982) has demonstrated how revealing it may be to delve into the frames of interpretation of marginal and powerless movements or subordinate classes that may lead a life detached from the societal mainstream.

the content of which is already presupposed in the formulation of the preceding account), and ideology and fields of action (Thesis 4). Starting with the relation between ideological meaning and the experiences or observations of community members, I propose the following:

Thesis 2: Ideology, because of its normative and common-sense nature, may be highly immune to experience and observation.

Note that I avoid specific claims about the emergence of ideological frames of interpretation. They may result from oft-repeated explicit statements, from processes of internalization, from shared experiences and observations, or from any combination of these. Lived experience and observation, however, form only a possible, not a necessary, source. And, once established, ways of seeing social reality may become entirely detached from what one personally experiences or observes.

How this works is easiest to observe when looking at processes taking place in a world that is not or no longer one's own (which, at the same time, serves as a reminder that the property pointed at here does not imply invariability or a lack of changeability). Take the following example from Lavisse (1902). In the short preface to this history textbook we read, after a succinct description of the contents of the book, the following sentence:

> A côté de ces œuvres de la politique et de la guerre, nous avons mis les œuvres de la paix: industrie, commerce, colonisation du monde.
>
> [Next to those works of politics and war, we have placed the works of peace: industry, trade, colonization of the world.]

The enumeration *industry, trade, colonization of the world* under the general label *works of peace* is likely to make most of us frown today. We no longer think of colonization as an acceptable way of handling international relations, and certainly not as a peaceful activity on a par with industry and trade. Clearly, the early twentieth-century perspective was sufficiently different to allow for such a categorization of colonization. Does this mean that today we know more about the violence involved in colonization? Maybe our documentation is more elaborate, but there was no attempt to hide that side of reality in Lavisse's textbook. On the contrary, colonial history is described as a history of conquests, wars, rebellions, repressions of rebellions – hardly peaceful activities. There are even visual presentations of rather unusual violence. Thus a one-paragraph account of a revolt of the sepoys (*cipayes* in French, the native – often Hindu – soldiers in the British army in India), supposedly spurred by a British decision to start using cow fat to coat cartridges (the tip of which had to be bitten off), and ending in the execution of the leaders, is accompanied by the illustration in Figure 1.

None of the information on and illustration of violence seemed capable of undermining the categorization of colonial activity as peaceful. The reason is

Fig. 10. — **Exécution des Cipayes.** Les soldats anglais marchèrent contre les Cipayes révoltés, reprirent la ville de Delhi et attachèrent les prisonniers hindous à la gueule des canons.

Figure 1. *"Execution of the Sepoys. The English soldiers marched against the revolting sepoys, recaptured the town of Delhi and attached the Hindu prisoners to the mouths of cannons."*)

simply that colonial activity *was categorized as* peaceful, as a result of hegemonic legitimations in terms of good intentions which turned forms of violent intrusion not only into a right but even into a duty. The peacefulness of colonization was part of common sense. Any accompanying violence was therefore a random and unfortunate side effect (not so different from today's 'collateral damage' when the West goes out to 'liberate' a country), usually provoked by the Other, unable to appreciate the colonizers' real intentions. In other words, the early twentieth-century perspective was simply different from the one that is dominant today (even though today striking parallels can be found). The meaning given to events is stronger than any objectively observable facts. The conclusion should *not* be that early twentieth-century Europeans were blind. Rather, it is possible to perfectly observe two phenomena without making the link or to link them without seeing the contrast. From this point of view, ideology may be defined as a way of linking things 'in the world.' Ideology research, then, should be aimed at pointing out how this works in specific cases and even what alternatives there are. Hence ideology research also opens the way to – and is often informed by – alternative frames of interpretation. This is what I have already referred to as the critical potential of such research. This cannot be an excuse, however, for simply superimposing researchers' ideologies on data. Hence the need for methodology.

Thesis 2 has further consequences for the forms of expression in which ideological meaning is couched:

> **Thesis 2.1:** *Just as there may be a discrepancy between ideology and direct experience, there may be discrepancies between the level of implicit meaning and what one would be willing to say explicitly.*

Thus this author does not subscribe to the vehicle view of language that may be detectable at the level of implicit meaning in the utterance closing the introduction to this book. But if a systematic discrepancy were to emerge between what I am willing to say explicitly about the functioning of language and the implications of the way in which I say it, questions would have to be asked about the underlying language ideology and, if the latter does not match beliefs, developing a different way of speaking about language would be useful in order to avoid the trap of being guided by a misleading type of common sense.[17]

In the realm of wider societal debates such as the one surrounding 'migrants' in Belgium (Blommaert and Verschueren 1998), glaring gaps may appear between the explicit and the implicit. If you study the rhetoric of the tolerant majority, as we did, there will be an abundance of overt expressions of acceptance of diversity. Yet a systematic analysis at the deeper levels of implicit meaning reveals that such acceptance is at best superficial. This observation raises serious theoretical and methodological questions. On the theoretical side we must say that, normally, explicit meaning is as important as implicit meaning, since meaning generation is always the product of both. But in the search for ideology, where meaning hinges on common sense, on what is taken for granted and remains unquestioned, the implicit plays a particularly important role (see Thesis 1.2) which is strengthened when discrepancies between the explicit and the implicit become very clear and systematic to the point of becoming contradictory. This may be the main reason why we should be careful, as I was at the beginning of this account, not to equate ideology with ideas, beliefs, or opinions as such. It is possible for one to 'believe' something that is inconsistent with one's own more global and habitual way of seeing and interpreting things, just as it is possible to express an opinion or to profess a belief that does not match one's more basic attitudes (even

---

[17] This is why the study of language ideologies is so important, not only because of what they do in the world as sources of principles of social structuring (see, e.g., Meeuwis 1999), but also because of their influence on scientific ways of looking at language (see, e.g., Silverstein 1979). Further useful reading: Blommaert (ed.) (1999b), Kroskrity (ed.) (2000), Lucy (ed.) (1993), Schieffelin, Woolard and Kroskrity (eds.) (1998), Verschueren (ed.) (1999a), Woolard and Schieffelin (1994).

without assuming insincerity), and just as it is possible to believe things that do not fit basic observations (as in the example above from Lavisse).[18]

The methodological question is: How can we devise analytical procedures that enable us to recover, with any degree of certainty, patterns in these incessantly intermeshing layers of meaning? The answer is what Chapters 2 and 3 of this book are intended to provide an approximation of. One thing should be clear by now: If implicitness plays the role described earlier, subjects cannot be *asked* about the patterns of meaning that make up ideology. Responses to questionnaire questions can never be taken at face value in the search for ideology.

There is no *empirical methodology* without an 'object' to apply it to. Thus we have to ask what *manifestations* of ideology should provide the data for empirical ideology research. The answer to that question is implicit in much of what has been said so far. The core issues I have declared an interest in are situated at the level of meaning. Meaning, however, needs to be expressed before it can be investigated. A strong case could even be made for saying that meaning does not exist without its expression or manifestation. Thesis 1.1 made reference to manifestations in discourse, a reference that was repeated in Thesis 1.1.1. Thesis 1.2 mentioned the contrast between implicit and explicit formulation, a distinction that was used again in Thesis 2.1. Clearly, it was the expression of meaning in *language* that I had in mind throughout. Note, however,

> that ideology is a matter of 'discourse' rather than 'language'. It concerns the actual uses of language between particular human subjects for the production of specific effects. You could not decide whether a statement was ideological or not by inspecting it in isolation from its discursive context, any more than you could decide in this way whether a piece of writing was a work of literary art.   (Eagleton 2007, p. 9)

The key concepts here are *language use* and *discourse*, which I will use as equivalents for the purposes of this book. Thus we can try the following formulation:

Thesis 3: (One of) the most visible manifestation(s) of ideology is LANGUAGE USE or DISCOURSE, which may reflect, construct, and/or maintain ideological patterns.

Ideology, like ideas, attitudes, and opinions, does not lead an abstract existence. It is not the filling of otherwise empty heads, but it exists in its being *used* and hence can be studied only in relation to that use. While the use of ideology in

---

[18] Frank Brisard (personal communication) has pointed out to me that there is a significant philosophical debate surrounding rationality and intentionality with implications for theories of the authority – or lack thereof – of the 'self' over his/her 'beliefs' (e.g., Anscombe 1957, Marcus 1983, Quine 1976). More could be said about all this in relation to the false consciousness view of ideology, as well as to psychoanalytic theories which allow for the possibility of explicit assent/ negation as an indicator of the opposite.

thinking is hard to observe, and therefore hardly a candidate for empirical analysis, there is direct access to its use in linguistic, discursive (rhetorical, argumentative, etc.) practices.[19] Language use or discourse not only reflects habitual
frames of interpretation, it also constructs, shapes, and reshapes them, and can
be observed to twist them around strategically or to avoid or pass over them
altogether. The term 'manifestation,' therefore, should be interpreted broadly.
The discursive manifestations of ideology are themselves part of the social
'reality' which the discourse pertains to, and they must be seen as *constitutive
practices* rather than mediating expressions.[20] No doubt there are other interesting manifestations as well, such as a flag symbolizing nationalist feelings
or aspirations.[21] But *language use* or *discourse* is the *only* medium or situated
practice in which one can literally *question* patterns of meaning as opposed
to *not questioning* them. This fact accords language use or discourse a privileged status *vis-à-vis* ideology because it relates to one of ideology's most basic
properties (see Thesis 1.1). Language use or discourse is also privileged as a
manifestation of ideology because it is no doubt the main instrument for spreading complex patterns of meaning. It is also related to the structures of dominance that are often involved, in that the ownership of the means of persuasive
rhetoric is unequally distributed in most societies.[22] The foregoing means that,
while responses to questionnaire questions provide dubitable data for ideology
research, sociological interviews may provide very interesting data indeed, on
condition that they are studied as discourse subject to all the processes of interaction that shape any other type of discourse rather than as straightforward and
factual reflections of ideological content.[23]

In addition, there are purely practical reasons for the centrality of language
use or discourse in ideology research. First, it is a highly observable or empirical

[19] What is 'directly observable' varies, of course, from practice to practice. Thus spoken interaction
provides more access to processes, while for writing the product is more tangible (in spite of the
availability of advanced techniques for writing research).
[20] Thus I adhere to a constructivist view of social reality (cf. Berger and Luckmann 1966). Yet, the
relativism that is often associated with constructivism should itself be seriously relativized: There
are things in the world, even in the social world, with an 'existence' prior to our discursive framing of them, even if our discursive framing provides them with added meaning. Note that the very
purpose of this monograph, the formulation of an adequate research methodology, implies that
there are evaluation criteria for research in relation to their 'object' (even if this object is largely
discursive), which implies a rejection of pure relativism. (See Searle 2009 for a useful discussion,
even though this review has a tendency to go too far in its rejection of constructivism and relativism by attacking some of its most absurd manifestations.)
[21] Because a flag may be the primordial symbolization of a nationalist ideology, Billig (1995)
talks about 'flaggings' of 'banal nationalism' (called 'banal' because what is investigated is precisely the category of ever-present and relatively superficial manifestations to which the 'flag'
belongs).
[22] Blommaert (1999a) provides a good example of rhetorical inequality in the institutional setting
of asylum procedures.
[23] For methodological reflections related to interviews in social science research, see e.g. Briggs
(1986); for an example of how interview data can be handled as discourse rather than as straightforward data, see e.g. Meeuwis (1997).

object of inquiry.[24] Second, present-day linguistic pragmatics[25] provides all the necessary tools for investigating the generation of meaning as a dynamic process, with a continuous mutual calibration of the explicit and the implicit in a context of social relations. It has developed these tools over the past three to four decades in response to one of its most basic premises, viz. that every utterance necessarily relies on a world of background assumptions, supposedly shared or presented as such, which combines with what is explicitly said in a process of generating meaning.[26]

Finally, and very briefly, a few words to summarize the way in which ideology can be seen to function in fields of action that make up social life, which is itself the reason for studying ideology:

> **Thesis 4: Discursively reflected, constructed, and/or supported ideological meanings may serve the purposes of framing, validating, explaining, or legitimating attitudes, states of affairs, and actions in the domains to which they are applicable.**

States of affairs, attitudes, and courses of action are made to look like they are normal or at least acceptable by framing, validating, explaining, or legitimating them in a way that appeals to the commonsensical core of ideology. It is in this way that ideology can support the perpetuation of existing relations of power and dominance.[27] However, social realities are rarely stable, so that reframings also occur, in which case forms of explanation and justification – often equally rooted in (possibly rivaling) common-sense patterns of meaning – can function as agents of change.[28] These various possibilities are meant to be captured in Thesis 4.

When relating ideology to fields of action, however important the link may be, it is also important to keep in mind that there is no predictable one-to-one

---

[24] Eagleton (2007, p. 194) makes essentially the same point, though not exactly for the same practical reasons, when he says, "there is a third way between thinking of ideology as disembodied ideas on the one hand, and as nothing but a matter of certain behaviour patterns on the other. This is to regard ideology as a discursive or semiotic phenomenon. And this at once emphasizes its materiality (since signs are material entities), and preserves the sense that it is essentially concerned with *meanings*."

[25] Linguistic pragmatics is seen as the general science of language use, taking the broadest possible interdisciplinary (i.e., cognitive, social, and cultural) perspective. This tradition is represented in the activities of the International Pragmatics Association (IPrA; ipra.ua.ac.be) and is reflected in Verschueren, Östman, Blommaert et al. (eds.) (1995 ff.) and in Verschueren (1999b).

[26] The term 'meaning generation' is preferred over the more common *meaning construction* to avoid an exclusive focus on the active and predominantly conscious involvement of the producer of utterances. A well-balanced theory of linguistic pragmatics must allow for the interpreter's contribution to meaning by means of the interpretation choices he/she makes, which feed back into the interaction. See Verschueren (1999b).

[27] Thompson (1990, p. 60) lists legitimation in a set of 'modes of operation' of ideology which also includes dissimulation, unification, fragmentation and reification. Much of what is meant by this will be dealt with in the form of specific discursive devices or strategies in Chapter 3.

[28] Antaki (1988b, p.1) suggests that explanations "have the power to challenge social realities" and "seem to be implicated in changes in people's behavior."

correspondence between frames of interpretation and behavioral choices. Thus a retired Flemish worker, finally able to read his newspaper every day, may come to realize the benefits of socialism; yet, loyalty to the Christian-democratic institutions that have provided security for him all his life may keep him from changing his voting behavior. This worker is real, not hypothetical. Cases involving more ambivalence can be imagined where discrepancies emerge between purposeful behavior (e.g., giving money to a beggar), which a person may feel he or she has to do, and a more general perspective (e.g., the belief that giving money to beggars keeps them dependent) which the same person shares and knows to be in conflict with his or her immediate actions.

Finally, the link between ideology and fields of action gets blurred by the mediating role of the uptake of discourse. Serious mismatches may emerge between the patterns of meaning that underlie specific types and samples of language use or discourse and the frames of interpretation that live and are generated in various audiences. This remark is especially relevant at the present point in history, when a communicative overflow makes consistent absorption of communicative content virtually impossible. Rather than to defeat the purposes of ideology research, however, this phenomenon makes it all the more relevant and necessary to search for underlying patterns of meaning that may inform seemingly diffuse forms of expression.

2   Pragmatic rules of engagement

Language- or discourse-based empirical ideology research is fundamentally concerned with *meaning* and the way in which it is generated. Therefore, a methodology – with a corresponding set of methods or procedures – should meet one basic requirement: *It must enable interpretation*[1] *with due regard for what can be intersubjectively established to count as evidence*. Details of how I hope to meet this requirement will be put forward in Chapter 3. For now I restrict myself to introducing some elementary pragmatics-based rules for engaging with language use and ideology. These are related to the formulation of research questions and the collection of data.

In actual research practice, most discourse-based studies of ideological processes start from basic *intuitions* that are not unrelated to the researcher's *involvement*. In our migrant research, for instance, the basic intuition was that 'something was wrong' with discourse on minorities as it was developing in Belgium, more specifically Flanders, in the late 1980s and early 1990s. There was a lot of obviously well-intended emphasis on integration processes, but at the same time it seemed as if diversity was not taken seriously and that minority members did not have a voice in the debate at all. A sense that 'something is wrong' can, of course, only be grounded in a personal position and opinion, i.e., in the way in which one feels 'involved.' Similarly, the history textbook materials that offer the second systematic point of reference for this book were collected because of an intuition that it might be interesting to look at presentations of colonization one hundred years ago, just because I was struck by what seemed like a 'strange' enumeration ("industrie, commerce, colonisation du monde") under a specific common category ("les oeuvres de la paix") in Lavisse (1902). The involvement

---

[1] Hence Thompson's definition of ideology research as a hermeneutic enterprise: "the object of analysis is a meaningful symbolic construction which calls for interpretation" (1990, p. 272), and

> If hermeneutics reminds us that the object domain of social inquiry is also a subject domain, so too it reminds us that *the subjects who make up the subject–object domain are, like social analysts themselves, subjects capable of understanding, of reflecting, and of acting on the basis of this understanding and reflection*.
>   (1990, p. 275; italics in original)

Following Ricoeur (1981), he proposes a 'depth hermeneutics' to relate the internal structuring of symbolic forms to their placement in historical and social context. In particular, he is concerned with interpretation that explicates the connection between symbolic forms and the establishment or sustenance of specific social relations.

factor in this case was a secret hope that by looking at such materials from the past some interesting and clarifying light could be shed on certain aspects of international relations today. Or, to take an example from someone else's work, involvement-related intuitions are referred to by Carbó (2001, p. 65) when she describes an "interested sense of strangeness" as the motivation for studying twentieth-century parliamentary discourse in Mexico after arriving there as an Argentinian refugee and observing "the apparent institutional and social stability of a painfully asymmetrical society, together with an official rhetoric that prided itself in being heir to an armed, popular, revolutionary movement."

Far from being inadmissible, such a starting point is no doubt a driving force for a lot of important (and critical) research in the humanities and social sciences. This is, however, a two-edged sword. There is the risk that research may be strongly guided by an initial intuition and in particular by the involvement-related personal position or opinion. Unfortunately, this happens in too many cases, resulting in various forms of bias.[2] In those cases, involvement turns into inadmissible subjectivity. In order to avoid this, *intuitions have to be shaped into researchable questions*, i.e., formulations of problems or questions that research can be designed to answer.[3] Researchability does not imply only that it is possible to find empirical evidence supporting a finding or an answer, but also that a systematic 'counterscreening' of one's data is feasible, by which identical methods can be applied to the same materials to see if there is any evidence contradicting the finding or the answer. In our migrant research, for instance, the initial intuitions gave rise to the suspicion that, in spite of overt invocations of tolerance, mainstream Flemish society was not ready to accept fundamental forms of diversity. What makes the questioning of such an intuition researchable is the fact that discourse data can be gathered that somehow represent 'mainstream Flemish society,' that linguistic tools are available that allow us to say something about underlying, non-overt forms of meaning, and that the same tools can be applied to the same data in a search for counterevidence. The same goes for the intuitive idea that late nineteenth- and early twentieth-century Europeans, in general, looked at or were led to look at colonization, including the violence it involved or required, as a perfectly legitimate way of dealing with the rest of the world. The first 'rule of engagement' in the study of ideology, then, goes as follows:

Rule 1: Formulate researchable questions, i.e., questions to which answers can be given, supported with empirical evidence and susceptible to counterscreening.

---

[2] For examples related to certain types of critical linguistics and critical discourse analysis, see Verschueren (1985a and 2001). Similar criticisms are to be found in Chilton (2005).

[3] Using intuitions of 'strangeness' in the search for researchable questions is fundamentally related to the detection of anomalies as a strategy in a variety of scientific endeavors. Well-known is Lévi-Strauss' *cherchez l'anomalie* as a guideline in ethnographic research, though we must be careful not to import the corresponding structuralist context.

Needless to say, the search for evidence and the counterscreening efforts are part of the same heuristic. This will be clear from the illustrations in Chapter 3, even if the point will not be made over and over again.

Note that I avoid using the term 'hypothesis.' I prefer 'research question' because discourse-based empirical ideology research can hardly be hypothesis-driven. A hypothesis takes the form of an assertion that can be verified or proven. Ideological phenomena and processes are usually too complex to be captured in straightforward statements, and research findings are themselves usually intricate narratives. *Rather than being hypothesis-driven, empirical ideology research is data-driven. But the data themselves have to be appropriate to a research question* – which is what the following paragraphs are about – *to be pursued with a theoretically grounded methodology for letting the data speak* – which is what Chapter 3 is designed to provide.

The construction of a corpus of researchable data is fundamentally connected with the formulated problems or questions. What we need are *criteria for data to count as (carriers of) evidence* in the search for ingredients of ideology of the type specified in the problem to be investigated.[4] Having said this much, I cannot overemphasize the fact that it is not merely data selection I need to talk about. Data selection principles must derive from a specific social-scientific approach or orientation. The approach we have in mind is summarized in the quite general second 'rule of engagement,' a starting point from which a number of more specific data selection principles will follow:

Rule 2: Before an aspect of meaning can be seen as an ingredient of ideology, it should emerge coherently from the data, both in terms of conceptual connectedness with other aspects of meaning and in terms of patterns of recurrence or of absence.

For a good interpretation of this rule, a serious warning is needed about the notion of *coherence*. The rule is *not* meant to suggest that ideologies are themselves coherent and solid wholes. For one thing, there is a reason why I have tried to avoid using the plural 'ideolog*ies*' or the singular '*an* ideology.' While it is neither possible nor necessary to carry this practice to its extreme, it is important

---

[4] For a useful discussion of 'evidence' and 'data' in pragmatics and discourse analysis, see Blommaert (2004). Compare with the notion of evidence in historiography, as stated by Hobsbawm (1997, p. 358):

> Without entering the theoretical debate on these matters, it is essential for historians to defend the foundation of their discipline: the supremacy of evidence. If their texts are fictions, as in some sense they are, being literary compositions, the raw material of these fictions is verifiable fact.

The added complication for discourse-based ideology research is that, while every aspect of every piece of text can be said to *be* a verifiable fact, what we are looking for requires interpretation, a step away from mere fact. This is what imposes specific requirements on data for them to be useful as evidence.

to point out that ideologies cannot be regarded as separable and self-contained 'entities.' In Eagleton's (2007, p. 193) words,

> We have seen that the concept of ideology embraces, among other things, the notion of reification; but it can be argued that it is a reification all of itself. Nobody has ever clapped eyes on an ideological formation, any more than on a Freudian unconscious or a mode of production. The word 'ideology' is just a convenient way of categorizing under a single heading a whole lot of different things we do with signs [...] It is probably more useful here to think along the lines of Ludwig Wittgenstein's doctrine of 'family resemblances' – of a network of overlapping features rather than some constant 'essence.'

Moreover, the very existence of what sometimes seem to be ideological certainties in a modern world otherwise dominated by epistemological skepticism can easily be seen as a contradiction in itself.[5] Or, to quote Billig,

> instead of beginning with the assumption that there is some deep-seated, possibly innate, desire for consistency, one might assert the natural ability of people to tolerate ambivalence.   (1982, p. 167)

Indeed, a desire for consistency and a tolerance for ambivalence both have a role to play in everyday life as well as in the development of ways of thinking. It would be a mistake, moreover, to ascribe consistency or coherence to ways of thinking as such, while relegating ambivalence or inconsistency to the domain of the individual. This is a serious error in George Lakoff's (1996, p. 15) analysis of the opposition between conservatism and liberalism as "two major categories of moral and political models for reasoning about politics." According to Lakoff, the models are fully coherent in their approach to issues as diverse as abortion, environmentalism, the minimum wage, affirmative action, and the like (to be explained in terms of two opposing models of the family: the Strict Father model and the Nurturant Parent model), while individuals can be seen to adhere to idealistic or more pragmatic versions of the models, to mix them in various ways depending on the circumstances, or to lean more toward one on a given occasion (e.g., in presidential elections) and to the other on a different occasion (e.g., when deciding how to vote in congressional elections). The reality of fully coherent models is not doubted in Lakoff's account: There are pure ideas as opposed to the less orderly reliance on ideas by people.[6]

Lakoff (1996) could have been a perfect example of the following observation by Foucault in *The Archaeology of Knowledge* (1972, p. 149): "The history of ideas usually credits the discourse that it analyses with coherence." Thus coherence tends to be 'found' either by considering contradictions as surface

---

[5] This point is made by Susser (1988).

[6] In a sense, with his emphasis on the cognitive-scientific analysis of pure conceptual models in the field of morality and politics, Lakoff comes very close to the ideals of the original French *idéologues* of the end of the eighteenth and the beginning of the nineteenth century, recalling in particular Destutt de Tracy's preoccupation with establishing a true science of thought or a science of ideas as a firm and stable basis for the moral and political sciences.

phenomena or by postulating contradiction as a basic fact of life, already given before the discourse as a precondition. Foucault then takes a position – labeled 'archaeological analysis' – that can best be rendered as a string of quotes:

> For archaeological analysis, contradictions are neither appearances to be overcome, nor secret principles to be uncovered. They are objects to be described for themselves, without any attempt being made to discover from what point of view they can be dissipated, or at what level they can be radicalized and effects become causes.   (1972, p. 151)

> In relation to a history of ideas that attempts to melt contradictions in the semi-nocturnal unity of an overall figure, or which attempts to transmute them into a general, abstract, uniform principle of interpretation or explanation, archaeology describes the different *spaces of dissension*.
> (1972, p. 152; italics in original)

> A discursive formation is not, therefore, an ideal, continuous, smooth text that runs beneath the multiplicity of contradictions, and resolves them in the calm unity of coherent thought; nor is it the surface in which, in a thousand different spaces, a contradiction is reflected that is always in retreat, but everywhere dominant. It is rather a space of multiple dissensions; a set of different oppositions whose levels and roles must be described.
> (1972, p. 155)

In the same vein, ideology research must recognize that real contradictions are as likely to occur as nicely coherent constellations of beliefs. Our migrant research, for instance, was sparked by the suspicion of a contradiction between overt and more covert layers of meaning. In the case of the old history textbooks it will not be possible to navigate around the discrepancy between attitudes to colonization and its violent corollaries on the one hand and the by then 100-year-old Declaration of the Rights of Man (in France) and the outspoken pride in taking ever more steps toward parliamentary democracy (in Britain).[7] In many ways, these are some of the more interesting facets of what happens in the world of ideology. Why, then, do we need Rule 2?

Rule 2 should be read literally: It concerns the way in which ingredients of ideology (with all their internal contradictions) emerge coherently from the corpus of investigated data. Coherence, in this sense, refers to *systematically observable conceptual connections between aspects of meaning* (e.g., reference to the importance of Flemish values to justify measures imposed on migrants, or reference to the character or behavior of the colonized to explain the need for military action) as well as to *systematic patterns of recurrence* (e.g., the consistent problematization of cultural diversity) *or of absence* (e.g., the complete absence of any reference to notions of freedom and equality in chapters on colonization, in contrast with their high-profile presence in other parts of the same work).

---

[7] Such discrepancies have continued throughout colonial history. Just think of the role of the British in Hong Kong, where real democracy was not made into a serious goal until the years preceding the handover to China.

In order to be able to establish such coherent emergence of aspects of meaning, the corpus under investigation must meet certain standards. Rules 2.1 through 2.4 are an attempt to capture the main criteria.

First of all, a demand for the coherent emergence of patterns of meaning would not make much sense if the chosen data type itself made this predictable. A certain degree of variability seems mandatory. Hence Rule 2.1:

Rule 2.1: *Types of data must be varied horizontally and vertically.*

Horizontal variation refers to *genre differences*. For instance, when we set out to investigate Flemish attitudes to diversity in society, it was not enough to focus exclusively on political policy statements. In fact, we studied four completely different types of data source in order to be able to draw some wide-ranging conclusions. First, we analyzed mainstream news reporting, mainly – but not exclusively – in the printed press. Second, we had a look at political policy statements. Third, social-scientific research reports (appealing to political policy makers and usually highly mediatized) were investigated. Fourth, we also attended and scrutinized a training program designed by a government institution for public officials, including police officers, to help them cope more efficiently with the challenges posed by a confrontation with minorities or 'migrants.' What all these data shared was their mainstream character and their availability in the public sphere. What is important at this point is their variability: journalistic, political, social-scientific, and educational; written versus oral; accessible to everyone versus more restricted (the training sessions, for example, though still in the public sphere, were targeted at specific selected audiences). Restricting one's investigation to only one specific genre could not lead to generalized conclusions bearing on a wider society, as one might be confronted exclusively with genre-specific idiosyncrasies. It is not until patterns can be found that recur across different genres that general conclusions can be drawn.

This does not mean that genre-specific studies would be uninteresting for ideology research; but, in those cases, the narrower scope of one's research results must be specified very clearly.[8] In that sense, the second case study to which I will make systematic reference, the history textbooks, cannot provide equally conclusive evidence in relation to views on colonization in late nineteenth- and early twentieth-century Europe. History textbooks form a very specific genre. These materials would have to be complemented with other generically different types of data in order to obtain generalizable outcomes. This is a clear reason why I have to stress that this case study serves only the purpose of illustrating a set of methods. However, to compensate minimally for this shortcoming, the

---

[8] This is not to say that our migrant research, by looking at four different discourse genres, captures all of mainstream Flemish society. We do claim, however, that we reach a better approximation, justifying a higher degree of generalization, than if we had restricted the research to just one genre.

textbook materials have themselves been varied as much as possible: French materials are contrasted with a range of British sources; the British sources themselves differ greatly in the amount of detail they provide, in the audiences they want to reach, and in the areas and periods they cover.

What is meant when Rule 2.1 requires *vertical variation* in addition to horizontal variation across genres? This requirement bears on *structural levels of analysis*. It is not enough, for instance, to study patterns of word choice. Interesting as this might be in its own right, it could never be enough to draw serious conclusions pertaining to ideology – though it might form the basis for serious questions to be investigated further. The reason is that all language use is always monitored by the users themselves.[9] Conscious self-monitoring, however, can never be accomplished at all levels of structure at the same time. When restricting one's analysis to one structural level (say, word choice) one might, without knowing, be stuck to a level that happens to be carefully monitored, thus distorting the picture of ingredients of ideology that, in this case, may only look like they are taken for granted and get carried along in the discourse while in fact they are inserted purposefully. This risk is avoided by varying the levels of analysis throughout the corpus under investigation. In our migrant research, for instance, we analyzed our (horizontally varied) data at the following (vertically related) levels of structural depth: patterns of word choice,[10] presupposition- and implication-carrying constructions,[11] interaction patterns,[12] and more global constructs (such as argumentation patterns).[13] Many more detailed distinctions can be drawn, as will be

[9] This is what a theory of pragmatics would refer to as metapragmatic awareness. Winch's (1958) idea of the 'meaningfulness' of all social action (in the sense of its being interpreted by the actors engaged in it) counts all the more for verbal action. The choices that people make when producing and interpreting utterances are constantly subject to reflection – even the most 'automatic' of choices do not fully escape this metapragmatic awareness which, in many ways, is the condition sine qua non for human language as we know it. This reflexivity often takes the form of self-monitoring, in the private as well as in the public sphere. See also Verschueren (2000).

[10] For instance, systematic contrasts can be observed in the wording of events that are structurally comparable but that involve different actors. Thus, a farmers' demonstration is systematically called a 'demonstration', emphasizing the legality of a form of protest, no matter how much damage the event does to a city, while the term 'riot', with its overtone of illegitimate social action, would be used for a group of migrant youngsters breaking in a few windows in protest against the shooting of one of their own by the police. The systematicity of such contrasts reveals basic differences in attitudes toward the actors involved.

[11] For instance, the phrase 'Towards a livable multicultural municipality' (the title of a social-scientific symposium) implies that a multicultural municipality, as such, is seen as problematic, requiring special measures to become 'livable.'

[12] E.g., if a member of the extreme right suggests that 'It must be possible to revise all naturalization procedures completed since 1974', then the tolerant majority member's response 'What about those who have adapted themselves?' implies acceptance of the premise that, under certain circumstances, taking away a migrant's Belgian citizenship is acceptable – only a condition is specified (adaptation to the mainstream), which itself implies hesitant acceptance of true diversity.

[13] The overall underlying argumentative model for the Belgian migrant debate turned out to be as follows: (Too much) diversity is inherently problematic; hence negative reactions to diversity (racism, xenophobia), though not to be applauded, are somehow 'normal'; hence a certain degree of homogeneity needs to be restored, which can be done by means of *integration* (a concept which, in the specific debate referred to, basically boils down to assimilation).

clear when I go into procedural specifics in Chapter 3. Rule 2.1 provides, as it were, built-in *triangulation* which, in combination with counterscreenability (see Rule 1) guards the trustworthiness of research results.

The next rule, bearing on the size of the data sample, almost goes without saying, even though pleas can be made for the validity of small samples:[14]

> **Rule 2.2:** *An appropriate amount of data is required.*

The key word here is 'appropriate,' and an evaluation of the extent to which a corpus meets this qualification will depend on the specific nature of one's research question. Clearly, any conclusions in our migrant research would have been unwarranted with a seriously restricted corpus. In fact, we gathered data over a three- to four-year period, amounting to thousands of pages of text representative of an ongoing debate about migrants and migration. Nothing similar can be said for the collection of history textbook materials introduced here for purposes of illustration. Yet I have collected and selected a corpus of books with a total of 4,740 pages (of which 149 are presented in the appendix, 38 in French and 111 in English). For a truly historically valid study of these discourse data on colonization, however, no doubt further relevant materials could and should have been looked at. In particular, detailed comparisons between different editions of the books could have shed some very interesting light on the findings.

Demanding a sizable corpus, however, is also not without its own risk. Given an extensive data base (e.g., of the proportions handled in our migrant research), it would not be difficult, in any given search for evidence supporting an initial guiding intuition, without a systematic balancing act of counterscreening (see Rule 1), to find – or construct – the 'desired' patterns of meaning. Indeed, it would be a very simple exercise to piece together an ideology of one's own choosing on the basis of bits of 'evidence' picked up from quite unconnected fragments of discourse, as long as there is enough discourse to play around with. Hence the usefulness of Rule 2.3:

> **Rule 2.3:** *Whatever is found throughout a wide corpus should also be recoverable in (at least a number of) individual instances of discourse.*

The suggestion is not that there would be a logical need for this. Given careful counterscreening in the course of the analysis, the risk of ideology construction taking over genuine empirical ideology research is minimized. In other words,

---

[14] Note that there is a significant difference between attempts to describe the relationship between language and ideology in general (where a cursory review of properties of language that lend themselves to ideological meaning construction may suffice; see e.g. Kress and Hodge 1979) and the kind of methodological advice I am trying to formulate for focusing on linguistic properties (in the wide sense embodied in a theory of pragmatics) of discourse that can be explored systematically in the search for evidence supporting or contradicting a specific interpretation related to meaning generation processes that can be seen as 'ideological.'

the influence of bias can be kept under control by the careful self-monitoring and self-critical application of research procedures (as outlined in Chapter 3). But experience teaches us that confidence regarding the validity of research findings based on a large corpus benefits significantly from the observation that the main ingredients of what one has identified as an ideological pattern co-occur in individual instances of the discourse under investigation. That is why Blommaert and Verschueren (1998) devote a chapter to the analysis of a single leaflet that was widely distributed by the official Belgian information bureau Inbel (through a wide range of high-exposure channels, such as the post offices). In fact, it turned out to be relatively easy to demonstrate that the entire skeleton of mainstream rhetoric of 'problems' of diversity and their solutions was reflected in this document (as well as in others of which an individualized analysis was not presented in the same way). There is no doubt that this strengthened the conclusions.

Having commented on the need for variation in the corpus, its size, and the inherent dangers of a large data set, the main guideline to be kept in mind for determining whether data can count as evidence in the search for answers to a certain research question is the following:

Rule 2.4: *The quality of the data must be carefully evaluated in view of the precise research goal.*

In other words, *data sampling is itself goal- or question-driven* (which provides one of the necessary qualifications of my claim that empirical ideology research is data-driven rather than hypothesis-driven). Going back again to the migrant research, remember that the initial intuitions gave rise to the suspicion that, in spite of overt invocations of tolerance, mainstream Flemish society was not ready to accept fundamental forms of diversity. This means that instances of discourse had to be collected that were characterized by a general appeal to tolerance, thus immediately excluding the rhetoric of the extreme right. Furthermore, 'mainstream' sources were needed, such as the main newspapers and magazines, policy statements issued by the major political parties, and research reports written by influential social scientists. Together, these two points of orientation led us to the coining of the term 'tolerant majority' to identify the corner of society whose discourse would be subject to analysis. Within the general discursive fields in question, further delimitations are possible on the basis of the motivated link between data sampling principles and research questions. For instance, in a search for widespread attitudes to diversity, regular news reports and news analyses provided by a newspaper's staff members tend to score more highly on a scale of relevance than letters to the editor; the reason is that they are not just expressions of personal opinions (though news analyses, especially, can be that, too), but that they are written with (assumptions about) the frames of reference of the paper's (intended or average) wider audience in mind.

Let me dwell a little longer, for the sake of illustration, on the criteria and considerations that have motivated my choice of materials for the history textbook case. Remember the test case intuition that late nineteenth-century and early twentieth-century Europeans, in general, looked at or were led to look at colonization, including the violence it involved or required, as a perfectly legitimate way of dealing with the rest of the world. As said before (in relation to Rule 2.1), a more varied set of data – along the horizontal genre axis – would have been required to ultimately warrant general conclusions. It would also have been necessary to look at voices of dissent[15] and to provide a good motivation if they were not allowed to enter the picture. Abstracting from that shortcoming, which would have been serious if the real purpose of this book had been to fully analyze attitudes to colonization, my motivations for the choice of materials must be situated in relation to (i) the history of mass education in the nineteenth century, (ii) traditions of history teaching, and (iii) traditions of historical writing. But let me first give an overview of the texts, fragments of which are to be found in Appendix 2; it is those fragments that will be referred to systematically throughout Chapter 3. The following sources were selected:

Lavisse, Ernest 1902 *Histoire générale: Notions sommaires d'histoire ancienne, du Moyen Âge et des temps modernes* (17th edn.) Paris: Librairie Armand Colin. [1st edn. 1882].

[Cassell's] 1903 *Cassell's Concise History of England – Being the Growth and Expansion of the British Empire from the Roman Invasion to the Diamond Jubilee.* Melbourne: Cassell & Company.

Fearenside, C. S. 1922 *Matriculation Modern History – Being English History from 1485 to 1901, with Some Reference to the Contemporary History of Europe and Colonial Developments* (2nd edn.). London: University Tutorial Press [1st edn. 1902].

Hearnshaw, F.J.C. 1930 *A First Book of English History – with Epilogue AD 1913–1927.* London: Macmillan & Co. [1st edn. 1914].

Innes, Arthur D. 1927 *History of England*, Part III, *1689–1918*. Cambridge: Cambridge University Press [1st edn. 1907; with additions 1921].

Kerr, P. H. and A. C. Kerr 1927 *The Growth of the British Empire.* London: Longmans, Green & Co. [1st edn. 1911; revised 1921].

Low, Sidney and Lloyd C. Sanders 1910 *The History of England During the Reign of Victoria (1837–1901)* (part XII of *The Political History of England*, ed. by William Hunt and Reginald L. Poole). London: Longmans, Green & Co.

McCarthy, Justin 1908 *A Short History of Our Own Times, from the Accession of Queen Victoria to the Accession of King Edward VII.* London: Chatto & Windus [1st edn., title ending in *[…] to the General Election of 1880*, published in 1888].

---

[15] Indeed, most periods have their voices of dissent. An example in the case of colonization at the very beginning of the twentieth century would be Hobson's (1902) critical account of imperialist policies.

Parkin, George R. 1911 *Round the Empire*. London: Cassell & Company [1892, revisions in 1898, 1903 and 1911].

Ransome, Cyril 1910 *A Short History of England, from the Earliest Times to the Death of King Edward VII*. London: Longmans, Green & Co. [12 earlier editions, gradually expanded with the course of events; 1st edn., with title ending in *[…] to the Present Day (1890)*, published by Rivingtons in 1890].

Richardson, E. M. 1924 *The Building of the British Empire*. London: G. Bell & Sons [1913, revisions and enlargement 1921, corrections 1924].

Synge, M. B. 1908 *The Great Victorian Age*. London: Hodder & Stoughton.

Warner, George Townsend and C.H.K. Marten 1912 *The Groundwork of British History*, Part II. *From the Union of the Crowns to the Present Day* (by C.H.K. Marten). London: Blackie & Son.

Woodward, William Harrison 1921 *An Outline History of the British Empire from 1500 to 1920*. Cambridge: Cambridge University Press [1901, 2nd edn. 1912, 3rd edn. 1921].

These sources differ from or are comparable to each other along a number of dimensions.

(1) Language

What distinguishes Lavisse (1902) from all the others is that it is in French. In fact, this was the book that triggered my interest in this case study. It was clear from the beginning that, if we were aiming for representations of colonization beyond a strictly French point of view, at least one point of comparison would have to be taken. Britain was an obvious choice, as it was definitely the most successful of the European colonial powers at the time, and because traditional British–French rivalry (persisting in spite of an absence of open conflict over almost a century) could be expected to produce differences of perspective, thus making similarities all the more interesting in a wider framework. Once the search for British materials started, it became clear that there was an abundance of historical writings to choose from, and that many of them focused very specifically on the building of the British Empire. In order to keep the data manageable (in such a way that they could be fully presented in Appendix 2), all colonization-related passages from Lavisse were selected, and it was decided that the specific point of comparison would be a single high-profile incident in British colonial history for which the relevant passages would be lifted out of a range of British sources. The chosen incident is generally known as the Indian Mutiny of 1857, a particularly appropriate case to look at from the point of view of the inevitable tension between legitimizations of colonization and the violence involved.

(2)   Temporal perspective

The temporal perspective of all the sources is pre-World War I, to be situated between 1882 and 1914, placing Lavisse, first published in 1882, at the very beginning of this period (its 1902 edition, the one I am using, being the seventeenth).[16] Some of the books I work with (in particular, Fearenside, Hearnshaw, Innes, Kerr and Kerr, Richardson, and Woodward) bear a later date, but this does not seem to alter the perspective, certainly not the perspective taken on the middle of the nineteenth century: Fearenside (1922) was first published in 1902, and its coverage ends in 1901, the original having been reproduced with little or no change; Hearnshaw (1930) was first published in 1914 and is very explicit – even in the subtitle – about changes, amounting to no more than an appendix covering the period 1913–1927; Innes (1927) is a reprint of a 1921 edition which itself contained only additions – also reflected in the subtitle ([...] *1689–1918*) – to the original 1907 publication; Kerr and Kerr (1927) is a pre-World War I publication, dated 1911, with a first revision bearing on the war period in 1921; Richardson (1924, p. v) is a 1913 publication, reissued in 1921 with "certain alterations and additions that the years since 1913 have made necessary"; Woodward (1921) is the third edition (with adapted title: [...] *from 1500 to 1920*) of a 1901 book with a second edition in 1912. Some of the other books I have used are also reprints or new editions of earlier works. Of these, Parkin (1911) was published for the first time in 1892, and for two others I have not been able to find the first date of publication; McCarthy (1908) is an update of an older edition, first published in 1888 and subtitled [...] *from the Accession of Queen Victoria to the General Election of 1880*, a condensed version of a more extensive and academic *A History of Our Own Time*; Ransome (1910) went through twelve earlier editions, expanding the period and adapting the title accordingly, the earliest version dating back to 1890 (the title ending in [...] *to the Present Day (1890)* instead of [...] *to the Death of King Edward VII* – which was 6 May 1910).

The choice for a consistent pre-World War I period is an important one. The historical reason is the same as why Hobsbawm (1987 and 1995) makes 1914 the transition point between his *Age of Empire* and his *Age of Extremes*: it is the moment when Europe was shocked out of its civilizational optimism, built up by a century without major armed conflicts between the established European powers (with a brief interruption by the Crimean War involving Russia on one side and France and Britain on the other), by steady advances in technology and education, and by a sense of unrivaled superiority in the world (with about one-third of the world population living in colonies around the globe controlled by European states).[17]

---

[16] The edition I am using makes reference to the *Programme de 1887*, the official school program that serves as a point of reference for French public education at the end of the nineteenth century (see Lavisse 1902, bottom of p. 2, just below the preface). Whether or not this implies major changes in relation to the first edition I have not been able to ascertain.

[17] Most of the ingredients of this civilizational optimism are captured in McCarthy's preface when he says, referring to the years that had passed since 1880: "We have had during these more recent

(3)   Geographical perspective

In keeping with the language distinction, there are also two focal points in the geographical perspective to be found in the materials: France and Britain. The French publication was published in Paris. All but one of the English-language publications were produced in London (ten) or Cambridge (two). The one exception has Melbourne as its place of publication. However, this is an anonymous work, specifically dealing with British history, intended for general use in schools, and published simultaneously in Britain and in Australia (still very much perceived as part of Britain at the time) by London-based Cassell & Company. There is only one (interesting) indication of the Melbourne edition possibly having been adapted for local Australian use: a glued-in separate sheet on the first page following the front cover, which says:

> ERRATUM
> Substitute the following somewhat detailed account of Captain Cook and his Voyages, for that given on Page 99.

This is then followed by a full-page narrative (twice the size of the paragraph it is meant to replace) emphasizing Cook's role in the discovery of Australia and, indeed, correcting some of the details (changing the date of discovery from 1788 to 1770, changing the reason for beaching the *Endeavour* in North Queensland from cleaning the vessel to repairing a hole caused by striking a coral reef, and ascribing the settlement at Sydney Cove to Captain Phillip in 1788, eighteen years after Cook's landing at Botany Bay, rather than to Cook himself in 1788). Whether this sheet with corrections was also put into the edition in Britain is unknown to me.

(4)   Size and degree of detail

Along this dimension, the different sources vary a great deal. Table 1 summarizes the main properties of the different texts, also giving the exact number of pages.

days some definite and I trust memorable attempts to bring about a combination among the great Powers of the world for the establishment of an international tribunal having for its work the adoption of a common code which should hold the war spirit in check and subject it to healthful control from the principles of equity and the spirit of peace [...] Nothing certainly can be more remarkable in the developments of later years than the growth which we can see in the influence of popular opinion all through the civilised world. Education has been spreading everywhere, and nowhere more, in proportion at least, than in our own country, where the work of genuine national education had been strangely neglected even until far down in our own times. [p. viii] [...] That reign [Queen Victoria's] will happily be memorable, above all things else, for its contribution towards the arts of peace. It had a literature of its own [...] Its poets were of their own time [...] It had a school of art all its own [...] Science conquered for herself entirely new kingdoms [...] proclaimed as a part of political science the principle of nationalities [...] We see its happy effects in our own colonial dominions [...] It changes reluctant and struggling peoples into willing and prosperous partners in the British State. [p. ix] [...] Our own times may, on the whole, be regarded as having created an ever memorable era in the development of civilisation [...]." (1908, pp. viii–x).

The closest equivalent to Lavisse (1902) in terms of size and degree of detail is Cassell's (1903). Purely in terms of size, Richardson (1924) would seem closer, but it differs much more from Lavisse because of the restricted scope, combined with a completely different form of presentation.

(5)   Coverage

The amount of detail that a textbook contains is directly related not only to its size, but also to its geographical and historical scope. Thus, Lavisse (1902) is no doubt the widest source, covering 'world history' from antiquity to the late nineteenth century, though from a clearly European perspective and always bearing the link with French history in mind (while being careful not to overrepresent France). None of the British sources has the same wide scope. Without a single exception, the focus is entirely on Britain and its empire, and many of the books select a recent period while some also go back to Roman times. See Table 1 for details.

(6)   Intended audience

Most of the books are quite explicit about the audience they are meant to reach. Only Low and Sanders (1910) and perhaps McCarthy (1908) are strictly 'academic,' the former being the last one of a twelve-volume series on the political history of Britain and the latter being a condensed version of a much more extensive academic work. All others have clearly educational goals (at various levels of formal schooling), though some of the British sources also hope to reach a general audience. Here is a brief overview:

Lavisse (1902) says on the title page:

À L'USAGE
DES CANDIDATS AU CERTIFICAT D' ÉTUDES PRIMAIRES
ET DES ÉLÈVES DE L'ENSEIGNEMENT SECONDAIRE

[FOR USE
BY CANDIDATES FOR THE PRIMARY EDUCATION CERTIFICATE
AND BY PUPILS IN SECONDARY EDUCATION]

This explicit indication clearly places the target audience at a level that is further specified as follows:

Programme de 1887. – **Histoire**.
(COURS SUPÉRIEUR, DE 11 À 13 ANS.)" (p. 2)

[*Program of 1887* – **History**.
(UPPER-LEVEL COURSE, FROM 11 TO 13 YEARS OF AGE.)]

The expected background knowledge is also specified (again on the title page, to be more fully explained in the preface):

Ce livre fait suite à **tous les cours** d'Histoire de France

[This book follows **all courses** of French History.]

This explains partly how overrepresentation of France in this textbook (see above, *Coverage*) could be easily avoided.

Cassell's (1903) describes itself on the title page as

For School and Home Use.

This book clearly casts its net as widely as possible, which is much further specified in the preface, from which I quote the relevant passages:

> The **clear** and **concise** form of this work will commend it to **busy people** who desire to refresh their memories in the important events which have taken place [...]
> As a **School History** this little book contains all that is essential, without being burdened by needless details – so bewildering to the opening mind of the scholar, and it is issued at a price within reach of all.
> [...]
> **General Readers** as well as **Teachers** will recognise the merits and usefulness of this **Concise History**, and **Scholars** will possess a book sufficiently full for all Home, School and Examination work."   (p. 3)

Fearenside (1922) places itself at the end of secondary education and at the beginning university level with *Matriculation* in its title. This is further explained as follows in the preface, sharply contrasting with the quote from Cassell's:

> This book is intended to meet the requirements of the London University Matriculation syllabus in Modern History [...]
> The syllabus states: "The questions will be framed to test the general conceptions of history and historical development rather than technical detail." In a text-book, however, technical detail is to some extent necessary in order that from it the reader may obtain conceptions which shall be duly in accordance with facts; and it is for the teacher to see that in endeavouring to fulfil the University requirements the learner founds his generalisations on a proper knowledge of leading events, persons, and dates, and also of the meaning of such common technical terms as must be used even in an elementary treatment of the subject."   (p. iii)

Hearnshaw (1930) says:

> This little book is intended in the first place for school children who, having passed through the early stages of instruction, in which legend and anecdote play the main part, are called upon to make their first systematic survey of authentic English History. It is hoped, however, that it may also be useful to those of more mature years who for one cause or another have not made acquaintance with their country's story, and desire to do so.
> In a sketch containing less than forty thousand words it has, of course, been found impossible to mention all the facts [...] The aim of the writer has been to select those facts which appear to him to be of prime significance,

and to weave them into a connected, intelligible, and (so far as possible) interesting narrative. It would have been easy, by adopting a method of analysis, summary, and tabulation, to pack ten times as much information into this book as it actually contains. But it is felt that to have done so would have involved so complete a sacrifice of movement, continuity, and life, that the results would have been fatal. It is incomparably more important that those who read a first sketch of English History should rise from their study with their reason satisfied, their curiosity aroused, and their interest quickened, than [p. v] that they should have their memories stored with a mass of detailed information.   (pp. v–vi)

It is not clear from this what is meant by "the early stages of instruction." However, the book itself looks as if it was probably intended for use in secondary education.

Innes (1927) presents itself as a book "For use in schools" (title page), which is further defined as follows:

This work is set forth as a School History, because it is specially designed to meet the needs of the middle and upper forms of schools [...]

[...] but the class whom the compiler has primarily to consider are those, roughly speaking, between the ages of fourteen and eighteen, and their teachers.   (p. v)

The school-orientedness is also abundantly clear from the rest of the preface, in which Innes explains how to weigh facts and insight, the demands of examinations, and the didactic organization of the text.

Kerr and Kerr (1927) does not give any explicit indication of its intended audience. From the style and structuring of the book, however, an educational purpose (whether or not in school contexts) can be gleaned. Just consider the following passages:

1. We hear a great deal nowadays about the British Empire; how great it is, how it is spread all over the face of the world, so that the sun is always shining on some part of it, and we feel very proud of belonging to it. But do we ever stop to think what we really mean by it? What is the British Empire? What is it made up of, and how did it ever come to be? What is it going to be in the future? [p. 1] [...] All these things we must know, if we are to understand about the British Empire.
   [...]
3. You know how, in a real family, the members are all different; some are big and old and like to walk by themselves, and some are still small and want to hold their mother's hand. So it is with the Empire. Some of England's children are quite grown up and can not only manage their own affairs, but can take their share in the conduct of the Empire's business. Some of them she still holds by the hand. But whatever their age, they are all fond of their Mother and of each other, and they all stand together whenever danger threatens or they have a common work to do.

(pp. 1–2)

Especially striking are the inclusive "*we*" in the first paragraph and the direct form of address in the third. But these are only two of the characteristics of a clearly didactic tone which persists throughout the book, the tone of a teacher telling a story to (probably relatively young) children.

Low and Sanders (1910), as said before, seems to be the only publication in the present collection that is clearly academic, addressing fellow scholars.

McCarthy (1908) does not have explicit educational goals either; rather, it seems first and foremost intended for a wide general audience, being a condensed version of a much bigger academic publication comparable to Low and Sanders (1910). Not only is there no reference to schools or schooling (except that the preface mentions the spread of national education as one of the major achievements of the final decades of the nineteenth century in Britain), the appeal to a wide audience is underscored by the inclusion, at the end of the volume, of a 32-page catalogue of Chatto & Windus' "popular two-shilling novels" and "general literature and fiction." From the preface:

> The 'Short History of Our Own Times' was [past tense is used because of reference to the first edition], I need hardly say, designed as a condensation of 'A History of Our Own Times,' and was meant to suit the especial wants and convenience of the large numbers who can find pleasure and profit in the reading of historical narrative but have not time to spare for much continuous study, and are therefore glad to have at hand a condensed narrative in some popular form not occupying extended space or elaborate shelves.
>
> (p. vii)

Parkin (1911) describes itself on the title page as "For the use of schools." This is further clarified in the introduction:

> This book has been written with the object of giving to boys and girls in our elementary schools a simple and connected account of those parts of our great Empire which are outside of the British Islands, and in which so many of them are likely to find homes.   [p. vii]
>   […]
> It is hoped that this little volume may find its way into many schools, and prove helpful to teachers who are interested in building up British patriotism on that basis of wider knowledge which is necessitated by the wonderful facts of our national growth.   (pp. vii–viii)

Ransome (1910) does not leave any doubts:

> The aim of this History of England is to give a short narrative of the growth of the British Empire and Constitution from the earliest times to the present day, in such a form and within such limits as shall supply the wants of middle and upper forms at schools, candidates for university and civil service examinations, and for the army and navy, pupil and assistant teachers at elementary schools, and students in training colleges, and also shall give a clear and intelligible account of those events and institutions a knowledge of which is so much needed by the student of modern political life.   (p. iii)

Table 1. *Overview of history textbook sources*

Source	Date	Size	Coverage	Audience
Lavisse	1902 [1882]	192	world history, antiquity to late nineteenth century, European–French perspective	(officially sanctioned) schoolbook, late primary to early secondary (ages 11 to 13); background in French history presupposed
[Cassell's]	1903	148	British history, from Roman times to Diamond Jubilee (= 1897), general	aimed at schools (probably late primary to early secondary) + general audience
Fearenside	1922 [1902]	xxii + 512 + index	British history 1485–1901, clear domestic focus, Europe and empire as sidelines	students at the end of secondary education, entering university
Hearnshaw	1930 [1914]	xii + 204	British history, from prehistory to 1913 (expanded 1913–1927), general	students (probably secondary level) + general audience
Innes	1927 [1907]	xii + 252	British history, (Part III) 1689–1901 (expanded 1901–1918), general but strong domestic focus	students at "middle and upper forms of schools" (ages 14–18) and their teachers
Kerr and Kerr	1927 [1911]	viii + 219	British imperial history, from age of discovery to early twentieth century	'educational' (school connection unclear; but clearly lower levels)
Low and Sanders	1910	xviii + 532	Victorian British history 1837–1901, general	academic audience
McCarthy	1908 [1888]	xii + 574	Victorian British history 1837–1901, general	general audience
Parkin	1911 [1892]	viii + 272	British imperial history, from age of discovery to early twentieth century	pupils at elementary schools and their teachers

Ransome	1910 [1890]	xliii + 500	British history, from prehistory to 1910, general	advanced students (middle and upper forms at schools, those preparing for university and civil service exams, and those training to be teachers)
Richardson	1924 [1913]	xii + 180	British imperial history, from age of discovery to early twentieth century	intended for schools (probably late primary level)
Synge	1908	xix +307	Victorian British history 1837–1901, general	probably a general children's book
Warner and Marten	1912	xii + 326a to 737 (= Part II)	British history, (Part II) 1603–1911, general	students at public schools for boys (probably upper levels)
Woodward	1921 [1901]	viii + 246	British imperial history, from 1500 to 1901 (expanded to 1920)	probably students at late secondary/ early university level

Richardson (1924) has "A reading book for schools" on the title page, but the target level is not clarified at all. Judging from the style and content, an educated guess would be the end of primary education.

Synge's (1908) title page says "For children." There are no special references to schools or schooling, though the edifying purpose of the prose is clear. In other words, it is a children's book in the widest sense.

Warner and Marten (1912)'s text states:

> the book strives to encourage the faculties of understanding and reason rather than mere memory; and to make boys think why things happened and what the consequences were [...]
>
> [...] but the book is intended for those who have got beyond the elementary outlines, and who require a general view of the broadening stream of our national history.   (p. vi)

That the audience is to be sought in public schools for boys is apparent not only from the consistent reference to "boys" throughout the preface, but was also to be expected from C.H.K. Marten's role as "Assistant Master at Eton College" (where at least one colleague offered his services for proofreading).

Woodward (1921), finally, does not contain direct clues, but the style and content are very close to those in Fearenside, suggesting a didactic target at the boundary between secondary education and university. There is a marked difference in size (Fearenside being about twice as voluminous as Woodward, both covering roughly the same period from the end of the fifteenth to the beginning of the twentieth century), but the degree of detail is comparable; this is the result of the fact that Woodward deals exclusively with empire-building aspects of British history.

Table 1 summarizes the main distinctions between the different sources used for the history textbook case study.

We must go back now to motivations for the choice of these specific materials in relation to (i) the history of mass education in the nineteenth century, (ii) traditions of history teaching, and (iii) traditions of historical writing. But, first of all, why choose history textbooks as an illustration for research methods in discourse-based empirical ideology research to begin with? The reason is best captured in Hanks' (1996) account of the two senses of the word 'history.' In a first sense, history refers to events of the past or strings of events over a long period of time that are already given and irrevocable; events are 'historic,' then, when they assume particular importance in that given past or if they (are expected to) have effects on the future. Hanks adds:

> In a second, closely related usage, 'history' designates a kind of study, the vocation of people we call historians. To 'do,' 'write,' or 'study' history is commonly understood as the reconstruction or recounting of history in the first sense. This ambiguity in the noun 'history' is different from what we find in nouns such as 'language' (cf. linguistics), 'culture' (cf. anthropology), 'society' (cf. sociology), and 'politics' (cf. political science). And the

> ambiguity is suggestive, I think, of a deeper assumption about the objectivity of history the process and the transparency of history the narrative genre. It is as if what happened can be discovered for what it was and retold as a story of chronology. (1996, p. 268)

Though few educated people, and even fewer professional historians, would today subscribe to the 'objective' nature of (past) events, the ambiguity Hanks describes is a basic characteristic of much unreflective thought, to be transcended only with conscious effort. Much history writing, therefore, *is* taken at face value, in spite of frequent recommendations to the contrary. Just as with journalism, even while claims to objectivity are recognized as unrealistic, still there is the demand of unbiased distance (basically just another word for the same phenomenon, no matter whether it is further qualified as journalistic or as academic), as well as the corresponding expectation that is put to work when interpreting, evaluating, rejecting, or accepting the communicated meaning. And, more often than not, interpretations and evaluations – just like the framing of the meaning itself – reflect the embeddedness of the 'content' of the narrative in a world of unquestioned assumptions that make up ideology. Such assumptions are always easier to detect in materials that do not belong to one's own epoch. That is why the sources I have chosen, in addition to their being characterized by the ambiguity described, suit training purposes very well.[18]

How are the sample data to be situated in *the history of mass education in the nineteenth century*, and how does this make them suitable for the type of research to be illustrated? The decisive observation is that, in both Britain and France, primary education touched the vast majority of the population by the end of the nineteenth century, thus acting as a powerful vehicle for the spread of ideas. The way in which this was achieved, however, followed different routes, which will have to be kept in mind when evaluating the role of the different sources I use.

In France,[19] an idea of universal education had already emerged during the Enlightenment, but at that time it was not agreed upon, let alone implemented in any way. Conceptually, the breakthrough was the French Revolution:

> the Revolution actually attempted to make a difference, for the National Convention not only imagined but created a "right to education" and a vehicle for implementing that right: *instruction publique* [...]
> [...] armed with the concept of [137] *instruction publique*, the revolutionary state undertook to promote and improve primary education. It began a campaign of state penetration that left its mark on the new civic order despite

[18] As Marnix Beyen (personal communication) correctly pointed out to me, the terminological ambiguity which Hanks indicates may also be explained by the fact that the object of knowledge (history in the first sense) cannot be known without the (subjective) stories told by knowing subjects. This complication (absent from sciences which allow for a strict distinction between known object and knowing subject) also characterizes accounts of current events (and hence also anthropology, political science, etc.). The advantage that temporal distance creates for illustrating ideological processes remains.

[19] See, for instance, Léon (1967) and Woloch (1993) for accounts of the development of education in post-Revolution France.

its equivocations and ultimate failures [...] Republicans came to regard universal primary schooling as the hallmark of a progressive nation and as a key
to the prospects of the French Republic. Schools would impart literacy and
numeracy, but would also inculcate republican values. In tandem with new
symbols, images, and public festivals for all citizens, republican primary
schools for the young would constitute a revolutionary pedagogy intended
to wean the French people from its ignorance and prejudices. The revolutionary passion for national integration, for spreading norms and institutions
uniformly across France, also shaped policy on education – as well it might,
considering the sharp disparities in schooling among regions and social
groups, between town and country, between male and female.

(Woloch 1993, pp. 137–138)

The idea of universal education was actually enshrined in the Declaration of the
Rights of Man in 1793: "Education is the need of everyone." The Jacobin premise was that only *éducation commune*, a 'common education,' could develop
equality and fraternity among children of diverse social backgrounds. Attempts
to implement the idea were made as early as 1794 (the so-called Lakanal Law),
but failed as the law was abandoned a year later when Daunou abolished both the
obligation for communities to organize public education and the complete public
funding that was inscribed in the Lakanal Law. However, the temporary return
to the demands of the marketplace, with locally organized and uncontrolled education (characterized by a complete separation between the little local primary
schools that were not at all homogeneous and where the only constant factor was
religious control, and the better-organized secondary education that was reserved
for the higher classes), was never complete:

primary schooling became normative for the nation in 1794, and the French
state never renounced for very long the mission of prodding local communities into accepting that norm.   (Woloch 1993, p. 149)

There were in fact two major exceptions which played their role until 1815:
first, the *idéologues* (the intellectual family to which Daunou belonged along
with Ginguené and Destutt de Tracy) took the position that local demand for
schooling should find its own level; second, Napoléon Bonaparte never gave pri-
ority to popular education. The period 1815–1875, then, sees a gradual introduction of measures favoring the goal of generalized primary education, with
public funding, centrally regulated quality control of teachers, a renewal of the
obligation (formulated in the Guizot Law, 1833) to organize primary education
in every municipality or commune as well as upper-primary education in every
community of 6,000 people or more. The Société pour l'instruction élémentaire was established in 1815, and a team of inspectors was created in 1835.
The number of primary schools went up between 1815 and 1820 from 20,000
to 27,000 and the number of students from 860,000 to 1,120,000. By 1829 there
were already 31,000 primary schools serving 1,370,000 pupils. The number of
teacher-training schools went up from 13 in 1829 to 47 in 1832. In 1848 there

were 63,000 primary schools (19,000 for girls) and 3,500,000 pupils (1,300,000 girls). Still, in the 1860s one-quarter of school-age children did not yet go to school. This proportion, however, diminished quickly. As of 1881, all public primary schools were completely state-funded. And in 1882 (the date of the first edition of Lavisse's *Histoire générale*) schooling became obligatory for ages 6 to 13, with the number of pupils going up from 5,300,000 in 1880 to 6,300,000 in 1900, while primary education was also secularized.

Britain, on the other hand, made a much slower start.[20] In the early decades of Victoria's reign, education remained completely decentralized. There was no regulation as to what was taught, who taught, where the teaching was done. In the 1850s, only half of the school-age children attended school. It is not until education was made compulsory for ages 7 to 10 in 1880 that primary education became more uniform. In contrast to primary education, secondary-level 'public' schools have a much longer tradition. As in Ancien Régime France, education throughout most of the nineteenth century in Britain remained extremely class-based. The 'public' schools (which acquired this name on the basis of the high level of organization they involved in contrast to purely private, often home-based, tutoring) educated gentlemen who would not really have to earn a living; their curriculum revolved around Latin and Greek; most of the students went directly from school into some kind of public service rather than to university; subjects such as science, history, literature, and foreign languages were added only in the 1880s as an 'army' or 'modern' curriculum. Other secondary schools (grammar schools) developed a more useful modern curriculum sooner and served as general academic education for the children of businessmen and farmers, while private business and technical schools taught vocational subjects. For lower-class students, a secondary education provided a route into the middle class by allowing them to become teachers. In 1902, the year after the end of Victoria's reign, an Education Act was passed which required local education authorities to provide secondary schools throughout the country.[21]

Briefly, by 1900 British public education had basically caught up with France in terms of the proportion of the population that it could reach. A decisive factor was the almost simultaneous introduction of compulsory education at the primary level (though one should not forget the difference in age groups for which the measures were meant: 6 to 13 in France, where all communities of 6,000

[20] See, for instance, Baudemont (1980), Goldstrom (1972), Hurt (1979), Mitchell (1996), and Sturt (1970).
[21] In light of this state of affairs of education in Britain in the course of the nineteenth century, it might be surprising to find that the British colonizer was very actively debating the need for education in India. This led, as early as 1813, to a first clause in the East India Company Act stating that education should be publicly funded. And, by the time of the 1854 Despatch from the Directors of the East India Company, there was quite general agreement on the goals of education in India (passing on European knowledge and values) as well as on the vehicle (the English language for higher levels of education, vernacular languages for mass education at a primary level). There were, of course, practical considerations involved: control over the colony required a class of educated local administrators as well as a population that could be effectively 'governed.' For a full discussion of the ingredients of the debate, see Pennycook (1998).

people had been obliged to organize upper-primary education since 1833, and 7 to 10 in Britain). As McCarthy (1908) says about the late Victorian period in Britain:

> Nothing certainly can be more remarkable in the developments of later years than the growth which we can see in the influence of popular opinion all through the civilised world. Education has been spreading everywhere, and nowhere more, in proportion at least, than in our own country, where the work of genuine national education had been strangely neglected even until far down in our own times.   (1908, p. viii)

We must keep in mind, however, that because state control over education in France was established earlier, the content of schooling was more guided and more homogeneous in France than it was in Britain. Hence, Lavisse (1902) was used much more widely and was much more authoritative than any of the British sources that I use for our case study.[22]

Coming to our second question, what about *the history of history teaching* in relation to our data? Remember Ferro's (1981) basic thesis that the images we have of others, and of ourselves, reflect the history we are taught as children. Also remember Harp's (1998) account of the role of primary schools – and the history taught there – in nation building; his test case is a region that changed hands often in the course of a century, Alsace-Lorraine, French until 1870, German 1871–1918, French again 1918–1940, German 1940–1944, and once more French since 1944. The development of public education in the course of the nineteenth century went hand in hand with conscious efforts to produce national unity and identity in a country like France, and the teaching of history was an obvious tool in that process. And even though there was less state regulation of education in Britain until the final decades of the nineteenth century, the mechanisms were very much the same. Textbooks for usage in schools, and especially history textbooks, were very much produced in view of a desired perspective on one's own society and the world at large. As Baudemont puts it:

> En effet, le choix du contenu de l'enseignement est à un double titre un choix d'adultes. Il est effectué par des adultes, en fonction non pas tant des enfants auxquels il s'adresse, que des futurs adultes en eux, des hommes dont la société aura besoin à la génération suivante. On peut donc considérer que le manuel scolaire, en particulier le manuel de base: le livre de lecture, représente une sorte d'index des idées approuvées par une société – ou du moins par ses classes [8] dirigeantes – et des modèles qu'elle propose à l'admiration et à l'imitation de sa jeunesse.   (1980, pp. 8–9)[23]

---

[22] Hence the stamp of officialdom which Lavisse bears at the bottom of the preface page: "*Programme de 1887. –* **Histoire**." This refers to a nationally imposed school program published by the Ministère de l'instruction publique in 1887 in Paris as *Règlements organiques de l'enseignement primaire*. The closest we come to a similar official character of a British text is in Fearenside (1922), which refers to the much more restricted matriculation requirements specifically for London University.

[23] "In fact, the choice of educational content is in two senses an adults' choice. It is made by adults, not so much in view of the children who are its addressees, but in view of the future adults in

She vividly describes how British textbooks in the latter part of the Victorian age can sing the praises of the benefits of industrialization while being entirely silent about the life of workers. In all of this, the presentation of the way in which the British Empire was built occupied a central position. This was, in fact, a success story if there ever was one. Expansion had followed the path of commerce, with Britain controlling 45 percent of all world trade in the 1830s. With a need for raw materials for their industry, with a desire for new (food) products, and with vast quantities of cheap manufactured goods to export, markets were opened, wars were fought to protect free trade, territories were annexed to protect the borders of existing colonies, etc.[24] In the sixtieth year of Queen Victoria's rule, the 1897 Diamond Jubilee, the British Empire contained one-quarter of the world's population. Educational attention to this fact was intense:

> Many of England's people felt a sense of unrivaled national importance. Explorers and soldiers were honored in newspapers, songs, and stories. Boys' magazines, in particular, played endless variations on the theme of conquest and adventure. 'Empire Day' on May 24 was celebrated with flags and school treats that made it a vastly popular holiday for children.
>
> (Mitchell 1996, p. 273)

With Britain's objective international weight going down toward the end of the nineteenth century in spite of its vast colonial holdings, there were extra reasons for trying to stimulate pride and patriotism:

> By the end of the century, however, US industry and German naval power threatened to challenge England's control of the seas and dominance of world markets. War against the Boers in South Africa revealed glaring weaknesses in the army's equipment and leadership. The response was a massive surge of patriotism. Symbols of the Empire and [288] images of subject peoples were virtually inescapable: in songs and advertising, on postage stamps, in the popular press, in fiction for adults as well as for boys and girls.
>
> (Mitchell 1996, pp. 288–289)

In all of this, there was a strong need for legitimation, and education had an important role to play in leading the next generations to believe in their duty to protect poor natives and to advance civilization. Schoolbooks in history and geography contributed to the process, as well as popular literature such as Rudyard Kipling's books,[25] which certainly supported a sense of superiority and which,

---

them, the people society will need in the next generation. One may therefore assume that school manuals, and in particular basic manuals such as reading books, represent a kind of index of the ideas approved by a society – or at least by its ruling classes – and of the models it presents to youngsters to be admired and imitated."

[24] An interesting link can be made between the success of British colonization and political and social stability at home: "The Empire may not have had much direct role in English life, but it supplied employment, adventure, and enterprise for ambitious people of all classes. The ease of emigration protected England from the social turmoil that many European countries experienced during the nineteenth century" (Mitchell 1996, p. 285).

[25] Kipling's popularity peaked in the 1890s, when he was one of the most widely read authors in Britain; he received the Nobel Prize in 1907.

by making engineers, regular soldiers, and children into heroes, put the pride of Empire within reach of ordinary British people.

If the preceding paragraphs have given the impression that the world view of broad layers of the population is determined by what elites decide should be communicated through (history) teaching, it is time to put this in its proper perspective. The influence of mass education is no doubt strong in the period under consideration, when nationhood is being actively constructed in Europe and elsewhere. As clearly argued by historians such as Van Ginderachter and Beyens (eds.) (in press), the construction of identities is not a simple top-down process but is the result of intricate interactions between elite views and objectives, attempts at guidance, receptiveness, resistance, appropriation, and input from below.[26] It is often the result of such processes that is to be found in the authoritative discourse of educational texts. The production of these texts involves the effects of audience design, but without making their functioning less authoritative. As a result, they can be said to reflect dominant ideologies without making specific claims about the sources of the content of domination.[27]

Keeping in mind the above background, the history textbooks for this case study can be predicted to be rich in what I would call 'ideological content.' Why, then, does the case remain interesting? Isn't a search for attitudes toward colonization in these materials similar to a search for attitudes to diversity in the discourse of the present-day European extreme right? Can we not expect that everything we are looking for is right there at the level of what is explicitly said? In fact, the data themselves contradict such an expectation. Though the supposed benefits of colonization for the colonized are often put in the limelight, much of the discourse under investigation is more subtle. This is related to our third question: the place which our sample data occupy in relation to *the history of history writing*.

History writing has not always been the same. The development of its various fashions and styles is too complicated to lend itself to a summary account. What is important for our purposes is that the materials in our sample corpus are all to be situated in the period of the rise of critical historical scholarship, in which an ideal of 'historical objectivity' had come to dominate. This characterization

---

[26] A classical and powerful description of the process of national identification is provided by Weber (1977). He clearly shows how schooling was one – but only one – of the important factors in the building of French nationhood. One aspect of the multidirectionality of influences is captured well in the following quote:

> It was only when what schools taught made sense that they became important to those they had to teach. It was only when what the schools said became relevant to recently created needs and demands that people listened to them; and listening, also heeded the rest of their offerings.   (Weber 1977, p. 303)

[27] While a historian may, for specific purposes of historical analysis, need to be able to identify sources that are predominantly revealing of a perspective from below, we do not necessarily have to be able to differentiate between sources of perspectives for the sake of ideology research, as all discursive expressions are by definition the product of variable influences that feed into the generated meaning – the end product being our real topic of research.

of the period we find in Barnes' (1962) pioneering account of historiography, in which he explicitly positions Lavisse, Innes, Hearnshaw, and Low and Sanders in such terms.[28] Iggers (1975) refers to the period as the era of 'scientific' historical scholarship, while Novick (1988) – with specific reference to American historical practice – talks of 'professionalization.' Though Bentley (1997) would prefer to reserve the term 'profession' without quotation marks for the period after World War I, his assessment clearly goes in the same direction:

> The years from 1860 to 1914 saw considerable change none the less and an observer surveying the background, working conditions, sources, production, expectations and theoretical sophistication of Western historians on the eve of Sarajevo, could hardly miss significant developments engendered over the past half-century.   (1997, p. 442)

In Barnes' words:

> Historical scholarship, by 1914, seemed to have attained a very high degree of impartiality. Patriotic sentiments were subordinated to the desire to tell the truth. Of course, important historical works were still being produced which were dominated by patriotic ardor, but these were the exception rather than the rule.   (1962, p. 277)

Thus the sources we are dealing with make a conscious attempt, or present themselves as making such an attempt, to apply rules of objectivity (while allowing patriotic ambitions to transpire to varying degrees). We find this explicitly in Lavisse's preface (1902, p. 2), where he combines the goals of 'sober' history writing with patriotic education:

> Ces notions d'histoire générale, pourvu qu'elles soient données sobrement, rendront grand service aux écoliers […] Elles seront aussi le complément de l'éducation patriotique […]

> [These notions of general history, if they are presented objectively, will render a great service to the students. […] They will also complete patriotic education […]]

The resulting discursive complexity is what makes the period of history writing we are looking at so interesting. Briefly, a restriction to materials from the period around the turn of the nineteenth to the twentieth century in France and in Britain seems sufficiently warranted for the illustrations in Chapter 3 on the basis of the tradition in history writing which they represent. This is not to suggest complete discontinuity with the following period. Barnes says:

> Then came the first World War, and there was a revival of patriotic enthusiasm on the part of the historians, which temporarily carried historical writing back, in psychological temper at least, to the generation before von Ranke.   (1962, p. 277)

---

[28] None of our other sources is mentioned by Barnes (1962), but most of them seem to fit the paradigm of their time.

But the very fact that we can use barely changed post-World War I reprints of pre-World War I textbooks shows that changes in approach as a result of the war should not be exaggerated.[29] Yet, materials from before and after 'our' period often have a markedly different style. A small anthology of excerpts may clarify this.

Earlier sources often make the account of the Indian Mutiny – the topic of our sample texts – more personalized:

> However, the topic of greatest interest, since the Russian war, has been the Mutiny of the Sepoys, toward the suppression of which the gallant Colin Campbell – afterwards Lord Clyde of Clydesdale – did so much. Its outbreak at Meerut in the spring of 1857, the story of the greased cartridges, the hideous massacre at Cawnpore, the siege of Delhi, the relief of Lucknow, the death of the heroic Havelock, and the fall of Bareilly are still fresh in every memory; and bitter tears are still dropping in Britain for those whose graves are far away.   (Collier 1875, p. 329)

Clearly, the events are close enough to require only the briefest reminder. Still this is also a schoolbook, while at the same time appealing to a wider audience. It is a general history of Britain, starting with the Roman empire. The above quote is all it contains about the Indian Mutiny.

At the other end, post-1914 history textbooks often show signs of serving the purpose of kindling patriotic sentiment. Thus Prothero's wartime account – the author having been in the Indian Educational Service, and being a Fellow of the Royal Historical Society of London and an Examiner in Indian History to the Civil Service Commissioners – does not leave any doubt about his allegiance:

> The British Empire maintains peace and good government amongst its subjects, it cares for human life by taking measures against disease and for the prevention and relief of famine, it exercises impartiality among rival religions, and it deals out even-handed justice to all its subjects. [76] [...] The Empire is a natural growth, statesmen have struggled against its expansion and the increase of their responsibilities; but their purpose was thwarted by various causes, and the Empire has expanded all the same.
>
> (1917, pp. 76–77)

The same tone emphasizing the inevitability and naturalness of the British Empire is still to be found in Williamson, the first edition of which was also published during World War I, in 1916:

> Wellesley, by a series of successful wars, had doubled the area of British jurisdiction in India [...] for a time the rate of expansion slackened. Yet expansion was steadily forced upon the British by the course of events, and India could not settle down to a stable condition until British power reached up to the natural mountain frontiers of the country, and until also the native

[29] I am grateful to Marnix Beyen for making this pertinent observation (personal communication).

> military forces within the country had been taught that it was useless to oppose themselves to the British peace.   (1956, p. 304)

On the other hand, there are also voices that relativize more than would have been possible in earlier days:

> The work of such Governors-General as Bentinck and Dalhousie had been of great benefit to the Indian people – or so, at least, it seemed to the British. It was not understood that the Indians did not like western ways and that they preferred to live as they always had done, without having railways, post offices, schools, and other things introduced by the British. The improvements in India were not wanted by the Indians.
>
> (Southgate 1947, p. 310)

Patriotic tendencies seem to be strongest in works originating in areas where nation building was still very much an issue, as for example in Australia. Thus the explicitly edifying purpose of Currey (1943), set against the background of two world wars which provided occasions for the construction of national myths, is clear. It is his intention to show "the slow but sure overthrow of the rule of Force by the rule of Right" (1943, p. 3), and to illustrate Australian national unity in this struggle against the "rule of Force":

> Australians think of themselves, not as Tasmanians or Queenslanders, but as Australians. They work together, play together, fight together. [9] [...] As Australians, the A.I.F., with their Allies, scaled the heights of Gallipoli, captured the forts of Bardia, and drove the Japanese from Papua.
>
> (1943, pp. 9–10)

Or, to quote Hobsbawm (1995, p. 23): "Australians and New Zealanders forged their national consciousness on a peninsula in the Aegean – 'Gallipoli' became their national myth [...]."

The theme of identity construction gradually becomes more subtle (and, therefore, maybe more interesting again for purposes of discourse-based ideology research) in the following decades. But the background of the world wars is kept in the foreground at least well into the 1950s, to the extent that even the terminology of the 'rule of force' persists, as witnessed in Clayton:

> The year 1945 saw the conclusion of the greatest conflict in history, a conflict in which neither territory nor trade was the principal issue at stake, but one that brought two orders of life face to face. The Axis Powers, comprising Germany, Japan, and Italy, advanced as the champions of despotism, world domination, and the rule of force. The British and American peoples accepted the challenge as the defenders of democracy, self-government and freedom.   (1958, p. 1)

This book does not show any qualms about presenting Britain as the champion of self-government (a path the British had not necessarily followed voluntarily in relation to all the dominions which by then had been granted self-government) and freedom (disregarding the many years of subjugation most parts of the British

Empire had been subjected to). Facing the title page of this 1958 book (which is presented as the "third revised edition" – leaving the identity of the earlier editions unclear, though it is essentially the same book as Clayton [1941] which bears a different title and which is itself a rewriting of the relevant portions of Clayton [1931] with yet another title and a somewhat wider scope) is a picture of Lord Durham, captioned "Champion of Self-Government" – obviously the leading theme of the book.[30]

From our point of view, such sources would have been less interesting to look at because there is less of a tension between professed views and the underlying message or frame of reference in relation to the colonial experience – though for many other purposes they are fascinating as well.

Appendix 2 to this book contains all the major portions from the selected textbooks which illustrations in Chapter 3 will be drawn from. As pages are always reproduced in full, and the materials will be presented in an easy-to-follow sequence (Lavisse first, and then all the British sources in alphabetical order by author), all examples and illustrations from this corpus will be referred to quite conventionally (name + date, page number); most of them will then be easy to find in their proper context, though occasionally it will be necessary to quote examples from non-reproduced portions of the same texts.

---

[30] The 'first' and 'second empires' in the title of the 1941 book, and used as terminology in the 1958 book as well, though the focus has by then shifted to the difference between the periods before and after the onset of the introduction of forms of self-government and the emergence of the 'Commonwealth,' refer to the British Empire before and after the loss of the thirteen colonies with the American Revolution.

3   Pragmatic guidelines and procedures

Chapter 1 of this book spells out some basic properties of ideology in the form of 'theses.' These properties give rise to the formulation of a number of 'rules' to be followed if we want to engage with ideology, as described in Chapter 2. This brings us to Chapter 3, which is a presentation of general 'guidelines' and practical 'procedures' to be followed in the actual process of investigation; these will be interspersed with a number of 'caveats' or warnings. What I hope to provide is *a package of methods grounded in a clear methodological perspective inspired by a general theory of linguistic pragmatics, viewed as the interdisciplinary science of language use.* The proposal will not at all contradict Thompson's claim that

> However rigorous and systematic the methods of formal or discursive analysis may be, they cannot abolish the need for a creative construction of meaning, that is, for an interpretative explication of what is represented or what is said.   (Thompson 1990, p. 289)

On the contrary, *rejecting a clear opposition between formal and non-formal analysis, steps will be described that ought to be taken in order to provide sufficient grounds for interpretation* (and for refuting certain interpretations). Clearly, *interpretation is an integral part of the research process.* It is not an add-on to formal analysis, even though the full-scale formulation of an interpretation – in the guise of a research report – may be the last step (in which not all preceding steps need to be fully spelled out). In other words, the following recipe-like admonitions are not just guidelines and procedures for self-contained descriptions of context and formal analyses; they are ingredients and building blocks of an overall act of interpretation.

A brief summary of the core elements of the theory of pragmatics that underlies my approach is not superfluous.[1] The starting point is that using language is essentially an activity that generates meaning. It consists in the continuous making of choices, not only at various levels of linguistic structure, but also pertaining to communicative strategies and even at the level of context. Choice-making characterizes both language production and language interpretation. It can be a process or activity that takes place with varying degrees of automaticity or consciousness. While not all choices are equivalent (some may be more marked than others), they always evoke or carry along their alternatives by way of contrast.

---

[1] For a more complete account, see Verschueren (1999b).

But choice-making can never be avoided, and it is always mediated by a human cognitive apparatus involving metapragmatic reflexivity and exerting a monitoring influence.

A first key notion to make sense of the process/activity of choice-making is *variability*, i.e., the property of language and the contexts of language use which define the range of possibilities from which choices can be made. This range is itself not stable; it is fundamentally changing and changeable. A first pitfall to watch out for in pragmatic analysis is, therefore, the underestimation of variability. A second essential notion is *negotiability*, referring to the fact that choices are not made mechanically or according to strict rules or fixed form–function relationships, but rather on the basis of highly flexible principles and strategies. This property is responsible for various forms of indeterminacy of meaning, but at the same time for the vast meaning potential of limited (though always expandable) means. Its methodological implications will be a major concern in what follows, as the temptation to draw conclusions mechanically from the observation of formal patterns is always there. Finally, *adaptability* is what enables people to make negotiable choices from a variable range of possibilities in such a way as to approach points of satisfaction for communicative needs.[2] The term refers essentially to the dynamic and negotiable interadaptability of forms and functions in the making of meaning. It is this notion that enables me to define four research angles, none of which should be ignored when approaching discourse data: Contextual correlates of adaptability have to be identified; processes have to be situated with reference to different structural objects of adaptability; the dynamics of adaptability must be accounted for; and we must keep in mind the salience of the adaptation processes, i.e., their status in relation to a human cognitive apparatus. Basically, context and structure form the locus of the processes to be investigated. They will also be the anchoring points for the methodological steps described in the remainder of this book, but always keeping in focus that what ultimately concerns us is the dynamics of meaning generation, which is the meaningful functioning of forms of expression in relation to human minds. Figure 2 summarizes the above remarks about the structure of a theory of pragmatics.[3]

Before embarking upon the research guidelines and principles, two initial warnings need to be formulated. The first one generalizes the earlier claim that interpretations presented in a final research report do not constitute a chronologically

---

[2] For a more extensive account of the complex notion of adaptability, which can be used to link evolutionary aspects of language with the processes involved in language use, see Verschueren and Brisard (2002).

[3] Note that, as the visualization in Figure 2 suggests, context and structure are intimately related (see, e.g., Verschueren 2008). For one thing, as soon as an utterance is made (i.e., as soon as a structure is produced) it becomes part of the context. Second, structural choices (e.g., the choice of an informal form of address) may affect properties of context (in the same example, aspects of social relations). Moreover, changes in context may cause shifts in basic properties of structural choices (e.g., in terms of markedness). Other aspects of the relationship will be clarified in the main body of this text (see, e.g., Guideline 2.3).

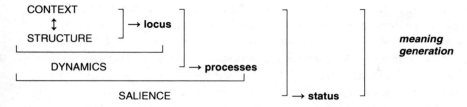

Figure 2. *The structure of a pragmatic theory*

later step in the overall investigation, by applying the same logic to the relationships between all other stages in the process:

> **Preliminary Caveat 1:** *The following guidelines and procedures may be followed*
> *step by step. However, actual research will develop cyclically rather than*
> *linearly. Some steps cannot be completed without going on to further steps, while*
> *sometimes a new step will force you to go back to earlier ones. Therefore: Get to*
> *know the entire set of guidelines and procedures before beginning to apply them.*

This warning pertaining to research practices has implications for the way in
which the following pages have to be interpreted. Since the presentation of
the guidelines can be ordered only in a linear fashion, while actual research is
cyclical, what I have been able to present is no more than a limited number of
illustrations. The remainder of this part of the book, therefore, should not be
interpreted as an example of a full-blown analysis. If the intention had been to
offer a well-founded account of the ideological underpinnings of late nineteenth-
and early twentieth-century history writing about colonial affairs, I would have
had to write a completely different book, the production of which would have
been preceded by a systematic (and, yes, cyclical) application of the guidelines
and procedures, which can now only be illustrated, to the entire corpus under
investigation (and, as suggested before, undoubtedly to a much more elaborate
one). Moreover, for specific research projects it is possible to concentrate on a
subset of guidelines and procedures; this may be necessary if a corpus is large; in
such cases, however, conclusions will have to be formulated in such a way that
their relative significance avoids being overgeneralized.

   In the same vein, a second preliminary caveat warns against looking at the
guidelines and procedures in this book as constituting a self-contained and complete methodology:

> **Preliminary Caveat 2:** *The following guidelines and procedures only serve the*
> *purpose of analyzing collected language use data in view of their relationship*
> *with ideological patterns and processes. A complete research project may have to*
> *involve other, in particular ethnographic, stages preceding or coinciding with the*
> *analysis stage.*

In particular when studying contemporary phenomena, an ethnographic approach may be required to collect the data (usually inevitable when spoken interaction is the topic, whether in institutional or informal settings) as well as for an accurate assessment of the contextual functioning of forms of language use (even if they consist in written texts). It is beyond the scope of this book, however, to spell out principles of linguistic ethnography. For a first introduction, the reader may consult articles on elicitation, ethnography, fieldwork, and interviewing in Senft, Östman and Verschueren (eds.) (2009). For a more extensive guide, see Hammersley and Atkinson (1995).[4]

The first guideline, then, is no doubt self-evident and would have to be respected irrespective of the theoretical background against which a study of discourse in view of ideological processes is to be situated:

Guideline 1: Get to know your data thoroughly.

Self-evident as this may be, its importance cannot be overemphasized. The practical procedures to be followed depend on the nature of the data, where a basic distinction can be drawn between the spoken and the written, and where for spoken data (in addition to their being preferably 'witnessed' in some kind of participant observation context – hence the need for ethnography as pointed out above) recording is a must. In the migrant research we carried out in the early 1990s, both types of data were represented; although there was a heavy emphasis on written materials, some television news programs were recorded and analyzed, and a full cycle of the training program organized by the then Royal Commissariat for Migrant Policies was attended, recorded, and transcribed.[5] Naturally, the sample data for the history teaching case study in this book are all of the written type, while it would be extremely useful in the case of a similar study of present-day history teaching materials to supplement printed text with the spoken words of teachers and their interaction with students. Minimally, the following procedures apply:

---

[4] It is equally beyond the scope of this book to go into the debate on the relations between historical and ethnographic scholarship. Ever since Lévi-Strauss (1958, 1963), a basic comparability between history and ethnography has been assumed, both being concerned with societies other than the one the researcher lives in, where 'Otherness' may be defined in terms of distance in time or space or simply in terms of the sociocultural heterogeneity of the here and now. Some work shows the need for ethnographic imagination in historiography (e.g., Sahlins 1992), while other authors emphasize the historical imagination required for good ethnography (e.g., Comaroff and Comaroff 1992). Also more recently, combinations of a historical and an ethnographic perspective are brought to bear on the study of specific social phenomena (e.g., Arborio et al. 2008 on 'labor'). While these efforts are commendable and the insights they produce are clearly useful, we should keep in mind that, at its core, ethnography requires painstaking fieldwork (so that presenting a discourse analysis of texts situated in a temporally and geographically distant place as 'ethnographic,' as Blommaert 2008 does, may be stretching things).

[5] I would like to repeat our debt of gratitude to Chris Bulcaen, who did all the time-consuming transcription work and the initial analyses.

Procedure 1.1: *In the case of audio-video-recorded data: Listen to/watch several times; transcribe all the data you want to subject to closer investigation.*

Serious research on spoken language data has become possible only since the availability of recording devices which allow one to listen to and/or look at the same stretches of discourse as often as one wants or needs to. For purposes of ideology research, in contrast to conversation analysis which would want to explore minute details of interaction processes for their own sake, relatively broad transcriptions marking the basic chunks of meaningful speech (and accompanying gaze and gesture if available) would usually suffice.[6] But it is important to keep in mind that transcriptions of that kind – or of any kind for that matter – are simplified renditions of the spoken sounds, and that the real data remain the sounds (and images) on tape, to go back to whenever necessary. In Silverstein and Urban's (eds.) (1996) terminology, any transcription would constitute a new *entextualization* which, moreover, introduces a "professional vision" (Goodwin 1994): The way in which talk is turned into text is inevitably guided by choices (comparable to the choice-making that is at the core of all language use) inspired by and contributing to a professional linguistic perspective that will facilitate certain types of observations at the expense of others. This type of researcher influence on the data is inevitable, but as long as it is not naïvely ignored in the analysis, it does not have to be more problematic than the very process of data selection, or than the observer's paradox in ethnography.[7]

Procedure 1.2: *In the case of written text: Read and re-read until you are fully familiar with the materials.*

Simple as this may sound, remember that Carbó (2001) does not hesitate to advocate 'reading' as a method in its own right. Of course, going this far requires a special understanding of reading, but the motivation behind the recommendation is a sound one. In particular, it is important to note that *there are no shortcuts* to avoid or facilitate this stage: *There are no mechanical coding systems that would make it possible to 'access' the data rather than to 'know' them*, even if

---

[6] Many kinds of transcription conventions are available. To make a choice appropriate to one's specific research goals, it is useful to have a look at some overview articles which contain references to more detailed proposals and descriptions. Two such articles are O'Connell and Kowal (1995) and Lenk (1999). More detailed descriptions of different systems are to be found in Edwards and Lampert (eds.) (1993). For a more recent overview of spoken language corpora, all using well-considered transcription conventions, see Aarts (2005). It is also worthwhile to familiarize oneself with the considerations underlying these approaches before engaging with currently available transcription software (which can easily be found on the internet).

[7] The observer's paradox states that the ethnographer must observe, but cannot do this without somehow being 'present,' thereby changing the context to be observed. Rather than to problematize the observer's paradox, this inevitable condition of observation can be seen to provide information that would otherwise have been hard to get. Good examples are Meeuwis (1997) and Jaspers (2005b).

coding systems can be devised – adapted to one's specific research purposes – to 'mine' certain aspects of texts to extract layers of structure and content that are useful to have available for purposes of analysis.[8] In addition to the practical need for reading as part of research practice, it must be kept in mind that texts in themselves do not 'mean'; they always require the sense-giving activity of reading (as is so well argued from an ethnomethodological point of view by Watson 2009) which, as a result, becomes part of the analyst's object as well as his/her method.[9]

It goes without saying that the preparatory Procedures 1.1 and/or 1.2 have already set the stage for or provide the researcher with many of the details or questions required to be able to comply with Guideline 2 (which may also require the kind of ethnographic venture pointed at in Preliminary caveat 2):

> **Guideline 2: Get to know the context of your data. Ask yourself what it is you need to know in order to interpret the data, i.e., about the linguistic context, the immediate context of situation, and the wider context (social, political, historical, geographical, etc.).**

Again, obvious as this may seem, much critical work on discourse fails to ask the relevant questions. Two different types of problems can be seen to emerge in a wide range of available analyses.

One problem is that the contextual embeddedness of the analyses themselves may escape the analyst's attention. Thus it seems not to have occurred to George Lakoff (1996) that his dichotomous analysis of the conservative vs. the liberal models in the moral political field may have been dictated by his own rather arbitrary political context dominated by a two-party system. The apparent limitation of political choice to two possibilities in a US context obfuscates a much wider diversity of political thought that is also available there. One would already have to assume that the two-party system is a 'natural' consequence of the existence of two opposing ideologies, rather than the product of real-world political processes that have as much to do with vested interests as with ideas, to be able to

---

[8] It is easy to imagine, for instance, the development of 'text mining' tools that could be used to facilitate certain procedures needed for a system of international communication monitoring, as proposed by Verschueren, Östman and Meeuwis (2002). But the risk of using such tools should be carefully evaluated in view of the principles of discourse-based ideology research set out in the rest of Chapter 3. With such evaluation in mind one can put to excellent use a number of available tools for qualitative analysis such as NVivo (as described, e.g., by Lyn Richards 2008, 2009) or Natural Language Toolkit (www.nltk.org). For a glimpse of some new methods of text analysis, see Mellet and Longrée (eds.) (2009), and specifically for text mining techniques Feldman and Sanger (2006), with a practical application compatible with the goals of this book in Pollak et al. (in press).

[9] Watson (2009, p. 30) correctly rejects "other analytic formulations which, in effect, reduce one 'half' of the text-reading pair to the other whilst at the same time tacitly relying upon the disattended 'half' in order to conduct the analysis of the other." In other words, ignoring the reading side, and trying to look only at the text as such, is in fact cheating.

take the analysis seriously. In an analysis of political discourse – whether in the United States or elsewhere – one should never lose sight of the contextual constraints imposed by existing political institutions embedded in a power structure. Otherwise one runs the risk of embarking, as Lakoff clearly does, upon an analysis that is itself subject to the same constraints as the discourse to be analyzed. (See also my earlier comments in Chapter 2.)

A second type of problem that should, in principle, be easier to avoid but which, nevertheless, emerges all the time is the simple neglect of (often obvious) aspects of context. Thus when Fairclough (1992, pp. 138–149) analyzes two samples of doctor–patient interaction, he engages in a metapragmatic framing of the contrasts (opposing, in his terms, a 'standard' medical interview, with a doctor controlling the interaction, following a preset agenda, showing no affinity and displaying an absence of politeness, etc., to an 'alternative' medical interview in which turn distribution is negotiated, the patient co-determines the topical development, the doctor shows a high degree of politeness, etc.) which completely ignores even the most basic contextual differences between the two events: Only in one of the two cases does the patient come to the doctor with a clear medical problem; and in one case doctor and patient know each other well whereas in the other case they do not.[10]

This is also the place to issue a warning related to the risk of introducing a gap, as is sometimes done, between (meaningful) forms (subject to formal analysis) and context (recoverable by non-linguistic means). Lähdesmäki and Solin (2000) correctly point out that an interdisciplinary approach, balancing linguistic and non-linguistic input, is important at all stages of the investigation: when asking the research questions, when engaged in analysis, when coming to interpretations. And though he seems to allow for a clear distinction between formal analysis and interpretation (a position I do not share), Thompson (1990, p. 291) may have a quite similar suggestion in mind when warning his readers that they should beware both of the *fallacy of reductionism* ("the fallacy of assuming that symbolic forms can be analysed exhaustively in terms of the social-historical conditions of their production and reception") and the *fallacy of internalism* ("the fallacy of assuming that one can read off the characteristics and consequences of symbolic forms by attending to the symbolic forms alone, without reference to the social-historical conditions and everyday processes within which and by means of which these symbolic forms are reproduced and received"). The point where my view deviates from Thompson's bears exclusively on the separability of formal and non-formal analysis. Before illustrating this, let me formulate the general warning in relation to the handling of context as follows:

---

[10] For a more detailed account of this example, see Verschueren (2001). Note that the contextual differences mentioned are not even referred to in Fairclough's analysis, though they are blatantly clear from the content of the interaction as such.

> **Caveat 2.1:** *Context is not a stable 'outside' reality, nor is it finite in any sense. Hence it cannot be described exhaustively. Those aspects of context may be deemed most relevant – without radically excluding others – which are actualized in the discourse (hence the dictum that discourse constructs context) and which may thus become recoverable in the analysis.*

This formulation contains a number of elements that require further clarification.

First of all, from a pragmatic perspective, 'context' is a cover term for any constellation of ingredients of a speech event, ranging from aspects of a physical world through social-historical phenomena, to mental properties and processes and aspects of the (immediate as well as intertextual) linguistic context. This is why context is by definition non-finite and cannot be described exhaustively – a fact that does not make the notion useless for analysis, as should become clear soon.

Further, there are three senses in which context is not an 'outside' reality that could therefore be described separately or appealed to autonomously in the search for interpretations. First, it includes discursive elements as well: co-text and wider linguistic context, including the properties of the communicative channels that carry both. Second, the very production of discourse itself has an impact on non-verbal aspects of context: Almost all social action involves discourse and is partly shaped by the discourse it involves.[11] Third, language users carve out 'lines of vision' from the unlimited potential of context: It is those aspects of context that language users orient to (as well as aspects that might be carefully or carelessly left out) that are the most relevant for interpretation. More often than not, such orientations leave traces in the discourse itself, which makes it possible to subject them to investigation. In other words, the way in which discourse itself 'constructs' or 'generates' its own context by choosing to select focal points from a vast continuum enables the researcher to find out what the relevant aspects of context are. That is why formal and non-formal analysis must be fundamentally intertwined.

One should also warn, however, against an interpretation of these observations as if they were to imply that all information relevant for interpretation is to be found in the texts to be studied: We cannot radically exclude all contextual information for which no obvious discourse traces can be found. That would be committing what Thompson calls the fallacy of internalism – while from a different perspective it would be inadmissibly reductionistic as well. Such a stance would ignore another basic principle of pragmatics – which will underlie another range of guidelines and procedures to be spelled out later – viz. the inevitability

---

[11] A good test for this is to take a newspaper and to ask oneself which articles bear on events that do not fundamentally involve communication. Chances are that you are not going to find any. Even natural disasters tend to become newsworthy only to the extent that people are directly affected, when action is undertaken which is communicatively prepared and verbally commented upon.

of implicitness. In a sense, of course, implicit meaning is *there*, in the discourse; but in many cases it cannot be accessed without recourse to information that is not expressed at all. In other words, these remarks do not only concern 'implicit meaning' in a strict sense ('carried' as it were by discourse choices): Elements of a more general contextual background of knowledge may become important for interpretation.

By way of illustration of the methodological consequences of this relatively complex state of affairs, have a look at the following example from one of the accounts of the Indian Mutiny:

> Bengal and the greater part of the Madras and Bombay Presidencies kept quiet; and the Sikhs of the Punjab *had been so well used by* Sir John Lawrence *that they helped* the British.   (Fearenside 1922, p. 433; italics added)

This fragment is characterized by what one could call *suggestive vagueness*: The nature of "had been so well used by" is left completely underspecified, yet a causal relation is proposed with "that they helped." This calls for contextual substantiation. The first thing to do is to look for elements of co-text that could provide the missing details. In the case of Fearenside's account, however, this does not really help very much. The furthest we get is the following reference to the same state of affairs:

> The Punjab, annexed [in 1849] after the Sikhs had been *defeated in hard-fought battles* at Chillianwallah and Gújrat, was *organised* by the brothers John and Henry Lawrence *in such a way that* the Sikhs proved the staunchest allies of Great Britain in the trying period of the Mutiny.
> (Fearenside 1922, p. 427; italics added)

At best, this reference is circular: it alludes to underspecified aspects of 'organization' which are in the same way causally linked to the Sikhs' behavior at the time of the Indian Mutiny. In fact, this earlier passage raises additional questions. If the Sikhs had to be defeated in "hard-fought battles," we can hardly assume them to have been natural allies of the British. Hence, crediting the Lawrence brothers (and in particular Sir John) for generating supportive behavior of the Sikhs only emphasizes the question as to what their 'organization' of the Sikhs, referred to as their "use" of the Sikhs in the first quote, involved precisely. Clearly, we are not going to find the answer to that kind of question in a book that refers to what happened in a vague, suggestive, and circular manner.

With this specific example, the rest of the corpus does not help either. Other texts, if they contain relevant references at all, remain equally vague. Consider:

> Sir John Lawrence, the Governor of the Punjaub, who had, by his humane treatment of the Sikhs, endeared those natives to him, now marched in command of a united British and Sikh force to Delhi, the rebel stronghold.
> (Cassell's 1903, p. 124)

> The Punjab was annexed [...] and placed under a commission of able officers, who not only disarmed and pacified the Sikhs, but contrived in the course

of a few years to turn them into the most loyal and contented subjects of the British ráj in Asia.   (Low and Sanders 1910, p. 134)

After great exertions Delhi was captured, mainly owing to the fidelity of the recently conquered Sikhs, which enabled Sir John Lawrence, the commissioner of the Punjab, whose admirable rule had in four years completely won over the Sikhs, to send large reinforcements to the besiegers of Delhi.   (Ransome 1910, p. 443)

Yet, it would be useful to have an explanation. The reason is not that the contemporary early twentieth-century user of the book would have been able to fill in the details, so that we would have to grasp those details in order to make an assessment of their interpretation at the time. In fact, it is quite likely that for those users the quoted passages were as vague as they are for us today, and that there was no additional background knowledge they could rely on to give further substance to the rather abstract expressions in the texts. The real reason is that we need to know, to the extent that we can achieve such knowledge, what it is that the author is leaving unsaid or implicit, whether or not by his own conscious design. Note that this is a case in which the language user's intentionality is not at issue – though we must assume that a serious historian would not make a suggestive appeal to background information without having access to that information him- or herself. What is at issue is the way in which the discourse carves out lines of vision in a historical 'reality,' and the obligation we have as researchers interested in ideological processes to gain whatever insight we can to be able to evaluate the discursive effects those lines have on a resulting picture of the described events. In other words, if this is necessary or useful or both, we cannot allow ourselves not to go beyond the texts. In other words, *though it is the texts that offers us clues as to what the relevant contextual parameters or phenomena may be, filling in the details may oblige us to look outside the texts.*

Going beyond the (corpus of) text(s) usually means going to other texts or other forms of discourse – and not only for historical topics, as most social events are profoundly communicative. For the specific case under consideration, we have a vast range of sources available. From reference works such as Lloyd (1996), Marshall (ed.) (1996), and Porter (ed.) (1999), as well as more specific scholarly studies of the East India Company's army,[12] such as Gupta and Deshpande (eds.) (2002), we can learn some of the basic 'facts' of the situation.[13] Thus the well-trained and well-equipped Sikh army, which had become a threat to the British by its rapid growth in a context of serious instability after the death of Ranjit Singh

[12] Until 1858, British affairs in India – commerce (until about 1850), government, and the military – were managed by the East India Company. The Company's position had already weakened by that time, and there was rivalry between officers directly employed by the Company and those who belonged to 'the Queen's service.' The events of 1857–1858 were used as an opportunity to end Company rule and to transfer India to the Crown.

[13] The extensive later Indian and British literature on the so-called Indian Mutiny includes Alavi (2007), Chaudhuri (1957), Dalrymple (2006, 2007), Embree (1987), Joshi (ed.) (1957), Khan (2000), Majumdar (1957), Mukharji (2007), Mukherjee (1984), Sen (2007), and Stokes (1986).

in 1839, was attacked and defeated by the British troops (consisting mostly of Indian sepoys[14]) in two wars in 1846 and 1849. After the final defeat in 1849, all of Punjab was annexed and the Sikhs were completely disarmed, leaving the area militarily occupied with regiments of the Bengal Army. As this left some 60,000 well-trained Sikh and Punjabi soldiers unemployed, the British soon decided to re-employ some to form extra regiments to guard the new northwestern border. In 1851 it was decided that by then it was safe enough to let Sikhs and Punjabis into the regular regiments of the Bengal Army, but this was heavily resisted by the Hindu sepoys.[15] Then, when the Mutiny broke out and significant parts of northern India were quickly under the control of mutineering parts of the Bengal Army, the British were not keen on turning to native regiments from Madras and Bombay for help, as they were not sure whether the discontent that sparked the Mutiny was shared by the sepoys there. All they could do was to regroup the British forces, to disarm the Hindustani majority of the Bengal Army regiments stationed in Punjab, and to risk a gamble with the few Sikh and Punjabi members of those regiments, giving them key positions in a newly composed military force consisting mainly of re-recruited Punjabis and Sikhs who had themselves been disarmed only a few years earlier. A gamble it was, and doubts remained among the British, including Sir John Lawrence, who knew very well that helping to crush the rebellion was not the Sikhs' and Punjabis' expression of loyalty. Various factors were involved. For one thing, there was a lot of resentment against the now mutineering sepoys of the Bengal Army who were looked upon as inferior by the Sikhs and Punjabis but who had nevertheless been instrumental in the British victory of 1849. Now there was an opportunity to avenge earlier humiliation and – maybe even more importantly – to loot Delhi. Moreover, they could now put themselves in a position of influence that would guarantee long-term benefits. Reopening Punjab as a military recruiting ground offered the

[14] At the time of the Mutiny, there were roughly five Indian soldiers for every British one. Figures given in our corpus vary slightly (257,000 vs. 45,000; 250,000 vs. 50,000; 290,000 vs. 50,000; nearly 300,000 vs. 43,000;? vs. 39,000). These approximations are confirmed by more recent studies. Bosma (2009), for instance, estimates average British garrison strength in India between 1851 and 1900 at 60,000 (compared to only 30,000 in the rest of the empire, and compared to an average of 21,500 before 1850) – where we must keep in mind that the number of British soldiers went up after 1857. In principle, with an annual replacement rate of 15 percent (bringing the estimated total for the period to about 450,000) and soldiers able to remain as a labor force after military duty, this could have resulted in significant white settlement in India. Bosma says: "British advocates of white settlement advanced the argument, for example, that a million Europeans in the hills of Darjeeling would be able to provide a military force that could nip in the bud any repetition of the Mutiny" (2009, p. 330). There were dreams of white agricultural enclaves in the healthier areas, but in fact mainly 'railway enclaves' emerged.

[15] The British Army in India consisted basically of three armies, corresponding to the three presidencies: Bengal, Madras, and Bombay. So, Fearenside's statement that "Bengal and the greater part of the Madras and Bombay Presidencies kept quiet" is somewhat confused and confusing, as there was no one else who could have been responsible for the revolt. The Mutiny was effectively started by regiments of the Bengal Army, stationed in the northern provinces bordering on Punjab. There is some clarification in Woodward (1921, p. 237): "In the Central Provinces the trouble was limited to the Ganges plain. Bombay, Madras, and Lower Bengal itself were untouched by it."

prospect of restoring fortunes lost by earlier defeat.[16] Because they realized that
loyalty could not be taken for granted, the British were very careful not to recruit
more men than was absolutely necessary to hold Punjab and to send reinforcements to Delhi, and Lawrence also paid special attention to the fact that in the
new regiments a single group should not become dominant. In Yong's words:

> Consequently, the composition of the new force came to be a mixed one,
> comprising Sikhs from the central Punjab, various Muslim tribes from the
> western Punjab (which had little in common except religion), Pathan and
> Baluch tribes from the frontier, hillmen, and Punjabi Hindus.
> The raising of a Punjab Force, and its subsequent despatch to Delhi, in
> addition to meeting British manpower needs at a crucial moment, provided
> the British with an important tactical advantage: it reduced the threat of an
> internal uprising by Punjabis by drawing in potentially dangerous elements
> and sending them out of the Punjab.   (2002, p. 20)

Against this background, Sir John Lawrence's "using" the Sikhs "so well"
that they turned into "staunch allies" clearly has two components based in facts:
First, the suggestion is that he must have availed himself of considerable skills
of diplomacy to 'pacify' the recently conquered area; second, a causal link is
introduced with the Sikhs' fighting on the British side. An unwarranted leap in
the description is its suggestion of the Sikhs' "being" – as if unconditionally –
on the British side as a result of good administration. In the years following the
Mutiny, these same staunch allies were still distrusted enough by the British to
make them keep the Punjabi and Sikh troops confined largely to the Punjabi regiments of the Bengal Army, rather than to use them to replace Hindustani elements altogether. The main guideline was a 'divide and rule' principle. It was not
until the late 1880s that Punjab would become the main recruiting ground and
backbone for the Indian Army, when the main threat was no longer perceived to
be internal instability but the possibility of attack from outside the empire, not-
ably by the Russians. It is likely that reliance on warriors from Punjab by the end
of the nineteenth century[17] colored turn-of-the-century perceptions and depic-
tions of their attitude at the time of the Mutiny.

[16] For all its shortcomings, the British raj in India was also known as a reliable source of income.
Soldiers did get their pay. This contrasted sharply with what happened to the rebelling sepoys
who could no longer rely on money or on supplies; as a result, for instance, many of the rebels
left occupied Delhi, reducing their number from about 100,000 to roughly 25,000 by the time the
city was recaptured; no doubt this was one of the major factors that contributed to the failure of
the Mutiny.

[17] During the final decades of the nineteenth century, the British tried to strengthen the Indian Army
(as a defense against potential Russian imperial ambitions) by recruiting what they saw as the best
fighting men in the region. To that effect, they relied on a theory of 'martial races': Some social
groups or 'races' were seen as providing inherently better warriors than others; these included the
Sikhs, Punjabis, Pathans, and Gurkhas – not surprisingly four categories that were also to be found
on the British side in the suppression of the Mutiny. (See Gupta and Deshpande 2002.)

Keeping these remarks in mind, let us now look systematically at and comment on different aspects of context to be investigated, moving from the most general level to the more specific ones.

Procedure 2.1: *Investigate the wider (social, political, historical, geographical, etc.) context, to the extent that it is accessible. In particular:*

2.1.1: *How does the context of the investigation relate to the context of the investigated discourse?*

2.1.2: *How does the context of the investigated discourse relate to the social, cultural, political, historical context which the discourse is (presenting itself as being) 'about'?*

2.1.3: *How does the investigated discourse carve out lines of vision in the 'world' it refers to?*

AD 2.1, IN GENERAL:

[Investigate the wider (social, political, historical, geographical, etc.) context, to the extent that it is accessible.]

As will be clear from the three questions that are formulated to give substance to an investigation of what is here called the 'wider context' (to be contrasted with an 'immediate context of situation' in Procedure 2.2 and the 'linguistic context' in Procedure 2.3), different aspects should be carefully distinguished. First, as already pointed out, a researcher engaging with language use and ideology should never forget his or her own positioning in relation to or involvement in the social structures, processes, and relations that are at issue. No doubt this is a tall order, requiring astute awareness of the (involvement-related) intuitions that lead to a researchable (set of) question(s), as described at the beginning of Chapter 2. A second layer of context pertains to the place occupied by the discourse under investigation. Third, discourse is always (presenting itself as being) 'about' something, and, as indicated before, it can never present a full picture of the 'world' it is about; the way in which 'lines of vision' are carved into that world is another layer of the wider context that can never be ignored, even if a good description of this would require recourse to data outside the object discourse (as illustrated with the example of Fearenside's mention of John Lawrence's good use of the Sikhs as an explanation for their support of the British at the time of the Indian Mutiny).

AD 2.1.1:

[How does the context of the investigation relate to the context of the investigated discourse?]

It is because of values and opinions prevalent in the world today that Lavisse's categorization of "industry, trade, colonization of the world" as "works of peace" triggered my interest in historical accounts of colonization at the time when colonization by European powers was still regarded by many Europeans as the natural thing to do. The investigated materials are full of elements that are judged worthy of our attention just because they highlight divergences of perspective in relation to the investigator's. Consider another example:

> This event closed a somewhat dragging war by compelling China to confirm a *Treaty of Tientsin*, made in 1858, which legalised the introduction into China of opium, ambassadors, and missionaries.
>
> (Fearenside 1922, p. 432)

The enumeration "opium, ambassadors, and missionaries" may not have been unmarked even when Fearenside wrote this, but from a present-day point of view it highlights phenomena (the British being the drug traders of the nineteenth century)[18] and connections (missionaries serving other than purely religious goals) in a particular way that cannot be disconnected from the researcher's own historical context and point of view.

This contextual 'positioning' of the investigation itself is harder to keep in focus when contemporary data are studied, which makes it all the more important if bias is to be kept at bay. The most useful application of ideology research may in fact be to show people how to detect naturalized, but possibly ill-founded, assumptions in texts they are inclined to fully agree with. By the same token, the best test for the validity of the proposed set of methods (and the best training for those learning how to handle them) would be to use them for the analysis of data one can feel aligned with, and then to come up with unexpected findings. This can be achieved only by carefully monitoring (and, when necessary, neutralizing or making explicit) the influence of one's own contextual involvement in the investigation.

Coming back to our case study, it should be clear that an answer to the question of how the context of the investigation relates to the context of the investigated discourse centers around the large distance between the two. We are looking at the history textbooks from a perspective determined by a century of later historical developments. The main difference between the research context and the context of the materials is no doubt the changed view of (the acceptability of) colonization, and hence of the actions and practices it involved. Two things should be kept in mind, however. First, already during the period in which our sample data are situated, colonial practices were not uncontested; Hobson's (1902) book on imperialism, for instance, offers a sharp critique of economic exploitation and exposes the idea of self-government as an imperial smokescreen. Second,

---

[18] Here Fearenside refers to the second of two nineteenth-century Anglo-Chinese 'Opium Wars,' fought from 1839 to 1842 and from 1856 to 1860. These wars were started in defense of British merchants who imported opium from British India into China, in defiance of Chinese anti-opium laws.

interesting parallels may emerge between the legitimation of colonization practices and a wide range of present-day assumptions (and rhetorical strategies) underscoring power relationships in the world.

> ***A*D *2.1.2:***
> [How does the context of the investigated discourse relate to the social, cultural, political, historical context which the discourse is (presenting itself as being) 'about'?]

Any complete attempt to describe the context of the investigation in relation to the context of the investigated discourse would of course bring forward most of the salient features of the latter and would thus reveal much of how the investigated discourse is to be situated socially, culturally, politically, historically in relation to what it is 'about'. The textbooks belong in a world strongly dominated by a few European powers controlling large portions of the globe. In that world, Britain was clearly the most successful of the colonizers, though in direct competition with France, and though the USA and Germany were rapidly expanding their influence while Russia had control over vast parts of Asia and was looking for a bridge to the Indian Ocean.

Clearly, our French source, Lavisse, is situated differently from the British sources. The difference could have been a symmetrical one, but in this case it is not, because of our main focus on an aspect of British colonial history as presented by both the French and the British sources. A simple visualization of the point of orientation is as follows:

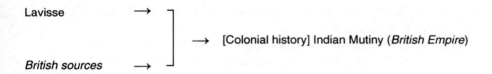

The 'involvement' of the British sources in the depicted events will not be without consequence; a persistent form of reflexivity transpires in the British discourse. Throughout most of the Lavisse corpus, on the other hand, there is a keen awareness of the context of competition for colonial possessions, fueling expressions of regret that France did not do more to prevent the British from acquiring their dominant position (e.g., in India as well as in North America).

What Lavisse shares with the British sources is an overall common outlook on processes of colonization and relations between colonizer and colonized, details of which will emerge from the remainder of this book. A sense of rivalry transpires, but the French and the British are competing in the same game.

AD 2.1.3:

[How does the investigated discourse carve out lines of vision in the 'world' it refers to?]

Finally, we need to devote more attention at this stage to the question of how the discourse under investigation carves out lines of vision in the 'world' it refers to. Far from pretending that we could tell the 'full' story behind the pieces of discourse in our case study sample, there are a number of things that can be put together from reading the sample sources themselves, as well as from more recent publications. I will restrict myself to two salient aspects of the historical 'world' which the texts are 'about': the causes of the Indian Mutiny, and the concatenation of events the term refers to. In relation to each, a table will be presented with an overview of the factors that our sources mention.

The reported *causes of the Mutiny* are quite wide-ranging and diverse. The following aspects seem to be involved:

(I)   Political discontent: 'Native princes,' who were still in control of parts of India in the period preceding the Mutiny, felt increasingly threatened by Lord Dalhousie's annexation policies.[19] Two aspects are repeatedly pointed at:

(a) It was decided that territories under the control of rulers who did not have a son would 'lapse' into the hands of the East India Company, and hence of the governor-general. Earlier, it was the practice that rulers without a son would pass on their authority and privileges to an adopted son. This practice was abolished by the British. (In fact, Nana Sahib, who became one of the leaders of the Mutiny, was the adopted son of a ruler who saw his eminence thus fade away.)

(b) In 1856, Dalhousie deposed the King of Oudh whom he regarded as too inefficient and corrupt, thus taking full control of one of the last relatively important independent kingdoms.

(II)   Social (rural) discontent: Some land reforms resulted in peasants feeling disfavored by taxation or by the gains of rival peasant communities.

(III)   Religious Unrest: Both Hindus and Muslims felt that the British were trying too hard to convert people to Christianity.

(IV)   Cultural unrest, based on the banning of old practices and the introduction of innovations representing westernization:

---

[19] Technically, the East India Company still governed India. But anticipating a transfer of the colony to the Crown (which was effectively carried out shortly after the Mutiny in 1858), the British government appointed a governor-general. In the period preceding the Mutiny, this was Lord Dalhousie, who had just returned to Britain (in early 1856) and had been replaced by Lord Canning.

(a) Government interfered with practices which the British regarded as barbaric (such as widow burning or infanticide).

(b) Roads were being constructed to unite the different parts of India, telegraph lines were being installed (at a very early time, just thirty years after their first appearance in the USA), a postal system was being developed, a railway system was under construction (though only a few dozen miles were already in place), and education was promoted (with emphasis on the teaching of English).[20]

(V) Discontent in the military:

(a) Compensatory allowances for sepoys serving in the Bengal Army in Punjab were cut in 1850 (after annexation of Punjab in 1849), as well as in Oudh after the king had been deposed (the argument being in both cases that now they were serving within their own borders rather than outside them).

(b) Service conditions were deteriorating; in particular, all sepoys were beginning to be considered liable for overseas duty, disregarding earlier respect for Hindu sensitivities: For high-caste recruits, crossing the seas meant loss of caste.

(c) Quasi-hereditary privileges and sources of economic well-being were under threat as a result of the intention of the British to broaden the recruitment base, e.g., by letting Sikhs and Punjabis serve.

(VI) Opportunity:

(a) The presence of British soldiers in India was particularly weak at this time (say about 50,000, as opposed to 250,000 native Indian soldiers), as many regiments had been withdrawn for duty in the Crimean and Persian Wars.[21]

(b) The British military had suffered a loss of prestige; they were no longer seen as invincible, in particular as a result of the disastrous campaigns in Afghanistan.[22]

(VII) Prophecy: there was a belief that British rule in India would last no more than 100 years; the starting date was 1757, the battle of Plassey, which gave the British control over most of the Bengal region.

---

[20] As explained by Pennycook (1998), the emphasis on English was not exclusive; there was a strong tendency to promote primary education in the vernacular and higher levels of education in English; the teaching of English at the primary level was preparatory to its use later. As far as different aspects of 'modernization' are concerned, most Indians were not really touched by this at all by 1857 (Marshall [ed.] 1996), an observation which certainly reduces the relative weight of this 'cause' of the Mutiny. The building of railroads and communication lines was seriously accelerated after 1858, mainly for strategic reasons (Sinha 2007).

[21] The Crimean War, 1853–1856 – a joint French and British action to limit Russian influence in Turkey – and the Persian War of 1856, also involving a struggle with Russia for control over the region.

[22] Particularly disastrous was the first Afghan war, 1838–1842, which ended in the complete annihilation of the withdrawing British troops.

(VIII)   The final trigger: The British army replaced the Brown Bess rifle with the Lee-Enfield rifle, which required greased cartridges, with ends that had to be bitten off, thus bringing the soldiers' lips into contact with the grease that was believed to be cow fat (an insult to the Hindus) or pig fat (an insult to Muslims) or a mixture of both.

We can see the distribution of these causes across our data samples in Table 2.

When interpreting a table like this, it should be kept in mind that categories are not as clear-cut as would be desirable when assigning plus- or minus-values. Thus Fearenside's and Synge's plus for I is based on implicit references to Ia and Ib (which have themselves been given a minus since they are not literally present in the text – this is also the reason why I occurs as a general item in addition to the more specific Ia and Ib, a distinction which was not necessary for the other categories of causes). Similarly, a plus for VIII always implies reference to religious factors, a more specific aspect of which is presented in III; clearly, then, VIII is not completely separable from III, as the greased cartridges were seen as a means of polluting sepoys in order to better prepare them for Christianization (nor, for that matter, are III and VIII completely separable from IVa and Vb).

Moreover, the absence of a clearly indicated cause does not mean that causes are not suggestively present. Thus the only source which does not go into causes at all, Parkin, still cannot avoid implicit reference to discontent which it is then suggested was basically a form of ungratefulness:

> In 1857 occurred the Sepoy Mutiny, when great numbers of the men whom we had drilled and armed so carefully rose in rebellion against our rule.
>
> (Parkin 1911, p. 213)

In the same way, the only two sources that explicitly recognize only one cause, namely the equipment of the army with guns requiring greased cartridges, refer suggestively to a wider context of discontent as well. This is clearest in the case of Cassell's, in which the discontent, which is itself left underspecified, is reduced to a product of manipulation:

> It [the Mutiny] had been long maturing, but the reason put forward by the mutineers was [...] Leaders had for a long time past been instilling feelings of dissatisfaction in the minds of the men, and this pretext was advanced to start the rebellion.   (1903, p. 124)

Lavisse is more opaque in his formulation. Just consider the following excerpts:

> Il y avait dans l'Inde, en 1857, 290 000 soldats; 240 000 étaient des Cipayes, c'est-à-dire des Hindous. Ils avaient encore la vieille religion de l'Inde; ils croyaient que la vache est un animal sacré. Les officiers anglais voulurent leur faire tirer des cartouches enduites de graisse de vache. Les Cipayes se révoltèrent [...]
>
> [...] depuis il n'y a plus eu de révolte, et les Hindous commencent à parler anglais et à adopter les usages des Anglais.   (1902, p. 152)

Table 2. *Causes of the Indian Mutiny*

Cause Source	I	Ia	Ib	II	III	IVa	IVb	Va	Vb	Vc	VIa	VIb	VII	VIII
Lavisse	–	–	–	–	–	–	–	–	–	–	–	–	–	+
[Cassell's]	–	–	–	–	–	–	–	–	–	–	–	–	–	+
Fearenside	+	–	–	+	–	–	–	–	–	–	+	–	–	+
Hearnshaw	+	–	+	–	–	+	+	–	–	–	+	+	–	+
Innes	+	+	+	–	+	–	+	–	+	–	+	–	+	+
Kerr and Kerr	+	–	–	–	+	–	–	–	–	–	+	–	–	–
Low and Sanders	+	+	+	+	+	+	+	–	+	–	–	+	–	+
McCarthy	+	+	+	–	+	+	+	–	+	–	–	+	–	+
Parkin	–	–	–	–	–	–	–	–	–	–	–	–	–	–
Ransome	+	–	+	–	+	–	–	–	–	–	–	–	+	+
Richardson	+	+	+	–	+	–	+	–	+	–	–	–	+	+
Synge	+	–	–	–	+	–	–	–	–	–	–	–	+	+
Warner and Marten	+	+	+	+	+	+	+	–	–	–	–	+	+	+
Woodward	+	+	+	–	–	–	+	–	–	–	+	–	+	+

> [In 1857 there were in India 290,000 soldiers; 240,000 were Sepoys, that is
> to say Hindus. They still had the old religion of India; they believed that the
> cow was a sacred animal. The English officers wanted to make them shoot
> cartridges coated with cow fat. The Sepoys revolted [...]
>
> [...] since then there have not been any revolts, and the Hindus are begin-
> ning to speak English and to adopt English customs.]

The first paragraph sticks to a factual account of the incident with the cartridges and explains why this was such an important matter for the sepoys. The
second paragraph, then, subtly introduces the idea of a *culture conflict* which
was resolved after the Mutiny: The Indians begin to go along with the ways of
the British, which – as is implied by contrast – they may have resisted before.
Thus these few words, pointing at some of the results of the British gaining the
upper hand again, open lines of vision toward factors that are otherwise left
unsaid but which are dealt with, sometimes in detail, by some of the British
sources.

A few sources also introduce causes that are left too vague for inclusion in
the above list, or that appear to be on a par with one of the factors that was
already listed. Thus Innes refers, without further explanation, to "an extensive Mohammedan conspiracy [...] for restoring the Mogul dynasty and the
Mohammedan ascendancy" (1927, p. 170), while Woodward says

> it had been unwise to leave the Moghul as nominal sovereign in the ancient
> capital, Delhi, where his enormous wealth and the prestige of his name
> enabled his household to create a network of anti-British intrigue.
>
> (1921, p. 236)

Both quotations refer to a political context; Innes suggests political discontent, giving rise to a 'conspiracy,' with religious overtones; Woodward adds an element of opportunity.[23] Similarly, Innes cites as a cause of discontent that "the strong hand of government had deprived the lawless sections of society of their old license" (1927, p. 169), a statement which is left unclear, but which may be similar in intent to Warner and Marten's observation that the government had suppressed "bands of hereditary assassins who roamed about India strangling travellers" (1912, p. 690) – something they clearly present, however, as a British course of action "directed to bettering the lot of their subjects," rather than as a possible cause of discontent. One of the additional causes, analogous to the cartridge story, which is mentioned twice (by Low and Sanders and by Richardson), is the circulation of a rumor that the dust of human bones would have been mixed with grain sold to the army. Moreover, directly related to the conditions of service that have already been mentioned as sources of unrest, there was the additional fact, pointed out by McCarthy, that the Indian Army had become "an army of native rank and file commanded by Englishmen" (1908, p. 174), a perfect recipe for lack of attention to the specific needs of the majority of the soldiers. Further, Hearnshaw sees in the Crimean War not only an event that drew away British troops from India, but also an event that, for reasons that are not clarified, "had excited the religious passions of the Mohammedan peoples of the peninsula" (1930, p. 154).[24] Low and Sanders, finally, mentions the average age of British officers as one of the reasons why the revolt could break out and spread so easily:

> Promoted by seniority, many of them were enfeebled by age and long residence in a trying climate [...] These elderly warriors, as events sadly proved, often broke down under the strain of sudden emergency.   (1910, p. 137)

[23] The Mogul (or Mughal) Dynasty ruled most of northern India from the early sixteenth to the middle of the eighteenth century. By the end of the eighteenth century, their dominion had been reduced to a small area around Delhi, first under Maratha and later under British control. In 1857 the Grand Mogul was Bahádur Shah II, no more than a puppet emperor.

[24] This reference provides a good example to illustrate the importance of contextual information. A causal link is introduced between the Crimean War and Muslim religious passions in India, but no explanation is provided. The question is: What explains this link in the mind of the author, and does the author's conceptualization match what was in the minds of Muslims in India at the time of the Mutiny? Conclusive answers to such questions would require serious historical research. Knowledge of some basic facts of the Crimean War seems to cast doubt on the causal link (though it may of course have been produced by a specific way of communicating or possibly manipulating those 'facts'). To the extent that religion was at all involved in the causes of the war, it concerned a dispute between Catholic and Orthodox Christians (in relation to who was granted authority over the holy places in then-Ottoman Palestine). In the war, both Britain and France fought against the Russians for the protection of the (Muslim!) Ottoman Empire – mainly to stop the spread of Russian influence rather than out of sympathy for the sultan. A further question could be, then: Were there, perhaps, consequences that were disadvantageous to Muslims in such a way as to 'excite religious passions' in India? As said before, only historical research can provide the answers. But the conclusion may very well be that the author is confusing a number of things: the weakening of the British presence in India as a result of the war on the one hand, and differently grounded fears that the British would want to interfere in religious affairs on the other. But then, this confusion may also have been there in the minds of some Indians at the time of the Mutiny.

In line with this comment, it is suggested that a faster reaction to the uprising at Meerut could have prevented mutineers from reaching Delhi, which became the center of the rebellion once they did.

Table 2 also reveals interesting patterns. Most obviously, perhaps, of all the sources that go into causes, only one (Kerr and Kerr) omits reference to the story of the greased cartridges. This source, in addition to mentioning the small numbers of British soldiers present in India at the time, reduces the entire account of the causes to one sentence:

> The native princes were jealous of the power of England, and the people thought that the British were going to interfere with their religion.
>
> (Kerr and Kerr 1927, p. 183)

Note also, at the other end, that none of the sources mentions the fact that extra compensations for the sepoys sent out to Punjab and serving in Oudh had been slashed (Va) and that there was unrest related to anticipated changes in recruitment (Vc), two factors about which later historical accounts agree. Obviously, these did not belong to the story as commonly told at the time.

Finally, it is also clear from Table 2 that quite a number of authors (at least including Innes, Low and Sanders, McCarthy, Richardson, and Warner and Marten) make a conscious attempt to be as complete as possible in their enumeration of causes; whatever was left out by them may be all the more important, as they may have regarded them as simply negligible (rather than the author's not being aware of them, since emergence in other sources shows accessibility). The most complete accounts usually also add a measure of surprise regarding the fact that, in spite of the many causes for discontent, the British (except, according to one source, Sir Henry Lawrence) had not seen the Mutiny coming.

More important than the actual occurrence of a specific cause in the explanation given by a certain author is the way in which the cause is presented. Some of the details will re-emerge when discussing additional research procedures in the following pages. But meanwhile it is worthwhile drawing the attention to a few of the more striking phenomena.

First, the theme of a cultural conflict is evoked more strongly in many of the British sources than in Lavisse, though, as pointed out, it is to be found there as well at an implicit level. Here are a few of the examples:

> Finally, the introduction of European education, the suppression of some cruel and obnoxious native religious customs, the zealous labours of Christian missionaries, the development of railways and other Western devices, appeared to forebode the total suppression of Eastern civilisation and the destruction of oriental faiths.   (Hearnshaw 1930, p. 154)

> Recent western innovations, and more particularly the introduction of railways and the telegraph, had shocked and alarmed the natives, who were encouraged by the Bráhmans to see in these inventions an attack upon their religion.   (Low and Sanders 1910, p. 136)

> Further, Lord Dalhousie made railways, and introduced the telegraph and the use of postage stamps. The rapid changes upset the natives [...].
>
> (Richardson 1924, p. 136)

> Western reforms mystified and unsettled the Eastern mind, and natives thought that the world was being turned upside down.
>
> (Warner and Marten 1912, p. 690)

> It is undoubtedly true that the very passion for honest government which animated Lord Dalhousie had stirred up discontent amongst those who benefited most by his policy. He had not allowed – as Lawrence did in the Punjab – for the intense conservatism of Oriental races, to whom oppression from their own kin is preferable sometimes to freedom at the hand of foreigners.   (Woodward 1921, p. 235)

> Perhaps Indian society had been passing too quickly through a period of change; the British temper was restless and pushing; steam, electricity, education, newspapers, betokened a future still more disturbed.
>
> (Woodward 1921, p. 236)

Though there is a suggestion of cultural backwardness on the part of the Indians, British measures are sometimes described as liable to criticism. In particular, many of the authors seem quite convinced that Dalhousie's annexation policies were a bit reckless:

> The reforms were sometimes carried out with too little regard for the prejudices and racial customs of the Hindus themselves, and several times Lord Dalhousie offended them very much.   (Richardson 1924, p. 136)

> Thus some of the leading princely houses of Northern India, Hindu and Mohammedan alike, were smarting under a sense of wrong, and their agents were active in promoting discontent.   (Low and Sanders 1910, p. 136)

Since, at the same time, most of our sources praise Dalhousie to the skies as a man with vision and real leadership, interesting attempts are made to balance criticism and justification:

> The violent changes in Oudh, well-meant from the English standpoint but injudicious in their suddenness, had been ill received.
>
> (Woodward 1921, p. 236)

> Necessary and justifiable as these proceedings were, they roused considerable alarm among the Indian princes and great landowners.
>
> (Low and Sanders 1910, p. 135)

Sometimes justification does not have to be spelled out, as it is driven home with absolute clarity by ascribing the revolt completely to attitudes inherent to the mutineers, as in

> It was not by any means a merely military mutiny. It was a combination of military grievance, national hatred and religious fanaticism, against the English occupiers of India.   (McCarthy 1908, p. 170)

or by discrediting the grounds for resentment:

> But we must above all other things take into account, when considering the position of the Hindoo Sepoy, the influence of the tremendous institution of caste. An Englishman or European of any country will have to call his imaginative faculties somewhat vigorously to his aid in order to get even an idea of the power of this monstrous superstition [...] No doubt there was in many instances a lack of consideration shown for the Hindoo's peculiar and very perplexing tenets. To many a man fresh from the ways of England, the Hindoo doctrines and practices appeared so ineffably absurd that he could not believe any human beings were serious in their devotion to them, and he took no pains to conceal his opinion as to the absurdity of the creed, and the hypocrisy of those who professed it.   (McCarthy 1908, p. 173)

The presentation of the key element, recognized by all (except Parkin) as the immediate trigger for the revolt, the story of the greased cartridges, is interesting in its own right. One source brands this cause as 'trivial':

> suddenly excited over a trivial dispute concerning greased cartridges
> (Hearnshaw 1930, p. 154)

Another one calls it a 'pretext':

> It [the Mutiny] had been long maturing, but the reason put forward by the mutineers was, that the cartridges served out to them were greased with cow's fat [...] Leaders had for a long time past been instilling feelings of dissatisfaction in the minds of the men, and this pretext was advanced to start the rebellion.   (Cassell's 1903, p. 124)

All seem to agree, however, that it would have been stupid for the British to have greased cartridges with cow fat (and/or pig fat), given the sensitivities of Hindus (and/or Muslims). The crucial question, then, is the factual basis of this account. Some sources jump to a denial:

> When the improved (Enfield) rifle was introduced into the Indian army in 1856, the idea got abroad that the cartridges [170] were made up in paper greased with a mixture of cow's fat and hog's lard. It appears that the paper was actually greased, but not with any such material as that which religious alarm suggested to the native troops.   (McCarthy 1908, pp. 170–171)

In most cases, truth judgements are avoided by sticking to a 'report' or (opening the way to the possibility of falsehood more directly) a 'rumor':

> And then came the report that Hindus and Mohammedans alike would suffer contamination by the use of the new rifles and cartridges just issued to the troops; since the cartridges were said to be greased with the fat of pigs which the Mohammedan reckons unclean, and of cows which the Hindu accounts sacred.   (Innes 1927, p. 170)

> Then came the rumour that the cartridges to fit the new rifles which had been lately given to them were greased with the fat of pigs and cows.
> (Richardson 1924, p. 137)

> It was rumoured that the new rifles required greased cartridges, and that they were greased with hog's lard, forbidden to Mohammedans.
>
> (Synge 1908, p. 113)

Two sources, however, mention explicitly that there may have been some facts behind the story:

> The soldiers were rapidly drifting into that state of panic which is capable of driving Orientals to frenzy. Stories were circulated that the dust of human bones was deliberately mixed with the grain sold to the army by government contractors. And then came a rumour, more alarming than any other, which ran like wild-fire through the sepoy lines in the late autumn. The old Brown Bess musket was being replaced by the Enfield rifle, and then ew [sic] cartridges were lubricated in order to fit the grooves of the barrel. It was universally believed that these cartridges, which the men had to bite with their teeth, were greased with a mixture of cow's fat and pig's lard. Thus the soldiers of both religions were outraged by the thought of touching with their lips the fat either of the unclean pig or the sacred cow.[2] The government tried to allay the excite-[138]ment by publishing a chemical analysis of the cartridge-grease, and instructing the officers to assure the troops on parade that the defiling ingredients were not employed. But the sepoys were filled with terror and suspicion, and fit for any violence.
>
> [2] It seems that some cartridges lubricated with the objectionable composition had actually passed into the hands of the troops before the issue was checked by the authorities. The evidence is however conflicting. See [...].
>
> (Low and Sanders 1910, pp. 138–139)

and

> The story may have had a slight foundation of truth in it.[1]
>
> [1] The cartridges had to be greased in order to fit into the groove of the barrel. Though the evidence is conflicting, it is probable that some of these cartridges – though they were almost immediately recalled – were smeared, by some mistake, with the ingredients to which objection was taken.
>
> (Warner and Marten 1912, p. 691)

Without going into this issue further, it may be interesting to note that more recent historical accounts also tend to be unclear on the issue. Thus Yong (2002, p. 15) talks of "Rumours that these cartridges were to be greased with cow and pork fat" Marshall (1996, p. 50) qualifies the cartridges as "apparently coated with ritually impure animal fat," and Lloyd (1996, pp. 174–175) says: "when the new rifle turned out to have cartridges of which the paper had to be bitten off, Hindus and Muslims were united in common outrage because it [174] appeared that the cartridge paper was waxed with a mixture of pig and cow fat." Others, e.g., Spear (1965) and Spilsbury (2007), clearly suggest that the first cartridges issued for the new Enfield rifle were indeed of the objectionable type, but that they were recalled and replaced quickly – though too late. Far from making claims about an objective truth, the preceding pages show the differential positionings *vis-à-vis* aspects of context and how they are achieved by linguistic means.

The reported *events of the Mutiny*, looking collectively at all of our data samples, can be summarized as follows, ordering them in episodes rather than trying to respect a strict timeline:

(A)   Early outbreaks of rebellion before the 'real' start of the Mutiny.

      (i)   Open insubordination is reported in a number of places from as early as 25 February 1857.

      (ii) These outbreaks are suppressed relatively quickly.

(B)   The outbreak of the revolt at Meerut.

      (i)   More than eighty sepoys refuse to obey their officers (in particular, they refuse to receive/use the greased cartridges); this is followed by a trial and prison sentences; sepoys are sent to jail on 9 May 1857.

      (ii) Sunday, 10 May, the prisoners are released by their fellow sepoys who murder officers and other Europeans.

      (iii) The revolt spreads to neighboring camps.

      (iv) The night after the revolt, the mutineers escape from Meerut and march on Delhi.

(C)   Delhi is occupied by the rebels.

      (i)   Sepoys arriving from Meerut cause a general uprising in Delhi and Europeans are attacked and killed.

      (ii) The old descendant of the Mogul kings, Bahádur Shah II, is set up as emperor.

      (iii) Some British soldiers (under Lieutenant Willoughby) keep defending the arsenal for a while and blow it up when they can no longer hold it.

(D)   The siege of Lucknow.

      (i)   Sir Henry Lawrence tries to keep control over Lucknow from May onwards, but is forced to retreat into the Residency on 30 June.

          (a) Sir Henry Lawrence is mortally wounded two days after retreat into the Residency, 2 July; he dies on 4 July.

      (ii) In September 1857, Sir Henry Havelock comes to the rescue (after defeating enemy forces at Cawnpore) and manages to break through the enemy lines on 25 September after having been joined by additional troops under General Outram (on 15 September).

          (a) General Outram, technically Havelock's superior, decides to serve under Havelock, to leave him the honor of victory.

      (iii) Havelock still does not have the manpower to break the siege and is forced to remain in the besieged city until more forces arrive.

(iv) 16 November 1857,[25] Sir Colin Campbell arrives and relieves Lucknow; withdrawal of the entrapped garrison is completed on 24 November.

(a)   Havelock dies on 24 November.

(E)   Cawnpore falls into the hands of the rebels.

(i)   From 5 June, Sir Hugh Wheeler, in command of a small British force in a hard-to-defend open structure, and with about 400 women and children under his protection, withstands a siege of 21 days.

(ii)   Out of food and ammunition, the besieged surrender 27 June 1857 on Nana Sahib's promise of free conduct out of the city. The promise is broken: The departing troops are attacked, all men are executed (except four who escape) and the women and children are locked up in a small prison house, the Bibigarh.

(iii) Eighteen days later, on 15 July, when British forces under Sir Henry Havelock are approaching, the women and children are murdered. Many sources have graphic descriptions of this event. It is also this that Lavisse refers to when he says:

Le chef des révoltés, Nana-Sahib, massacrait les Anglais, les femmes comme les hommes, et faisait jeter les enfants au feu.

(Lavisse 1902, p. 152)

[The leader of the rebels, Nana Sahib, massacred the English, women and men alike, and ordered the children to be thrown into the fire.]

The final detail of this account does not occur in any of the other descriptions, most of which mention a well which all the bodies are thrown into.

(F)   Havelock defeats the rebel forces at Cawnpore, but arrives too late to rescue anyone; he cannot keep the city occupied, as he has to move on to Lucknow.

(G)   Delhi is recaptured.

(i)   Almost immediately after Delhi is occupied by the rebels, a long siege starts, from May to September 1857; several commanding officers follow each other: first General Barnard (who dies in June), then General Reed (who becomes ill), then Archdale Wilson, who holds on until sufficient reinforcements have arrived.

(ii)   14 August 1857, John Nicholson (sent by Sir John Lawrence, who governs Punjab) arrives from Punjab with a combined British and Sikh army.

(iii) 14 September 1857: A successful attack on the city is led by John Nicholson; Delhi is recaptured completely on 21 September.

---

[25] Synge (1908, p. 122) mentions 17 November; this date may bear on the actual relief of Lucknow rather than on Campbell's arrival.

(a) John Nicholson is mortally wounded when he attacks the Lahore gate (the only gate which the British do not manage to take from the outside) from inside the city.

(iv) The puppet emperor is captured and deported as a state prisoner to Rangoon.

(v) There are massive reprisals and executions.[26]

(H) Campbell moves back from Lucknow with the rescued soldiers and civilians, and meets and defeats a rebel army from Gwalior (headed by Nana Sahib and Tántia Topí) before being able to take firm control over Cawnpore.

(I) There is a second siege of Lucknow (where only General Outram has stayed behind with a small force in a fortress) in March 1858; British control of Lucknow is now complete.

(J) A further campaign (including the capture of Jhánsi) by Sir Hugh Rose and Sir Colin Campbell, lasts well into 1858.

(K) The Rání (princess) of Jhánsi, whose adopted son was one of those disinherited by Dalhousie's measures, retires with Tántia Topí into Gwalior, which is finally recaptured in June 1858.

(L) By the end of 1858, all remnants of the revolt have been crushed, though Tántia Topí is not captured and hanged until April 1959; Nana Sahib espaced and was never heard of again.

Converting this into a timeline, we get Table 3.

An overview of the events, as mentioned in each of the data samples individually, is given in Table 4.

---

[26] The detail introduced by Lavisse concerning the use of cannons to execute leaders of the revolt is not to be found in any of the British sources. The closest we come is in McCarthy's account of the disarming of sepoys at Meean Meer soon after the outbreak of the revolt:

> There was no actual reason to assume the Sepoys in Meean Meer intended to join the rebellion. There would be a certain danger of converting them into rebels if any rash movement were to be made for the purpose of guarding against treachery on their part. Either way was a serious responsibility, a momentous risk. The authorities soon made up their minds. Any risk would be better than that of leaving it in the power of the native troops to join the rebellion. A ball and supper were to be given at Lahore that night. To avoid creating any alarm it was arranged that the entertainments should take place [...] A parade was ordered for daybreak at Meean Meer; and on the parade ground an order was given for a military movement which brought the heads of four columns of the native troops in front of twelve guns charged with grape, the artillerymen with their port-fires lighted, and the soldiers of one of the Queen's regiments standing behind with loaded muskets. A command was given to the Sepoys to pile arms. They had immediate death before them if they disobeyed. They stood literally at the cannon's mouth. (McCarthy 1908, p. 180)

Also in later sources, very little is said about this manner of execution ('blowing from guns') which seems to have been used under Mogul rule – not a British invention. Nayar (2007, p. 110) indicates 1825 as the last date of its use. Spilsbury (2007, pp. 82–83), however, quotes eyewitness accounts of British recourse to the practice at the early stages of the revolt (not after its suppression) for the sake of deterrence. He mentions Nicholson's banning of the practice as a waste of gunpowder (p. 87), but Havelock's making at least one exception (pp. 208–209).

Table 3. *Timeline of events*

from 25 February 1857	Ai+ii	Early outbreaks
9 May 1857	Bi	Sepoys jailed at Meerut
10 May 1857	Bii+iii	Revolt at Meerut
10–11 May 1857	Biv	March of mutineers to Delhi
11 May 1857	Ci+ii+iii	Delhi occupied
mid-May 1857	Gi	Siege of Delhi starts
5 June 1857	Ei	Siege of Wheeler's British force in Cawnpore
early June		Neill's mass executions in Benares and Allahabad
27 June 1857	Eii	Surrender and massacre at Cawnpore
30 June 1857	Di	Lucknow, Lawrence's withdrawal into the Residency
2 July 1857	Dia	Sir Henry Lawrence mortally wounded
4 July 1857	Dia	Lawrence dies
15 July 1857	Eiii	murder of women and children in Cawnpore
16? July 1857	F	Havelock defeats rebels at Cawnpore
14 August 1857	Gii	Nicholson arriving at Delhi with reinforcements
14–21 September 1857	Giii+iv+v	Recapturing of Delhi
15 September 1857	Diia	Outram joins Havelock for assault on Lucknow
25 September 1857	Dii+iii	Havelock breaks through enemy lines at Lucknow
16 November 1857	Div	Sir Colin Campbell relieves Lucknow
17–24 November 1857	Div	Rescued soldiers and civilians withdrawn from Lucknow
24 November 1857	Diva	Sir Henry Havelock dies
6 December 1857	H	Definitive recapturing of Cawnpore by Campbell
March 1858	I	Second siege and definitive recapturing of Lucknow
June 1858	K	Ráni of Jhánsi and Tántia Topí defeated at Gwalior
throughout 1858	J+L	Further campaigns against remnants of the revolt.
April 1859	L	Tántia Topí captured and hanged

As in the case of Table 2, in Table 4 a minus-value does not necessarily mean complete absence of an event from the discourse. Thus, when Lavisse talks about the British recapturing Delhi, this implies that Delhi had been captured – an event that is not mentioned as such. On the other hand, a plus does not always mean that an event is presented individually. Thus Cassell's does not distinguish between the two separable episodes Eii (the attack on the troops trying to depart from Cawnpore under a false promise of free conduct) and Eiii (the murder of

Table 4. *Events of the Indian Mutiny*

	Lavisse	[Cassell's]	Fearenside	Hearnshaw	Innes	Kerr and Kerr	Low & Sanders	McCarthy	Parkin	Ransome	Richardson	Synge	Marten	Warner & Woodward
A	–	–	–	–	+	–	+	+	–	–	–	–	–	+
Ai	–	–	–	–	+	–	+	+	–	–	–	–	–	+
Aii	–	–	–	–	+	–	+	+	–	–	–	–	–	–
B	+	+	+	+	+	+	+	+	+	+	+	+	+	+
Bi	–	+	–	–	+	–	+	+	–	+	+	+	–	–
Bii	+	+	+	+	+	–	+	+	–	+	+	+	+	–
Biii	+	–	+	+	–	–	+	–	–	–	+	–	–	+
Biv	–	–	–	–	+	–	+	+	–	+	+	+	+	+
C	+	+	+	+	+	–	+	+	–	+	+	+	+	–
Ci	–	–	–	+	+	–	+	+	–	–	+	+	+	+
Cii	+	+	+	–	+	–	+	–	–	+	–	–	+	+
Ciii	–	–	–	–	+	–	+	+	–	–	–	+	–	–
D	+	+	+	+	+	+	+	+	–	+	+	+	+	+
Di	–	–	+	–	+	–	+	–	–	+	+	+	+	–
Dia	–	–	–	–	+	–	+	+	–	–	+	+	+	–
Dii	–	+	+	–	+	+	+	+	–	+	+	+	–	–
Diia	–	+	+	–	–	–	+	+	–	+	–	+	+	–
Diii	–	+	+	–	–	–	+	+	–	+	+	+	+	–
Div	–	+	–	+	+	+	+	+	–	+	–	+	–	+
Diva	–	–	–	–	–	–	+	+	–	–	–	+	+	–
E	+	+	+	+	+	–	+	+	–	+	+	+	+	+
Ei	–	+	+	–	+	–	+	+	–	–	+	+	+	–

Table 4. (cont.)

	Lavisse	[Cassell's]	Fearenside	Hearnshaw	Innes	Kerr	Kerr and Low & Kerr	Sanders	McCarthy	Parkin	Ransome	Richardson	Synge	Marten	Warner & Woodward
Eii	−	+	−	−	+	−	+	+	−	+	+	+	+	+	+
Eiii	+	+	+	−	+	−	+	+	−	+	+	+	+	+	+
F	−	−	+	−	+	−	−	−	−	−	+	+	+	−
G	+	+	+	+	+	+	+	+	−	+	+	+	+	+
Gi	−	−	+	+	+	+	+	+	−	+	+	+	+	−
Gii	+	−	+	−	+	−	+	+	−	+	+	+	+	+
Giii	−	−	+	−	+	+	+	+	+	+	+	+	+	+
Giiia	−	−	+	−	+	+	+	+	−	+	+	+	−	−
Giv	−	−	−	−	−	−	+	−	−	−	−	−	−	+
Gv	+	−	+	−	−	−	+	+	−	−	−	−	−	−
H	−	−	−	−	+	−	+	+	−	−	−	−	−	−
I	−	−	−	−	+	−	+	+	−	−	−	−	−	−
J	−	+	−	−	+	−	+	+	−	+	−	+	+	+
K	+	−	+	−	+	+	+	+	+	+	−	−	−	−
L	−	−	−	−	+	+	+	+	−	−	−	−	−	−

the women and children a few days later). The two episodes are lumped together as follows:

> The promise was broken: all except four, who escaped, were foully massacred, and their bodies thrown into a well.   (Cassell's 1903, p. 124)

Similarly, Fearenside sums it all up under 'the massacre of Cawnpore,' further described as follows:

> The Europeans at Cawnpore surrendered in June, after a month's siege, and were butchered.   (Fearenside 1922, p. 433)

The topical overview in Table 4 shows that there is strong agreement on the main ingredients of the story line. It leads directly to an assessment of the overall weighting of certain reported events. All sources mention the outbreak of the revolt (B), though some do not provide details of the circumstances. Lavisse, for instance, restricts himself to a four-word sentence, omitting even the most commonly cited placename (Meerut) and continuing immediately to emphasize the general spread of the uprising:

> Les Cipayes se révoltèrent. Ce fut une **révolte générale**.
>
>   (Lavisse 1902, p.152; bold in original)
>
> [The Sepoys revolted. It was a **general revolt**.]

Equally sparse is the information provided by Parkin, who, however, stresses the fortunate fact that the revolt was *not* completely general:

> For a short time it seemed probable that British power in India would be overthrown. Had the whole of the people of India joined in the rebellion, this would no doubt have taken place. But they did not do so, and of the Sepoys themselves many regiments remained faithful, and helped us to fight the mutineers.   (Parkin 1911, p. 213)

In addition to the outbreak of the revolt, the events that attract most attention are the occupation and recapturing of Delhi (as the events marking the initial success and the final failure of the revolt), the siege of Lucknow (testifying to British resilience), and the Cawnpore massacre (symbolizing the mutineers' treacherous nature and cruelty).

What is not immediately clear from the overview is the systematicity with which certain events are downplayed or entirely passed over. Thus the everpresent emphasis on Nana Sahib's treachery and cruelty in Cawnpore completely overshadows the excessive brutality with which James Neill took control over Benares and Allahabad in early June, when the slightest suspicion of complicity or intent was sufficient to execute soldiers and civilians alike. If mentioned at all, it is done so fleetingly that making it into a separate 'episode' in the above overview could hardly be justified on the basis of our data. Yet later sources (e.g., Hibbert 1978, Nayar 2007, Spilsbury 2007) are unanimous about its importance, and its relevance is no doubt clear from inserting it in the timeline in Table 3 (the highlighted line): the events took place weeks before Cawnpore. Though this may remain a matter of historical interpretation, Nayar assigns a causal link between Neill's actions in Benares and Allahabad and the Cawnpore massacre:

> Often ignored is this sequence: Neill's actions at Benares and Allahabad *preceded* Cawnpore, and to see Cawnpore as having provoked Neill's brutalities is to forget chronology. It is more than possible that it was Neill's horrific massacres that provoked Nana Sahib.   (2007, p. 125)

It is true that, far from being denied in our sources, British brutalities are usually portrayed as vengeance for Cawnpore.

While there is obviously a correlation between the length of the text extracts and the amount of detail that is provided, it is not a straightforward one. For instance, while Lavisse and Parkin devote comparable amounts of text to the Indian Mutiny, Lavisse is considerably more specific on a number of event details. On the other hand, Innes puts as many factual details concerning the concatenation of events in three pages and a half as McCarthy in twenty-five, though of course with less extensive descriptions.

What is most important in relation to Table 4 is to see how texts that look very similar in terms of topical 'content' can be organized in very different ways, with different effects on the generated meaning, and how the same topic or event can be presented in very different ways. These phenomena, which have the deepest possible effect on the 'lines of vision' which the discourse carves out in the 'world' it refers to, will be clear from later illustrations. One example was already adduced. Neither Lavisse, emphasizing the generality of the revolt, nor Parkin, stressing its non-general nature, can be said to misrepresent a state of affairs. They simply highlight different aspects, but with clear rhetorical goals and implications. What is most interesting for Lavisse (and presumably for the French school children he writes for) is the fact of the revolt. Parkin, on the other hand, is primarily interested in educating British children about 'their' empire, the unity of which needed to be stressed in spite of obvious eruptions of dissent – a unity that was, furthermore, not simply imposed but that involved "the good government of our fellow-subjects in India" (Parkin 1911, p. 214).

Procedure 2.2: *Investigate the immediate context of situation that presents itself, i.e., the way in which the discourse carves out lines of vision into its own physical, social, mental world. In particular:*

    2.2.1: *Who are the utterers and interpreters involved in the discourse? In particular:*
        2.2.1.1:   What system of person deixis is used?
        2.2.1.2:   What types of voices are involved on the utterer's side?
        2.2.1.3:   What types of interpreter roles are involved?
    2.2.2: *What mental states are expressed or appealed to?*
    2.2.3: *What (aspects of) social settings or institutions are involved/invoked?*
    2.2.4: *How is the discourse anchored temporally and spatially? In particular:*
        2.2.4.1:   How do event time, time of utterance, and reference time relate to each other?

2.2.4.2:   What aspects of temporal ordering are involved?

2.2.4.3:   What spatial orientations are involved/invoked?

2.2.4.4:   Are there any temporal and/or spatial constraints on the production of the discourse itself?

2.2.4.5:   Are there any 'material' conditions that constrain/orient the discourse production or interpretation?

2.2.5:   *In the case of (video-taped) spoken data: What relevant aspects of bodily posture, gesture, gaze, appearance can be pointed out for the discourse participants? In the case of written data: What graphic features (typography, pictorial representations) are used?*

AD 2.2, IN GENERAL:

[Investigate the immediate context of situation that presents itself, i.e., the way in which the discourse carves out lines of vision into its own physical, social, mental world.]

The overall question that is addressed here can be rephrased as follows: How do the 'actors' involved in the discourse (in the case of our sample data, mainly the author, but with clear assumptions about the targeted readers as well) position themselves and their discourse? Note that this is a very different question from the one asked in Procedure 2.1. The distinction is made, for lack of a better formulation, by contrasting *wider context* (in 2.1), referring to the social, political, historical, geographical world which the investigated discourse is *topically* related to (i.e., the world that it is somehow 'about' – with 2.1.1 trying to link that world with the one which the investigation itself is situated in), with *context of situation*[27] (in 2.2), referring to the immediate context which the discourse is itself *communicatively* situated in as a speech activity (i.e., the world of which the investigated discourse is an ingredient).

AD 2.2.1:

[Who are the utterers and interpreters involved in the discourse?]

Whenever discourse is investigated, it is important to be clear about the 'actors' involved and how they relate to each other. All the utterers (i.e., authors) of our sample data have academic and/or educational ambitions with the work they produce. In keeping with those ambitions, the targeted interpreters, i.e., the intended audience types, range from various levels of pupils or students (and their teachers

---

[27] A brief note on terminology: the terms 'context of situation'/'context of culture' were originally introduced by Malinowski (1923, p. 307) in contrast to 'linguistic context' (see also Senft 1997); what I am referring to as the 'wider context,' for lack of a better term, would also be included in his context of situation/context of culture, whereas my use of 'context of situation' comes closer to the more restricted sense the term acquired in certain trends of linguistic research (such as Firthian linguistics; see Östman and Simon-Vandenbergen 1995).

and sometimes even their parents) in formal education, via an academic to a general audience. For an overview, see Table 1 (in Chapter 2). Reference will have to be made to specific properties of this utterer–interpreter relationship to explain certain discursive phenomena (as I have already done, however briefly, when commenting on a point of comparison between Lavisse and Parkin in the last paragraph of 2.1.).

AD 2.2.1.1:
[What system of person deixis is used?][28]

Anticipating a point to be dealt with extensively later (see 3.1), it is clear that the genre of academic or semi-academic writing to which our sample data belong has a great influence on the way in which the authors refer to themselves and address their intended audience. The general expectation for scholarly textbooks would be a backgrounding of both the utterer and the interpreter, and a clear dominance of topic-related third-person reference. Though this expectation fits most of our data, there is still some serious variability. Both utterer and inter- preter, author and reader, are present in the discourse, though under different guises and to different degrees, and with clear differences between prefaces and the main body of the texts.

Direct first-person reference in the singular is exceptional, but it can be found in some prefaces, and quite prominently so in Ransome:

> In deciding what subjects to admit, I have had with great regret to omit [...] I have omitted [...] I am led to think [...] I have been guided by [...] I have contented myself with [...] I have spared no pains [...] I have been guided by what I have learnt [...] I have tried to bear in mind [...] I have in the earl- ier part of the work followed [...] I have rejected [...] I have followed [...] I have not attempted to [...] I have taken pains not to [...] published by Mr. A. H. Dyke and myself [...] I can only add that I am as conscious as anyone can be of the many shortcomings of the book. I have done my best [...] I should specially mention [...] to all of whom I owe a great debt of thanks.
> (Ransome 1910, pp. iii–vi)

This preface contrasts sharply with the remainder of the book, which fits the expectation of a depersonalized style flawlessly. Clearly, Ransome feels the need to justify a number of choices he made in the selection of materials and in the style of presentation (including terminological choices) in view of outspoken scholarly and pedagogical principles. Such an overwhelming presence of 'I,' however, is rare, though it can still be found in other sources more sparingly, as in

---

[28] 'Deixis' is the term linguists use to describe a variety of ways in which language use is 'anchored' into a surrounding world by 'pointing' at variables along a number of dimensions (social, tem- poral, spatial, etc.) of that world.

> I hope, then, […].   (Parkin 1911, p. iv – note that the preface from which this is quoted was written by someone other that the author of the book)

But to the extent that the first-person singular pronoun occurs at all, it is usually more backgrounded, as in the following:

> It has therefore been found necessary to add to the 'Short History' a summarised but, as I hope, in every sense symmetrical reproduction in this volume of the story told in the longer narrative.   (McCarthy 1908, p. vii)

> Our own times may, on the whole, be regarded as having created an ever memorable era in the development of civilisation, and I feel it an honour to have had a share, however limited and imperfect, in describing its progress.   (McCarthy 1908, p. x)

Note that both these examples of the usage of the first-person singular pronoun embed it in a larger construction containing other devices as well to position the author in relation to his own communicative act ("It has therefore been found necessary […]") as well as its subject matter ("Our own times […]"). Both of these devices will be commented on again later.

Direct first-person reference in the plural is slightly more common. This may take the form of a 'royal *we*' as in

> Nous l'avons divisée en quatre périodes […].   (Lavisse 1902, p. 2)

> [We have divided it [i.e., the history of the world] into four periods […].]

> The country owes much to these two princes, for the part they took at her hour of need; and she has not, we are glad to think, proved herself ungrateful.
>   (McCarthy 1908, p. 194)

or of an 'inclusive *we*' incorporating both author and readers, as in

> We hear a great deal nowadays about […].   (Kerr and Kerr 1927, p. 1)

> We have seen how India was conquered for us largely by the help of natives [sic] troops, or Sepoys.   (Parkin 1911, p. 213)

Not surprisingly, both Kerr and Kerr and Parkin, the sources of these two quotes, show a strong didactic orientation, supported by the use of this device. Occasionally, the 'inclusion' established by the use of *we* goes beyond utterer and interpreter:

> Jusqu'au xve siècle, les Européens ne connaissaient qu'un *coin du monde*. Depuis les grandes découvertes, nous connaissons le **monde entier**.
>   (Lavisse 1902, p. 68; italic and bold in original)

> [Until the 15th century, the Europeans knew only a *corner of the world*. After the great discoveries, we know the **whole world**.]

Here the first-person plural pronoun "nous" is co-referential with "les Européens." This is an example of how person deixis may serve identity construction.

Much more frequent, however, is indirect first-person reference. Several tools serve that purpose. First, the authors can realize self-reference by means of a third-person description:

> The author takes this opportunity to gratefully acknowledge [...].
>
> (Fearenside 1922)

> The aim of the writer has been to select those facts which appear to him to be of prime significance [...].   (Hearnshaw 1930, p. v)

> The author then has not overlooked the demands of Examiners and examinations; he has indeed [...] But he is satisfied that [...] His aim therefore has been [...].   (Innes 1927, p. vi)

> The writer has tried to tell the story of [...].   (Richardson 1924, p. vi)

> In giving the name *The Groundwork of British History* to this book, the writers seek to make clear the plan on which it is constructed.
>
> (Warner and Marten 1912, p. v)

All these examples belong to an unmistakable preface-style. Second, in the same vein, but replacing the authors with their product, there are references to "our book" or "our aim":

> It is to meet such difficulties that our book is directed. Our aim is to provide the reader with [...].   (Warner and Marten 1912, p. vi)

Third, a slightly depersonalized version of the same device yields:

> This book is intended to meet the requirements of [...].
>
> (Fearenside 1922, p. iii)

> This little book is intended in the first place for [...].
>
> (Hearnshaw 1930, p. v)

> the aim of the book is rather to suggest than inform
>
> (Synge 1908, pp. vii–viii)

Fourth, we come across various indirect ways of positioning the author personally in relation to his own communicative act, as in

> It has therefore been found necessary to add [...].
>
> (McCarthy 1908, p. vii)

> It is hoped, however, that [...].
> [...] it has, of course, been found impossible to mention all the facts [...] But it is felt that to have done so [...].
> It is hoped that [...] The words used, if often long and sometimes uncommon, are, it is believed, [...].
> It was originally intended [...], but it was found impossible [...].
>
> (Hearnshaw 1930, pp. v–vi)

> The illustrations will, it is believed, [...].   (Cassell's 1903)

or in relation to the subject matter of the discourse, as in

> Our own times may, on the whole, be regarded as [...].
>
> (McCarthy 1908, p. x)

Moving from the utterer to the interpreter, the reader is addressed directly on a number of occasions by means of a second-person pronoun:

> There are some facts which must be known about the population of the country before you can understand how English people got India, or how and why they keep it.   (Parkin 1911, p. 207)

Note that in an example like this, "you" is of course interpretable as referring to 'anyone,' and not just as 'you, the reader.' In addition, readers are often appealed to in the form of imperatives (whether or not combined with further use of the second-person pronoun):

> Substitute the following somewhat detailed account of [...].
>
> (Cassell's 1903)

> Look at the map at the beginning of the book and you will see that [...].
>
> (Kerr and Kerr 1927, p. 2)

As with the utterer's self-reference, interpreter-reference takes an indirect third-person form more often than a direct one:

> will commend it to **busy people** who desire to refresh their memories [...]
> **General Readers** as well as **Teachers** will recognise [...] and **Scholars** will possess [...].   (Cassell's 1903; bold in original)

> that the youth of our race will learn from this book   (Parkin 1911, p. iv)

> to inspire the children of to-day   (Synge 1908, p. ix)

> If in reading it a boy comes to carry with him some idea of [...].
>
> (Warner and Marten 1912, p. v)

> Our aim is to provide the reader with [...].
>
> (Warner and Marten 1912, p. vi)

And sometimes this type of indirect reference gets somewhat personalized in the following way:

> the primary purpose is to remind our children that [...].
>
> (Parkin 1911, p. iii)

> nos enfants doivent apprendre [...].   (Lavisse 1902, p. 2)

> [our children must learn [...].]

Here a personal connection is established between the author and the target audience, though the addressee is ambiguous in this case: The authors seem to be addressing other adults as well, persuading them of the suitability of the books for children.

When making a detailed analysis of person deixis in a given text (and of most other phenomena, as will become clear later), however, the most interesting observations tend to bear on apparent breaches of expected or discovered patterns. Thus Lavisse is a textbook example of a textbook, adhering to the expected norms almost without exception. The author positions himself in the preface in the first-person plural, only to move entirely to the background from then onwards. Similarly, the target audience remains in the third person in the preface ("nos enfants"). But all of a sudden, in the main body of the text, a form of direct address emerges:

> Dans toutes ces guerres, les *colons* et les *marins français ont fait leur devoir bravement*. Mais la France était alors gouvernée par Louis XV, dont vous connaissez le triste règne.   (Lavisse 1902, p. 96)

> [In all those wars, the *colonizers* and the *French seamen did their duties bravely*. But at the time France was governed by Louis XV, whose sad rule you know.]

This switch of footing[29] may be motivated by the nature of this episode that seems painfully in need of explanation: Namely, how was it possible for the British to take over dominance of both India and North America from the French, who were there first? A similar form of direct address comes up in a passage that is meant to appeal directly to the school children's imagination, after explaining the principles of human rights:

> La plupart de ces règles vous paraissent toutes naturelles. Peut-être ne vous figurez-vouz pas comment on peut vivre dans un pays où l'on n'est libre ni de travailler, ni de parler, ni de penser; où [...] Songez pourtant qu'encore aujourd'hui [...].   (Lavisse 1902, p. 100)

> [Most of these rules seem very natural to you. Maybe you cannot imagine how one can live in a country where one is neither free to work, nor to speak, nor to think; where [...] Yet, know that still today [...].]

Clearly, specific communicative effects are aimed at when such switches are made. As with other phenomena, their full effect on the meaning generation process can be evaluated only in the totality of the discourse. It will be useful, therefore, to keep in mind these two examples while looking at other phenomena. Meanwhile, note that they function as clear indicators of the way in which the context of the investigated discourse relates to what the discourse is about (cf. 2.1.2).

---

[29] The term 'footing' refers to possible shifts in the social capacity in which an interactant is involved in an interaction; here a switch is involved that moves from addressing pupils as pupils to addressing them as French citizens or pupils knowledgeable about and somehow involved in French history. (See Goffman 1979.)

Ad 2.2.1.2:

[What types of voices are involved on the utterer's side?][30]

History books contain information of which the authors/utterers themselves are rarely the source. Rather, a chain of communicative acts underlies what ends up in the historical narratives, with an ultimate source that is usually many times removed and often unknown to the author.[31] Yet, in our sample data, an explicit acknowledgement of sources is to be found only in a few footnotes, and this only in the single more academically oriented publication, Low and Sanders. In combination with the backgrounding of the author's own involvement, as discussed above in relation to person deixis, this strongly contributes to the creation of an impression that, as Hanks (1996) put it, history can be told as an objective story of chronology. The discrepancy between the manifest reality of non-personally witnessed events and their manifold subsequent entextualizations on the one hand, and the discursively produced impression of mere factuality and immediate accessibility on the other, hiding the modulations and calibrations introduced by intervening voices, results in a close connection between the investigated texts and a world view in which the author's (and the targeted readers') own temporal, geographical, and social deictic center abundantly prevails, thus making these materials eminently suitable for ideology research.

It is remarkable, in this context, that many of the prefaces situate the current texts in opposition to supposed or real alternatives and/or predecessors in terms of style (e.g., more concise, with fewer difficult words, etc.) and/or pedagogical considerations (e.g., principles of selecting or deselecting details, emphasis on perspective versus facts, etc.), but never in terms of content (except in relation to scope). Thus the other (real or virtual) voices that are invoked in the prefaces by way of contrast are not brought to life as sources of information. Occasionally, however, a virtual utterer is invoked to anticipate criticism, as in

> These events are related, not in a spirit of boastful pride, but rather to inspire the children of to-day with a love of the country for which their near kinsmen have died, and a feeling of individual responsibility as members of so great

[30] 'Voice' is used as a cover term to distinguish different sources of the content of an utterance; the utterer may or may not be the source him- or herself; sources may be real or imagined; sources may be specified or remain vague; and so forth. To indicate the diversity of voices that may be involved in an utterance, the term 'polyphony' is used. For an overview article, see Roulet (2003).

[31] The basic training of the historian involves acquiring the knowledge and skills needed to get at and to interpret sources which are usually fragmentary, sometimes isolated, sometimes related to each other along interesting dimensions of intertextuality. In fact, scholars dealing with present-day phenomena would also benefit greatly from a similar training. Intertextuality will therefore have to be brought in later as an important angle from which to look at data. In the case of the Indian Mutiny, there is a sizeable archive, the 'Mutiny Papers,' consisting of thousands of catalogued and indexed pages of original documents stored in the National Archives of India. Naturally, none of the authors in our corpus ever had direct access to those. Nor would it have helped, unless the authors were able to read Shikastah Urdu (Farooqui 2007, p. 14).

> a heritage, remembering that 'to whom much has been given, of him shall
> much be required.'   (Synge 1908, p. ix)

Here the possible criticism that Synge's tale of great deeds could be seen as
boastful is 'controlled' by giving it a voice, negating it, and contrasting it with
all that follows "but."[32]

Virtual utterers are strikingly absent from the main body of the texts, further
strengthening the impression of mere factuality. Even negative forms of expression (normally invoking their opposites) are extremely rare. And in the few
examples where they occur, as in

> For a short time it seemed probable that British power in India would be
> overthrown. Had the whole of the people of India joined in the rebellion, this
> would no doubt have taken place. But they did not do so [...].
> (Parkin 1911, p. 213)

the power of the negative to invoke its opposite (the virtual utterer suggesting that
all Indians joined in the revolt) is undermined by the preceding hypothetical and
counterfactual constructions.

On a number of occasions, authors leave their own voice carefully implicit
while not really hiding it. For instance, when they contrast the many causes of
the revolt with the British unpreparedness, criticism transpires that is rarely made
explicit but that is nevertheless clearly and consciously there.

There is a serious discrepancy, finally, between the extent to which British
and Indian voices are brought in. A possible Indian voice is very much backgrounded, but our sources differ significantly in that respect, ranging from complete absence to subtle presence. Consider, for instance the contrast between the
following:

> Leaders had for a long time past been instilling feelings of dissatisfaction
> in the minds of the men, and this pretext [i.e., the greased cartridges] was
> advanced to start the rebellion.   (Cassell's 1903, p. 124)

> Thus some of the leading princely houses of Northern India, Hindu and
> Mohammedan alike, were smarting under a sense of wrong, and their agents
> were active in promoting discontent.   (Low and Sanders 1910, p. 136)

While in the first quotation "feelings of dissatisfaction" are presented as the
products of manipulation, Low and Sanders recognizes grounds for a "sense
of wrong," which then leads to manipulation. But none of the textbooks feels
the need to engage in anticipatory response to possible defenders of the Mutiny
(e.g., by saying something like "The rebellion was not without grounds, but ..."),
which means that no one in the intended readership is expected to undertake such
a defense.

---

[32] This type of discursive pattern was aptly called 'response-controlling *but*-prefaces' by Baker
(1975).

Occasionally, a mixing of mental spaces[33] also brings in the Indian voice, as in the following example:

> They burst open the prison, released the eighty-five martyrs, and then proceeded to fire on their officers. (Synge 1908, p. 113)

The characterization of imprisoned sepoys in Meerut on 10 May 1857 as martyrs (which is what this sentence refers to) fits the mindset of the Indians involved at that time and at that place, rather than the author's own voice. The same device, however, usually moves the Indian voice to the background, as in

> Lord Canning saw that the one important thing was to strike at Delhi, which had proclaimed itself the head-quarters of the rebellion.
> (McCarthy 1908, p. 178)

It is unlikely that the mutineering sepoys would have used terms translatable as "rebellion" and "headquarters" in any act of 'proclamation,' as their goals – or hopes – were far more ambitious.

AD 2.2.1.3:
[What types of interpreter roles are involved?]

Also with respect to interpreter roles, there are differences between the preface and the main body of most of our text samples. Many types of interpreters are involved, though they mainly fit into two categories which we can label 'primary' and 'secondary' audience. The *primary audience* consists of those the author wants to inform or teach about the narrated historical events: students, other scholars, or members of a general readership outside schools or academia. But in many cases (in particular: in all cases in which the texts are written for teaching purposes), there is also a *secondary audience*: fellow historians who may not want to read the book for the information it contains, but rather to check out the mode of presentation, its adequacy in relation to content and/or educational goals, etc.; parents who may be interested in getting acquainted with the stories their children will read or hear about; school supervisors or other people with the authority to select textbooks.

While the primary audience is always the addressee of the main body of the text (whether or not direct forms of address are used – see 2.2.1.1), it may be either the addressee or merely a side participant in relation to the preface. A typical textbook such as Lavisse, for instance, does not treat the school children for which it was written as addressees of its preface. Rather, they figure as third persons ("nos enfants," "our children") in discourse that is obviously addressed to others: parents and/or those responsible for (adhering to guidelines pertaining

---

[33] For the original use of the term 'mental spaces,' see Fauconnier (1985). It refers to frames of interpretation that may be evoked by specific patterns of wording a state of affairs. Different conceptual frames may be mixed or blended in the same utterance.

Table 5. *Interpreter roles*

	PREFACE	MAIN BODY OF THE TEXT
PRIMARY AUDIENCE: scholars, students, general readership	**addressee** *or* **side participant**	**addressee**
SECONDARY AUDIENCE: others (colleagues, parents, school supervisors, and so forth)	**addressee**	**side participant**

to) curriculum choices. But since the school children are not excluded from read-ing the preface, they still act as side participants whose presence must be taken into account.

Conversely, members of the secondary audience may be the direct addressees of the preface, while they remain side participants (whose presence is not with-out influence for the choices made by the author) for the main body of the text. This overall structure of interpreter roles is presented in Table 5.

Needless to say, not everything is so easily captured in a neat table. For one thing, there is the role of the history teacher who will use the textbook in class and who incorporates properties of both audience types. The complexity of the issue may appear from the following lines from Fearenside's preface:

> This book is intended to meet the requirements of the London University Matriculation syllabus in Modern History, [...].
> The syllabus states: "The questions will be framed to test the general con-ceptions of history and historical development rather than technical detail." In a text-book, however, technical detail is to some extent necessary in order that from it the reader may obtain conceptions which shall be duly in accordance with facts; and it is for the teacher to see that in endeavouring to fulfil the University requirements the learner founds his generalisations on a proper knowledge of leading events, persons, and dates, and also of the meaning of such common technical terms as must be used even in an elem-entary treatment of the subject.   (Fearenside 1922, p. iii)

In this fragment, norms are invoked (the Matriculation syllabus) that will no doubt be handled by some members of the secondary audience to evaluate the book and the meeting of which is also crucial for members of the primary audi-ence ("the reader," "the learner"). At the same time, it highlights the mediating role of the teacher, who must have a close affinity with the world of evaluators in order to be able to help students in their reading so as to achieve the required level of competence; thus the teacher must also be able to take on the interpreter roles associated with both audience types.

In addition, just like other discourse genres, the textbooks under consideration show clear traces of *audience design*: Forms of expression are adapted to interpreter roles; in other words, utterances are designed specifically for a target audience so as to ensure continued attention and the required level of understanding. This becomes very explicit, for instance, in the following footnote in Lavisse:

> 1. Les mots marqués d'un astérisque sont expliqués dans le lexique placé à la fin de cet ouvrage.   (Lavisse 1902, p. 1)

> [1. The words marked with an asterisk are explained in the lexicon at the end of this work.]

Indeed, conscious efforts are made to keep or make the text intelligible for those it is intended for. This is also the case in many of the British sources, and some of the quotes above bear witness to that fact. Audience design, however, does not end with these explicit statements of purpose. Basically, all linguistic choices that are made are somehow related to this phenomenon. For example, consider a simple declarative of the following kind:

> Le pays est très chaud et très malsain […].   (Lavisse 1902, p. 151)

> [The country is very hot and very unhealthy […].]

This statement is inevitably comparative and incorporates assumptions about the life world of the audience which, consequently, is a clear point of reference, the standard of comparison. This could not be explained without the author's having a clear design of the audience in mind – however trivial this may seem.

Ad 2.2.2:
[What mental states are expressed or appealed to?]

In spite of the overall descriptive purpose of the history textbooks, the texts are full of expressions that reveal beliefs, goals, aspirations, intentions, etc., and topics are often clearly anchored into concerns that are 'personal' for the author, at least in his/her capacity as a citizen of the nation he/she represents.

I have already referred to some of the expressions of *regret* to be found in Lavisse, i.e., regret regarding the lost chances for France in India and in North America. Here is what he says:

> Le directeur de la Compagnie française, **Dupleix**, avait commencé à conquérir les Indes. Cela n'était pas très difficile, car […] C'eût été une **très belle conquête**, car l'Inde a aujourd'hui plus de 200 millions d'habitants, et elle produit en quantité du coton, du riz, du poivre, de la soie.
>
> Les Anglais demandèrent au gouvernement français de destituer Dupleix, et le gouvernement le *destitua* (1754) […]
>
> Ce fut la même chose en Amérique […]
>
>   (Lavisse 1902, pp. 93–95; bold and italics in original)

> [The director of the French company, **Dupleix**, had started to conquer the Indies. That was not difficult, because […] It would have been a **very nice conquest**, as India today has over 200 million inhabitants, produces great quantities of cotton, rice, pepper, and silk.

> The English asked the French government to dismiss Dupleix, and the government *did* (1754) [...]
> It was the same thing in America [...]]

It would have been nice indeed to have control over India and North America. All the more lamentable is the reason why that did not happen:

> On dépensait beaucoup d'argent et de soldats à des guerres en Allemagne et en Italie, où la France n'avait rien à gagner, et on refusait d'envoyer aux colonies 4 ou 5 000 soldats qui auraient donné à la France l'*empire du monde*.
> (Lavisse 1902, p. 96; italics in original)

> [A lot of money and many soldiers were expended on wars in Germany and Italy, where France had nothing to gain, and there was a refusal to send the 4 or 5,000 soldiers to the colonies that would have given to France the *empire of the world*.]

And even somewhat more bitterly this state of affairs is summarized as follows in the *résumé* ending this chapter:

> La France a laissé échapper alors, par la faute de son gouvernement, l'*empire du monde*; ce sont les Anglais qui l'ont pris.
> (Lavisse 1902, p. 96; italics in original)

> [Thus, France let escape the *empire of the world*, as a result of the mistakes of its goverment; it was the English who took it.]

The other side of this regret is the *pride* of the British, as voiced, for instance, by Synge:

> These events are related, not in a spirit of boastful pride, but rather to inspire the children of to-day with a love of the country for which their near kinsmen have died, and a feeling of individual responsibility as members of so great a heritage, remembering that "to whom much has been given, of him shall much be required."   (Synge 1908, p. ix)

There are, of course, many more subtle examples throughout the narrative accounts, where linguistic choices betray clear attitudes, whether cognitive or emotive. Thus an unmistakable personal *opinion* emerges from "under ill advice" in

> In 1856 Dalhousie was replaced by Lord Canning, who, under ill advice, issued an Act under which all recruits in the Bengal army would in future be liable for service abroad.   (Innes 1927, p. 169)

and *affect* or *involvement* (again in the form of pride) are equally clear in

> Here a stubborn defence had been maintained, with a success chiefly due to the unceasing vigilance and energy of the Engineer department, whose counter-mines frustrated no fewer than twenty-five of the enemy's mines.
> (Innes 1927, p. 171)

Choices such as "stubborn" or "unceasing vigilance and energy," as qualities ascribed to the British side, occur frequently. On the Indian side they are to be found in only a few of the sources, and they are reserved for two protagonists, Tántia Topí and the Ráni of Jhánsi:

> Tántia Topí, the Nana's former minister, and the most able military leader on the rebel side during the entire campaign.
>
> (Low and Sanders 1910, p. 151)

> But the undaunted Ráni had an audacious scheme in reserve [...] Dressed like a man, the Ráni of Jhánsi charged with the cavalry of the Gwalior contingent, and was killed in the rout by a sword-stroke [...].
>
> (Low and Sanders 1910, p. 157)

> for his [Tántia Topí's] courage and indomitable resolution could not save him from the doom he had earned by his participation in the infamies of Cawnpore.   (Low and Sanders 1910, p. 158)

Here a certain admiration is transparent, based in the case of the Ráni at least partly on the fact that she was a woman fighting like a man and in the case of Tántia Topí on his military strategic skills.

It is important to note, in this context, that the systematic attempts at attitudinal *distancing* that characterize the bulk of the corpus are themselves fundamentally *attitudinal* as well (a point to be commented on again, from a different angle, in relation to 2.2.3). Trying to approach the neutral rhetorical position of a scholarly text is itself the product of a decision to engage in a form of intellectual activity that neutralizes the cognitive or emotive interference of attitudes that are deemed inadmissible for the activity in question. This makes the surfacing of attitudes all the more interesting, as will be pointed out again later.

AD 2.2.3:

[What (aspects of) social settings or institutions are involved/invoked?]

It is not only details of the wider political-historical context to which the investigated discourse relates itself (as discussed in 2.1.2) that are important for an understanding of the discourse data. At least as important is the 'local' institutional embedding of the discourse itself. What we are dealing with is discourse that embodies a form of authority: the socially and politically sanctioned authority of the institution of education (though more centrally regulated in France at the time than in Britain), and the academically sanctioned authority of scholarship (making a bid for 'objectivity,' though in a diversity of ways and to differing degrees). Many of the relevant aspects of this contextual dimension were dealt with at length at the end of Chapter 2, where I situated the data in the history of mass education in the nineteenth century, in the history of history teaching, and in the history of history writing.

There are obvious processes of institutional identity construction at work beyond what is already reflected in specific usages of person deixis, identifiable voices, and interpreter roles. Most of them are easy to find in the prefaces or title pages which, by their very nature, position the texts in a world of discourse and of real-world social relations. Lavisse, for instance, makes explicit reference to "études primaries" and "l'enseignement secondaire" ("primary education" and "secondary education"; on the title page) as well as a "Programme de 1887. – Histoire" ("Program of 1887 – History"; at the bottom of the preface page). The institutional embedding of the text could not be any clearer. Similar devices are used in many of the British sources. The clearest parallel is "matriculation" in Fearenside's title, while more fuzzy boundaries – but boundaries nonetheless – are suggested in Cassell's "For School and Home Use," Innes' "For use in schools," Parkin's "For the use of schools," and Richardson's "A reading book for schools."

Further, institutional identity construction also takes the form of opinions that are voiced about the educational role of history teaching. Thus Lavisse describes the teaching of history as "le complément de l'education patriotique" (loosely translated, "complementary to patriotic training"). A more intellectual goal is set by Hearnshaw in expressing the wish

> that those who read a first sketch of English History should rise from their study with their reason satisfied, their curiosity aroused, and their interest quickened […].   (Hearnshaw 1930, p. v)

More practical aspirations, related to a similar intellectual goal, are voiced by Ransome, whose book

> shall give a clear and intelligible account of those events and institutions a knowledge of which is so much needed by the student of modern political life.   (Ransome 1910, p. iii)

A role that is both patriotic and cosmopolitan is ascribed to history teaching by McCarthy. Not only is it a contribution to "national education," but also

> Now it may be taken as almost a scientific fact that the spread of national education in all countries must lead to the [viii] development of the arts of peace and the suppression of impulses towards the work of war.
> (McCarthy 1908, pp. viii–ix)

In addition, there are also expressions of opinions about educational practices. Lavisse's "pourvu qu'elles soient données sobrement" (about notions of general history: "on condition that they are presented in a restrained manner" or "if they are presented objectively") defines the conditions under which notions of general history can be of service to students. It is with respect to such opinions that many of the authors seem to exercise the least restraint. Consider the following example:

> Such a volume may be produced with a single eye to examinations – to simplify the process of acquiring and imparting knowledge which is intended

> to be, not assimilated, but committed to memory in such a manner as to be readily reproduced at the end of a few weeks or months, and then wiped out of the mind. This method, however, is, educationally, worse than useless for intelligent pupils, because it inevitably inspires a strong distaste for the subject. On the other hand, if details and aids to memory are neglected, there is nothing for the less intelligent pupil to lay hold of, while the impressions received by the more intelligent are misty and inaccurate.
>
> (Innes 1927, p. v)

Similarly:

> It would have been easy, by adopting a method of analysis, summary, and tabulation, to pack ten times as much information into this book as it actually contains. But it is felt that to have done so would have involved so complete a sacrifice of movement, continuity, and life, that the result would have been fatal.   (Hearnshaw 1930, p. v)

Clearly, the authors stake their claims in the institutional territory of education.

While such highly explicit processes are almost completely absent from the main body of the texts, it would be wrong to assume that institutional identity construction is not at work at that level as well. All of the above is to be situated against the background of the struggles for *authority* and authorization that are involved in language use. As Bourdieu (1991) has so accurately described, individual language users may derive authority from the way in which they fit into an institutional context, which always involves relations of power. The discursive reflection of authority is the right to speak on behalf of an institution, a group. In an educational or academic context, this combines with an assumption that the institution itself stands for objective knowledge. As a result, authority is established – or attempts at establishing authority are made – by distancing, the avoidance of personal positioning. In other words, educational or academic face is established by being faceless. Most of our data fit that paradigm, and occasional breaches further underscore the norm.

Ad 2.2.4:

[How is the discourse anchored temporally and spatially?]

At the most trivial level, all publications carry a date and place of publication. Both were discussed at length in relation to Rule 2.4. But in the main body of the texts, all temporal and spatial anchoring tools come in, as will be shown.

Ad 2.2.4.1:

[How do event time, time of utterance, and reference time relate to each other?]

Event time and *reference time* clearly dominate. Event time is simply the time at which an event takes place, which, in the history textbooks, is usually indicated by means of a temporal description or a date:

> Au XVe siècle [...] En 1484 [...] le 11 octobre 1492 [...] En 1520 [...].
> (Lavisse 1902, p. 64)
>
> [In the 15th century [...]. In 1484 [...] on 11 October 1492 [...] In 1520
> [...].]

Temporal adverbs (e.g., 'then') are often used to concatenate series of event times, though usually this is not even necessary. A more complex example of linking event times is the following:

> The long-delayed assault took place at dawn on September 14. [149] [...]
> It was not till five days after the original assault that the Lahore gate was
> taken.   (Low and Sanders 1910, pp. 149–150)

When event time becomes the deictic center in relation to which other events are positioned, it functions as reference time:

> En 1519, l'Espagnol **Fernand Cortez** débarquait au Mexique avec 700
> soldats, 18 chevaux et 10 canons. Les Mexicains n'avaient jamais vu ni
> Européens ni chevaux [...].   (Lavisse 1902, p. 65; bold in original)
>
> [In 1519, the Spaniard **Fernand Cortez** disembarked in Mexico with 700
> soldiers, 18 horses and 10 cannons. The Mexicans had never seen Europeans
> or horses [...].]

The phrase "n'avaient jamais vu" ("had never seen") refers to a past preceding 1519, an event time which thus functions as reference time. Similarly:

> **1857**. The Indian Mutiny, a rising of native Indian troops, broke out this year.
> It had been long maturing [...].
>
> (Cassell's 1903, p. 124; bold in original)

Here "this year" is co-referential with '1857,' which serves as reference time for "had been long maturing." Sometimes, of course, a future is referred to in relation to a given reference time:

> In 1856 Dalhousie was replaced by Lord Canning, who, under ill advice,
> issued an Act under which all recruits in the Bengal army would in future be
> liable for service abroad.   (Innes 1927, p. 169)

In spite of the clear dominance of event time and reference time, *time of utterance* also comes in occasionally (and significantly). This is unmistakably the case when "today" is referred to, as in

> Songez pourtant qu'encore aujourd'hui [...].   (Lavisse 1902, p. 100)
>
> [Yet, know that still today [...].]

the special significance of which was already hinted at in relation to our discussion of person deixis (see 2.2.1.1). The same effect of establishing the time of utterance as deictic center can also be achieved by means of tense usage. Consider the following:

> Inside India, British rule has only once been in real danger, and that was in the year 1857. For some time there had been [...].
>
> (Kerr and Kerr 1927, p. 183)

Here the present perfect "has [...] been" means "up to now". The same quote illustrates the interrelations between the different temporal perspectives by also bringing in event time ("in the year 1857"), which is turned into reference time by means of "there had been." At a more implicit level, a link with the author's present is made by emphasizing, paradoxically, discontinuity between a moment in the past and the present:

> La France a laissé échapper alors, par la faute de son gouvernement, l'*empire du monde*; ce sont les Anglais qui l'ont pris.
>
> (Lavisse 1902, p. 96; italics in original)
>
> [Thus, France let escape the *empire of the world*, as a result of the mistakes of its goverment; it was the English who took it.]

It is clear that the French government talked about here is not to be associated with the French government running France's affairs at the time of writing.

Not surprisingly for history writing, past reference is the most frequent orientation. Sometimes, however, the relevance of past events for a present state of affairs is emphasized, as in

> The Civil Service gained in status by the changes of 1858. It is through the strong, upright, and experienced men who from one end of India to the other, hold in their hands the local administration of justice, order, revenue, and public works, that the influence of British rule most makes itself felt.   (Woodward 1921, p. 238)

Future tenses are used occasionally to highlight a general truth (a function for which also the present can be used, sometimes in combination with a future) or to give expression to expectations. Some examples:

> Now a true Hindoo will not kill a cow, nor allow the meat of it to touch his lips.   (Cassell's 1903, p. 124)
>
> The Hindu believes that his life beyond the grave is affected by caste; to preserve caste he will suffer anything.   (Innes 1927, p. 169)
>
> The Mutiny proved that India was not, and probably never will be, a country which can be united to oppose our rule.   (Parkin 1911, p. 214)

Ad 2.2.4.2:
[What aspects of temporal ordering are involved?]

Within the tradition of history writing to which our samples belong, there is a clear tendency to find a story line in which the linear ordering in the text iconically matches sequences of event times.[34] Especially in shorter accounts (e.g., Lavisse, Cassell's, Fearenside, or Hearnshaw) the match is nearly complete, with minor expansions that go into circumstances that color or explain the chain of events. The longer the accounts become (e.g., Low and Sanders, or McCarthy), and the more details the authors want to provide, the more we see an inevitable tendency to let coherent 'episodes' take over whenever purely temporal ordering in the text would become impossible because of simultaneity or insufficiently documented temporal precision. In those cases, the result is very much like the ordering of events in Table 4, with a temporal baseline (presented in Table 3) and a superimposed episodic structure whenever useful. In the longer accounts, more – not surprisingly – than in the shorter ones, we also find expansions into circumstances as well as causes and consequences. While event time defines the temporal baseline, the expansions make use of the interplay between event time and reference time, and occasionally they also bring in the time of utterance. (More will be said about this when discussing sequencing in 2.3.3.)

Ad 2.2.4.3:

[What spatial orientations are involved/invoked?]

As will be clear from Table 4, 'episodes' in the chain of events are generally – i.e., not only in sources that sometimes let episodes take precedence over purely chronological ordering – defined in terms of *spatial points of reference* or place names. Just a few illustrations:

> The main incidents in the struggle were the massacre of Cawnpore and the sieges of Delhi and Lucknow.   (Fearenside 1922, p. 433)

> Horrible barbarities and fierce fights were witnessed at Delhi, Lucknow, and Cawnpore.   (Hearnshaw 1930, p. 154)

> There were six main theatres of operations: Delhi; Cawnpore and Lucknow; the Punjab; Central India; the rural districts of Oudh and Rohilkhand; and parts of Upper Bengal and Behar extending to the Nipál frontier.
> (Low and Sanders 1910, p. 142)

Even the key actors involved in the events associated with those places, however highly profiled they are, do not have the same definitional value in the presentation of the events. While the actors' behavior (mostly heroic if they are British) determines the manner in which events take place, the predominantly spatial orientation toward the events themselves manifests the strongly military-strategic perspective taken by the authors.

---

[34] The notion of 'iconicity' that is appealed to here stands for the property of language that allows for non-arbitrary similarity between form and meaning. An example is indeed the correspondence between a sequence of events and the structuring of a narrative following the same sequence. History books that reverse the order are exceptional, but they simply switch perspectives rather than breaking the iconic pattern.

In addition, all the sources share, predictably, a Eurocentric spatial world view. Thus Lavisse describes India as a faraway place that is too hot and too unhealthy for Europeans to live ("c'est de l'Inde que nous vient le choléra," Lavisse 1902, p. 151; "it is from India that cholera has come to us"): the British only go there for trade, government, and military control. Yet, switches of perspective can also be found, as in

> Lord Canning [...] issued an Act under which all recruits in the Bengal army would in future be liable for service abroad.   (Innes 1927, p. 169)

Here "abroad" must, of course, be interpreted from the Indian recruits' point of view.

Spatial *distance and distribution* are frequently an issue. Thus Cawnpore is characterized as "a short distance from Lucknow" (Cassell's 1903, p. 124), British troops in India are said to be "few and scattered" while the discontent "was most widespread in the native regiments in the North-West Provinces" (Fearenside 1922, p. 433), the revolt "rapidly spread throughout Upper Bengal and Oudh" (Hearnshaw 1930, p. 154), but "did not spread all over India" (Fearenside 1922, p. 434) or "did not extend beyond the Ganges valley" (Hearnshaw 1930, p. 154). Related to this is spatial *movement*, as in "the war had drawn away a [153] large part of the British garrison in India" (Hearnshaw 1930, pp. 153–154). The overall event being a string of military campaigns, reference to movements are very prominent indeed: The rebels "marched to and took possession of Delhi," Havelock "succeeded with his troops in getting through the rebel lines into the city" (Cassell's 1903, p. 124), and the British government "hurried reinforcements to India" (Hearnshaw 1930, p. 154). Or, to give a more elaborate example:

> if no relief had arrived before the end of the month, they [the loyal sepoys] would probably have marched out. But relief came. Havelock [...] advanced with sharp fighting to Cawnpore [...] Then he marched towards Lucknow, but was forced to fall back. In the middle of September he was joined by Outram with fresh forces. On the 23rd the troops were four miles from Lucknow; on the 25th they fought their way in [...]
> By this time Sir Colin Campbell had come out to Calcutta [...]; troops had arrived; others, on the way to the China War, had been diverted to help in the much more serious emergency in India.   (Innes 1927, p. 171)

Permeating all of this we find two types of spatial concepts: points in space (that can be approached or moved away from) and contained spaces (that one can move into or out of). Both support the overall strategic-military approach.

Ad 2.2.4.4:
[Are there any temporal and/or spatial constraints on the production of the discourse itself?]

Most trivially, the available printing space imposes constraints on the authors. The exact size of a history book may be self-imposed by the author. In most cases it is, to a certain extent. Thus it is McCarthy's (1908) own decision to write a *short* 'history of our times' as a condensation of the more extensive *A History of Our Own Times*. And it is Lavisse's (1902) own decision to write a compact history textbook for primary school children. The Lavisse example, however, immediately points at the role of the intended audience as a co-determiner of size. It is only one step further to indicate the decisive role of the economics of book publishing which often leads to strict guidelines, even in terms of the number of characters to be used. It is worth inquiring to what extent such guidelines influenced writing at the beginning of the twentieth century. But no matter how many pages the authors had or decided to have available, the twin constraints of writing time and printing space always necessitate at least two types of non-trivial choices.

First of all, how dense or how expansive is the writing going to be? In general, our data show a high *degree of density*. There is an unmistakable preoccupation with the presentation of as many facts as possible in the smallest possible space. Consider the following sentence:

> Les soldats anglais marchèrent contre les Cipayes révoltés, reprirent la ville de Delhi et attachèrent les prisonniers hindous à la gueule des canons (fig. 10).   (Lavisse 1902, p. 152)

> [The English soldiers marched against the revolting Sepoys, recaptured the city of Delhi, and tied the Hindu prisoners to the mouths of cannons.]

Here the initiation of the counterattack, its end result, and punishment for the instigators of the Mutiny require only this one syntactic structure. This is not untypical for the entire corpus, the main exception being Synge (1908), whose main concern is the telling of an entertaining story:

> Such a time [when a nation must either fight or go down] had come now. Swiftly, silently the blow fell, and heroically, alone, without an ally, against odds too great to be counted, England in the face of the world set to work to re-conquer India.   (Synge 1908, p. 111)

Capturing only the first steps toward the action described in the first phrase of Lavisse's sentence above, the emphasis is more on expansive description than on relating facts.

Second, what choices are made exactly as to *what is and what is not going to be communicated*? Here the most remarkable observation is that, no matter how much space is available (which, by definition, is always restricted so that choices have to be made, just like in any other form of communicative language use), and no matter how dense the account is (the longer texts often being just as dense as Lavisse, though at a different level of detail), the focus remains (as was already to be suspected from looking at the pattern of spatial orientations; see 2.2.4.3) on the military and strategic nature of the events. The meaning generating effects of such choices are not to be ignored: This episode of colonial history is clearly cast in terms of power relationships, without ever going into what it means to be relatively powerless and how this could explain certain actions.

AD 2.2.4.5:

[Are there any 'material' conditions that constrain/orient the discourse production or interpretation?]

One type of material circumstance that helps to shape the discourse was just mentioned with reference to the economics of book publishing: The production of a book requires an investment justifiable in terms of an expected return. This is not an equally pressing demand for all the books in our corpus. Though commercial considerations no doubt play some role for all of them, circumstances may significantly diminish the urgency involved. In the case of Lavisse (1902), for instance, the prescribed French school curriculum, combined with Lavisse's academic status,[35] minimize the risks. On the side of the British sources, similarly ameliorating factors may be at play for Fearenside (1922), published by the London University Tutorial Press specifically to help students in their matriculation exams, so that students with such ambitions could not afford to ignore the book.

Needless to say, the material conditions of production and interpretation of books as physical and commercial objects are relatively simple when compared to what is happening with newer media. Especially the fast-developing technological possibilities and constraints of audio-visual and internet-based communication condition discourse production and interpretation in highly specific ways. Ideology research based on discourse in the new media will have to address most of the issues reviewed in this book, but will have to take into account the specificities produced by the highly different material conditions.[36]

An important 'material' factor for most history writing as well as much journalistic discourse, as already mentioned when discussing 'voices' (2.2.1.2), is the lack of direct access to what it is one is writing about, because of temporal and spatial distance. While – remarkably – sources other than the author are rarely acknowledged explicitly in our sample data, this comment on the absence of observability for both utterer and interpreter feeds directly into what will later have to be said about intertextuality (2.3.2).

---

[35] Born in 1842, Lavisse studied Prussian history for a few years in Germany in the 1870s. He returned to France in 1875. In 1880 (two years before the first edition of his *Histoire générale*), he replaced the French historian Fustel de Coulanges at the Sorbonne, where he became adjunct professor in 1883 and succeeded Henri Wallon in 1888 as chair for modern history. Moreover, from the beginning of his career he was actively involved in the shaping of educational policies at all levels.

[36] For a first glimpse at the properties of audio-visual and computer-mediated forms of communication that have to be kept in mind while analyzing, the reader is referred to Slembrouck (1995) and Georgakopoulou (2005). On multimodality in general, see Jewitt (ed.) (2009).

Ad 2.2.5:

[In the case of (video-taped) spoken data: What relevant aspects of bodily posture, gesture, gaze, appearance can be pointed out for the discourse participants? In the case of written data: What graphic features (typography, pictorial representations) are used?]

I use only textual data for purposes of illustration in this book, but we should not forget that spoken data incorporate physical properties and physical types of behavior that are relevant in the overall process of meaning generation. Bodily posture, gesture, gaze, and general appearance are the most obvious examples.[37] There are parallel phenomena in writing as well. Thus font changes and layout could be seen, to some extent, as counterparts to gesture in writing. They will be discussed in relation to information chunking (under 3.3.1).

Of direct interest here are those graphic features that are specific to the channel of writing: pictorial representations. There are four types in our corpus:

(i)   A *photograph* (or what looks like one): In Richardson (1924, p. 140) there is a picture of Calcutta, the textual function of which may simply be that the reader get a glimpse of a well-known Indian city, an important point of entry; it presents a tranquil port scene, very much detached from the story line, even though early on during the period of the Mutiny there were fears that this city would be affected too; it is not unambiguously clear what historical period the picture should be situated in (the time of the Mutiny? the time of writing?); it is somehow suggestive, but suggestive of what? Do the larger ships in the background represent vessels that carried British troops that came to the rescue? We cannot answer such questions without access to more information (e.g., about Calcutta in various periods in the nineteenth century, about types of vessels and their changes over time, etc.).

(ii)   A *photograph of a painting* (or what looks like one): In Cassell's (1903, p. 123), we get a pictorial representation of one scene from the narrative, the meeting of Sir Colin Campbell and General Havelock at the relief of Lucknow; what we get is the layout of a classical painting with the protagonists taking center stage, backed by a force of rescuers, with the victims of earlier violence in the left bottom corner, and with the smoking buildings of Lucknow in the background; here the suggestive force unmistakably underscores a tale of British heroism.

Somewhat surprisingly, these are the only two examples in the British texts of our corpus. By contrast, Lavisse (1902) makes extensive use of two other types of pictorial representations throughout his book, and both are represented in the relevant extracts:

[37] See Payrató (2006) for an overview and further references.

(iii)   *Drawings*, most probably specifically designed for the book, illustrating events in much the same way as (ii): On p. 65 we see Cortez
entering Mexico, and on p. 153 the execution of the sepoys. While (ii)
displays heroism, both of these pictures show power and superiority.
Just consider Cortez, high up on his horse, in armor, backed by soldiers with spears and cannons, looking down on half-naked Indians,
bowing their heads and assuming a humble posture. The picture is
certainly in full harmony with its caption:

> Les Mexicains prirent les hommes blancs pour des fils du Dieu-Soleil, les
> reçurent avec honneur et les laissèrent entrer à Mexico.
>
> (Lavisse 1902, p. 65)

> [The Mexicans took the white men for the sons of the Sun-God, received
> them with honor and let them enter Mexico.]

Note that the caption line is taken literally from the main historical
narrative, where the Indians' respectful behavior contrasts sharply
with the Spanish abuse of their trust:

> Les Espagnols en profitèrent pour s'emparer des trésors du roi [...].
>
> (Lavisse 1902, p. 65)

> [The Spanish took advantage of this to grab the king's treasures [...].]

Thus, while both drawings show European power and superiority,
they also emphasize more objectionable qualities of the Spanish
(treachery) and the British (cruelty). This fits in with the undercur-
rent of global competition that was already said to be noticeable in
Lavisse.

(iv)   There are three *maps* in our extracts from Lavisse (1902): pp. 66–67,
94–95, 156–157. All three are in fact maps of the world, which are
progressively filled in with
    – possessions of the Spanish and the Portuguese in the sixteenth
       century
    – European colonies in the eighteenth century
    – Europeans in the world in the nineteenth century
showing ever-increasing European presence outside Europe. They
occur in chapters labeled, respectively,
    – 'inventions and discoveries'
    – 'the formation of the English empire'
    – 'Europeans outside of Europe'.

The naturalization of Europeans' presence all over the world becomes a simple
story of chronology.

   The embeddedness of pictorial representations in the text, and their interaction
with the text in generating meaning, should be clear (except perhaps for (i)), and
goes as far as to involve a pattern of sequencing (in the case of (iv)).

Procedure 2.3: *Investigate the linguistic context. In particular:*

2.3.1.   *What linguistic channel(s) is/are involved?*
2.3.2.   *What intertextual links are required and how are they appealed to?*
2.3.3.   *Is sequencing an issue?*
2.3.4.   *What kinds of contextual cohesion are established, and how? (Think of conjunctions, anaphora, co-reference, self-reference, exemplification, explanation, ellipsis, enumeration, highlighting, contrasting, comparison, repetition, substitution, etc.)*

AD 2.3, IN GENERAL:

[Investigate the linguistic context.]

There is a *linguistic* – in our case *textual* – *dimension* to the accomplishment of *contextualization*: That is what 'linguistic context' is about. At this point I should highlight an observation that, so far, was relegated to a footnote accompanying Figure 2: Context and structure are intimately related (as further explored in Verschueren 2008). The notion of linguistic context bears on the simple fact that, as soon as an utterance is produced, it becomes part of the context of whatever else is said. This should not be looked at in a strictly linear way: Discourse also anticipates what is going to be said, thus turning future utterances into (first virtual, then real) linguistic context as well. The linking of utterances, turning them into each other's contexts, which is what the topics under 2.3.2, 2.3.3, and 2.3.4 are about, is a particularly conscious activity in writing, but is by no means restricted to that channel.

AD 2.3.1:

[What linguistic channel(s) is/are involved?]

All of our sample data use the channel of writing. Non-verbal elements, such as the pictorial representations discussed in 2.2.5 are functionally integrated as part of the same physical object, a text published as a book. Their contribution to the meaning generation process is significant, as pictures attract a reader's attention.

Many of the sources are completely understandable on the basis of their being largely 'monologic' published written texts, with all the properties, restrictions, and possibilities this entails.[38] Though belonging to a common genre (if defined broadly enough), they display a wide range of styles. Some are clearly meant

---

[38] In this context, 'monologic' simply means 'written by an author and unidirectionally addressed to an audience.' This is not to deny the fundamentally 'dialogic' nature of all discourse, including this type of 'monologic' text. The fact that utterances are adapted to an intended audience, or that voices other than the author's are invoked, produces polyphony in every text. See Angermüller (2011) for an example of the complex dialogical organization of print media discourse.

as reading materials only, whether or not oriented to other types of interaction (such as Fearenside 1922, meant to help students prepare for exams). Others show features typical for use in teaching contexts, and hence in assumed combination with spoken discourse; in some of those texts, features of dialogue are also brought in, such as direct forms of address (as reviewed in 2.2.1.1).

Lavisse (1902) goes furthest in bringing in elements of the channel of spoken language. At the end of each chapter, there is a section with the following heading:

> **Résumé** *(à réciter)*.
>
> [**Summary** *(for recitation)*.]

Those sections, summarizing the main points from the preceding chapters, are meant to be read aloud and/or recited after memorizing them. They belong to prescripted spoken language, utterances written-to-be-spoken, serving a pedagogical purpose.

Moreover, Lavisse (1902) brings in a dialogic element that is not to be found in the other texts: At the bottom of every page there are questions corresponding to one or more sentences in the text. Clearly, they can be used by pupils to test their own knowledge or understanding, or by teachers to interrogate pupils. In the latter case, there is again a possible orientation toward spoken language. But unless the whole set of questions is gone through sequentially, the teacher has to adapt (mainly by making more explicit) the questions, so that their prescripted nature is less solid.

AD 2.3.2:
[What intertextual links are required and how are they appealed to?]

Various types of intertextuality are involved in our sample texts. In other words, interpreting the texts often requires awareness of intertextual links.

A first type of intertextuality concerns *the positioning of parts of a text in relation to each other*. There is a reason, for instance, why prefaces tend to behave differently from the main bodies of the texts with regard to aspects of person deixis (see 2.2.1.1). Because of their special status, they are allowed to deviate from certain norms which the rest of the text is expected to adhere to. Prefaces are typically written (or at least rewritten) after completion of the full texts, upon which they reflect so that the author can ascribe certain (intended) qualities to them, to the point of becoming self-congratulatory. McCarthy is a mild example:

> [...] I have [vii] endeavoured to make the compressed version, contained in this new volume, not merely accurate as a record, but also clear, suggestive, and vivid [...] [viii] [...] Our own times may, on the whole, be regarded as having created an ever memorable era in the development of civilisation, and I feel it an honour to have had a share, however limited and imperfect, in describing its progress.   (McCarthy 1908, pp. vii–x)

Such distancing, allowing for less subdued laudation, increases when the author of the preface is not the author of the book, as in Parkin (1911), where a certain Rosebery writes:

> Mr. Parkin, the author of this book, whose earnest eloquence is inspired by a single zeal, pursues the picturesque and instructive method of a tour round the British Empire. He himself is best known as the untiring advocate of a cause which represents the high resolve to maintain Imperial unity [...] Such a cause can only be furthered and fostered by this little book.
>
> (Parkin 1911, p. iv)

Other examples of intertextual links between functionally separate parts of the same overall text are provided by Lavisse's summaries and questions, as just mentioned (in 2.3.1). In relation to Lavisse I should add that he goes even further with the structuring of his book into separable parts that are intertextually linked. The book is divided into four 'livres' (or 'books'). At the end of each 'livre' there is (i) a section of "**Réflections sur le Livre** N" ("**Reflections on Book** N"), which provides a summary – sometimes with additional thoughts – on a higher level of topical structure, as well as (ii) a section entitled "DEVOIRS DE RÉDACTION SUR LE LIVRE N" ("WRITING TASKS ON BOOK N"), giving a number of topics which pupils can be asked to write about, presumably by way of exam. Furthermore, at the end of the book (pp. 167–182) there is a section entitled

RÉVISION
DE L'HISTOIRE DE CHAQUE ÉTAT
PAR ORDRE ALPHABÉTIQUE

[REVIEW
OF THE HISTORY OF EACH STATE
IN ALPHABETICAL ORDER]

Here we find a summary of the main points that have been made about twenty-six states or regions in the course of the book. Finally, to top it all off, there is a "LEXIQUE" (pp. 183–185), a glossary of key terms marked with an asterisk in the main text – not to mention the more predictable "TABLE ALPHABÉTIQUE" or index.

Second, for a proper understanding of the texts, their *intertextual positioning in relation to a wider body of literature* belonging to the institutional contexts of education and scholarship must be appealed to. This institutional embedding has already been illustrated (under 2.2.3). Here I just want to draw attention to the intertextual dimension involved. It is worth noting, however, that a very explicit intertextual (and even sequential) link is indicated by Lavisse (1902) on his title page:

> Ce livre fait suite à **tous les cours** d'Histoire de France
>
> [This book follows **all courses** in French History.]

This is further motivated in the preface:

> Ces notions d'histoire générale [...] seront le complément naturel de l'histoire de la France; car on ne sait pas toute l'histoire de son pays, si l'on n'a point appris quelle place il occupe dans le monde.
>
> [These notions of general history [...] will be the natural complement to French history; because one does not know the entire history of one's country, if one has not at all learnt what place it occupies in the world.]

In other words, one cannot understand one's own history if one cannot place it in a wider framework – a framework that, in an educational setting, necessarily involves other texts.

Somewhere between these first two types of intertextuality, there is the frequent establishment (in the preliminary pages of the book, including the preface) of links and/or contrasts with earlier editions of the same work.

Remembering what was said about the material conditions of historical book publishing (see 2.2.4.5), and in particular the absence of direct accessibility of the reported events to the authors, it is surprising that there are almost no explicit references to specific items in the wider body of literature that is intertextually assumed, except in the footnotes to Low and Sanders (1910), the one source that is clearly directed at an academic audience. A quick quote from Sir George Trevelyan (who himself served in India for several years from 1862 onwards) is inserted by Synge (1908, pp. 144–145) to indirectly describe the dramatic conditions of the besieged British garrison in Cawnpore. We find in Kerr and Kerr an appeal to other literature, which is not further specified:

> The story is too long to tell here. But if you want to know how [...] you must read the story in another book.   (Kerr and Kerr 1927, p. 183)

And literature of a different type, Tennyson's poetry, is quoted at length by Synge (1908).

Coming to a third type of intertextuality, relatively limited use is made of *reported speech* or *direct quotations*, though the different texts vary a great deal in this respect. In Low and Sanders' footnotes, reported speech is often used together with an identification of the written sources the authors rely on as evidence. Synge (1908) uses a great deal of direct quotation, often without source indications at all, to liven up his narrative. In all other instances, both reported speech and direct quotations serve the recounting of communicative actions or events that are part of the story to be told. *Reported speech*, marked with linguistic action verbs and verb-like phrases[39] or related nouns (underlined in the examples below), occurs regularly. Here is a small sample:

> Les Anglais <u>demandèrent</u> au gouvernement français de <u>destituer</u> Dupleix, et le gouvernement le *destitua* (1754).   (Lavisse 1902, p. 94)
>
> [The English asked the French government to discharge Dupleix, and the government discharged him (1754).]

---

[39] 'Linguistic action verbs' is used here as a cover term for all verbs that are used to describe instances of verbal or communicative behavior (including the more restricted set of speech act verbs). See Verschueren (1980, 1985b) for an approach to the semantics of these lexical items. For a general introduction to the topic of reported speech, see Holt (2009).

Les colons <u>déclarèrent</u> qu'ils ne payeraient pas [...] Les colons de chaque province <u>nommèrent</u> alors des députés qui se réunirent en *congrès** à Philadelphie. Le 4 juillet 1776, ce congrès <u>proclama</u> que les États étaient indépendants* [...].   (Lavisse 1902, p. 97)

[The colonists declared that they would not pay [...] The colonists of each province then appointed deputies who gathered in congress* in Philadelphia. On 4 July 1776, this congress proclaimed that the States were independent* [...].]

Depuis le XVIIIe siècle, les libéraux <u>réclamaient</u> qu'on rendit la liberté à ces nègres [...] Mais les colons <u>disaient</u> qu'on ne pouvait se passer de nègres pour cultiver le coton et le café [...] Dans les États du Nord [...] ils <u>demand-èrent</u> qu'on abolit l'esclavage."   (Lavisse 1902, p. 122)

[From the 18th century on, the liberals demanded that liberty be given back to these negroes [...] But the colonists said they could not manage without the negroes to cultivate cotton and coffee [...] In the Northern States, they asked to abolish slavery.]

The Hindoos <u>objected</u> to do this and mutinied [...] this pretext <u>was advanced</u> to start the rebellion.
     [...] Regiments of soldiers <u>refused</u> to obey their officers [...]
     [...] they surrendered to that chief on <u>the promise that</u> their lives should be spared.   (Cassell's 1903, p. 124)

Lord Canning, who, under ill advice, <u>issued</u> an Act under which [...].
(Innes 1927, p. 169)

And then came <u>the report that</u> [...]; since the cartridges <u>were said to</u> be greased with [...].   (Innes 1927, p. 170)

[...] the governor-general had <u>made it known</u> that he would regard a state as "lapsed" when [...].   (Low and Sanders 1910, pp. 135)

Rumours <u>were circulated</u> that the government intended to compel the people to embrace Christianity [...].   (Low and Sanders 1910, p. 136)

Sir Henry Lawrence foresaw the approach of the revolt, and <u>warned</u> the government to prepare for it.   (Low and Sanders 1910, p. 138)

Bahádur Sháh [...] <u>was proclaimed</u> emperor.
(Low and Sanders 1910, p. 142)

He <u>asked for</u> large reinforcements from England [...]; he <u>summoned</u> reinforcements to Bengal from Ceylon [...] [142]; he <u>ordered</u> back to Calcutta [...] the troops under Outram [...]; and he took upon himself the responsibility of <u>requesting</u> Lord Elgin to land in India [...].
(Low and Sanders 1910, pp. 142–143)

On July 31 he <u>issued an order</u>, intended to […].
(Low and Sanders 1910, p. 143)

Nana Sahib, who <u>agreed to</u> send them down the river under safe conduct […].   (Low and Sanders 1910, p. 144)

Even Outram <u>suggested</u> that […].   (Low and Sanders 1910, p. 150)

She <u>persuaded</u> Tántia Topí to retire to Gwalior […].
(Low and Sanders 1910, p. 157)

He had taken great interest in <u>the framing of</u> [174] <u>regulations</u> for the railway legislation […].   (McCarthy 1908, pp. 174–175)

Mr. Disraeli, to do him justice, <u>raised his voice in remonstrance against</u> […] He <u>declared</u> that […].   (McCarthy 1908, p. 178)

What all these examples have in common is the public nature of the acts described or of their consequences, whether or not the acts themselves belong to a formal, institutionalized, official type. Except in Synge (1908), *direct quotations* are rare. A few examples:

"I will not govern in anger," <u>said</u> Canning.
(Low and Sanders 1910, p. 143)

Two days afterwards Henry Lawrence, the statesman, soldier, and saint, who <u>asked</u> only that it should be <u>recorded</u> of him that he had "tried to do his duty," was mortally wounded by a shell.   (Low and Sanders 1910, p. 145)

<u>argued for</u> a bolder policy, and they <u>were encouraged</u> by the governor-general, who <u>bade</u> Lawrence "hold on to Peshάwar [148] to the last."
(Low and Sanders 1910, pp. 148–149)

the officer […] <u>called out</u>, 'Sir Henry, are you hurt?' 'I am killed,' <u>was the answer</u> that came faintly but firmly from Sir Henry Lawrence's lips.
(McCarthy 1908, p. 181)

He <u>desired that</u> on his tomb <u>should be engraven</u> merely the words, 'Here lies Henry Lawrence, who tried to do his duty.'   (McCarthy 1908, p. 181)

"Sir Henry, are you hurt?" <u>cried</u> a friend who was with him.
    There was a moment's silence.
    "I am killed," <u>answered</u> the wounded man firmly.
    […]
    "Let every man die at his post – never make terms – God help the poor women and children!" he <u>said</u> in [119] broken snatches to those around him as he lay dying. Then, speaking rather to himself than to others, he <u>murmured</u> the now historic words, "Here lies Henry Lawrence, who tried to do his duty," words which <u>were carved</u> on his tombstone […].
(Synge 1908, pp. 119–120)

While some of these examples also refer to acts or consequences of a public nature, most of them highlight individual character traits – especially those the author deems laudable – of the persons quoted. Quotation marks are also used to point at labeling practices that are relevant to the story line without being attributed to anyone in particular. A recurrent example is the following:

> the calmness that earned him the sobriquet of "Clemency Canning" […].
>
> (Low and Sanders 1910, p. 143)

> he was nicknamed 'Clemency Canning' […].   (McCarthy 1908, p. 104)

> He was called "Clemency Canning" […].
>
> (Warner and Marten 1912, p. 694)

But there are numerous other examples: Low and Sanders (1910, p. 147) makes use of quotes to refer to General Outram as "the Bayard of India," Synge (1908) mentions "Havelock's Saints" (p. 116) and describes John Nicholson as the "Lion of the Punjab" (p. 123).

While functioning differently, as specified above, the way in which both reported speech and direct quotation are used underscores the factuality of the told communicative events. This is accomplished by the matter-of-factness of the descriptions. No doubt this is related to the norms associated with the genre of history writing. But that deviations from expected patterns are possible should be clear from the more flowery and effect-oriented way in which Synge (1908) describes Henry Lawrence's famous words.[40]

Fourth, a comparison between the texts of the sample corpus shows reliance of the different accounts on a number of *common 'master narratives.'* Thus there is the overall dominance of the themes of the greased cartridges and of the Cawnpore massacre which emerge with a great deal of consistency throughout. But similar patterns are to be found at lower levels of structure. For instance, the theme of John Lawrence 'using' the Sikhs so well (commented on earlier with reference to Fearenside – see Caveat 2.1) recurs, as was also pointed out, in equally vague and suggestive terms in a number of the other sources:

> Sir John Lawrence, the Governor of the Punjaub, who had, by his humane treatment of the Sikhs, endeared those natives to him […].
>
> (Cassell's 1903, p. 124)

> The Punjab was […] placed under a commission of able officers, who not only disarmed and pacified the Sikhs, but contrived in the course of a few years to turn them into the most loyal and contented subjects of the British ráj in Asia.   (Low and Sanders 1910, p. 134)

Fifth, intertextual links also take the shape of *identical or near-identical phrasings* for the same actors, actions, and events. Examples are to be found in the above presentation of forms of direct quotation (the nicknaming of Canning as 'Clemency Canning,' Henry Lawrence's words after having been wounded

---

[40] The natural-language description of verbal behavior may also be called 'metapragmatic description.' A good illustration of how much metapragmatic descriptions can deviate from a matter-of-fact style, even in a genre such as international news reporting, can be found in Verschueren (1985a).

and his own suggestion for an epitaph). Another example relates to the master narrative of the Cawnpore massacre:

> the bodies were thrown, "the dying, with the dead," down a well near by.
> (Low and Sanders 1910, p. 145)

> and the bodies, the dead with the dying, were thrown down a well (July 15).
> (Warner and Marten 1912, p. 692)

> and threw their bodies, "the dying with the dead," into a well.
> (Richardson 1924, p. 138)

Low and Sanders adds in a footnote attached to the quoted phrase "the dying with the dead": "Inscription on the Memorial at Cawnpore." If this is a correct indication, the quote certainly does not exhaust the complete inscription, but it explains the consistency of the phrasing across the sample texts as there is an identifiable source tapped by all of them (no doubt mostly indirectly). In other cases as well, identical wordings betray intertextual relations, though the ultimate source or the direction of borrowing is hard to determine – nor would that usually be important. Thus there is the story of William Hodson, who, after the surrender of the newly installed Mogul emperor in Delhi, takes the three Mogul princes from their hiding place and

> shot them dead with his own hand.

which is told in identical terms – though narratively framed differently – by Low and Sanders (1910, p. 150) and McCarthy (1908, p. 191). A systematic search will no doubt reveal many instances of this type.

Ad 2.3.3:

[Is sequencing an issue?]

As there is no language use without the linear ordering of utterances, sequencing is always a property to be looked at. While the topic has been most intensively investigated in relation to turn-taking, adjacency pairs, repair, openings and closings and other conversational phenomena,[41] it is equally basic for an understanding of written text. There are two major differences between spoken and written discourse in this respect. First, the written text, once published or 'issued' in a different way, acquires a frozen structure that does not allow for further manipulation on the utterer's side, whereas spoken discourse, as long as it is actually 'in use' rather than simply accessed by memory, may undergo continued prospective and retrospective build-up moves. Second, oral language use, unless it is strictly monologic, is built up collaboratively, which results in an interactional dynamics that affects the build-up in a way that is only implicitly mirrored in an author's interaction with a virtual reader.

---

[41] For an introductory look at conversational sequencing phenomena, see Clift, Drew and Hutchby (2006), Sidnell (2006a, 2006b).

Though the surface structure is necessarily linear (in the case of a romanized writing tradition: left to right, top to bottom), sequential structuring frees itself from this restriction by means of retrospective and prospective moves. Typically prospective are the prefaces (even if written after completion of the books), while typically retrospective are, for instance, Lavisse's summaries (at the end of each chapter) and reflections (at the end of each 'book'). And throughout the texts, though sparingly, we find intratextual cross-references such as

> We have already noted that [...].   (Innes 1927, p. 169)

> as we have already seen [...].   (McCarthy 1908, p. 194)

Even hypothetical future discourse is evoked:

> he will have to say that [...].   (McCarthy 1908, p. 182)

I have already commented upon sequentiality in the section on temporal ordering (see 2.2.4.2), where an iconic relationship was pointed out between the temporal order of events and narrative sequence, a relationship that was ignored only in longer accounts leading to episodic structuring. In addition to episodic structuring, however, longer accounts also deviate from merely temporal ordering in other ways. Take Low and Sanders (1910) as an example:

> The news that the Indian native army had broken out into revolt in the late spring of 1857 came upon England like a thunder-clap [...]
> Yet the state of affairs in the Asiatic empire might well have justified uneasiness [...] [132]
> [...] [132–139]
> Yet in that fateful spring of 1857 the danger signs were blowing thickly over the lowering skies of Northern India [...] The military revolt was imminent; but even then, if vigour and energy had been displayed, it might have been quelled at the outset.
> Such qualities were conspicuously wanting when the disaffection first blazed into a flame of violent rebellion early in May, 1857, at Meerut, forty miles from Delhi. At this large [139] station [...]
> (Low and Sanders 1910, pp. 132–140)

Here the events of May 1857 are first mentioned. Then many pages of digression are devoted to a detailed description of anterior circumstances and events (explaining why the 'thunder-clap' should not have been a thunder-clap). After this digression, the author gets back to the starting point from which then the narrative continues.

I have also mentioned (in 2.2.5) the sequential ordering of Lavisse's maps, describing a progressive presence of Europeans throughout the world. Obvious as this may seem, the sequential ordering, following the main story line and physically located at the 'right' places (without references to the maps in the text), is necessary for a good understanding; switching the maps around (even though the captions are explicit enough) would be most confusing.

Also, texts are subdivided into chapters, sections, and paragraphs. All of these are ordered consecutively. In some texts (Lavisse being an extreme case) they are also numbered accordingly.

AD 2.3.4:

[What kinds of contextual cohesion are established, and how? (Think of conjunctions, anaphora, co-reference, self-reference, exemplification, explanation, ellipsis, enumeration, highlighting, contrasting, comparison, repetition, substitution, etc.).]

All texts contain formal markers of contextual (or co-textual) cohesion (closely related to, but still distinct from, discursive coherence, as discussed in 3.3.6.3). As this is a matter of great detail, it is worth looking closely at a specific text fragment, a more extensive extract, for which I have chosen paragraph 213 of Lavisse (1902, pp. 154–155), of which I am here presenting the English translation only.

> **213. Chinese wars**. – **5. China** is a very rich and densely populated country. **6**. It has at least **400 million inhabitants**, more than all of Europe together. **7**. The Chinese produce a lot of rice, tea, cotton; they manufacture porcelain and silk. **8**. One could trade with them on a large scale. **9**. But the Chinese government *does not like foreigners*, and did not want to let Europeans enter China.
>
> **10**. Many Chinese have a habit of smoking **opium**. **11**. Those who smoke it go mad or die, because opium is a poison. **12**. The English sell a lot of opium in China. The Chinese government banned its purchase, and in 1839, it let 22,000 cases of opium, brought in by English ships, be thrown into the sea. **13**. The English waged war on China and, in 1842, forced the Chinese to open five ports where the Europeans would have the right to disembark and to sell their goods.
>
> **14**. But the Chinese government had only accepted this treaty by force, and it continued to maltreat the French missionaries* and the English tradesmen. **15**. England and France then made an alliance and undertook two expeditions against [154] China (1857 and 1860). **1**. A small army of 12,000 Frenchmen defeated 40,000 Tatar cavalry, and entered **Peking**, the Chinese capital (1860). **2**. The Chinese government signed a treaty which allowed the Europeans to trade with China in certain ports.
>
> **3**. Yet it is still very dangerous for a European to enter the interior of China alone; he would risk being murdered there. **4**. The *Mandarins** who govern China despise and detest Europeans, whom they call *barbarians*. **5**. A small railroad had been built in China. The Chinese government *had it destroyed*, in order not to change the old customs.   (Lavisse 1902, pp. 154–155)

Markers of cohesion in this fragment include:

- *Conjunctions* such as "very rich <u>and</u> densely populated" (in 5, both conjoined elements being further substantiated in the following sentences, 6 and 7), "<u>But</u> the Chinese government does not like for-eigners, <u>and</u> did not want to let Europeans enter China" (sentence 9), "<u>because</u> opium is a poison" (in 11), "the French missionaries <u>and</u> the English tradesmen" (in 14), "<u>Yet</u> it is still very dangerous" (in 3).

- *Anaphora* establishing co-reference, such as the personal pronouns "It" (in 6 and 11), "they" (in 7), the demonstative "Those" (in 11), the relative pronoun "whom" (in 4), the possessive "its" (in 12). Look, for instance, at the anaphoric interrelations between 10 and 11: "those" in 11 refers back to the "many Chinese" of 10, but it may also carry a more general reference to all (also non-Chinese) smokers of opium; "it" in 11 both refers back to "opium" in 10 and forward to "opium" (further characterized as poison) later in the same sentence.

- *Juxtaposition*, as with sentences 5 to 8, which are not linked expli-citly, but where 6 and 7 provide a substantiation for the conjoined adjectives in 5 and together lead to 8 as a logical conclusion.

- What I have just referred to as 'substantiation' could also be called *explanation* (such as sentence 6 in relation to "densely populated" in 5) and *exemplification* (such as 7 in relation to "very rich" in 5). Other instances of explanation, of two quite different types, are the definite description "the Chinese capital" in relation to "Peking" (in 1), and "in order not to change the old customs" (in 5 on p. 155); the former explains the nature of a named entity, the latter explains reported action in terms of an attribution of intentions to the actors.

- Many sentences (such as 9, the second sentence in 12, 13, and 1) show *ellipsis*, as the subjects of the second verb phrase following the conjunction "and" are not repeated (or replaced by a pronoun).

- There is *highlighting* by means of italics and the use of bold face. But it is also accomplished by means of *(near-)repetition*, as in "despise and detest" (in 4).

- In this fragment, *contrasting* is also accomplished by means of juxta-position, as when the sentence on the Chinese view of Europeans as barbarians (in 4) is immediately followed by a description of their own anti-modern behavior (5 on p. 155). Contrasts, in this case *com-parisons*, are also made with the use of *numbers* (12,000 vs. 40,000 in 1).

- Forms of *substitution* occur, as when "the Chinese government" (in 9, 12, 14, and 2) is replaced by "The Mandarins who govern China" (in 4), to be replaced again by "the Chinese government" in the last sentence.

This is just a partial overview of some of the typical formal markers of cohesion that can be found in the corpus. As to their contribution to meaning generation processes, suffice it to say that all instances of conjoining, juxtaposing, contrast-ing, comparing, and the like may give rise to implicit meanings. Thus, stating that a small army of Frenchmen defeated a much larger force suggests, without the author's 'saying' so, serious superiority in warfare. Formulating the Chinese view of Europeans as barbarians, followed by a statement concerning their willful destruction of a railroad (presumably built by Europeans) introduces an implicit contrast that, in this context, suggests the 'strangeness' (if not backwardness) of Chinese perspectives. Similarly, saying that opium is a poison, immediately followed by the observation that the English sell a lot of the stuff in China fits in nicely with Lavisse's recurrent attempts to covertly frown upon the behavior of France's competitors in colonial affairs; it also makes the Chinese government's reaction understandable; that the French join forces with the British later requires the prior description of a legitimating context in which not only British (opium?) traders but also French missionaries are victims of harassment.[42]

It is, of course, not enough to look at such text fragments in isolation. Comparable patterns of cohesion extend across wider streches of discourse. Consider, for instance, a few paragraphs further down the text in a section on Europeans in Japan:

> Depuis ce temps, les Japonais ont fait connaissance avec les Européens, et au lieu de nous mépriser, comme les Chinois, ils se sont mis à **nous imiter**.
>
> (Lavisse 1902, p. 156)

> [Since that time, the Japanese have become acquainted with the Europeans, and instead of despising us, like the Chinese, they started to **imitate us**.]

Here a contrast is made textually explicit between two types of reaction to European progress, both of which imply European superiority: backward rejection or imitation – culture clash or adjustment.

> **Guideline 3: The core task consists in tracing the dynamics of meaning generation in relation to issues pertaining to social structures, processes, and relations.**

Note, first of all, that there is a stronger continuity between the preceding pages and what follows than what the transition to a new guideline might suggest. Tracing the dynamics of meaning generation requires attention to levels of structure that are all ingredients of the linguistic context which embody meaning generating operations and processes. Before going into further details, a few preliminary warnings have to be formulated.

> **Caveat 3.1:** *There are hardly any fixed form–function relationships. Hence there are no interpretation rules that can be applied mechanically.*

---

[42] During the Second Opium War from 1856 to 1860, the French joined British anti-Chinese campaigns. In addition to securing open ports for the opium trade from British India into China, a number of concessions were forced upon China, such as the permission for foreigners, including missionaries, to travel freely. One of the French motives for engaging in this war – in addition to their own trading demands – had been the murder of a French missionary in Canton.

In order for communication to be successful, utterers and interpreters must be able to share meaning. Such an achievement would not be possible without conventions of language use. Conventions may guide interpretations, but they are not like rules that could be straightforwardly applied.[43] This has important implications for analysis. It would be most convenient if we could analyze texts with reference to a set of forms that would immediately yield specific interpretations. Unfortunately, this is out of the question. It is true that languages allow us to identify relatively stable grammatical rules, that grammar has a relation to meaning, and that there is a level of meaning that is strongly guided by linguistic form. It is even true that regularities can be observed in the relationship between forms and the ways in which they are habitually used, or that aspects of use can be seen to restrict choices of form. But the meaningful functioning of language in use allows for near-infinite manipulations of all those relationships, even if principles and strategies can usually be identified that underlie such operations. Thus interpretations can never be arrived at mechanically. Interpretation processes have to take into account variability and negotiability, basic properties of language use that characterize the contextual emergence of meanings. Contextual embeddedness, with all the dimensions of variation this entails (taking into account the complexity of context – see Caveat 2.1), must at all times be fully taken into account.

A couple of simple examples may help. Consider the use of quotation marks. They may serve two completely opposite functions. They may be used to strengthen a claim by invoking someone's authority. But they may also be used to weaken it by creating distance. In addition, as illustrated above (under 2.3.2), they may also simply be used to liven up an otherwise relatively dry narrative. Local processes of interpretation are required to determine the function of such forms.

As a second example, passive voice may serve – as is often, and quite correctly, pointed out in the critical discourse analysis literature – to allow an author to avoid identifying agentivity and responsibility for actions or events described. But this effect is considerably weakened, if not eliminated, by certain types of genre-specific stylistic conventions, even if the basis for the convention itself may be to facilitate 'evasion' as a general property of the genre (a point to be illustrated at length under 3.3.3).

> **Caveat 3.2:** *Though Caveat 3.1 does not allow jumping from the observation of forms to interpretations, whatever can be detected with a reasonable degree of certainty on the basis of a 'formal' analysis can never be ignored.*

However important it may be to warn against the temptation to formulate quick conclusions on the basis of observed formal properties of a stretch of discourse,

---

[43] Donald Davidson (1986, 2001) goes so far as to suggest that convention (unlike beliefs, desires, and intentions) is not a necessary element in language, but that language is a condition for having conventions.

it is equally important to point out that *describable patterns do matter for interpretation*. Remember Rule 1: What we need is empirical evidence to support answers to questions, and if a counterscreening of the data reveals formal patterns that contradict a possible conclusion, the conclusion loses its validity.

Caveat 3.3: *Because form–function relationships are never absolute, ideology research is necessarily comparative and contrastive.*

In *The Archaeology of Knowledge*, Foucault writes a chapter entitled 'The Comparative Facts,' in which he says the following:

> Archaeological analysis individualizes and describes discursive formations. That is, it must compare them, oppose them to one another in the simultaneity in which they are presented, distinguish them from those that do not belong to the same time-scale, relate them, on the basis of their specificity, to the non-discursive practices that surround them and serve as a general element for them.   (Foucault 1972, p. 157)

As might already be gleaned from some of the examples given above (under 2.3.4), close scrutiny of elements of comparison and contrast is a powerful tool for the interpretation of texts, as often patterns of implicit meaning are involved. Comparison may involve the contrasting of equivalent forms in different languages[44] or in variants of the same language, but it may also concern intertextual, intratextual, even intrasentential processes of conveying added meaning by

---

[44] Here is a simple example from our earlier migrant research, involving variability across languages and speech communities, situated at the lexical level. Consider the way in which a term such as 'integration' figures in debates surrounding ethnic diversity in different societies. In Dutch the term 'integratie' contrasts primarily with concepts such as 'assimilatie'. In this context, a policy aimed at integration gets rhetorically associated with an open and tolerant attitude toward diversity: It is meant to accept groups of newcomers into the society without demanding their full assimilation, i.e., their abandoning their difference from mainstream society. In an American context, however, the primary contrast set is between *integration* and *segregation*, as in "the racial integration of public schools." The integration concept thus comes to stand for full participation at every level of social and political life. It is the ethnic equivalent to *emancipation* in gender relations. Much more variability is possible. Elements of both contrast sets are incorporated into the concept of 'integration' as it is handled in the following excerpt from a Slovenian Ministry of Education and Sports report on the treatment of Bosnian refugees:

> Thus the children are not integrated into our compulsory programme, for such integration would signify the first step toward the assimilation of these children. With the fact that lessons for the children proceed in their mother tongue, the national and cultural identity of these children is preserved and the psychological stress of their coming into a foreign environment is minimized. Also, the children will be able to join in normal life after their return to their homeland.

Here 'integration' is (i) contrasted with 'segregation,' and (ii) both contrasted and associated with 'assimilation.' This Slovenian political usage shares with Dutch usage the negative connotations attached to 'assimilation,' but while in the usage of the Dutch term the contrast with assimilation is focused upon to defend integration, the Slovenian usage zooms in on a link with assimilation (in terms of a continuum which makes integration lead toward assimilation) to argue against integration and in favor of segregation. With the American usage, the rhetoric of the Slovenian Ministry shares a semantic contrast, but none of the social and political considerations.

describing comparable phenomena in different terms or different phenomena in comparable terms.[45] The contribution which contrasts make to the meaning generation process will emerge from many of the following sections, perhaps most forcefully from the discussion of aspects of categorization (as in 3.3.2.1). It will be hinted at repeatedly, but should be kept in mind throughout.

Procedure 3.1: *Define the activity type or speech event type (providing a general frame of interpretation) to which the investigated discourse belongs. In addition:*

3.1.1: *Identify the speech acts or language games of which the activity or event predominantly consists.*

AD 3.1, IN GENERAL:

[Define the activity type or speech event type (providing a general frame of interpretation) to which the investigated discourse belongs.]

Many properties of the investigated discourse (e.g., the high frequency of passives – see 3.3.3) clearly are a function of the style that is *typical of a certain specific verbal activity type*, namely 'academic writing.' This activity type – one manifestation of the more general *genre* of academic discourse – is metapragmatically defined at the beginning of most of the books, where the publications literally define their own status (as further explained under 3.6). Like any other activity type, academic writing imposes *its own rules* and sets *its own boundaries of interpretability*. The emergence of verbal activity types is simply one aspect of the variability that sets the context within which strategies of meaning generation are negotiated.[46] In other words, a jump from the observation of certain forms to their interpretation in terms of specific functions, without taking into account this highly meaning-related type of variability, could never be justified. Such a

---

[45] For instance, consider the following sentence, which is a subtitle to an article in the *International Herald Tribune* (9 March 1993) on the social and economic situation in the former East Germany, a couple of years after the unification of the two Germanies:

> In East and West, Resentment at Costs.

The mere juxtaposition expressed by the connector *and* gives the impression that East and West have something in common, viz. a *resentment at costs*, i.e., the costs of German unification. This phrasing, however, blurs the fact that the object of resentment, the cost of unification – talked about as if it were one single phenomenon – is completely different for East and West: For the West the cost involved is merely economic and financial (the only type of 'cost' called by that name in the article) whereas for the East the cost is a personal and social one (in particular the high rate of unemployment and the feeling of utter uselessness resulting from the dismantlement of uncompetitive industries). Thus an underlying contrast between incompatible phenomena is de-emphasized by a unifying description. (For more examples, see Verschueren 1996.)

[46] Other examples of speech activity types (or speech events) would be: classroom teaching, police interrogations, job interviews, wedding ceremonies, dinner conversations, story telling, service encounters, poetry readings, business meetings, and the like. These are all associated with norms or expectations related to properties which they typically display. Since they are 'types,' actual 'tokens' may of course deviate in various ways, but rarely without an effect on meaning.

jump from form to meaning would violate some of the most basic principles of pragmatics. But, remembering the centrality of the notions of variability and negotiability in general, the same principles would be at risk if we were to regard activity types as immutable grids for interpretation. Analysis, therefore, is always a balancing act: There is a rope to support us, but we are up in the air above it, responding to ethereal impulses – and grabbing the rope really is the end of the performance.

Keeping these remarks in mind, some prototypical properties of the activity type of academic writing, as found in the sample data, are the following:

- The *transparent structuring* of the texts: Not only Lavisse (the extreme case), but also the British sources make efforts to subdivide the text into clearly distinguishable parts, with dates, numbers, and/or titles that immediately clarify what these parts are about.

- An *expository style*: Except for Lavisse's didactically motivated questions at the bottom of every page, the texts consist mainly of straightforward statements of known or assumed facts (see 3.1.1). The emphasis on factual recounting also implies an attempt at *personal distancing*: Authors present their accounts of actions and events as *objective*, if not quite neutral.

- An endeavor at maximal *explicitness*: The authors are clearly concerned with attempts to avoid vagueness, hedges, and ambiguity. Thus, terms or names that are introduced are quickly defined or further identified, as in

  The Indian Mutiny, a rising of native Indian troops, […].
  (Cassell's 1903, p. 124)

  Sir John Lawrence, the Governor of the Punjaub, […].
  (Cassell's 1903, p. 124)

  The British government (immensely aided by the electric telegraph, a new invention which had recently been installed) […].
  (Hearnshaw 1930, p. 154)

  a policy of annexation; broadly speaking, of bringing under direct British dominion […].   (Innes 1927, p. 169)

- Attention for *explanation*: Reported actions and events are linked by pointing out motivations, intentions, and causes. Thus Fearenside's (1922, p. 433) paragraph about the causes of the Mutiny is labeled "Causes of […]" and further contains elements such as "One reason why […]" and "[…] caused […]." Similarly, 'because' (or its French equivalents 'parce que' or 'car') occurs regularly throughout the texts. Or consider the following extracts from Hearnshaw (1930), not at all untypical for the rest of the corpus, and illustrating in addition to an attempt at explanation also the transparent structuring of his expository discourse:

> The Crimean War was one of the causes of the Indian Mutiny which broke out in 1857. On the one hand [...] [153] [...]; on the other hand [...] Other causes, however, were more potent. The Afghan disaster of 1842 had lowered British prestige. At the same time [...] Finally [...]
>   Hence [...]   (Hearnshaw 1930, pp. 153–154)

All of these features are indeed easy to illustrate in all of the sample texts.

What is particularly interesting, however, is the observation of aspects of use that (seem to) violate the self-imposed rules and expectations of the adopted activity type. If violations are random, not much attention should be paid to them, but if they show systematicity, they become meaningful. Thus, I have already observed, with reference to Sir John Lawrence's commendable treatment of the Sikhs, that in spite of overall attempts at explicitness, significant episodes may show a serious degree of suggestive *vagueness* (see the discussion under Caveat 2.1). It is assumed, to stick to this example, that readers will know what a good treatment of colonial subjects involves, but it is unlikely that they will have more than an utterly vague idea about this. Such an occurrence of vagueness in relation to a core issue of the colonial process is a clear sign of the ideological embedding of the discourse in a context of colonization that is not itself questioned.

While true *ambiguity* (contributing to the discursive meaning generation process – as opposed to ambiguity that is simply part of the language system) is hard to find, *hedges* are more frequent in our sample than one might expect from typical academic writing.[47] Some examples (in which hedging constructions are underlined):

> if no relief had arrived before the end of the month, they would probably have marched out.   (Innes 1927, p. 171)

> Yet the state of affairs in the Asiatic empire might well have justified uneasiness.   (Low and Sanders 1910, p. 132)

> The military revolt was imminent; but even then, if vigour and energy had been displayed, it might have been quelled at the outset.
>   (Low and Sanders 1910, p. 139)

> It is possible that if the Meerut rebels had been followed [...] the incipient rising might have been checked.   (Low and Sanders 1910, p. 141)

> If the mutineers flying from Meerut had been promptly pursued [...] the tale we have to tell might have been shorter and very different.
>   (McCarthy 1908, p. 172)

> He could not, perhaps, always conceal [...].   (McCarthy 1908, p. 178)

> It seems that some cartridges [...].   (Low and Sanders 1910, p. 138)

---

[47] 'Hedges' are linguistic devices that are used to modify an expressed proposition, usually by adding unclarity as to the utterer's commitment to truth or certainty. The most common ones are modal auxiliaries, certain linguistic action or mental state verbs, and hypothetical constructions, as well as a variety of adjectives, nouns, and adverbs that emphasize probability, possibility, likeliness.

There were peculiar reasons too why, <u>if</u> religious and political distrust <u>did</u> prevail, the moment of Lord Canning's accession to the supreme authority in India <u>should seem</u> inviting and favourable for schemes of sedition.

(McCarthy 1908, p. 176)

<u>It must be owned that</u>, given the existence of a seditious spirit, it <u>would have been hardly possible</u> for it to find conditions more <u>seemingly</u> favourable and tempting.   (McCarthy 1908, p. 177)

there were moments when <u>it began to seem almost possible</u> that they <u>might actually</u> keep back their assailants until […].   (McCarthy 1908, p. 112)

For a short time <u>it seemed probable that</u> the British power in India <u>would be</u> overthrown.   (Parkin 1911, p. 125)

The outbreak was <u>probably</u> premature, a concerted rising having been arranged for a <u>somewhat</u> later date.   (Woodward 1921, p. 236)

Dalhousie, <u>somewhat</u> against his own will, […].

(Low and Sanders 1910, p. 135)

<u>C'eût été</u> une **très belle conquête** […].   (Lavisse 1902, p. 94)

[It would have been a **very nice conquest** […].]

on refusait d'envoyer aux colonies 4 ou 5 000 soldats qui <u>auraient</u> donné à la France l'*empire du monde*.   (Lavisse 1902, p. 96)

[they refused to send 4 or 5,000 soldiers to the colonies who would have given France the *empire of the world*.]

All these examples show that the authors do not restrict themselves to the mere reporting of what they regard as facts. They make suggestions concerning unattested circumstances, and they formulate hypotheses for alternative scenarios. None of this seems to be random, and in all cases there is a rhetorical effect. When assumptions are voiced, they contribute to a pattern of explanation. When a contrast is introduced between what happened and what could have happened, an element of evaluation seeps in. Thus, a certain measure of blame is laid on those who failed to pursue the Meerut mutineers in their march on Delhi – actually, in spite of its hypothetical nature, this assumes the character of an intertextual master narrative.

When such evaluation is at stake, hedging defies the norm of *neutrality*, the overall academic attempt to keep some *personal distance*. This norm, though explicitly invoked in a number of the book prefaces, is deviated from in a variety of ways, adding a distinct scent of *personal opinion* or *attitude* to the narratives:

The rulers of India were at length alarmed, <u>as well they might be</u>, for Bengal lay at the mercy of the native soldiers.   (Low and Sanders 1910, p. 139)

On dépensait beaucoup d'argent et de soldats à des guerres en Allemagne et en Italie, <u>où la France n'avait rien à gagner</u> […].   (Lavisse 1902, p. 96)

> [A lot of money and many soldiers were expended on wars in Germany and
> Italy, where France had nothing to gain […].]

More fully explicit still are the attitudes and opinions voiced by Lavisse in the
sections with reflections at the end of the 'books.' A telling example, particularly
relevant in relation to attitudes toward colonization, is the following:

> Mais il n'est pas trop tard. Il reste encore bien des *pays à occuper*, et dans les
> pays occupés bien de la *place vide*.   (Lavisse 1902, p. 166)
>
> [But it is not too late. There are still quite a few *countries to occupy*, and in
> the occupied countries there is still quite a lot of *empty space*.]

This sentence is followed by a straightforward exhortation to consider serving
France by going to one of these countries to be occupied or spaces to be filled.

In keeping with the expectations created by 'academic writing' as an activity type, our texts show a high degree of rational, analytical, unemotional
discourse. Yet there are plenty of deviations from this norm, also in terms of
reference to emotions. Take for example Fearenside's paragraph about the
causes of the Mutiny (Fearenside 1922, p. 433). It contains the following terms
and phrases:

> anxiety and vexation
> had annoyed
> religious prejudices
> been offended
> cherished […] grievances
> vengeance
> discontent

Here emotions are focused on quite straightforwardly. Whenever such deviations
from activity-internal norms emerge, the task of the discourse analyst is to see if
there is a pattern. In this case, there clearly is: Emotions are ascribed only to the
'Others,' the Indians. By implication, British actions are presented as *not* driven
by emotions: The British soldiers do not want revenge, they are not angry, they
are simply doing their job as good professionals in crushing the revolt (see also
3.4.3). Though emotions cannot be ascribed to the British, virtues such as courage may be suggested:

> a handful of British troops […] held the ill-fortified Residency

See also, in this respect, the following less-than-dryly academic description by
the same author:

> The rising failed partly because it was, for the most part, a military, [433] not
> a national movement; partly because it did not spread all over India; partly
> because the Hindus and the Muhammadans did not work well together; but
> above all because nearly all the British officers displayed a resourcefulness
> which matched the courage and endurance of the troops and civilians under
> their care.   (Fearenside 1922, pp. 433–434)

Needless to say, such patterns become part of a process of legitimation underlying the dry academic discourse. What is also involved is implicit interactivity, as audience expectations are clearly oriented toward.

It would be wrong, however, to quickly generalize from a pattern as the one observed in this individual Fearenside extract. Counterscreening of the data reveals that non-reference to emotions or possible emotions (including feelings of vengeance) on the part of the British is not a general property of all the sources. Most of the texts conform to the patterns, but some deviate from it in significant ways. British anger and revenge are turned into explicit points of attention by Low and Sanders (1910):

> He [the governor-general] retained his sense of justice even in the excitement produced by the outbreak; and he deprecated undue and excessive reprisals with the calmness that earned him the sobriquet "Clemency Canning" from some less able than himself to temper with mercy the uncontrolled and natural resentment kindled in English hearts by the news of the first massacres. "I will not govern in anger," said Canning. On July 31 he issued an order, intended to check the summary execution of sepoys suspected of mutiny or of complicity in the murder of their officers.   (p. 143)

> rescuing the European residents and inflicting stern vengeance on the rebels.
>
> (p. 143)

> His [Havelock's] troops were fainting with fatigue, and some of them died of sunstroke and exhaustion on the field of battle. But the British soldiers had heard rumours of the Cawnpore butcheries, and nothing could stop them. They carried the enemy's guns and drove the sepoys before them in a furious rush. The Nana fled; and Havelock's wearied followers tottered into Cawnpore, to look down into the well where the still uncovered bodies of the 200 murdered women and children met their gaze. It was too late to save them – not too late for signal vengeance. Some of those who had taken a prominent part in the massacres [...] were forced by Neill under the lash to clean the [146] blood from the walls and floors of the Bibigarh, and then executed.
>
> But there was little time to linger in Cawnpore either for revenge or for repose.   (pp. 146–147)

> before they could [...] amid a scene of tumultuous emotion at length enter the enclosure.   (p. 148)

It may not be surprising that this side of the story is so clearly highlighted by our one source that is primarily, if not exclusively, directed at an academic audience. A true academic inclination must allow for a balanced presentation of differing perspectives. Low and Sanders obviously tries to accomplish this. Yet, descriptions such as "natural resentment" attenuate brutality on the British side by making it more comprehensible, as does the emphasis on Lord Canning's role. The authors do their best to also empathically introduce explanations for the Indians' decision to revolt; they are said to be "smarting under a sense of wrong" (p. 136) which was understandable on the basis of British acts of government. But then those acts are also said to be "necessary and justifiable" (p. 135), and never will the mutineers' violence be 'normalized' in a comparable fashion. That is how ultimately the balance breaks even in this text, which also does not shy from overt expressions of admiration for the authors' countrymen – "Henry Lawrence, the statesman, soldier, and saint" (p. 145), "Herbert Edwardes, John Nicholson, Neville Chamberlain, Montgomery, and Sydney Cotton, the ardent and daring spirits of the border province" (p. 148).

An extensive exploration of the same theme of British emotional involvement and Canning-like attempts to temper it, is offered by McCarthy (1908, p. 178), who does his utter best to make British anger understandable:

> It is worthy of record as an evidence of the temper aroused even in men from whom better things might have been expected, that Nicholson strongly urged the passing of a law to authorize flaying alive, impalement, or burning of the murderers of the women and children in Delhi. He urged this view again and again, and deliberately argued it on grounds alike of policy and principle. The fact is recorded here not in mere disparagement of a brave soldier, but as an illustration of the manner in which the old elementary passions of man's untamed condition can return upon him in his pride of civilisation and culture, and make him their slave again.   (McCarthy 1908, p. 191) ·

In the case of McCarthy, there is never any lack of clarity about whose side he is on, in spite of admissions of extreme violence. His descriptions easily turn into hero-worship:

> Amid all the excitement, of hope and fear, passion and panic, in England, there was time for the whole heart of the nation to feel pride in Havelock's career and sorrow for his untimely death. Untimely? Was it after all untimely? Since when has it not been held the crown of a great career that the hero dies at the moment of accomplished victory?   (McCarthy 1908, p. 193)

In this episode, there is a distinct smell of hagiography – further supported with phrases such as "Havelock's Saints" (p. 193), which also surfaces in Synge (1908, p. 116).

Ad 3.1.1:

[Identify the speech acts or language games of which the activity or event predominantly consists.]

Activity or event types are always 'meaningful' in the sense that, like any other form of social action, they are interpreted by the actors (in this case language users) involved.[48] Those interpretations use 'types' as anchoring points, definable in terms of (proto)typical properties and corresponding normative expectations. Being 'types,' these are abstractions which allow for variable tokens and even

---

[48] Remember earlier references to Winch (1958).

outright deviations from the norms. But as the preceding examples show, deviations usually add meaning. Activities and events, 'interpreted' in terms of types, provide frames of meaning for the speech acts or language games of which they consist.[49] At that lower level of structure, the same processes can be observed.

I mentioned (in 3.1) the *expository style* typically expected of academic texts, consisting mainly of straightforward statements of known or assumed facts. The vast majority of sentence-level speech acts in the sample texts are indeed simple statements or assertives (sometimes framed as reminders). Their essential property is that they commit the utterer to the truth of the propositional content. Such a commitment is made by the authors. Nothing could be more straightforward than utterances such as

> Le dernier roi fut mis sur des charbons ardents, et le Mexique devint une *colonie espagnole* (1521).   (Lavisse 1902, p. 65)
>
> [The last king was put on hot coals, and Mexico became a *Spanish colony* (1521).]

or

> At Cawnpur Nana Sahib led the mutineers.   (Richardson 1924, p. 138)

Looked at in isolation, such assertions almost sound as if Lavisse was in Mexico and Richardson in Cawnpore at the time of the reported events. The historical nature of the related events, however, defeats assumptions of first-hand knowledge. Thus the commitment to truth is somewhat diluted by the authors' reliance on their sources' assumed commitment to truth as implicated in their statements. The surface expression of such diluted commitment is the hedging described above.

Lavisse's text is the only one reflecting stages in the educational process it is intended to be part of: exposition (the main historical narrative), rehearsal (the summaries at the end of each chapter), testing (at the bottom of every page), further reflection or discussion (at the end of each 'book'), and writing tasks. These different stages all have their typically associated speech acts or language games. The main narrative and the summaries exhibit the expository style consisting of assertives. The 'testing' fragments are all questions. But they are not ordinary questions. First of all, like many interrogatives in an educational context, they are

---

[49] Note the gradient terminology: I have used 'genre' for general worlds of discourse associated with spheres of human activity (e.g., the genre of academic discourse in general) and 'activity type' or '(speech) event type' for a more specific, but still general, manifestation of a genre (e.g., the activity type of academic writing); activity types, in turn, consist of lower-level acts or events which I now label 'speech acts' or 'language games.' There is an obvious reference here to speech act theory (Searle 1969) and Wittgenstein's (1958) notion of language games. But these are merely parallel concepts and I do not feel bound by the technical restrictions which an orthodox reading might impose. In fact, on earlier occasions (Verschueren 1999b) I tried to steer away from constraining technicalities by replacing 'speech act' with 'speech genre,' making use of Bakhtin's allowance for the use of 'genre' with reference to wide ranges of utterance types (from single-word utterances to complex discourses). But I am here abandoning that practice in order to avoid confusion with the use of 'genre' at a higher level of abstraction.

not asked by someone interested in learning the answer, but rather by someone interested to know whether the addressee knows the answer; they may, moreover, also be used by pupils for self-testing. Second, if one were to pick out one of the questions at random, it would usually not be possible for anyone to answer. Take the following example:

> Que possèdaient-ils?   (Lavisse 1902, p. 68)
>
> [What did they possess?]

What we find are strings of interconnected questions. Who 'they' are is clear from the preceding question only ("Où dominaient les Espagnols?," p. 67; "Where did the Spanish dominate?"). Moreover, the question depends for its proper interpretation on the topical and deictic anchoring of the main narrative. What does "que" relevantly refer to? What period are we talking about? In the "further reflection" parts, we also find a majority of assertives of the same kind as those in the main body of the text and in the summaries. On one occasion, one of the reflections assumes the nature of a prediction (grounds for which are to be introduced in the discourse that follows):

> La France ne conduit plus, comme auparavant, les destinées de l'Europe; mais elle va prendre, par la **Révolution**, la direction de l'humanité.
>
>   (Lavisse 1902, p. 98)
>
> [France no longer drives, like before, the destinies of Europe; but it will take, with the **Revolution**, the leadership of humanity.]

At the very end, there is even an exhortation:

> VIII. Souvenez-vous que si on sert bien la France on combattant pour elle, on la sert aussi en allant au loin fonder une famille française, qui répandra notre langue, nos idées, nos habitudes, et qui fera respecter et aimer la France dans le monde entier.   (Lavisse 1902, p. 166)
>
> [VIII. Remember that if one serves France well by fighting for her, one serves her also by going and founding a French family far away, which will spread our language, our ideas, our habits, and which will make France respected and loved in the whole world.]

In other words, French school children are actively encouraged here to take part in the colonial process. The 'writing tasks,' finally, do not contain full propositions, but only themes that can serve as titles.

In the British texts, the dominant pattern of assertion (whether or not hedged) leaves room for little else. The main exceptions are summary renditions of conversations intended to liven up the story (e.g., Synge 1908, p. 119), and utterances in the form of questions. As to questions, only McCarthy seems to make use of them. They are, moreover, all of a rhetorical type, implicitly making claims though in the form of an interrogative:

> Those walls might have been leaped over as easily as that of Romulus; but of what avail to know that, when from behind them always came the fatal fire of the Englishmen?   (McCarthy 1908, p. 186)

> his untimely death. Untimely? Was it after all untimely? Since when has it not been held the crown of a great career that the hero dies at the moment of accomplished victory?   (McCarthy 1908, p. 193)

> Not the faintest suspicion crossed any mind of the treachery that was awaiting them. How, indeed, could there be any such suspicion? Not for years and years had even Oriental warfare given example of such practice [...].   (McCarthy 1908, p. 186)

The latter example combines the force of a rhetorical question with the function of a question used to introduce a topic to be further explored or commented upon.

Procedure 3.2: *Investigate the use of languages, codes, and styles. In particular:*

3.2.1.   *What language(s) is/are used? And how does this relate to the wider linguistic context of the society/community in which the discourse is to be found?*

3.2.2.   *What codes are used? Is there any code switching? Is a specific communicative style involved?*

3.2.3.   *Is the style formal, informal, ...?*

AD 3.2, IN GENERAL:

[Investigate the use of languages, codes, and styles.]

AD 3.2.1:

[What language(s) is/are used? And how does this relate to the wider linguistic context of the society/community in which the discourse is to be found?]

For our sample data, the answer to this question is uncomplicated at first sight, French being the language for Lavisse, English for all the other texts. There is, however, more to be said about that. Already from the spelling it is clear that the English sources are British, and this identification is, as goes without saying, not trivial with regard to the topic at hand. Only one (Cassell's 1903) was actually printed outside England (in Australia, with a population that still had a very strong affinity with Britain at the time), though some of the publishers also had establishments in Bombay and Calcutta. The linguistic uniformity is nearly complete. As to the French materials, since there is only one source, there is no variation whatsoever. Moreover, being published in Paris, it fits all assumptions of French centripetal tendencies.

As to the temporal identification of the language forms used, differences between present-day French and English and the French and English from the turn of the nineteenth to the twentieth century are minimal. Yet, analysis must remain attentive to possible differences. Therefore, rather than to attach hasty interpretations to observed choices, an attempt must be made to reach a (historically) correct assessment. For instance, when I first read

> There were peculiar reasons too why, if religious and political distrust did prevail, the moment of Lord Canning's accession to the supreme authority in India should seem inviting and favourable for schemes of sedition. The Afghan war had told the Sepoy that British troops are not absolutely invincible in battle. The impression produced almost everywhere in India by the Crimean war was a conviction that the strength of England was on the wane. The Sepoy saw that the English force in Northern India was very small [...].   (McCarthy 1908, p. 176)

I wondered what was so "peculiar" about the enumerated reasons. Upon closer inspection, however, I learnt that the strong overtone of 'strangeness' attached to 'peculiar' in common usage today was not necessarily there at the time of writing. 'Peculiar' could still simply be used in the sense of 'distinctive' or 'specific' (even if this was already often associated with 'strange' or 'odd', as in other examples in the same text, as when McCarthy mentions "the Hindoo's peculiar and very perplexing tenets," p. 173, or "the peculiar baptismal custom of the Mohammedans," p. 174).

Clearly, when spoken discourse is analyzed, a much wider relevant range of variability must be taken into account. Participants in a conversation, for instance, may use distinct linguistic repertoires as resource, even in a so-called monolingual context, not to mention multilingual settings.[50]

Ad 3.2.2:

[What codes are used? Is there any code switching? Is a specific communicative style involved?]

The code in all our samples is written standard language. Unlike in many oral contexts, especially – though not only – when multilingualism is involved, code switching[51] is not an issue, except when Synge (1908) moves back and forth between his own narrative and the fragments of poetry that he quotes.

The overall communicative style[52] is one typical for communities with long-standing traditions of literacy and schooling; it is within this style, allowing for

---

[50] For an example of sociolinguistic ethnography in an urban multilingual institutional context, in which a wide range of repertoires is drawn from, see Jaspers (2005a, 2005b, 2006, 2008).

[51] 'Code' may be used for any distinguishable variant of a language. But 'code switching' not only refers to the switching between intra-language variable codes, but also between languages that are in use in the same (multilingual) setting. For the analysis of oral discourse, code switching must often be attended to. For an introduction to the topic, see Auer (ed.) (1998) or Auer and Eastman (2010).

[52] The concept of 'communicative style' has been most often used in discussions of interethnic or intercultural communication, where members of ethnically and/or socioculturally definable groups can sometimes be observed to be socialized into distinctive habits of communicative

certain degrees of abstraction beyond the immediate demands of the here-and-now, that the normative properties and patterns of the activity type of academic writing have developed. We are confronted with discourse that takes itself very seriously. The texts have been written to teach, not to amuse, even if attempts are made to make the reading enjoyable. This contributes in no small measure to the seriousness with which interpreters are expected to gather meaning from the texts: They are supposed to get information, to learn facts, and they are supposed to do so at a cognitive level that abstracts from their own everyday situation. Even the patriotic sentiments that are appealed to – in ways I have already been able to illustrate – are not 'personal'; they are more abstract, to be situated at the level of what is seen as advantageous to the wider community, the country, the nation. This is why the communicative style itself turns these texts into powerful ideology-sustaining tools.

Ad 3.2.3:
[Is the style formal, informal, …?]

The sample texts, though parading a highly literate communicative style as manifested in typical examples of academic writing, differ significantly along the dimension of formality, but all are at the formal end of the scale. Choices producing this variability are in the first place the result of an assessment of the needs of the different primary audiences addressed. Thus compare Synge (1908), which reads as a general children's book, with Low and Sanders (1910), the book for an academic audience. The former introduces the sepoys as follows:

> every one, both in India and at home, believed in the loyalty of the native soldiers, or Sepoys as they were called.   (Synge 1908, p. 112)

By way of contrast, Low and Sanders, when first mentioning sepoys, add a footnote:

> The word should be written *sipáhi* according to the rules of orthography now officially recognised in the transliteration of Indian names; but in this, as in some other cases, the spelling consecrated by tradition and usage has been retained.   (Low and Sanders 1910, p. 137)

Many more subtle examples can be found.

Most interesting would be cases in which an author lapses from an adopted style into choices typical for a different one. The styles of all of the individual texts are, however, strikingly consistent. This mainly means that, when using examples from different texts, the differences in style typical for each of them must be fully taken into account. Consider the following three extracts:

behavior. Typically oral vs. typically literate traditions, for instance, give rise to differences in communicative style.

Havelock […] encountered the Nana, with over 5,000 men and eight guns, drawn up to dispute the entrance to Cawnpore […] They carried the enemy's guns and drove the sepoys before them in a furious rush.
(Low and Sanders 1910, p. 146)

He made one last stand against the victorious English in front of Cawnpore, and was completely defeated.   (McCarthy 1908, p. 190)

They were resting […] when, with wild shouts, a huge mass of native cavalry rushed upon them. Fiercely and swiftly the little English band advanced; in ten minutes they had captured the rebel guns and the Nana's troops were in full flight.   (Synge 1908, p. 116)

These are three stylistically different descriptions of one and the same event. Compare "drawn up to dispute the entrance to," "made one last stand against," and "with wild shouts […] rushed upon them." Or "carried the enemy's guns and drove the sepoys before them in a furious rush" and "captured the rebel guns and the Nana's troops were in full flight." The wording does not leave any doubt about an orientation toward different audiences. Underlying these differences, the perspective is conspicuously similar.

Procedure 3.3: *Look for overt carriers of information structure. In particular:*

3.3.1: *How is information 'chunked' prosodically (with spoken data) or in writing?*

3.3.2: *What patterns of word choice can be found? In particular:*
   3.3.2.1:   How are people, events, relations categorized?

3.3.3: *At the sentence level: How are grammatical relations, case categories, and semantic roles handled when describing events, actions, or relations between (groups of) people?*

3.3.4: *Still at the sentence level: How are moods, modalities, negation, and evidentiality handled?*

3.3.5: *And still at the sentence level: What is the calibration between given, new, and accessible information, and between highlighting/foregrounding and backgrounding?*

3.3.6: *At the suprasentential level: How is coherence/relevance established? In particular:*
   3.3.6.1:   What discourse topics are established?
   3.3.6.2:   How do central discourse topics relate to peripheral ones?
   3.3.6.3:   What does the discourse progresssion or rhetorical structure look like (in terms of relations such as juxtaposition, justification, explanation, proving, elaborating, motivating, etc.)?

3.3.7: *In a wider corpus: How do discourse topics and rhetorical patterns develop/change across the different parts of the corpus?*

AD 3.3, IN GENERAL:

[Look for overt carriers of information structure.]

The term 'information structure' is often reserved for the relation between given and new information at the sentence level. Gundel and Fretheim (2002) provide an excellent introduction to that specific phenomenon, which I will here deal with (under 3.3.5) within a broader spectrum of devices for information 'packaging' in discourse at varying levels of structure.

Ad 3.3.1:

[How is information 'chunked' prosodically (with spoken data) or in writing?]

In spoken discourse, prosody, intonation, pausing, hesitations, stress, rhythm, voice quality, and loudness, as well as paralinguistic signs (such as sighing), may overtly signal the way in which information is put into 'chunks.' There are parallels to these phenomena in writing: (numbered) chapters and paragraphs, punctuation, font changes, and layout. In our corpus, such devices are used most extensively by Lavisse. Consider the following fragment:

> **99. La boussole. – 2**. La **boussole** est une aiguille aimantée qui *se tourne toujours vers le nord*. **3**. Les Européens la connaissent aussi depuis de XIVe siècle, et elle a fait *une révolution dans la marine*.
>
> **4**. Avant d'avoir la boussole, les marians n'osaient pas s'éloigner des côtes. **5**. Avec la boussole, ils ont pu **aller en pleine mer** sans peur de se perdre, puisque la boussole leur indiquait le nord. **6**. Les Espagnols et les Portugais en ont profité pour **découvrir le Nouveau Monde** (carte, p. 66).
>
> (Lavisse 1902, p. 64)

> [**99. The compass. – 2**. The **compass** is a magnetic needle which *always turns to the north*. **3**. The Europeans have also known it since the 14th century, and it has made *a revolution in navigation*.
>
> **4**. Before they had the compass, seamen did not dare to move away from the coasts. **5**. With the compass, they could **go out on the open sea** without fear of getting lost, because the compass showed them where the north was. **6**. The Spanish and the Portuguese made use of it to **discover the New World** (map, p. 66).]

As competent, literate language users, we normally process the semiotic signals with the same automaticity as prosodic features in spoken discourse. None of it, however, is random, and especially the effect on the interpretation side of meaning generation is significant. Pupils using the book will understand that there is a clear connection between the compass, visually as well as textually identified as the main topic of section 99, and the following sections 100 and 101 which are about the discovery of Africa and India (100) and the discovery of America (101). This connection is also propositionally expressed in sentence 6, and graphically highlighted with the boldface "découvrir le Nouveau Monde" which visually links the discoveries about to be made with – also in bold – the invented instrument (the compass, in the title of the section as well as in the first sentence, 2) and what it allowed people to do (to go out on the open sea, 5).

Furthermore, the explanation for how the instrument allowed people to go out on the open sea (by "always turning to the north") as well as the historical signifi-cance this had (a revolution in navigation – further explained in the oppositional "before" and "after" of sentences 4 and 5) are emphasized by means of italics. Furthermore, the section number, 99, makes explicit the fact that whatever falls under its scope is a chunk of information following and preceding other separable chunks which, however, are linearly (in this case not just temporally but also logically) connected. The sentence numbers, on the other hand, serve the purpose of crossreferencing (with the questions at the bottom of the page), as does the page number between brackets at the end of the fragment, which serves as an instruction for the reader to look at a different page where they are told to expect a map that explains what "découvrir le Nouveau Monde" means. Within section 99, finally, there is a typographical break between sentences 2–3, of a more intro-ductory background nature, and 4–6, containing the main point.

The British sources make use of similar devices, though less extensively. Cassell's (1903) uses numbered sections, where the numbers are consecutive relevant dates, emphasizing the linear temporal progress of history as well as a 'critical periods' view of history; the content of longer sections is chunked by means of paragraphs. Fearenside (1922) and Hearnshaw (1930) are built up around consecutively numbered sections which usually coincide with paragraphs (though sometimes there are two or three, rarely four, paragraphs), with bold-face titles that clearly indicate the topic. Innes (1927) uses longer sections with centered titles in italics and dates indicating a time frame; these sections contain paragraphs, the topics of which are highlighted by means of smaller-print mar-gin insets – sometimes more than one for a single (longer) paragraph. Low and Sanders (1910) write a long uninterrupted chapter on the Indian Mutiny, but the running titles mention themes or episodes (on the recto side) and contain dates (both recto and verso). No need to describe all the others here. Basically, subsets of the same overall set of conventions are used, with the same types of informa-tion-chunking functionality.

Not surprisingly, the structuring of the texts shows a common paradigm of thinking about history as a chain of events that can be told as a story of chron-ology in which causes, events, and consequences can be distinguished. There is also a strong parallelism in the choice of structurally highlighted topics in the sources where such highlighting occurs. Basic to this is, indeed, the distinc-tion between causes or circumstances, actions and events, and the end result. Differences in the labeling of chunks of text are sometimes driven by the cho-sen conventions (e.g., paragraph titles vs. margin insets vs. running titles); if, for instance, multiple topics occur on two pages covered by one (recto) running title, a choice must be made to the neglect of another possible choice. There are also some differences in focus (both within and between texts), where a major dimension seems to be event-centeredness vs. person-centeredness. Practically all the chunking labels are as purely descriptive (from one specific point of view, of course) as they can be; but evaluative items occur as well, such as "The Caste panic" (Innes 1927) and "Social progress" (Warner and Marten 1912). Table 6 makes it easy to compare five of the sources.

The labeling of information chunks is easy for our sample data because there is a transparently told story line. For other types of texts, labeling might not be so easy. But information chunking is a general process, though it may not always lead to similar parallels between related texts.

AD 3.3.2, IN GENERAL:

[What patterns of word choice can be found?]

Words are always chosen from sets of possible alternatives. Whatever choice is made, it carries along in its shade the sense potential of those alternatives. The implicit contrasts which are thus evoked are fully integrated in the meaning generating process. Consider the following sentence:

> Calumnies of most extraordinary nature were spread and accepted with credulity.   (Woodward 1921, p. 235)

"Calumnies" could have been '(false) claims,' '(false) rumors,' 'untruths,' or even 'lies.' But within this contrast set 'calumnies' emphasizes maliciousness and an unmistakable intent to injure or hurt someone or someone's cause. Similarly, "accepted with credulity" could simply have been 'believed.' But "credulity" foregrounds a predisposition to believe, implying not so much naiveté as an extension of a form of maliciousness (even if only by way of prejudice) from the sources of the calumnies to their recipients. The terms chosen are clearly *marked*.[53]

Even when the terminology seems more *neutral*, still *evaluations* often come in. Consider the following:

> recent land settlements had annoyed the larger landowners, especially in Oudh, by favouring the actual cultivators of the soil [...].
> (Fearenside 1922, p. 433)

The contrast between "larger landowners" and "actual cultivators of the soil" implies that the landowners did not actually cultivate the soil themselves; hence, "favouring" those who do the work seems very democratic, and reflects favorably upon the land settlements and negatively upon the annoyance of the landowners. That an old and probably stable social order is thus disrupted is backgrounded completely by this apparently objective description of events.

One type of markedness is the *euphemistic* nature of some choices. A striking example in the British texts is to be found in the numerous accounts of one of

---

[53] Sets of lexical choices within the same semantic field are usually called lexical or semantic fields. A useful approach to lexical fields is to place the items they contain along a number of salient dimensions of meaning variation (in the example from Woodward above, dimensions related to 'maliciousness,' 'intent to injure,' 'predisposition to believe'). For a book-length set of examples, specifically in relation to the domain of linguistic action verbs, see Verschueren (1985b).

Table 6. *Chunking labels*

Innes (1927)	Low & Sanders (1910)	Synge (1908)	Warner & Marten (1912)	Woodward (1921)
India and the Great Mutiny	**The Indian Mutiny**	**The Indian Mutiny**	**Causes of Indian Mutiny**	**Lord Canning, 1856–1862**
- Dalhousie's policy	- The Sikh wars	- Troubles in India	- Social progress 1823–56	- The mutiny 1857: its symptoms
- Sources of unrest	- Annexation of Oudh	- Mutiny at Delhi	- Causes of mutiny of 1857 The Indian Mutiny	- Its causes
- The Caste panic	- The sepoy army	- Spread of the mutiny	- Outbreak of Mutiny, May, 1857	- The outbreak at Meerut, May 10, 1857
- 1857 The Moghul proclaimed (May)	- The first outbreaks	- Cawnpore	- The massacre of Cawnpore, July, 1857	- Characteristics of the Mutiny
- June	- Spread of the revolt	- General Havelock	- British heroism	- The danger at an end, Dec. 1857. The east India Company dissolved, 1858. The new Government of India
- Limits of the Revolt	- First attempts at Delhi	- The price of empire	- Native loyalty	
- Delhi captured (Sept.)	- Cawnpore and Lucknow	**Lucknow and Delhi**	- Storming of Delhi (Sept.) and relief of Lucknow (Sept. and Nov.), 1857	
- Lucknow (June–Sept.)	- Havelock's march to Lucknow	- Siege of Lucknow		
- Sir Colin Campbell 1857–8	- Nicholson at Delhi	- Death of Sir Henry Lawrence		
- India transferred to the crown 1858	- Second relief of Lucknow	- Relief of Lucknow		
	- Lucknow taken	- Sir Colin Campbell		
	- Operations in Oudh	- John Nicholson		
	- Capture of Gwalior	- End of the mutiny		

Dalhousie's new annexation practices which consisted in letting full authority over a given territory, already controlled but not ruled by the East India Company, 'lapse' into company hands when the native ruler did not have a natural son (while earlier Indian practice in such cases had been to pass on authority to an adopted son). Though this is also a technical legal term (referring to the loss of a right or privilege due to neglect, disuse, death, or failure of some sort), which was no doubt used in the texts regulating the new practice, the uncritical adoption (even if sometimes in quotation marks) of the term in the historical narratives, turns it into a euphemism for 'taking possession of,' 'appropriating,' 'confiscating,' 'terminating native rule,' 'dispossessing/divesting native rulers,' etc.

In addition to such compliance with institutionalized euphemism, euphemistic descriptions are to be found, for instance, in accounts of British actions in the crushing of the revolt. Even though, as pointed out earlier, excessive violence is not denied, it tends to be described in vague and general terms. Thus "inflicting stern vengeance on the rebels" is Low and Sanders' (1910, p. 143) account of one of the bloodiest episodes (preceding the Cawnpore massacre) at the hands of Neill in Benares and Allahabad, and later "signal vengeance" (p. 146) is said to follow the recapturing of Cawnpore. Both "stern" and "signal" strengthen "vengeance," but the abstract generality of the description is far removed from what was to be described, as is also the case in the following:

> That considerable severity should be shown in revenge was inevitable
> [...].   (Warner and Marten 1912, p. 694)

And when McCarthy (1908, p. 178) talks about "the most savage and sanguinary measures of revenge," this is embedded in a sentence that talks about such measures as merely being proposed, and followed by a sentence emphasizing the rejection of such proposals.

Other lexical means of deviating from mere narrative neutrality are provided by *comparative and superlative* forms, which permeate the sample texts. Circumstances and people are said to be "most extraordinary," "most formidable," "most loyal and contented," "most capable," "most valuable," "most able," etc. Standards of comparison are, needless to say, left implicit. Also, choices of *adjectives and adverbs* in general are interesting devices to mark perspectives on entities and events, and hence important objects of scrutiny at the lexical level.

A final general point of attention in relation to patterns of word choice is the use of a group-specific lexis or *jargon*. Especially in the more educational and academic texts, terminologies are used that appeal to membership of the category of readers familiar with historical narratives. Lavisse (1902), with his obviously pedagogical goals, makes a point of explaining all jargon-like terms in the appended "Lexique" ("Glossary"), to make sure his young readers will be able to understand. Thus, while the British sources just talk about practices such as 'annexation,' in Lavisse this term will be explained in simple language:

> **Annexer**, réunir un pays à un autre.   (Lavisse 1902, p. 183)
>
> [**To annex**, unite one country with another.]

Needless to say, this definition leaves out an important element of perspective that must also be understood – and that probably was understood by the pupils using the book – for a proper placement of the practice in the context of colonization.

AD 3.3.2.1:
[How are people, events, relations categorized?]

Patterns of lexical choice are basic linguistic tools for categorizing people, institutions, events, actions, practices, relationships, and hence for discursively making sense of the social world.[54] They are central to processes of ideological meaning construction because they always invoke contrasts or comparisons, whether implicitly (carrying along the possibility of alternative choices, as explained earlier) or explicitly. Discursive practices of categorization reflect and have an impact on how aspects of the social world are actually 'seen.' They are, as it were, conceptual and practice-related operations on that social world. The effects are not trivial. Thus, categorization in discourse enables us to *describe different phenomena as if they were comparable or even identical.* Consider the following:

> 3. Avant la Révolution de 89, l'Espagne, l'Italie, l'Allemagne, la Russie, la France, l'Amérique du Sud étaient, comme la Turquie aujourd'hui, gouvernées par **le bon plaisir** des rois et de leurs ministres. **4.** Excepté la Hollande, l'Angleterre, la Suisse et les Etats-Unis, aucun peuple ne se gouvernait lui-même. **5.** Il n'y avait **pas de nations**, mais seulement des **sujets**. (Lavisse 1902, p. 100)

> [3. Before the Revolution of 89, Spain, Italy, Germany, Russia, France, South America, like Turkey today, were governed by **the whims** of the kings and their ministers. **4.** Except for Holland, England, Switzerland and the United States, no people governed itself. **5.** There were **no nations**, but only **subjects**.]

In sentences like these, lots of entities are lumped together under the same categories as if they are fully comparable. For instance, what are called Italy, Germany, and South America in sentence 3, is fundamentally different from Spain, Russia, and France in the period talked about (before the French Revolution of 1789). Italy was a patchwork of little states, sometimes independent, sometimes ruled in various combinations by outside powers. Germany consisted of numerous sovereign or virtually sovereign entities with feudal rulers. And South America was a collection of colonies, none of which were independent from Spain or Portugal as yet. So, also the extent to which "kings and their ministers" could be talked about with reference to the complete enumeration in 3 is dubious, whereas such identification of rulers would have been perfectly acceptable for two of the three

---

[54] One of the basic notions in ethnomethodology is 'membership categorization,' precisely because of the centrality of assigning categories and relationships for an understanding of the social world. For an example of how the ethnomethodological notion (often associated with analyses of conversational interaction) can be applied to textual analysis, see Watson (2009).

entities enumerated in 4 (Holland and England), though this set is supposed to be fully opposite to the first set in terms of ways of being governed. Lavisse being a knowledgeable historian, however, details of fact are quite consciously glossed over to drive home a rhetorical point: the difference between countries or states with a form of democracy (even if incipient) and autocratic ones, the French Revolution being presented as symbolic for the transition from the one to the other. This rhetorical strategy is then topped with the introduction of two new categories, nations vs. subjects, which again gloss over distinctions worth going into (such as the serious differences in content of the concept of 'nation' in the French context vs. the German or Italian contexts, where the term had also become applicable by the time Lavisse was writing his book).

At the other end, categorization also enables us to *give differential treatment to comparable phenomena.* In our corpus, this is easiest to illustrate with reference to the ways in which *events, actions and practices* are portrayed. Consider, again from Lavisse:

> **7.** […] Le chef des révoltés, Nana-Sahib, massacrait les Anglais, les femmes comme les hommes, et faisait jeter les enfants au feu.
> **8.** Les soldats anglais marchèrent contre les Cipayes révoltés, reprirent la ville de Delhi, et attachèrent les prisonniers hindous à la gueule des canons (fig. 10).   (Lavisse 1902, p. 152)

> [**7.** […] The leader of the rebels, Nana Sahib, massacred the English, women and men alike, and ordered the children to be thrown into the fire.
> **8.** The English soldiers marched against the revolting sepoys, recaptured the city of Delhi, and tied the Hindu prisoners to the mouths of cannons (fig. 10).]

Sentences 7 and 8 describe two sides of the fighting of a war, offering significantly different views of those two sides, partly by picking out different subactions or subevents, partly by categorizing actions and events differently. Sentence 7, the Indian side, focuses on excessive violence, an indiscriminate "massacre." Sentence 8, the British side, focuses on 'regular' military action: marching, recapturing, executing. The same differential presentation of involvement in the common activity of warfare, is to be found in the British texts. Fearenside (1922, p. 433), for instance, lists under the category of "the main incidents":

> the massacre of Cawnpore
> the sieges of Delhi and Lucknow
> the capture of Gwalior

It is significant that from the events at Cawnpore, one event is picked out that can be categorized as a "massacre," while the military-strategic overarching concepts of "siege" and "capture" are used when talking about Delhi, Lucknow, and Gwalior, though these general events also involved what could be called massacres. From later sources, we know about the British plundering recaptured Delhi and Lucknow (efficiently assisted by those well-used loyal Sikhs) while killing anyone coming in their way, about their burning of villages that resisted, and their indiscriminate killing 'out of hand' of mutineers and supposed supporters. Lloyd says:

> the deaths of the captives at Cawnpore, in what seemed to be an outrageous blend of cruelty and treachery, left the British thirsting for revenge. And this they took: as they advanced against the mutineers they proceeded on the principle that any mutineers, or anyone who had helped the mutineers, or anyone who was thought to have helped the mutineers, should be executed.
>
> (1996, p. 175)

But even this account presents British violence as a reaction (while, as said before, it is not impossible to assume that Cawnpore was already a reaction to earlier extreme violence by Neill and his troops in Benares and Allahabad – which itself, as is usual with violence, can in turn be seen as a reaction against, etc.). Also, "execution," with its ring of legitimacy, remains the word. These aspects of the events are completely absent from most of the British sources, except McCarthy (1908) and Low and Sanders (1910) both of which address the issue quite directly. Low and Sanders is quite explicit about revenge, and suggest that summary executions took place:

> On the day after his [the 'puppet emperor's'] surrender, Hodson dragged out the Mughal princes from Humayun's tomb and was escorting them to the city when, fearing as he alleged that they would be rescued by the turbulent crowd of armed Mohammedan spectators, he caused them to descend from their palanquins and shot them dead with his own hand.[1] It was but one of many deeds of blood which conquered Delhi witnessed; for heavy indeed was the retribution that fell on the guilty city, and martial law, not always discriminating in its wrath, hurried hundreds of its citizens from their wrecked and pillaged homes to the gallows.
>
> [1] [...] Hodson's statement that the slaughter of the princes was justified by his situation was not accepted at the time or afterwards by those best competent to judge. [...]
>
> (1910, pp. 150)

Next to the explicitness of the admissions, however, there is also the reference to "martial law," providing an – albeit feeble – frame of legitimacy, as well as disapproval by other British actors involved, as spelled out in the footnote (following a discursive strategy comparable to the emphasis we observed in 3.1 on British attempts to temper admitted British emotional involvement leading to revenge). The pattern is clear: Truly despicable acts are ascribed to the Indian side, while highly comparable acts on the British side either remain hidden, or are embedded in a context of direct British criticism reducing the likelihood of a generalization of guilt,[55] or get the cloak of action or event categories which make description and explanation spill over into justification and legitimation work.

---

[55] It must be added here that many of the British sources also make an effort to make sure that guilt does not attach to all Indians: The contribution of those who remained loyal is often described extensively (e.g., in Parkin 1911, p. 213, where it gets as much attention as the events themselves).

In this context it is interesting to point out that the facts of violence during the crushing of the revolt were reasonably well known. Some twenty years after the events, Jules Verne wrote *La maison à vapeur* (*The Steam House*; 1880). This novel tells the story of a certain Colonel Munro, whose wife had been killed during the massacre of Cawnpore, and who is taken along by a bunch of friends on an adventurous trip through northern India ten years after the revolt, in 1867, traveling in a comfortable mobile home pulled by a giant steel elephant (in fact a sophisticated steam engine – hence the title of the book). In order to build up some dramatic tension around the shadowy figure of Nana Sahib, who had never been captured by the British, Verne gives a full history of the sepoy rebellion in chapter 3. This chapter also contains a detailed account of the crushing of the revolt, including details of extreme violence, supposedly leading to the death of 120,000 sepoys and 200,000 civilians. This chapter was left out of the English translations.[56]

The *categorization of people*, as collectivities or as actors involved in specific events, is another important point of attention. Consider the following categorizations of the native peoples of America and Australia:

> **2**. L'Amérique était habitée par *des sauvages*. **3**. Mais il y avait *deux grands royaumes*: dans l'Amérique du Nord, le **Mexique**; dans l'Amérique du Sud, le **Pérou**.   (Lavisse 1902, p. 65)

> [**2**. America was inhabited by *savages*. **3**. But there were *two great kingdoms*: in North America, **Mexico**; in South America, **Peru**.]

> **17**. Il y a cent ans, [158] **l'Australie** n'était encore habitée que par des sauvages stupides et misérables, qui n'avaient ni maisons ni troupeaux, et parcouraient les déserts, n'ayant souvent à manger que des insectes et des bêtes mortes.   (Lavisse 1902, pp. 158–159)

> [**17**. A hundred years ago, **Australia** was still only inhabited by stupid and miserable savages, who had neither houses nor herds, and traveled the deserts, often without anything to eat other than insects and dead animals.]

> **14**. Aux États-Unis et dans l'Amérique anglaise, il ne reste presque plus de sauvages; les Anglais en ont massacré beaucoup, les autres ont été tués par l'eau-de-vie ou les maladies.
> [...] [163]
> [...] **1**. La plupart des Mexicains ne sont que les descendants des *anciens Indiens*. **2**. Ces sauvages, mal civilisés, ne savent ni travailler ni se gouverner.   (Lavisse 1902, pp. 163–164)

> [**14**. In the United States and English-speaking America, there are hardly any savages left; the English have massacred many of them, the others have been killed by brandy or diseases.
> [...]

[56] Swati Dasgupta drew my attention to the novel and the interesting detail about its English translations. She is now engaged in a study of French newspapers of the period, in search of the sources of Jules Verne's account.

[...] **1**. Most of the Mexicans are only descendants of the *old Indians*. **2**. Those savages, poorly civilized, are neither able to work nor to govern themselves.]

The views expressed here are hardly flattering. Though consistent in its denigration of Indians and Aboriginals, there are some textual tensions, illustrative of the property of ideology in discourse that it may contain elements of apparent or real contradiction. For instance, how does the categorization of American Indians as "savages" chime in with the observation that there were "two great kingdoms," which implies a recognizable level of civilization? And how can this be reconciled with the incapability to work or to govern themselves ascribed as inherent properties to those poorly civilized savages who are said to be the descendants of the same Indians who ran this great kingdom in Mexico? By way of explanation, one could of course point at the "but" introducing 3, possibly indicating a contrast between a majority and some exceptions, or at the "only" ("ne sont que") which qualifies the Mexicans' descendency from the old Mexican Indians in 1. There are tensions at a deeper level as well. Contrasting with the categorization of the Indians, there are descriptions of the violent and deceitful way in which the Spanish colonizers, characterized as "avonturiers féroces" (fierce – not to use savage – adventurers) only interested in stealing gold, got hold of Indian territory, as well as the massacres of Indians which the British were guilty of (in 14). The tension here is one between the ascription of inherent properties to members of a collectivity (the American Indians) and the attribution of responsibility for specific forms of behavior to members of a differently viewed collectivity: savage behavior does not seem to necessitate a categorization as 'savage', while non-European lineage, in combination with a non-European way of living, does.

For a different, though equally interesting, type of observation about the categorization of people, turn to Fearenside (1922, p. 433). Looking at the paragraph on causes of the Mutiny, we find many categorizations which, in line with the expectations raised by the activity type of academic writing, have a perfectly dry and descriptive appearance. Here is the full list:

> British forces
> the native princes
> the larger landowners
> the actual cultivators of the soil
> the native sepoys
> those who cherished
> the British troops
> the native regiments
> their officers
> the Sikhs of the Punjab
> Sir John Lawrence
> the British

the Europeans
a descendent of the Moguls/Emperor
the mutineers
troops from the Punjab
John Nicholson
(a handful of) British troops
Sir Henry Lawrence
Sir Henry Havelock
Lord Clyde, the Sir Colin Campbell of Crimea fame
Clyde

Ordinary as this may seem, interesting patterns emerge, and at least two phe-nomena should be pointed out. First, only on the British side do we find individ-uals. Yet, keeping in mind that one-to-one form–function relationships cannot be assumed, we should be careful with conclusions. Does this pattern function as a depersonalization of the enemy? Positing a direct link between the (non-)use of names and (de)personalization for strategic purposes would clearly be in violation of a basic principle of pragmatics (cf. Caveat 3.1). For one thing, it also happens that enemies are demonized precisely by giving them high-profile individualized names (such as Osama bin Laden, Saddam Hussein, or – depending on one's per-spective – George W. Bush). Moreover, treating Indians as a native 'mass' (except for the Sikhs) may be simply a matter of audience design: Categories are chosen in view of what the readers are supposed to know or recognize. The British pro-tagonists can be supposed to be rather well known to the users of Fearenside's history textbook. After all, Sir Henry Havelock has a statue on Trafalgar Square. But also this cannot be handled mechanically as an explanation for the pattern. When we go back to Lavisse (1902), for instance, we do find the name of one of the protagonists of the Indian Mutiny, even though this is a much more concise textbook than Fearenside and though the name in question is certainly not more recognizable for a French audience of school children (at the end of elementary education) than for British students (ready to go to university) – unless we assume widespread familiarity with Jules Verne's *La maison à vapeur*. Such issues can-not be settled without wider research within the analyzed texts as well as inter-textually. Many of the other British sources do give Indian names. Nana Sahib (mentioned in Lavisse) also occurs in Cassell's (as concise as Lavisse), Innes, Low and Sanders (both much more elaborate), etc. A number of soures, e.g., Low and Sanders (1910, p. 141), also give several additional Indian names (three of which, Bahádur Shah II, Tántia Topí, and the Ráni of Jhánsi, recur often enough through the texts for inclusion in the overview of events given earlier in 2.1.3). Yet, when looking at the totality of the texts, a pattern persists: Either Indians remain unnamed (as in Fearenside), or else the names are accompanied by quali-fications – making heavy use of adjectival characterizations – that are markedly less favorable than those accompanying British individuals. Thus, nothing good is said about Nana Sahib or Bahádur Shah. To give just one example:

> The Nana Sahib was among the last of the fugitives, and the English missed the satisfaction of sending this bloodthirsty and perfidious scoundrel to the gallows.   (Low and Sanders 1910, p. 155)

The only positive words about the other two Indian protagonists concern Tántia Topí's military and strategic skills (he was the last major obstacle to British victory) and the Ráni's equally remarkable military skills and courage. Low and Sanders (1910, p. 156) talks about Ganga Bhai, "the Ráni of Jhánsi," as "the fiery Maráthá princess." The authors continue:

> In this engagement the young Marátha heroine, whose fertile brain and valiant heart had cost the English so many lives, lost her own.
> (Low and Sanders 1910, p. 157)

What provides her with such exceptional distinction among the enemies of the British is her being a woman who, as is emphasized in several sources, fought like a man and died on the battlefield.

A second interesting observation (mentioned in 3.3.2) is the contrast between "the larger landowners" and "the actual cultivators of the soil." Here legitimation is at work for the "land settlements" imposed by the British. "Actual cultivators" refers negatively to those who are not, which turns the land settlements into a democratic measure.

Our sample texts also contain *categorizations of relations* between (categorized) groups of actors involved in the described events and states of affairs. Especially in Lavisse, the dominant way of categorizing the relationship between colonizer and colony is one of possession and mastery following from conquest, occupation, annexation:

> **4.** Les Portugais et les Espagnols possédèrent alors des *pays immenses hors de l'Europe.*   (Lavisse 1902, p. 66; similar phrasings on pp. 67 and 68)

> [**4.** The Portuguese and the Spanish thus possessed *vast lands outside Europe.*]

> **9.** Aujourd'hui la Cochinchine et le Tonkin appartiennent à la France. **10.** Le Cambodge et l'Annam sont sous le *protectorat* français, c'est à dire qu'ils obéissent à des gouverneurs français. Les Français pourront bientôt, s'ils veulent, être **maîtres de l'Indo-Chine**, comme les Anglais sont maîtres de l'Inde.
> [...] **11.** La France a occupé, en 1853, la **Nouvelle-Calédonie**. [...]
> **14.** En 1879, la France a annexé l'île de **Taïti** et les îles de la Société [...]
> **16.** Les sauvages qui habitaient l'île disparaissent, il en meurt plus qu'il n'en nait; les Français les remplaceront.   (Lavisse 1902, p. 158)

> [**9.** Today Cochinchina and Tonkin belong to France. **10.** Cambodia and Annam are under French *protectorate*, which means that they obey French governors. The French can soon, if they want, be **the masters of Indo-China**, like the English are the masters of India.
> [...] **11.** France occupied, in 1853, **New Caledonia**. [...]

14. In 1879, France annexed the island of **Tahiti** and the Society Islands […] **16**. The savages who lived on the island are disappearing, more die than are born; the French will replace them.]

1. En 1830, les Français prirent Alger, ils ont conquis ensuite toute [160] l'**Algérie** […] **2**. Beaucoup de Français sont allés s'y établir; ils ont semé du blé, planté des vignes, bâti des villes, et l'Algérie est devenue un **pays français**.
    3. La France a fondé, de 1855 à 1860, la colonie du **Sénégal**. […]
    5. En 1882, la France a conquis la **Tunisie**, qui touche à l'Algérie. **6**. Elle ne l'a pas annexée,* mais elle y a établi un gouvernement français, et la Tunisie sera bientôt habitée par des colons français.
(Lavisse 1902, pp. 160–161)

[**1**. In 1830, the French captured Algiers, since then they have conquered all of [160] **Algeria** […] **2**. Many Frenchmen have gone to settle there; they have sown wheat, planted vines, built towns, and Algeria has become a **French country**.
    3. France founded, from 1855 to 1860, the colony of **Senegal**. […]
    5. In 1882, France conquered **Tunisia**, which borders on Algeria. **6**. It did not annex* it, but it established a French government there, and Tunisia will soon be inhabited by French colonists.]

The picture is very similar in the British sources. Being 'masters' implies a clear division of labor:

> We have only to repeat here, that as a matter of fact no indignities, other than that of the compulsory corn-grinding, were put upon the English ladies.
>
> (McCarthy 1908, p. 188)

Clearly, corn-grinding did not belong to the regular duties of English ladies, if such work can be classified as an 'indignity.' The British sources also pay more detailed attention to the manner in which India was ruled by the British after conquest, acquisition, the establishment of control, annexation:

> The East India Company, which till then had ruled India, transferred its rights over that country to the Crown of England, and a proclamation was issued by the British Government taking over the administration of the country. Since then India has been ruled by a Viceroy, or Governor-General and Council, on behalf of the Sovereign of Great Britain and Ireland.
>
> (Cassell's 1903, p. 124)

> Dalhousie's annexations […]
>   […] [433] […] the transfer of Indian administration from the Company to the Crown […] The *Indian Government Act* of 1858 placed the control of British India in the hands of a new Secretary of State, responsible to Parliament, and represented in India by a Governor-General.
>
> (Fearenside 1922, pp. 433–434)

> the East India Company had been rapidly extending its dominions and its protectorates. […] had been brought under control; […] had been forcibly annexed; […] incorporated; […] acquired […].

> [...] the [154] East India Company was abolished and its functions trans-
> ferred to the Crown; [...] British methods of governing India were thor-
> oughly revised and remodelled.   (Hearnshaw 1930, pp. 154–155)

In addition to this attention to manner of government, triggered by the changes
which the Mutiny brought about, there is a complete naturalization of a full state
of dominance underlying the description. Control is taken for granted; it just needs
to be 'transferred.' Parkin (1911) makes this explicit and adds a prediction:

> The Mutiny proved that India was not, and probably never will be, a country
> which can be united to oppose our rule.   (Parkin 1911, p. 214)

The section on the Indian Mutiny is only a small part of Parkin's chapter on
British rule in India. Elsewhere, outside the sample in this book's Appendix 2, he
goes more deeply into the nature of the relationship with India:

> If another nation, such as Russia, should conquer India, and take it from us,
> or if we left the country, and it fell back into the disorder which prevailed
> when we began to rule it, almost all these sources of income, which make so
> many of our people comfortable and prosperous, would disappear.
>   [...]
> On the other hand, British rule has done a great deal for India. We can truly
> say that British people now wish to govern India for the good of the people
> in it. So we send out many of our ablest public men to make and carry out
> just laws, and they have given to the country peace, order, and justice, such
> as it knew little about in old times. Of all our exports to India none are [226]
> so valuable to the country as the honest and upright men which we have sent
> to it.   (Parkin 1911, pp. 226–227)

Again this illustrates ideological tensions, and to a certain extent contradictions.
While obviously the reason for being in India is the material benefits this pro-
duces for Britain, India is said to be governed by the British for the good of the
Indians. Like Lavisse, Parkin would categorize colonization as a work of peace.

Categorization is a matter of perspective. Hence the mixing of perspectives or
mental spaces, as already illustrated at the end of section 2.2.1.2, is also relevant
here. Usually, however, the perspective from which a categorization emanates is
crystal clear. Just think of the cover term for the events in India in 1857–1858.
In all our sources it is called 'the Indian Mutiny.' This choice of terms takes a
British perspective, emphasizing rebellion against legitimate authority. In later
Indian history writing, the same events have come to be labeled 'the great uprising' (stressing insurrection under conditions of domination and repression) or
'the First Indian War of Independence.'

AD 3.3.3.:

[At the sentence level: How are grammatical relations, case categories, and semantic
roles handled when describing events, actions, or relations between (groups of)
people?]

One of the tools for discursively varying perspectives on events, actions, and the relations between (groups of) people is the system of functional relations between nominal constituents and the expressed activity, event, or state of affairs.[57] Have a look at the Agent–Patient and Subject–Object positions in the following (partial) description of the outbreak of the revolt in Meerut.

> [1] The sepoys rushed across to the European quarter, and [2] were joined by all the rabble of the native city. [3] Officers, civilians, women, and children were assaulted and murdered, [4] the defenceless bungalows were attacked, and [5] the ruffians of the bazaar kept up the orgy of bloodshed and plunder till morning.
>
> [6] The mutineers went back to the lines, eager to make their escape from the scene of their crime. [7] With deplorable weakness they were suffered to depart without a blow struck against them. [8] The British troops were held inactive while the mutineers hastened through the night to Delhi; [9] and the next morning their cavalry rode into that city, with the infantry following. [10] They had marched on the wings of fear, never doubting that the tramp of English horse and the rumble of English cannon would speedily be heard behind them. [11] But there was no one to do with the cavalry and horse artillery at Meerut what Gillespie had done with the dragoons and galloper-guns at Vellore half a century earlier. [12] Hewitt was incapable of giving a decisive order; [13] Archdale Wilson, his brigadier, was weighed down by the responsibility of protecting the stores and residents at Meerut, and [14] he too kept the troops inactive.
>
> (Low and Sanders 1910, p. 140; proposition numbering added)

Looking at this fragment proposition by proposition, we get the structure shown in Table 7. From a simple table like this, where I have highlighted the positions occupied by the rebeling sepoys and their supporters, one can read the agentivity structure of the recounted episode. The grammatical relations and semantic roles show how clearly the sepoys are described as having the initiative. Not until [7] and [8] do the British emerge in an Agent role – and then it is only implicitly, and their Agent role consists in their not doing anything to prevent the sepoys from keeping the initiative. Similarly, [11] through [14] underscore British inactivity. Though this reads like – and is – a criticism of local British leadership in Meerut, it is at the same time an explanation for how the revolt could succeed to begin with, i.e., through individual failure (which is contrasted with a show of ability (in [11]) by a different British leader under comparable circumstances half a century earlier). Note that, in passing, the second in command is slightly exculpated by his being made (in [13]) into the Patient of being 'weighed down by' responsibilities.

[57] The term 'grammatical relations' refers to subject, direct object, indirect object, etc.; 'case categories' are nominative, accusative, dative, etc.; 'semantic roles' are agent, patient, experiencer, etc. There are interrelationships between these three, but not all are equally relevant for all languages; for English, with virtually no case marking, grammatical relations and semantic roles are the most relevant points of reference. For further background, see Rudzka-Ostyn (1995) and Ahearn (2010).

Table 7. *Grammatical relations and semantic roles*

	Subject	Agent	VERB	Object	Patient
[1]	the sepoys	the sepoys	rushed across to	[destination: the European quarter]	
[2]	the sepoys	all the rabble of the native city	were joined by		the sepoys
[3]	officers, civilians, women, and children	[implicit: the sepoys + all the rabble of the native city]	were assaulted and murdered		officers, civilians, women, and children
[4]	the defenceless bungalows	[implicit: the sepoys + all the rabble of the native city]	were attacked		the defenceless bungalows
[5]	the ruffians of the bazaar	the ruffians of the bazaar	kept up	the orgy of bloodshed and plunder	[implicit: officers, civilians, women, and children + the defenceless bungalows]
[6]	the mutineers	the mutineers	went back to	[destination: the lines] [purpose: eager to make their escape from the scene of their crime]	
[7]	they [the mutineers]	[implicit: the British, 'with deplorable weakness']	were suffered to depart without a blow being struck against them		they [the mutineers]
[8]	the British troops	[implicit: the British]	were held inactive		the British troops
[9]	their cavalry	their cavalry	rode into	[destination: that city]	
[10]	they [the mutineers]	they [the mutineers]	had marched	[manner: on the wings of fear]	
[11]	no one	no one	there was	[to do what …]	
[12]	Hewitt	Hewitt	was incapable of giving	a decisive order	
[13]	Archdale Wilson, his brigadier	the responsibility of protecting the stores and residents of Meerut	was weighed down by		Archdale Wilson, his brigadier
[14]	he [Archdale Wilson]	he [Archdale Wilson]	kept inactive	the troops	the troops

In isolation, such observations would not be so remarkable. But again looking at this contrastively, we see that a similar pattern in the other direction is absent. When the British get the initiative back, their successes are due to intrinsic British merits rather than to failures or *laissez faire* on the part of the Indians.

Similar observations can be made and comparable patterns found by going beyond the elementary Agent–Patient distinction when charting semantic roles.[58] Consider:

> Sir Colin Campbell arrived later on with an army, which fought its way through the streets of Lucknow to the fort.   (Cassell's 1903, p. 124)

The semantic role structure of this sentence looks as follows:

> Agent *arrived* Time ⌐Accompaniment
>   └ Agent *fought* Result – Locative – Goal

This structure, again nothing remarkable in itself, combines with its referents to encapsulate a typical story of liberation for which parallels will be hard to find describing what could be objectively similar actions with Indian rebels as Agents.

Two grammatical forms which express a different relation between subjects and the action expressed by the verb, and of which there are already examples in Table 7, are active vs. passive voice. The difference provides a favorite example for authors in the critical literature on discourse bent on finding direct mappings between forms and functions. Consider Fairclough's statement of the functions of the passive (which he further links up with the discursive functioning of nominalizations):

---

[58] A few of the frequently distinguished semantic roles are the following:

- Accompaniment: person or thing participating in an action or event.
- Agent: a person or thing who is the 'doer' of an action or event; often this is the subject of an active verb; prototypically the agent is a conscious being, acting on purpose, and the action has a visible result. ('Force' is sometimes used for a non-volitional agent.)
- Beneficiary: the person or thing who/that is advantaged or disadvantaged by an action or event.
- Counteragent: force or resistance against which an action is carried out.
- Experiencer: the one who receives or experiences the named action or event.
- Goal: place toward which something moves or person/thing at which an action is directed.
- Instrument: thing used to implement an action or event.
- Locative: location or spatial orientation of an action or event.
- Manner: how the action, experience, process, or event is taking place.
- Patient: the affected or undergoer of an action or event; often the object of an active verb.
- Result: what is produced by an action or event.
- Source: place or entity of origin.
- Time: temporal placement of an action or event.

Active is the 'unmarked' choice, the form selected when there are no specific reasons for choosing the passive. And motivations for choosing the passive are various. One is that it allows for the *omission of the agent*, though this may itself be variously motivated by the fact that the agent is self-evident, irrelevant, or unknown. Another political or ideological reason for an agent-less passive may be *to obfuscate agency, and hence causality and responsibility* [...] Passives are also motivated by considerations related to the textual function of the clause. A passive shifts the goal into initial 'theme' position, which usually means presenting it as 'given' or already known information; it also shifts the agent, if it is not omitted, into the prominent position at the end of a clause where we usually find new information [...]

Nominalization shares with the passive the potentiality of omitting the agent, and the variety of motivations for doing so. [..]

(1992, p. 182; italics added)

There is nothing wrong, as such, with this careful wording of the links between certain *forms* and the *functions* they are typically supposed to have. But problems may emerge as soon as this general observation of typical form–function relationships is mechanically handled as an analytical instrument. Take Fearenside's (1922, p. 433) section on the causes of the Mutiny as an example. We find the following verb phrases:

> X dragged on
> X had caused Y among Z
> X had annoyed Y by favouring Z
> X had been offended by Y
> X thought that they had Y
> X were few and scattered
> X was most widespread in Y
> X broke out in open mutiny, shot Y, and stirred up Z
> X kept quiet
> X had been so well used by Y that they helped Z
> X were Y
> X surrendered and were butchered
> X had been set up as Y
> X themselves were besieged by Y
> X held Y
> X were relieved by Y
> X were brought away by Y
> X reoccupied Y
> X was finally crushed by Y

And here are some nominalizations:

> the preoccupation of British forces in India
> Dalhousie's annexations
> recent land settlements
> the equipment of the native sepoys with rifles that required greased cartridges
> the capture of Gwalior

Of the verb phrases, about half are passive, and all these nominalizations capture complex actions, events, or circumstances. But in both the passives and the nominalizations, agentivity is always clear, i.e., an agent is identified or unmistakably identifiable from the discourse itself. Thus one of their basic functions, as attributed by Fairclough, does not seem to emerge. Nor could it be said that there is anything 'marked' about them. Their high frequency is most probably simply a function of the style that is *typical of a certain specific verbal activity type*, namely 'academic writing'; see the remarks about this under 3.1. There is no doubt a reason why certain features become expected properties of specific activity types. But their capacity to obfuscate agency and responsibility does not seem to be a generalizable reason for the high frequency of passives in academic discourse. This does not mean that in a corpus such as ours such functionality does not occur. But in order for the passive to clearly serve purposes of taking away responsibility, more is needed than the passive alone: a 'local' context must support the interpretation. For example (from the introduction to Kerr and Kerr's 1927 chapter on "India in the nineteenth century," from which the fragment in Appendix 2 is taken):

> You remember how the English first went to India, because of its trade, and how the British East [179] India Company was drawn into war, first with the French, and then, after the Black Hole of Calcutta, with the native princes. Once the Company began to interfere with native affairs it found that it could not stop."   (Kerr and Kerr 1927, pp. 179–181)

Here "was drawn into war" is a way of using the passive that clearly de-emphasizes the East India Company's own initiative in the endeavors of war: The passive effectively serves as a device to remove responsibility. It is hard to assume the Company's reluctance to engage with the French; after all, they were actively disputing each other's access to and control over the trade lines they were in India for in the first place – as is presupposed in the first part of the quotation. As to war with "native princes," the burden of guilt is put on Indian shoulders: Warfare is presented as a natural consequence of the 'Black Hole of Calcutta' incident[59] rather than the Company's own decision. And subsequent wars are presented as an equally natural inability to stop 'interfering with native affairs' once this course of action had started.[60]

---

[59] Reference is to a highly mythologized (and disputed) event in 1756, when the Bengal nawab imprisoned East India Company soldiers in a small lockup for petty offenders (the 'Black Hole') – far too many for the available space – and most of them died.

[60] Note that, in the relationship between active and passive, active can be marked. In the article "In East and West, resentment at costs" (referred to in n. 44, and taken from the *International Herald Tribune*, 9 March 1993, on the social and economic situation in the former East Germany, a couple of years after the unification of the two Germanies), the following subtitle occurs:

East Germans Weigh Down Europe.

This sentence refers to the fact that Europe's economic prosperity could have been greater at that point in time if the former East Germany had not needed support. But rather than to describe this as an effect of circumstances, an agentive role is assigned to the East Germans.

Note that taking away personal responsibility, which is sometimes accomplished with the choice of a passive voice or the nominalization of a complex event, may also be achieved by different means. For instance:

> The mutineers fled along the road to Delhi; and some evil fate directed that they were not to be pursued or stopped on their way.
>
> (McCarthy 1908, p. 172)

Here the personification of "some evil fate," made into an agent, does the same.

AD 3.3.4:
[Still at the sentence level: How are moods, modalities, negation, and evidentiality handled?]

'Modality' is a term for what utterers do with a proposition to indicate (degrees of) necessity, possibility, certainty, likelihood. The linguistic means used for this purpose include grammatical mood (indicative, subjunctive, imperative – a system that is more elaborate in French than in English), modal auxiliaries, adjectives, adverbs, sentence adverbs, and particles.[61] Most of these have been extensively illustrated in 3.1, when hedging constructions were discussed. Hedging is indeed a common way of modifying or specifying the attitude with which a proposition is expressed. Sometimes hedging co-occurs with the strengthening of a claim; look at the underscored items in the following:

> It seems that some cartridges lubricated with the objectionable composition had actually passed into the hands of the troops before the issue was checked by the authorities.   (Low and Sanders 1910, p. 138, footnote)

"Actually" emphasizes the factuality of the claim which is at the same time weakened by "It seems that." McCarthy combines the same attenuated admission with a negation bearing on the composition of the lubricant:

> It appears that the paper was actually greased, but not with any such material as that which religious alarm suggested to the native troops.
>
> (McCarthy 1908, p. 171)

It is hardly surprising that this modal tension is so clearly present in the recounting of a somewhat embarrassing episode. But strengthening also occurs with hypothetical claims:

> Their government was abominably oppressive and [134] corrupt, and at the same time so feeble that they would certainly have fallen before external attack or domestic rebellion, but for the support of the English.
>
> (Low and Sanders 1910, pp. 134–135)

For a more straightforward strengthening of propositional content, a variety of devices can be found in the following examples:

[61] For some basic literature, see Aijmer and Simon-Vandenbergen (2009), Foolen (1996), Kiefer (1998), Lenk (1997).

> In fact, the native princes all held aloof from the revolt [...].
>
> (Innes 1927, p. 170)

> They had chains put on them in the presence of their comrades, who no doubt regarded them as martyrs [...].   (McCarthy 1908, p. 171)

> If, however, each of these acts of policy were not only justifiable but actually inevitable, none the less must a succession of such acts produce a profound emotion among the races in whose midst they were accomplished [...] they yet felt that national resentment which any manner of foreign intervention is almost certain to provoke.   (McCarthy 1908, p. 176)

> He must have begun to know by this time that he had no chance of establishing himself [188] as a ruler anywhere in India.
>
> (McCarthy 1908, pp. 188–189)

> It is undoubtedly true that the very passion for honest government which animated Lord Dalhousie had stirred up discontent amongst those who benefited most by his policy.   (Woodward 1921, p. 235)

The pragmatic particles "in fact" and "no doubt," as well as the adjective "certain," the adverb–adjective combination "undoubtedly true," and the modal auxiliary "must," indicate a heightened certainty with regard to the statement that is made. In general, while hedging was said to be quite common in spite of the expectation of factuality accompanying the activity type of academic writing, a true strengthening of expressed propositional meaning is relatively rare. No doubt this is related to the historical nature of the topic which does not allow for direct observation as a basis of certainty. That is what may be behind the reflex underlying the insertion of "almost" in "is almost certain to" – absolute certainty seems like a tall order.

Another type of modality, not so much related to parameters of necessity, possibility, or certainty, is found in the use of the particles "still" and "yet" in the following sentences:

> Still the idea was strong among the troops that some design against their religion was meditated.   (McCarthy 1908, p. 171)

> they yet felt that national resentment which any manner of foreign intervention is almost certain to provoke.   (McCarthy 1908, p. 176)

Such expressions evoke alternative possible worlds which, in spite of considerations already voiced in the immediately preceding discourse, were not realized.

All examples so far bear on what is commonly known as 'epistemic modality,' modalizations related to 'knowledge.' By way of contrast, so-called deontic modality, related to 'obligation,' is rare, just as imperatives are rare (except in the few cases in which the authors of our sample data directly address their audience). Yet, here are a couple of examples:

> Il faut se garder de vouloir tout dire [...].   (Lavisse 1902, p. 2)

> [One must refrain from wanting to say everything [...].]

> But if you want to know [...], <u>you must</u> read the story in another book.
>   (Kerr and Kerr 1927, p. 183)

> One name <u>must not</u> be forgotten among those who endured the siege of Lucknow.   (McCarthy 1908, p. 194)

While the first two are simple pieces of advice (the first one self-addressed as much as aimed at the reader), the third carries with it some moral urgency. Lavisse (1902) contains a passage in which deontic modality is used in a legal context, spelling out the human rights principles of 1789; e.g.:

> La loi <u>doit</u> être la même pour tous.   (Lavisse 1902, p. 99)

> [The law must be the same for all.]

In most of the cases in which the modal auxiliary "must" occurs, however, we are confronted with an obligation that bears on a way of handling knowledge:

> Une histoire des principaux peuples anciens et modernes <u>doit</u> être enseignée avec *discrétion*, car elle est immense.   (Lavisse 1902, p. 2)

> [A history of the principal ancient and modern peoples <u>must</u> be taught with *discretion*, as it is boundless.]

> <u>To all this must be added that</u> the English had suffered con-[136]siderable loss of prestige through the Afghan disasters of 1841–42, and subsequently through the Russian war, of which very misleading accounts had been circulated.   (Low and Sanders 1910, pp. 136–137)

> But <u>we must above all other things take into account</u>, when considering the position of the Hindoo Sepoy, the influence of the tremendous institution of caste.   (McCarthy 1908, p. 173)

> So far we have been concerned with the extension of the British control in India, but it <u>must not be supposed that</u> the efforts of British rulers were not directed to bettering the lot of their subjects.
>   (Warner and Marten 1912, p. 690)

This mixture of the deontic and the epistemic is an appeal to intellectual honesty.

Of particular importance for our data is the phenomenon of *evidentiality*. Utterances may not only indicate (degrees of) certainty, necessity, possibility – the province of modality proper – but also the manner in which the utterer had access to the communicated meaning. Such linking with a source of information is what the term 'evidentiality' refers to. One type of source is direct perception.[62] Clearly, this is not a relevant option in our sample (though even for historical

---

[62] A common categorization of types of evidentiality (proposed by Willett 1988) is as follows:

>   - Direct, i.e., attested/perceived (visually, auditorily, ...)
>   - Indirect
>   • reported (second-hand, third-hand, folklore)
>   • inferred (from results, or through reasoning)

For further reading, see Dendale and Tasmowski-De Ryck (eds.) (2001), Kiefer (1998).

accounts, if bearing on events more recent relative to the moment of writing, this would not be impossible). When discussing the utterer's voices (in 2.2.1.2), we already observed the nature of historical writing as the product of a chain of entextualizations, adding that, however, transparent reference to earlier texts is almost completely absent. This 'appropriation' of the propositional content, where indirect evidentiality in the form of 'reporting' is largely absent (reported speech being restricted to recounted speech events that are part of the told history – see 2.3.2), contributes to a taken-for-granted objectivity or factuality of the story. Even implicit and vague source attributions (common, for instance, in journalistic writing)[63] do not occur. The closest we come is in the appeal to (what is presented as) common or encyclopedic knowledge:

> Mais la France était alors gouvernée par Louis XV, <u>dont vous connaissez</u> le triste règne.   (Lavisse 1902, p. 96)
>
> [But at the time France was governed by Louis XV, whose sad rule you know.]
>
> The story of the mysterious *chupatties* <u>is well known</u>.
> (McCarthy 1908, p. 177)
>
> alarming news was reaching England of a native revolt in another part of her Dominions, a revolt <u>known to history as</u> the Indian Mutiny.
> (Synge 1908, p. 111)

On the other hand, indirect evidentiality in the form of 'inferring' is common in our sample texts. The devices used for expressing an inference are often the same as those expressing an epistemic modality, whether of the strengthening or the hedging type; e.g.:

> If, however, these acts of policy were not only justifiable but actually inevitable, none the less <u>must</u> a succession of such acts produce a profound emotion among the races in whose midst they were accomplished.
> (McCarthy 1908, p. 176)
>
> He <u>must</u> have begun to know by this time that he had no chance of establishing himself [188] as a ruler anywhere in India.
> (McCarthy 1908, pp. 188–189)
>
> His faithful lieutenant, Tantia Topee, had given orders, <u>it seems</u>, that when a trumpet sounded […].   (McCarthy 1908, p. 187)
>
> This they did, but <u>apparently</u> without doing much harm.
> (McCarthy 1908, p. 189)

Devices specific to the signaling of inference are used too:

> Les Portugais et les Espagnols possédèrent <u>alors</u> des *pays immenses hors de l'Europe*.   (Lavisse 1902, p. 66)

---

[63] E.g. of the type 'X was said to have done Y,' or in French 'X aurait Y.'

[The Portuguese and the Spanish thus possessed *vast lands outside Europe*.]

Tous sont <u>donc</u> **égaux** devant la loi.   (Lavisse 1902, p. 100)

[All are thus **equal** before the law.]

Les Chinois mangent peu, supportent bien le froid et la chaleur, et sont très économes; ils peuvent <u>donc</u> travailler partout à bien meilleur marché que les ouvriers Européens.   (Lavisse 1902, p. 155)

[The Chinese eat little, withstand the cold and the heat well, and are very thrifty; therefore they can work everywhere much more cheaply than European workers.]

<u>Thus</u>, when the rulers of *Nagpur* and of *Jhansi*, in Central India, died without direct heirs, their territories "lapsed" to the Company.
                                                            (Warner and Marten 1912, p. 690)

George Canning's son, Lord Canning, who had succeeded Dalhousie, was continued in office and was <u>thus</u> the first Governor-General in India who can be called "Viceroy."   (Fearenside 1922, p. 434)

<u>Consequently</u>, in the Mutiny, the landowners of Oudh were against the British.   (Warner and Marten 1912, p. 691)

The main conclusion we can draw from a look at the functioning of evidentiality in our data is that, while obviously there must be extensive reliance on prior sources, this dependence is not really acknowledged. Hence, except in the form of hedging, there is no real distancing from the propositional content, the truth value of which is thus stressed.

Though controversy surrounds the appropriateness of doing so, *negation* is often dealt with in conjunction with modality. After all, negating is something an utterer does with a proposition. There are, however, many negation-specific phenomena that would justify making it into a grammatical-semantic-pragmatic category in its own right (see Miestamo 2006 for an introduction). For one thing, negation is a marked form in relation to affirmative sentences. This is why (as pointed out in 2.2.1.2) a negation always evokes a voice presenting its opposite. Consider the following:

One name <u>must</u> not be forgotten among those who endured the siege of Lucknow.   (McCarthy 1908, p. 194)

So far we have been concerned with the extension of the British control in India, but it <u>must not be supposed that</u> the efforts of British rulers were not directed to bettering the lot of their subjects.
                                                            (Warner and Marten 1912, p. 690)

Yet the heroism of British soldiers <u>must not lead us to forget</u> the services of those natives who were loyal.   (Warner and Marten 1912, p. 693)

These negative prescriptions suggest that under normal circumstances there would be a good chance of 'forgetting' (or, in fact, ignoring) a name considered important by the author, or the fact that there were loyal Indians as well as rebels, and of 'supposing' that the British rulers were not interested in the lot of their subjects (the latter thus placing another negative within the scope of the negative prescription). What is involved here is the dialogic property of (even 'mono-logic') discourse, making use of the ability to negate or deny, one of the basic language-related human capacities. Note how this relates to what was identified (in Thesis 1.1) as a property of ideological meaning, namely its being rarely questioned. What negations of the above type do is to present a point of view which the author assumes could be somehow 'questioned' (by way of forgetting or ignoring or, more directly, by way of supposing the opposite). From the point of view of a study of ideology, therefore, it is interesting to look at precisely what meanings negation is used to try and prevent.

Equally interesting is the low frequency of occurrence of negation in our corpus (as also pointed out in 2.2.1.2). Again this contributes to the creation of an impression of factuality: Not very much of what is communicated is presented as open to dispute. The evocation of the opposite often serves merely the function of rhetorical contrast. Consider

> Car le gouvernement anglais a l'habitude de *ne pas tracasser les colons anglais, et de ne pas se mêler de leurs affaires.*   (Lavisse 1902, p. 97)

> [Since the English government usually *does not harass the* English *colonists*, and *does not mingle in their affairs*.]

which introduces an episode in which, straying from this habit, the British government did mingle too much in the affairs of colonists in North America by levying heavy taxes, which then led to the fight for independence. In many cases, therefore, a clause with 'not' is followed by one introduced with 'but.' As said elsewhere, contrasts are always interesting to look at.[64]

Ad 3.3.5:
[And still at the sentence level: What is the calibration between given, new, and accessible information, and between highlighting/foregrounding and backgrounding?]

Sentence-level information structuring is most commonly looked at in terms of the givenness vs. the newness of information. Gundel and Fretheim (2002) make a useful distinction between referential givenness/newness and relational givenness/newness. *Referential givenness/newness* pertains to the relation between a linguistic expression and a non-linguistic entity (whether in the language user's

---

[64] When investigating different, especially spoken, types of discourse, the pragmatics of negation is more complex. For a quick review, see Miestamo (2006); for a more detailed account, see e.g. Horn (1989).

mind, the discourse, or a real or a possible world).[65] For 'reference' to be successful, all referring expressions must show a certain degree of referential givenness or accessibility. Consider the following sentence:

> The main incidents in the struggle were the massacre of Cawnpore and the sieges of Delhi and Lucknow.   (Fearenside 1922, p. 433)

Here "the struggle" refers to the Indian Mutiny, uniquely identifiable from the preceding paragraph in the same text. What the sentence brings into focus is "The main incidents in the struggle"; they are clearly identifiable as types; world knowledge tells the reader that any armed struggle must have incidents, and that some are more important or decisive than others. Both "the massacre of Cawnpore" and "the sieges of Delhi and Lucknow" provide new information; there is no real referential givenness yet, but accessibility is assured, partly by what a reader can imagine terms such as "massacre" and "siege" in a warlike context to cover, partly by the ensuing text which briefly describes the events referred to. In other words, referential givenness/newness relates what is said to the audience's assumed background knowledge and/or information still to be provided. To the extent that background knowledge is appealed to, elements of what is taken for granted may come in, making the phenomenon of referential givenness relevant for ideology research. (There is also a link here with the phenomenon of presupposition, further to be explained in 3.4.1.)

Relational givenness/newness, on the other hand, distinguishes what a sentence is about (the 'given' part X, often coinciding with what could be called the 'theme' or 'topic') from what is predicated about X (i.e., the 'new information' or Y, the 'rheme' or 'comment').[66] Y is new in relation to X. Quoting Gundel and Fretheim (2002), "Relational givenness/newness thus reflects how the informational content of a particular event or state of affairs expressed by a sentence is represented and how its truth value is to be assessed." Needless to say, this is a phenomenon central to a sentence's contribution to discursive meaning generation, in which the utterer's choices are important (while the referential givenness status of a linguistic expression is more dependent on the interpreter). Consider the following sentences:

> One reason why the Second Chinese War dragged on so long was the preoccupation of British forces in India.   (Fearenside 1922, p. 433)

> Before the war with China had gone far, the country was startled by the news of a mutiny among the Bengal sepoys in India.   (Ransome 1910, p. 442)

---

[65] The distinction is borrowed from Gundel, Hedberg and Zacharski (1993), where a 'givenness hierarchy' (in focus > activated > familiar > uniquely identifiable > referential > type identifiable) is proposed and explained in detail.

[66] Note that terms such as 'given,' 'theme,' 'topic' on the one hand, and 'new,' 'rheme,' 'comment' (to which could be added 'focus') on the other, do not fully overlap. Details of the way in which they are used in the linguistic literature are not crucial for present purposes. I will, therefore, restrict myself to using only the contrast 'given/new,' in those terms.

Both authors start from the givenness of the ongoing war with China (framed in slightly different ways) as a background against which the new information of events in India is introduced. In the new information part, India is specified clearly in both cases, but the nature of the events to be reported on is kept vague in Fearenside (suggesting only that they were such as to form a "preoccupation" for British forces), while Ransome summarizes the entire situation (news that startled "the country," a mutiny, Bengal sepoys as perpetrators).

The specific choices that are made within the two structures that show a strong parallelism in terms of a givenness/newness articulation score different effects in terms of *highlighting* or *foregrounding* and *backgrounding*.[67] While keeping the new information vague, merely anticipating further details and thus rousing the reader's curiosity, Fearenside draws attention to a specific aspect of the war with China, namely that it "dragged on so long" (an element already emphasized in a preceding part of the text), and by using as opening words "One reason why" he highlights or foregrounds the explanatory power of the events he is about to tell for another event. In the process, nothing gets really backgrounded. Ransome, on the other hand, merely uses the Chinese war as background to situate the events in India historically (suggesting only that the war with China had just begun), thus literally backgrounding it and bringing India clearly into the foreground.

Close attention is required to the types of contrast introduced by highlighting and backgrounding, as well as to the systematicity with which some things are handled as given and others are introduced as new.

AD 3.3.6, IN GENERAL:
[At the suprasentential level: How is coherence/relevance established?]

Devices for structuring information at the sentence level are building blocks for the meaning generation work utterers set out to do at the suprasentential discourse level. The organizational principles handled at that higher level, making use of sequencing principles (see 2.3.3) and all the devices for establishing contextual cohesion (see 2.3.4), may be captured with the labels coherence and relevance.[68]

Pertinent questions include: What does the overall message of a piece of analyzed discourse look like? How does the discourse 'build' the message? What distinguishable and significant parts is it composed of? How do these parts hang together, i.e., how do they 'cohere'? What is the relevance of one in relation to the others? Answers to such questions search for the 'why?' behind topical choices. We must keep in mind, however, that it is not just utterers' intentions we are after, but primarily likely effects at the level of conveyable meaning.

[67] For the notion of 'grounding,' see Wårvik (2006).
[68] A basic introduction to the notions of cohesion and coherence is to be found in Bublitz (1998). In this book I am using an everyday notion of relevance, not the technical notion it is within relevance theory (see Blakemore 1995, Wilson 2010).

A_D 3.3.6.1:

[What discourse topics are established?]

Table 4, with its overview of distinguishable events in the story of the Mutiny, gives part of the answer to this question. But topics, of course, are not restricted to events. By way of illustration, consider Fearenside again:

> [1] **537. Causes of the Indian Mutiny, 1857**. – [2] One reason why the Second Chinese War dragged on so long was the preoccupation of British forces in India. [3] There Dalhousie's annexations had caused considerable anxiety and vexation among the native princes; [4] recent land settlements had annoyed the larger landowners, especially in Oudh, by favoring the actual cultivators of the soil; [5] and religious prejudices had been offended by the equipment of the native sepoys with rifles which required greased cartridges. [6] Those who cherished these and other grievances thought that they had a good opportunity for vengeance in the fact that the British troops in India were few and scattered. [7] The discontent was most widespread in the native regiments in the North-West Provinces; [8] and in May 1857 some of these, stationed at Meerut, broke out in open mutiny, shot their officers, and stirred up similar mutinies in the neighbouring camps. [9] Bengal and the greater part of the Madras and Bombay Presidencies kept quiet; [10] and the Sikhs of the Punjab had been so well used by Sir John Lawrence that they helped the British.
>
> [11] The main incidents in the struggle were the massacre of Cawnpore and the sieges of Delhi and Lucknow. [12] [...]
>
> (Fearenside 1922, p. 433; numbering of propositions added)

A simple list of the topics brought up in this extract would include at least the following:

[1], [3]–[6]:	*causes* of the Mutiny
[2]:	the Second Chinese War
[2]:	preoccupations of British forces
[2], [8]–[12]:	the Mutiny
[3]:	local reaction to annexations
[4]:	local reaction to land settlements
[5]:	reaction to the new rifles
[6]–[7], [9]–[10]:	*circumstances/properties* of the Mutiny
[6]:	low presence of British troops as opportunity
[7]:	spread of the discontent
[8], [11]–[12]:	*events* of the Mutiny
[8]:	start of the Mutiny
[9]:	non-participation in Bengal, Madras, Bombay
[10]:	support from the Sikhs – result of good government
[11]–[11]:	further events

Of course, such topics do not occur as a mere list. They are related to each other in a variety of ways.

A<small>D</small> 3.3.6.2:

[How do central discourse topics relate to peripheral ones?]

In the above Fearenside (1922) extract, the *Indian Mutiny* is clearly the central discourse topic, its treatment falling apart into *causes* and *events* (even if the title in boldface refers to causes only, in contrast to results, on which the next numbered section of the book concentrates), but also *circumstances/properties*. In the wider structure of the book, this topic is subsidiary to the general issue of *British war efforts in the middle of the nineteenth century*, from the Crimean War (1853–1856, concluded with the Peace of Paris in 1856), via the Persian War (1856) and the Second Chinese War (1856–1860) – qualified as "a somewhat dragging war" (p. 432) – to the Indian Mutiny, all of which the category 'preoccupations of the British forces' in [2] would be applicable to.

In this extract, the only two topics that are peripheral to the central one(s), are (i) the Second Chinese War, brought in in [2], where at the sentential level it is somehow highlighted (as explained in 3.3.5), and (ii) the suggestion of good government that is supposed to explain the support from the Sikhs. Nothing else in the extract can be said to be peripheral, which means that it is a topically well-focused piece of text. There is, however, a distinction between the central topics and the subtopics, including the individual causes, circumstances/properties, and events.

There is a significant amount of variation in the way in which the different texts in the sample corpus handle topics. Longer accounts of the Mutiny allow for the insertion of more peripheral topics or digressions. They are able, for instance, to expand on aspects of the climate, structural properties of cities and fortifications, details of (British) heroism and suffering, often going beyond the main story line while still underscoring it. Looking at these in detail, rather clear patterns emerge, as it is usually the same types of information that are used for digressions.

Variability is also to be found in the foregrounding or backgrounding of subtopics and, also at that level, patterns emerge. For instance, the events in Cawnpore are an absolute favorite for expanding upon.

A<small>D</small> 3.3.6.3:

[What does the discourse progresssion or rhetorical structure look like (in terms of relations such as juxtaposition, justification, explanation, proving, elaborating, motivating, etc.)?]

The topical progression of the above extract from Fearenside (1922) can be described as follows.

[1]   as title of section 537, *contrasts* causes of the Indian Mutiny with its
           results, described in the following section (538)

[2]   *situates* the Indian Mutiny in the context of a superordinate discourse topic, the British war efforts in the middle of the nineteenth century, and frames the entire episode, somewhat euphemistically categorized as "the preoccupation of British forces in India," as an *explanation* for why another event in the wider context "dragged on so long."

[3]   zooms in on India ("there") and starts an *enumeration* of causes

[3]   local reaction ("considerable anxiety and vexation among the native princes") to annexations (by Dalhousie)

[4]   local reaction ("annoyed the larger landowners") to "recent land settlements", for which an *explanation* is offered: the land settlements favored "the actual cultivators of the soil"

[5]   reaction ("religious prejudices had been offended") to "the equipment of the native sepoys with rifles which required greased cartridges"

[6]   makes a *transition* from causes to circumstances: the low numbers of British troops in India provides a context that may itself also have served as a trigger ("a good opportunity for vengeance") for "those who cherished these and other grievances"; at the same time, [6] *summarizes* the enumerated causes (only *juxtaposed* in [3] to [5]) with the label "grievances," and reference to "other grievances" turns the enumeration of causes into an open-ended list of *examples*

[7]   *elaborates* on circumstances by describing the spread of the "discontent" (used as an equivalent for "grievances") that caused the Mutiny

[8]   opens with "and," *conjoining* information on causes and circumstances with their result, and it describes the start of the Mutiny as a string of *juxtaposed but sequentially related* subevents: "broke out in open mutiny," "shot their officers," "stirred up similar mutinies in the neighbouring camps"

[9] and [10] further *elaborate* on circumstances, singling out two aspects that *contrast* with the spread of the discontent described in [7]

[9]   Bengal, Madras, and Bombay mostly "kept quiet"

[10]   the Sikhs of Punjab "helped the British," which is *explained* by their having been "so well used by Sir John Lawrence"

[11]   switches the focus to events following the start of the Mutiny, and *enumerates* the "main incidents," which are then individually *elaborated* upon in [12].

Making rhetorical links explicit in this way helps us to observe important aspects of the meaning generating potential of a stretch of discourse. Just a few observations in passing:

–   The 'framing' of the episode, as in [2], detracts from the importance of the Indian Mutiny in its own right; the importance of the event is defined in terms of its effect on the war with China, and (in section 538) its function as a trigger to implement measures (such as the reorganization of the Indian Army and the transfer of Indian administration from the East India Company to the British Crown) which were needed anyway and which had already been contemplated before.

– The explanation offered for the "annoyance" of "the larger landowners" (in [4]) serves – as pointed out before – as justification for the land settlements (which are not further specified, neither in this extract, nor elsewhere in the book).

– Since land settlements were justified, the negative Indian reaction was not; in contrast to [4] it is interesting to observe that there does not even seem to be any need for explanation or justification in [3] and [5]; Dalhousie's annexations are taken for granted (as they were justified earlier in the book as "made partly for purposes of frontier defense and partly to secure better government," p. 427); and the negative reaction to the new cartridges is not deemed worthy of any explanation (how can "greased cartridges," as such, be objectionable?) as it can be reduced to "religious prejudices."

Such aspects of a text allow us to look at general patterns of argumentation or global meaning constructs that are left largely implicit.

Often it suffices to observe very simple patterns such as parallelism, repetition, juxtaposition, and sequential ordering. Using juxtaposition and sequential ordering as an example, see how they are mobilized by Lavisse (1902) – in two parallel and almost repetitious episodes – to establish the relationship between violent action and colonization (which is ignored in the categorization of colonization as a work of peace in his Preface):

> […] 7. Les Mexicains n'avaient jamais vu ni Européens ni chevaux; ils prirent les *hommes blancs* pour des fils du Dieu-Soleil, les reçurent avec honneur et les laissèrent entrer à Mexico (fig. 5).
>
> 8. Les Espagnols en profitèrent pour s'emparer des trésors du roi; les Mexicains se révoltèrent, et plus de 100 000 guerriers vinrent assiéger Cortez, qui pourtant finit par les vaincre. 9. Le dernier roi fut mis sur des charbons ardents, et le Mexique devint une *colonie espagnole* (1521).   (p. 65)

> [[…] 7. The Mexicans had never seen Europeans or horses; they took the *white men* for sons of the Sun-God, received them with honor and let them enter Mexico (fig. 5).
>
> 8. The Spanish took advantage of this to grab the king's treasures; the Mexicans revolted, and more than 100,000 warriors came to besiege Cortez, who still managed to defeat them. 9. The last king was put on hot coals, and Mexico became a *Spanish colony* (1521).]

> 1. Une autre bande espagnole, commandée par **Pizarre**, entra dans le Pérou et prit le roi (1529). 2. On le força à payer pour sa rançon une *chambre pleine d'or*, puis on l'étrangla. 3. Et le Pérou fut *conquis par les Espagnols*.
>
> (p. 66)

[**1**. Another Spanish unit, commanded by Pizarro, entered Peru and captured the king (1529). **2**. They forced him to pay a *room full of gold* as ransom, then they strangled him. **3**. And Peru was *conquered by the Spanish.*]

As could be expected on the basis of the activity type (see 3.1), a noticeable amount of attention goes to the explaining of events, albeit in a very elementary way. Look at Lavisse's (1902) explanation for slavery:

> **2**. Les Espagnols qui allaient en Amérique étaient presque tous des *aventuriers* féroces*. **3**. Ils voulaient se procurer *de l'argent* et ils *forçaient les habitants du pays* à travailler dans les mines, les tourmentaient, les faisaient chasser par leurs chiens. Les habitants mouraient tous.
>
> **4**. On envoya alors acheter des nègres en Afrique, on les ramenait en Amérique où on les faisait travailler comme **esclaves**. **5**. Ce commerce inhumain s'appelait la **traite des noirs**.   (Lavisse 1902, p. 68)

> [**2**. The Spaniards who went to America were almost all *fierce adventurers.**
> **3**. They wanted to gain *money* and they *forced the inhabitants of the country* to work in the mines, they tormented them, and had them chased by their dogs. The inhabitants all died.
>
> **4**. They then sent for negroes to be bought in Africa, they brought them back to America where they made them work as **slaves**. **5**. This inhuman trade was called the **slave trade** [literally: "trade of blacks"].]

Explanations usually carry an evaluation with them. The point of view from which this passage is written is one that no longer takes the slave trade as an acceptable practice. The fact that it emerged in the context of colonization thus again creates some tension with the positive view Lavisse espouses of colonization in general. This passage also gives a clue as to how Lavisse manages to escape from a looming contradiction. Slavery is presented, as are the feats of Cortez and Pizarro, as a historical past that no longer has an essential link with his colonial present.

AD 3.3.7:

[In a wider corpus: How do discourse topics and rhetorical patterns develop/change across the different parts of the corpus?]

Since we are not working with a single extended corpus, rhetorical pattern development is hardly an issue.[69] A few hints can be given here, however, of types of phenomena to look at. In particular, it is interesting to see how certain connections do *not* get established in a wider discourse context. Thus Lavisse (1902, p. 99) elaborates on the 1789 French Declaration of the Rights of Man as meant not only for the French ("les droits que doivent avoir non seulement les Français")

[69] By way of contrast, it would be most interesting, for instance, to study the way in which the Belgian migrant debate (as analyzed in Blommaert and Verschueren 1998) has developed and changed over the past ten to fifteen years. A usable corpus would be easy to compose in which transformations of rhetorical patterns could be traced.

but for all other peoples ("tous les autres peuples"). Still the need for colonial possessions, necessarily implying control over other people, is taken for granted, while the link with the "inhuman" practice of the slave trade is properly made and its abolishment is proudly presented as a French achievement:

> **5.** Les *Français avaient donné l'exemple* en 1789, en abolissant l'esclavage.
> **6.** Mais les colons disaient qu'on ne pouvait se passer de nègres pour cultiver le coton et le café, et ils avaient fait rétablir l'esclavage.
> **7.** Les Français l'ont aboli de nouveau en 1848, et tous les autres Européens les ont imités.   (Lavisse 1902, p. 122)

> [**5.** The *French had set the example* in 1789, by abolishing slavery. **6.** But the colonists said they could not manage without the negroes to cultivate cotton and coffee, and they had slavery re-established.
> **7.** The French abolished it again in 1848, and all other Europeans followed their example.]

Similarly, some of the British textbooks take pride in the increasing establishment of democratic principles at home. Rhetorically, the ideas are sometimes presented as if fully extended to subjects in various parts of the empire:

> But the most important thing to be noted about the [4] British Empire is that it is not an Empire in the old-fashioned sense of the word, that is to say, a number of races and peoples held together, largely by force, under a strong centralised government. It is rather an association of peoples united by their common love of liberty, justice, and self-government, and by political institutions which protect their rights against attack from within and without [...] As we shall show later, the people, first of England and later of the rest of the Empire, have been safe and prosperous just in proportion as they were faithful to the ideals and principles upon which their Commonwealth was founded. And the history of the Empire is largely concerned with the growth of freedom and self-government within its boundaries, and with the attempts of less free and progressive peoples to interfere with that freedom and to prevent it spreading over the world.
>
> (Kerr and Kerr 1927, pp. 4–5)

This general view of the British Empire brackets all the stories of war and violence, even though they are fully told. Conceptually, the contradiction is evaded by defining violence as a necessary evil if subjects do not faithfully accept the ideals and principles that are provided for them.

In Lavisse there is also a noticeable contrast between the cursory way in which the 'taking' of colonies is described, and the pains it takes to explain that expansion in Europe by France after the French Revolution was subject to the consent of the people involved:

> Les Français n'avaient pas fait toutes ces guerres pour agrandir leur territoire. Ils se contentèrent d'annexer* à la [103] France la *Savoie*, la *Belgique*, et la *rive gauche du Rhin*, après avoir demandé aux habitants de ces pays *s'ils consentaient à devenir Français*.   (Lavisse, 1902, pp. 103–104)

> [The French had not conducted all these wars to enlarge their territory. They were satisfied with the annexation* to France of *Savoy*, *Belgium*, and the *left bank of the Rhine*, after having asked the inhabitants of those countries *whether they consented to becoming French.*

All other European conquests are presented as having been made to free the people, i.e., to establish republics. Napoleon is then presented as a later aberration, disrespecting the French constitution.

Procedure 3.4: *Look systematically for carriers of implicit meaning. In particular:*

3.4.1: *Find presupposition-carrying expressions and constructions (e.g., definite descriptions, change-of-state verbs, factive verbs, implicative verbs, cleft constructions, scalar notions).*

3.4.2: *Find logical implications and entailments.*

3.4.3: *Find implicatures.*

3.4.4: *Investigate tropes, i.e., cases of simile, metonymy, metaphor, irony, overstatement and understatement, rhetorical questions (as well as cases of humor, politeness, and the like).*

AD 3.4, IN GENERAL:

[Look systematically for carriers of implicit meaning.]

If ideological meaning is defined (cf. Thesis 1.2) as often being carried along implicitly rather than to be formulated explicitly (though there is always an interaction between the explicit and the implicit), screening different types of carriers of implicit meaning in the discourse under investigation is of central importance to empirical ideology research – bearing in mind the need for counterscreening as soon as one is inclined to draw conclusions from the observed data (see Rule 1).

AD 3.4.1:

[Find presupposition-carrying expressions and constructions (e.g., definite descriptions, change-of-state verbs, factive verbs, implicative verbs, cleft constructions, scalar notions).]

The most ubiquitous type of presupposition is what is usually called 'existential presupposition.'[70] A sentence such as

> The main incidents in the struggle were the massacre of Cawnpore and the sieges of Delhi and Lucknow.   (Fearenside 1922, p. 433)

---

[70] For an introduction to the topic of presupposition, see Bertuccelli Papi (1997) and Delogu (2007). An extremely useful list of types of presupposition triggers is to be found in Levinson (1983, pp. 181–185).

presupposes the 'existence' (or possible referential substantiation – which makes the notion akin to, though not identical with, 'referential givenness' as discussed in 3.3.5) of

–   a specific struggle
–   incidents in that struggle
–   the main incidents in that struggle
–   cities called Cawnpore (present-day Kanpur), Delhi, and Lucknow
–   the massacre of Cawnpore
–   the siege of Delhi
–   the siege of Lucknow

Such presuppositions have to be satisfied – i.e., the corresponding entities or events must exist or have occurred at a given time and/or place – for the sentences in which they occur to be 'meaningful.' This does not mean that a reader, or even an author, of our textbook samples is necessarily able to identify, describe, ascertain such 'existence' or 'occurrence'; there are just too many people, places, and events mentioned for such personal knowledge to be possible. But it is one of the assumptions behind a history textbook as activity type that none of the entities or events talked about is fantasized. In other words, an entire world, not accessible to individual observation, is assumed to be there for the historian to talk about. This does not imply that one should not be attentive to factual errors at the level of existential presuppositions. More important, however, is the observation that the typical function of presuppositions, which is to ground an utterance in assumed shared knowledge, is systematically deviated from in texts of this kind: Most of the entities or events that figure in definite descriptions, thus presupposing their 'existence,' are not familiar to the average intended reader. In other words, what is formally presupposed is in fact new information. Sometimes this new information is subsequently provided with further substance, as when "the preoccupation of British forces in India" (in [2] of Fearenside's section 537) introduces a topic that is then expanded upon. But in many cases the "information" remains at the level of a mere assumption of "existence," as when "the larger landowners" contrasted with "the actual cultivators of the soil" (in [4] of the same extract) suggests a social structure that is not further explained, or when "the neighbouring camps" (in [8]) are nowhere specified.

Different types of presuppositions are triggered by a variety of lexical items and grammatical forms. An extremely common type consists of the verbs of motion that reflect the military-strategic preoccupations of the narrative: Leaving X presupposes prior presence in X, entering X presupposes prior presence outside X, returning to X presupposes both absence from and earlier presence in/ at X. Here is a brief overview of other types, with examples from the corpus (in which presupposition triggers are underlined):

> It was unfortunate [...] that *Lord Canning* [...] [690] [...] was not made aware of the peculiar conditions of land tenure in Oudh, and that his subordinates

aroused the hostility of the great landowners in that province by a settlement of the land which did the landed aristocracy grievous injustice.

(Warner and Marten 1912, pp. 690–691)

→ 'Aware of' presupposes the factuality of what follows.

Outram was content to remain quiescent, <u>knowing</u> when he entered Lucknow <u>that</u> Delhi, the heart and centre of the rebellion, had already fallen.

(Low and Sanders 1910, p. 148)

Therefore in the opening days of 1857, it was <u>known</u> among the native populations of India <u>that</u> the East India Company was at war with Persia <u>and that</u> England had on her hands a [176] quarrel with China.

(McCarthy 1908, pp. 176–177)

They did not <u>know of</u> the help even now approaching.

(Synge 1908, p. 116)

When the sepoys <u>realised</u> their strength, [...].

(Kerr and Kerr 1927, p. 183)

He was worn with deep anxiety, for he <u>realised</u> as no other Indian official how deep-seated was the discontent of the Sepoys.   (Synge 1908, p. 118)

The Mohammedan and the Hindoo <u>forgot</u> their own religious antipathies to join against the Christian.   (McCarthy 1908, p. 170)

D'ailleurs presque personne ne <u>comprenait que</u> *les colonies sont nécessaires à une nation.*   (Lavisse 1902, p. 96)

[Besides, almost no one understood that *colonies are necessary for a nation.*]

→ "Knowing" and "known" presuppose the factuality of what is within the scope of "that" (in contrast, e.g., to 'thinking,' which does not carry such a presupposition). Similarly, "know of" presupposes that there was really help on its way and "realised" presupposes the reality of the sepoys' strength (in Kerr and Kerr) and the deep-seatedness of their discontent (in Synge), just as "forgot" presupposes a more usual context of mutual religious antipathies. And "comprenait que" presupposes the truth of the following proposition.

Yet the telegraph operator had first <u>managed</u> to flash half his warning message through to the Panjab; and the Europeans had <u>succeeded</u> in blowing up the arsenal.   (Innes 1927, p. 170)

The troops sent up from the coast just <u>managed</u> to secure Benares and Allahábád [...].   (Low and Sanders 1910, p. 143)

Nana Sahib himself <u>managed</u> to escape [...].

(Low and Sanders 1910, p. 152)

Après la grande guerre civile de 1865, ils avaient une dette de 20 milliards, qu'ils <u>sont arrivés à</u> payer.   (Lavisse 1902, p. 163)

[After the great civil war of 1865, they had a debt of 20 billion, which they managed to pay.]

Les Espagnols en profitèrent pour s'emparer des trésors du roi; les Mexicains se révoltèrent, et plus de 100 000 guerriers vinrent assiéger Cortez, qui pourtant <u>finit par</u> les vaincre.   (Lavisse 1902, p. 65)

[The Spanish took advantage of this to grab the king's treasures; the Mexicans revolted, and more than 100,000 warriors came to besiege Cortez, who still managed to defeat them.]

Il <u>parvint</u> enfin <u>à</u> décider le roi d'Espagne à lui donner trois mauvais navires.
(Lavisse 1902, p. 64)

[At last he managed to persuade the king of Spain to give him three bad ships.]

Ils <u>réussirent à</u> reprendre l'Inde [...]."   (Lavisse 1902, p. 152)

[They succeeded in regaining control over India [...].]

→ "Managed," "succeeded," "sont arrivés à," "finit par," "parvint à," and "réussirent à" all presuppose that the subjects of the sentences tried to do what they are said to have done, and that it may not have been easy.

<u>As it happened</u>, Sir John Lawrence was then away at Rawul Pindee, in the Upper Punjaub [...].   (McCarthy 1908, p. 179)

The English themselves began to show a perplexing kind of aggressive enterprise, and took to making little sallies in small numbers indeed, but with astonishing effect, on any bodies of Sepoys who <u>happened to be</u> anywhere near.   (McCarthy 1908, p. 186)

→ 'Happened' presupposes the absence of conscious planning in relation to the relevant circumstances.

5. Ce commerce inhumain s'appelait la **traite des noirs**. 6. Les Espagnols l'<u>avaient commencé</u> en 1517 [...].   (Lavisse 1902, p. 68)

[5. This inhuman trade was called the **slave trade** [literally: 'trade of blacks']. 6. The Spanish had started it in 1517 [...].]

11. Le directeur de la Compagnie française, **Dupleix**, <u>avait commencé à</u> conquérir les Indes. [...] [93] [...]
     [...] 3. Alors les Anglais <u>commencèrent</u> eux-mêmes à conquérir [94] les Indes.   (Lavisse 1902, pp. 93–95)

[11. The director of the French Company, **Dupleix**, had started to conquer India. [...] [93] [...]
     [...] 3. Then the English started to conquer [94] India themselves.]

et les Hindous <u>commencent à</u> parler anglais et à adopter les usages des Anglais.   (Lavisse 1902, p. 152)

[and the Hindus begin to speak English and to adopt English customs.]

and the first Sikh war <u>began</u>.   (Low and Sanders 1910, p. 133)

Rangoon <u>became</u> the capital of British Burma, and <u>began</u> to make a rapid advance towards its present standard of population and prosperity.

(Low and Sanders 1910, p. 134)

A mutinous spirit <u>began</u> to spread itself abroad.

(McCarthy 1908, p. 171)

A section among the native Indians <u>began</u> to demand some share in the government of the country [...].   (Richardson 1924, p. 141)

His troops were <u>growing tired</u> and <u>began</u> to drag behind.

(Synge 1908, p. 123)

But the loyal sepoys were <u>beginning</u> to lose heart [...].

(Innes 1927, p. 171)

➔ All underlined verb forms indicate a change of state; in particular, they presuppose that what is beginning to be done or to take place was not done or did not take place before.

Depuis le XVIIIe siècle, les libéraux réclamaient qu'on <u>rendit</u> la liberté à ces nègres et qu'on <u>cessât</u> d'en acheter de nouveaux.

(Lavisse 1902, p. 122)

[From the 18th century on, liberals demanded that liberty be given back to these negroes and that new ones would no longer be bought.]

It was resolved that the Company's control should <u>cease</u>, and the government of India should be <u>transferred</u> to the Crown.

(Innes 1927, p. 172)

The use of the cartridges complained of was <u>discontinued</u> by orders issued in January 1857.   (McCarthy 1908, p. 171)

➔ Here again the underlined verb forms indicate a change of state, presupposing liberty that had been taken away before, earlier practices of buying slaves, prior control of the East India Company over India, and earlier use of a certain type of cartridge.

Ils <u>augmentent sans cesse</u> et on ne sait si un jour les Chinois n'occuperont pas l'Océanie et la moitié de l'Amérique.   (Lavisse 1902, p. 155)

[Their numbers keep growing and one does not know whether one day the Chinese won't occupy Oceania and half of America.]

Lord Canning [...] <u>was continued</u> in office [...].

(Fearenside 1922, p. 434)

Havelock was enabled to <u>continue</u> his victorious march [...].

(McCarthy 1908, p. 192)

➔ A continuation of a process, condition, or activity presupposes that it had already started.

Puis ils détruisirent les colonies françaises (1763), et ils devinrent les **maîtres de l'Inde**. Ils le sont <u>encore</u>.   (Lavisse 1902, p. 95)

[Then they destroyed the French colonies (1763), and they became the **masters of India**. They still are.]

Songez pourtant qu'<u>encore</u> aujourd'hui presque tous les peuples de l'Orient [...] *vivent sous un régime arbitraire.* *   (Lavisse 1902, p. 100)

[Yet, know that still today almost all the peoples of the Orient *live under arbitrary* regimes*.]

La France <u>ne</u> conduit <u>plus</u>, comme auparavant, les destinées de l'Europe [...].   (Lavisse 1902, p. 98)

[France no longer drives, like before, the destinies of Europe [...].]

→ The adverb "encore" presupposes a pre-existent state of affairs which continues, while "ne ... plus" presupposes an earlier state of affairs that has ceased.

Meanwhile the Chinese war was also apparently brought to a satisfactory conclusion [...] It broke out <u>again,</u> however, [...].   (Innes 1927, p. 172)

On July 13 Havelock's first battle was won at Fatehpur, where the rebels were scattered, losing eleven of their guns; and they were <u>again</u> defeated in two actions on the 15th.   (Low and Sanders 1910, p. 146)

We have only to <u>repeat</u> here, that as a matter of fact no indignities, other than that of the compulsory corn-grinding, were put upon the English ladies.
      (McCarthy 1908, p. 188)

The same scenes of murder were <u>repeated</u> at Delhi [...].
      (Richardson 1924, p. 137)

→ Both the adverb "again" and the iterative verb "repeat" presuppose earlier occurrence of what is described; more specifically, "we have only to repeat here" presupposes that what is about to be said has been said before (in this case not in the same text, but in a wider world of discourse).

<u>Avant d</u>'avoir la boussole, les marins n'osaient pas s'éloigner des côtes.
      (Lavisse 1902, p. 64)

[Before they had the compass, seamen did not dare to move away from the coasts.]

Mais <u>depuis qu</u>'on a creusé le *canal de Suez* <u>et que</u> beaucoup de marchands européens se sont établis au Caire et à Alexandrie [...].
      (Lavisse 1902, p. 128)

[But since the *Suez Canal* was dug and many European merchants have established themselves in Cairo and Alexandria [...].]

It seems that some cartridges lubricated with the objectionable composition had actually passed into the hands of the troops <u>before</u> the issue was checked by the authorities.   (Low and Sanders 1910, p. 138)

a sepoy attacked the adjutant, <u>while</u> his comrades looked on and some even assisted him.   (Low and Sanders 1910, p. 139)

it was just a hundred years <u>since</u> the battle of Plassy was fought.
(Richardson 1924, p. 136)

➔ The temporal clauses introduced with "avant de," "depuis que," "before," "while," and "since" presuppose that now seamen have compasses, that the Suez Canal has been dug and that European merchants have moved to Egypt, that the issue of the cartridges was indeed investigated by the authorities, that the sepoy's comrades were looking on and assisted him, and that the battle of Plassy did take place.

<u>C'était la première fois qu</u>'on faisait le *tour du monde*.
(Lavisse 1902, p. 65)

[It was the first time that a *trip around the world* was made.]

<u>It was not</u>, however, <u>till September that</u> the force on the Delhi Ridge had been sufficiently strengthened to make an attack on the city.
(Innes 1927, p. 171)

➔ The underscored temporal clauses bring in the subsequent propositions by way of presupposition.

it was <u>Canning who</u> suggested the transfer.
(Low and Sanders 1910, p. 143)

<u>It was to Nana Sahib</u>, then, <u>that</u> poor old Sir Hugh Wheeler in the hour of his distress applied for assistance.   (McCarthy 1908, p. 184)

<u>Ce sont les Chinois</u> qui ont construit les chemins de fer de l'Amérique [...].
(Lavisse 1902, p. 155)

[It is the Chinese who constructed the American railroads [...].]

➔ The first of these cleft sentences presupposes that someone suggested the transfer, the second that Wheeler turned to someone for assistance, the third that someone built railroads in America.

Les Européens la [la boussole] connaissent <u>aussi</u> [...].
(Lavisse 1902, p. 64)

[The Europeans were familiar with it [the compass] also [...].]

Les Russes se sont avancés <u>aussi</u> au sud de la Sibérie.
(Lavisse 1902, p. 154)

[The Russians have also moved south of Siberia.]

Outside the Ganges basin, the sepoys in the districts to the south and southwest of Agra <u>also</u> revolted.   (Innes 1927, p. 170)

Meanwhile the Chinese war was <u>also</u> apparently brought to a satisfactory conclusion [...].   (Innes 1927, p. 172)

Hewitt was incapable of giving a decisive order; Archdale Wilson, his brigadier, was weighed down by the responsibility of protecting the stores and residents at Meerut, and he <u>too</u> kept the troops inactive.

(Low and Sanders 1910, p. 140)

➔ In these sentences, "aussi" and "also" presuppose that others (in addition to the Europeans) were familiar with the compass, that the Russians had advanced elsewhere, that sepoys inside the Ganges basin had revolted, and that other wars had been brought to a satisfactory conclusion. Similarly, "too" presupposes that not only Wilson keep the troops inactive.

others, on the way to the China War, had been diverted to help in the <u>much more serious</u> emergency in India.   (Innes 1927, p. 171)

The administration of this veteran soldier was <u>no more peaceful than</u> that of his predecessor [...].   (Low and Sanders 1910, p. 133)

Another annexation which attracted <u>more</u> attention at the time was that of Oudh.   (Low and Sanders 1910, p. 134)

It was arranged that [...] a <u>better</u> system of government should be established.   (Synge 1908, p. 124)

<u>Stranger still</u>, their blind indifference to the portents about them was shared by many of the officers commanding the native regiments [...].

(Low and Sanders 1910, p. 139)

➔ These comparative constructions presuppose that the China War was a serious emergency, that the predecessor's administration was not peaceful, that other annexations also attracted attention, that there was already a good (though improvable) system of government, and that something else has just been said that could also be a source of surprise.

Les États-Unis, <u>qui n'ont pas de voisins à redouter</u>, n'ont pas besoin d'une armée.   (Lavisse 1902, p. 163)

[The United States, which has no neighbors to fear, does not need an army.]

Many of the *tálukdárs*, or revenue collectors, <u>who exercised ownership rights over the villages</u>, were dispossessed.   (Low and Sanders 1910, p. 138)

➔ The non-restrictive relative clauses contain presupposed information.

But the loyal sepoys were beginning to lose heart, in the belief that the defence was hopeless; and, <u>if no relief had arrived before the end of the month</u>, they would probably have marched out.   (Innes 1927, p. 171)

➔ The counterfactual conditional presupposes that relief arrived before the end of the month.

Many of these examples, when looked at in isolation, do not necessarily contribute much to an ideological level of meaning generation. As with other formal phenomena, the point is that their local functioning in combination with other discourse features should be attended to. Moreover, there are also the more exceptional individually significant examples, such as

> D'ailleurs presque personne ne <u>comprenait que</u> les colonies sont nécessaires à une nation.   (Lavisse 1902, p. 96)

> [Besides, almost no one understood that colonies are necessary for a nation.]

to which we can add

> The fact is recorded here not in mere disparagement of a brave soldier, but as an illustration of the manner in which <u>the old elementary passions of man's untamed condition</u> can <u>return</u> upon him in <u>his pride of civilisation and culture</u>, and make him their slave <u>again</u>.   (McCarthy 1908, p. 191)

which manifests a strong belief in civilizational progress, which is in no way shaken by the facts of warfare, though aberrations are admitted – and presented as aberrations. Note the multiple embedding of presuppositions in the latter sentence. The phrase "an illustration of the manner in which" presupposes the factuality of what follows, and hence the correctness of the perspective that is taken. The brave soldier's "pride of civilisation and culture" is supposed to have removed him from "the old elementary passions" that are attributed to "man's untamed condition"; being removed from them, however, they can (actively – note the semantic roles involved, as discussed in 3.3.3) "return upon him" and "make him their slave again".

Though not all individual examples have such immediate relevance, all of them contribute to the way in which an overall discursive perspective is generated, so that systematic attention to the functioning of presuppositions (keeping in mind that some of them are used to communicate new information, and that many of them are dependent for their interpretation on what is said explicitly elsewhere in the immediate or wider discourse, while others convey meaning that remains fully implicit) is an essential ingredient of a methodology for ideology research.

Ad 3.4.2:
[Find logical implications and entailments.]

The interpretation of presuppositions requires inferences that take into account contextual information. There are also forms of implicit meaning, however, that can be logically deduced from certain forms of expression. They form a general category of phenomena that have been given various labels such as (logical) implication, entailment, or sometimes conventional implicatures.[71] Though making

---

[71] Making detailed distinctions would lead us too far here. For basic sources of information on such phenomena, as well as those in 3.4.3, see Grice (1989), Levinson (1983), R. Lakoff (1995), and Huang (2007).

the implications explicit may often be tedious and sometimes sound trivial, their contribution to the overall pattern of discursive meaning generation is crucial, as the following examples (with implication triggers underlined) will show.

> **2.** Ils [les Portugais et les Espagnols] se sont emparés, en Amérique, en Afrique, en Asie, en Océanie, des pays qui leur convenaient, et ils ont pris *les pays les plus riches*. **3.** <u>Mais</u> comme ils gouvernaient très mal, leurs colonies sont devenues pauvres et faibles.   (Lavisse 1902, p. 93)

> [**2.** They [the Portuguese and the Spanish] have seized, in America, in Africa, in Asia, in Oceania, the countries that appealed to them, and they have taken the richest countries. **3.** But since they governed very badly, their colonies have become poor and weak.]

> It [the Indian Mutiny] had been long maturing, <u>but</u> the reason put forward by the mutineers was, that the cartridges served out to them were greased with cow's fat.   (Cassell's 1903, p. 124)

> <u>Yet</u>, with hardly an exception, the authorities in India were perfectly unsuspicious.   (Innes 1927, p. 170)

> <u>Even then</u> Canning and his council and the commander-in-chief, General Anson, saw no occasion for special anxiety.
>   (Low and Sanders 1910, p. 139)

➜ "Mais" establishes a *contrast* between the situation of certain parts of the world before and after colonization by the Portuguese and the Spanish, while "comme" indicates a *causal connection* between the fate of the Portuguese and Spanish colonies and their being poorly governed (an element that is brought in by way of presupposition). "But" introduces a contrast between "the reason put forward by the mutineers" and a prior context with unspecified circumstances which are thus implicitly presented as the real reasons for the Mutiny. A strong contrastive marker is "yet," which in the above example suggests that what follows should not have been the case given the facts observed in the paragraphs preceding this sentence; somehow, what we get here is the opposite of a causal connection; in other words, what was observed in the previous paragraphs should have led to the opposite of what is said in the sentence introduced with "yet." "Even then" functions in much the same way.

> Tous les citoyens doivent payer les mêmes impôts. Tous sont <u>donc</u> **égaux** devant la loi.   (Lavisse 1902, p. 100)

> [All citizens have to pay the same taxes. Therefore they are all **equal** before the law.]

> At one time it was intended that the native troops should be commanded for the most part by native officers. The men would, <u>therefore</u>, have had something like sufficient security that their religious scruples were regarded and respected.   (McCarthy 1908, p. 174)

➔ "Donc" and "therefore" present the proposition with which they occur as a *logical conclusions* from preceding propositions. In cases like these, it is always interesting to look closely at the precise statements that are introduced as sufficient grounds for the conclusion. What is particularly striking in the British example is the logical connection that is established between a clearly unrealized antecedent at the level of intentionality and a vaguely formulated ("something like") counterfactual ("would have had").

"There was great danger of a Sikh rising, and of an attack from the frontier clans and the Afghans. <u>Even</u> Lawrence hesitated for a moment, and was disposed to hand over Peshàwar to the Amír Dost Muhammad in return for his assistance [...].   (Low and Sanders 1910, p. 148)

Not for years and years had <u>even</u> Oriental warfare given example of such practice as that which Nana Sahib and the graceful and civilised Azimoolah Khan had now in preparation.   (McCarthy 1908, p. 186)

➔ "Even" evokes a *scalar contrast*. If "even Lawrence" hesitated, this implies that others, lower on a scale of being resistant to hesitation, would certainly have done so (and probably did). If what Nana Sahib and Azimoolah Khan "had now in preparation" surpassed what "even Oriental warfare" usually offered, this places "Oriental warfare" fairly high on a scale of expected atrocities and suggests that what happened during this particular episode of the Indian Mutiny would have been less likely elsewhere.

AD 3.4.3:

[Find implicatures.]

Implicatures (see Grice 1989, Levinson 1983, R. Lakoff 1995, Huang 2007 for more details) are forms of unexpressed or unsaid meaning inferred by an interpreter from an utterance on the basis of assumed standard adherence to general communicative principles. Such principles include: that one would normally try to give the amount of information needed at a given moment – not more, not less (quantity); that one would say what one believes to be true, or for which one has sufficient evidence (quality); that one would make an attempt to say relevant things (relation or relevance); that one would try to make one's communication succinct, clear, orderly (manner).

The quality principle is by definition strong in academic writing. Hence the preponderance of assertive speech acts. Authors are assumed to communicate what they 'know,' even if only indirectly through other sources. The fact that they can expect to be judged by such norms is no doubt partly responsible for the significant amount of hedging that occurs (see 3.1). But even hedged assertions implicate that the author believes, has evidence for, what is said. If questions were asked – other than Lavisse's testing questions or rhetorical questions – this would implicate that the author does not know the answer. Since they do not occur, our sample texts take a clear position of authority.

As to the manner principle, history book authors write under similar constraints. The expected orderliness is responsible for the fact, for instance, that events that are recounted in a specific order are interpreted as having occurred in that temporal order, even if there are no explicit temporal markers, and unless such markers lead to a different conclusion (see 2.3.3 on sequencing). Most narratives, including those in history textbooks, do not abide by a strict rule of providing information in as succinct a manner as possible. Consider the following:

> It was not till five days after the original assault that the Lahore gate was taken. Fighting their way through the streets, the assailants reached the palace and gradually mastered the city, though not before 1,145 officers and men had been slain in the process of capture.
>
> (Low and Sanders 1910, p. 150)

It would have been sufficient to say "Five days after the original assault, the Lahore gate was taken and the city was mastered, at the cost of 1,145 lives." The lengthier description carries added meaning beyond the literal content of the extra propositions; in particular, it evokes the difficulties experienced and the heroism needed to recapture Delhi.

As to the need for an appropriate quantity of information, take the fact – already observed in 3.1 – that Fearenside (1922, p. 433) ascribes emotions only to the mutineering Indians. The assumption that Fearenside is trying to give as much information as is needed in this narrative, combined with the fact that, in contrast to the account that is given of the involvement of the Indians, nothing is said about the emotional side of British involvement in the conflict, communicates the implicit message that British emotionality is not relevant to the story. In other words, British actions are implicitly presented as *not* driven by emotions: The British soldiers do not want revenge, they are not angry, they are simply doing their job as good professionals in crushing the revolt. Though some (two) other British sources do not follow this pattern, and therefore do not carry a similar implicature, it is clearly there in Fearenside and in some of the others. Also consider the following:

> The soldiers were rapidly drifting into that state of panic which is capable of driving Orientals to frenzy.   (Low and Sanders 1910, p. 138)

> There were frightful massacres of our people.   (Parkin 1911, p. 213)

The specificity with which susceptibility to frenzy is attributed to Orientals implicates that others, in general, are not equally susceptible; hence implicature serves as a categorization device in this example. Similarly, specifying "our people" as the victims of massacres during the events of the Indian Mutiny, if the sentence is supposed to abide by a principle of quantity that says that sufficient relevant information must be given, implicates that there were no other comparable victims.

As to a principle of relation or relevance, look at just two examples. First:

> In 1857 occurred the Sepoy Mutiny, when great numbers of the men we had drilled and armed so carefully rose in rebellion against our rule.
>
> (Parkin 1911, p. 213)

If the restrictive relative clause is assumed to be relevant, it implicates ungratefulness on the part of the rebelling repoys. The second:

> Fighting their way through the streets, the assailants reached the palace and gradually mastered the city, though not before 1,145 officers and men had been slain in the process of capture.   (Low and Sanders 1910, p. 150)

This passage being written so clearly from the point of view of the British assailants whose courage is evoked with the longer-than-necessary description, mentioning the "1,145 officers and men" who were slain would be less relevant without the implicature that those officers and men were British – a fact that therefore does not have to be stated explicitly.

AD 3.4.4:

[Investigate tropes, i.e., cases of simile, metonymy, metaphor, irony, overstatement and understatement, rhetorical questions (as well as cases of humor, politeness, and the like).]

A wide range of tropes or figures of speech (see, e.g., Kienpointner 2005) is used to communicate implicature-type added meaning, as the literal meaning of the chosen forms of expression would not make sufficient sense or might even clearly violate general communicative principles.[72] Some examples (with underlining of the relevant stretches added):

> A conviction began to spread among the mutineers that it was of no use attempting to conquer these terrible British sahibs; that so long as one of them was alive he would be as formidable <u>as a wild beast in its lair</u>.
> (McCarthy 1908, p. 186)

➜ In a different context, the comparison of British soldiers with wild beasts would be avoided. And it is certainly not the intention to equate the two. Here the *simile* evokes certain properties such as strength and courage.

> the transfer of Indian administration from the Company to <u>the Crown</u>.
> (Fearenside 1922, p. 434)

➜ Here 'the Crown' *metonymically* refers to British government, with the monarch as head of state.

> But it was not till the end of the year that <u>the last embers of the great revolt</u> were finally stamped out.   (Innes 1927, p. 171)

> Before the end of the year all danger was over, though Sir Colin Campbell and Sir Hugh Rose had still work to do in <u>stamping out the last embers of revolt</u>.   (Woodward 1921, p. 237)

---

[72] I am here avoiding the discussion concerning the generality of the communicative principles in question. There is evidence that at least their universality can be questioned. But for the interpretation of a number of phenomena in the types of discourse under investigation, they remain useful.

This success broke the neck of the mutiny.   (Ransome 1910, p. 443)

The news that the Indian native army had broken out into revolt in the late spring of 1857 came upon England like a thunder-clap.

(Low and Sanders 1910, p. 132)

The news of the outbreak at Meerut, and the proclamation in Delhi, broke upon Calcutta with the shock of a thunder clap.

(McCarthy 1908, p. 177)

And then came a rumour, more alarming than any other, which ran like wildfire through the sepoy lines in the late autumn.

(Low and Sanders 1910, p. 138)

Yet in that fateful spring of 1857 the danger signs were blowing thickly over the lowering skies of Northern India.   (Low and Sanders 1910, p. 139)

when the disaffection first blazed into a flame of violent rebellion

(Low and Sanders 1910, p. 139)

They had marched on the wings of fear [...]

(Low and Sanders 1910, p. 140)

➔ All of our sample texts contain numerous *metaphors* of the above types. Even this small selection of examples shows that there are intertextual consistencies in the choices of metaphors. They are not random; rather, they emphasize aspects which the authors deem important, such as the surprise element and startling effect evoked by "thunder clap," of the difficult-to-control force-of-nature character of the revolt suggested by the many fire-related metaphors. In addition to those, there are of course many stock metaphors that form essential ingredients of the texts (e.g., the 'spreading' of rumors, etc.).

Not for years and years had even Oriental warfare given example of such practice as that which Nana Sahib and the graceful and civilised Azimoolah Khan had now in preparation.   (McCarthy 1908, p. 186)

They burst open the prison, released the eighty-five martyrs, and then proceeded to fire on their officers.   (Synge 1908, p. 113)

➔ It is hard to assume that "graceful and civilised" is literally meant to characterize Azimoolah Khan in this context (even though elsewhere in the text it is said that he is fully capable of presenting himself as such). Similarly, "martyrs" does not correspond to the really intended categorization of the imprisoned sepoys (even though it would be the applicable category in the mental world of the other rebels – see 2.2.1.2). In both examples, where quite the opposite is meant, we are confronted with cases of *irony* – which are predictably rare in our sample texts, as they belong to an activity type supporting expectations of seriousness.

The little garrison, thinning in numbers every day and almost every hour, held out with splendid obstinacy, and always sent those who assailed it scampering back – except of course for such assailants as perforce kept their ground by the persuasion of the English bullets.

(McCarthy 1908, p. 185)

➜ Even more exceptional than mere irony in our corpus – for the same reason – is a sentence like this which overtly tries to be *humorous*.

Utterly, overwhelmingly, preposterously outnumbered as the Englishmen were […].   (McCarthy 1908, p. 186)

He had under his command only some 5,000 men, a force miserably inferior in number to that of the enemy; but in those days an English officer thought himself in good condition to attack if the foe did not outnumber him by more than four or five to one.   (McCarthy 1908, p. 192)

but for the grand courage of Havelock, the fierce energy of Nicholson, the unsleeping toil and forethought of Lawrence, this prophecy would have come true.   (Synge 1908, p. 112)

➜ These *hyperbolic* utterances or *overstatements* clearly deviate from simple adherence to a principle of quantity; as a result they put heavy emphasis on the odds faced by the British soldiers and the latter's resourcefulness.

He was a brave and clever soldier, but one who unfortunately allowed a fierce [191] temper to overrule the better instincts of his nature and the guidance of a cool judgment.   (McCarthy 1908, pp. 191–192)

➜ Here *understatement* is used to downplay or mitigate the graveness of Hodson's killing of the three royal princes of Delhi.

his untimely death. Untimely? Was it after all untimely? Since when has it not been held the crown of a great career that the hero dies at the moment of accomplished victory?   (McCarthy 1908, p. 193)

➜ These *rhetorical questions*, deviating from the principle that one does not ask a question to which one knows the answer, are indirect ways of making a statement, which strengthens its rhetorical effect by implicating that the very asking of the questions is in fact senseless.

When analyzing interactional types of discourse, it is under this rubric that it would make sense to inquire into issues of *politeness* (see Kasper 1996, Eelen 2001). The closest we come in written academic discourse to strategies for avoiding face threats or for supporting positive face is in the flattering ways in which the earlier acts of compatriots are described and the mitigating phrasing for possible points of criticism and blame.

Procedure 3.5: *Investigate interactional aspects. In particular:*

3.5.1: *In the case of overtly interactional data (e.g., conversations, correspondence), investigate the sequential organization and patterns of mutual engagement.*

3.5.2: *In the case of covertly interactional data (anything that looks like it is purely 'monologic'), look for aspects of dialogic organization, i.e., implicit patterns of interaction.*

AD 3.5, IN GENERAL:

[Investigate interactional aspects.]

When investigating data that are literally interactive, with two or more participants who are all uttering and interpreting, the study of interactional aspects is one of the more crucial angles from which to approach the discursive generation of meaning.[73] It would be a mistake, however, to believe that no such angle can be taken to look at written, apparently 'monologic,' data. As Watson's (2009) work clearly demonstrates, authors install 'events-in-the-world' into their texts; they do so on the basis of their own interpretative engagement with earlier entextualizations; moreover, they do so in such a manner as to render their own categorizations and representations credible; and the meaning generation process is not complete until 'readings' are produced. As discourse analysts without direct access to others' readings, we have to keep these fundamentally interactive structural processes in mind to achieve a balanced picture of the meaning potential of a text.

AD 3.5.1:

[In the case of overtly interactional data (e.g., conversations, correspondence), investigate the sequential organization and patterns of mutual engagement.]

For conversational data, various aspects of sequential organization (see Sidnell 2006b) have to be studied in detail, including openings and closings, adjacency pairs, pre-sequences and insertion sequences, interruptions and overlaps, pauses, hesitations, false starts, and repairs. Patterns of mutual engagement must also be investigated: Who introduces what topics when and how? How are they accepted and elaborated? Is there a dominant party in the interaction? How is attentiveness signaled? Furthermore, all of this must be looked at with due attention to prosody, gaze, gesture, and bodily positioning.

In our sample corpus, the closest we come to these kinds of phenomena is in the summary rendition of some reported cases of interaction. An example that occurs more than once (thus becoming indicative of an intertextual master narrative) is the following:

---

[73] For a number of introductory texts on a variety of interactional phenomena, see D'hondt, Östman and Verschueren (eds.) (2009).

> "Sir Henry, are you hurt?" cried a friend who was with him.
> There was a moment's silence.
> "I am killed," answered the wounded man firmly.
>
> (Synge 1908, p. 119)

The opening turn is a simple yes–no question. It is followed by a pause, punctuating the weight of the following answer. Then the answer comes, which does more than to respond to the literal import of the question. It reinterprets the question as "How badly are you hurt?," and, in answering that question, Sir Henry takes the unexpected further step – which makes the story worth reporting – not to describe the current situation but the anticipated outcome, which he does in such a way that the utterance he produces, if taken literally, would not make sense.

AD 3.5.2:

[In the case of covertly interactional data (anything that looks like it is purely 'monologic'), look for aspects of dialogic organization, i.e., implicit patterns of interaction.]

The texts in our sample corpus are not simply representations of (assumed/believed) facts. As Watson (2009, p. 53) would put it, they are "representations for particular types of recipients" who all bring their own interpretation categories into the reading of the texts. All features of audience design, already touched upon under Rule 2.4 and Procedure 2.2.1.3, are relevant here. In addition, the features I have repeatedly highlighted in Lavisse (1902), with its overt structuring for classroom use (left more implicit in the British sources, except in some of their prefaces), openly define the texts as central ingredients in "textually-mediated social action" (Watson 2009, p. 93). Furthermore, what has been said (under 2.2.1.2) about the various voices involved or invoked in the discourse also signals covert interactionality.

Our largely 'monologic' printed texts, moreover, sometimes show phenomena directly analogous to dialogic units. Thus the questions that are sometimes asked (in the British texts), even if rhetorical, do get answered. There are interest-arousing openings such as

> In May 1857 the great Indian Mutiny shook to its foundations the whole fabric of British rule in Hindostan.   (McCarthy 1908, p. 170)

with twenty-five pages later an unmistakable closing:

> On December 20, 1858, Lord Clyde, who had been Sir Colin Campbell, announced to the Governor-General that the rebellion was at an end, and on May 1, 1859, there was a public thanksgiving in England for the pacification of India.   (McCarthy 1908, p. 195)

There are also parallels to repair strategies:

> The Queen created him a baronet, <u>or rather</u> affixed that honour to his name on the 27th of the same month, not knowing then that the soldier's time for struggle and for honour was over.   (McCarthy 1908, p. 193)

Finally, in some parts of the narratives, clear *interaction profiles* are set up. One type we find in Low and Sanders' use of footnotes:

> Tántia Topí, the Nana's former minister, and the most able leader on the rebel side during the entire campaign.[1]
>
> [1] With the possible exceptions of the Oudh maulvi and the Ráni of Jhánsi, Sir Hugh Rose thought that the Maráthá princess was "the best and bravest military leader of the rebels."   (Low and Sanders 1910, p. 151)

A different device for letting different opinions/views interact, this time without identifying the sources (though the stability of the same opposition across texts suggests some sort of 'common knowledge' status):

> He is commonly thought to have died of fever in the jungle, though it was long rumoured that he had escaped to Tibet, or was hiding in India.
>   (Low and Sanders 1910, p. 155)

> Nana Sahib escaped, and is thought to have died of fever in the jungle, though there is some reason to believe that he escaped, and lived in concealment in Nepal.   (Richardson 1924, p. 139)

Sometimes an outside voice is contradicted by the author, as in

> On July 2 he had been up with the dawn, and after a great amount of work he lay on the sofa, not, as it has been well said, to rest, but to transact business in a recumbent position.   (McCarthy 1908, p. 181)

or simply invoked:

> He had just time left, it is said, to order the murder of a separate captive, a woman who had previously been overlooked or purposely left behind.
>   (McCarthy 1908, p. 190)

Not surprisingly, these examples also take us back to the discussion of evidentiality (see under 3.3.4).

Procedure 3.6: *Investigate metapragmatic functioning. In particular:*

3.6.1: *Look for indicators of metapragmatic awareness (ranging from verba dicendi, to sentence adverbs, question tags, hedges, quotations, and reported speech).*

AD 3.6, IN GENERAL:

[Investigate metapragmatic functioning.]

As was pointed out at the beginning of Chapter 3, in the discussion of a background theory of pragmatics, metapragmatic reflexivity is an essential ingredient of language use. In fact, language as we know it would be unthinkable without reflexive awareness of what it is that one is doing when using language; it would not be possible, for instance, to decide on what needs to be said explicitly and what kinds of information can be left implicit as they can be assumed to be 'computed' by the interpreter. Or to repeat my earlier formulation (when explaining Thesis 1), language use shares with any other form of social action the basic property of its being 'meaningful' in the sense that it is always interpreted by the people involved, and that these reflexive interpretations need to be understood if we want to make sense of observed behavior. This is not only a basic premise of linguistic pragmatics; it is shared by philosophers (Winch 1958 – one of the first to drive home this point in relation to the social sciences), sociologists (Thompson's 1984 'hermeneutics of everyday life' depends on it), and ethnomethodologists (see e.g. Watson 2009).

At a general level, we cannot even ignore the role of ideologies of language and communication when investigating discourse. Our sample texts very clearly define their own status, and this status is often associated with normative expectations. Lavisse's (1902) title page provides a clearly reflexive definition of the book:

> Notions sommaires [...]
> Leçons – résumés – réflexions
>
> [Basic notions [...]
> Lessons – summaries – reflections]

He further specifies the speech act purpose of the "résumés" with "(*à réciter*)," whenever they occur. His preface, furthermore, clearly spells out self-imposed communicative norms:

> Une histoire des principaux peuples anciens et modernes doit être enseignée avec *discrétion*, car elle est immense. Il faut se garder de vouloir tout dire, et sacrifier résolument les details: nous les avons sacrifiés.
> [...]
> Ces notions d'histoire générale, pourvu qu'elles soient données sobrement, rendront grand service aux écoliers. Elles seront le complément naturel de l'histoire de la France; car [...]. Elles seront aussi le complément de l'éducation patriotique: nos enfants doivent [...].   (Lavisse 1902, p. 2)
>
> [A history of the principal ancient and modern peoples must be taught with *discretion*, as it is boundless. One must refrain from wanting to say everything, and sacrifice the details resolutely: we have sacrificed them.
> [...]
> These notions of general history, if they are presented objectively, will render a great service to the students. They will be the natural complement to the history of France; since [...]. They will also complete patriotic education: our children must [...].]

Lavisse also provides comments on content organization, defending his decision to take a 'universal' perspective rather than dealing with different 'peoples' one after the other.

Similarly, Hearnshaw's preface introduces a contrast between authentic history, legend, and anecdote:

> This little book is intended in the first place for school children who, having passed through the early stages of instruction, in which legend and anecdote play the main part, are called upon to make their first systematic survey of authentic English History.   (Hearnshaw 1930, p. v)

Hearnshaw also makes a normative statement about language use:

> The attempt to tell a complex story entirely in Anglo-Saxon monosyllables may give the narrative an air of child-like simplicity; but, as one or two well-known and awful examples show, the simplicity is delusive and the monotony deadly.   (Hearnshaw 1930, p. vi)

Most of the other sources contain similarly reflexive and normative judgements, recommendations, and expressions of intention. Some also give a further characterization of the type of prose to be expected; thus McCarthy's preface, like many of the others, describes what follows as the telling of a 'story' or a 'narrative.'

Ad 3.6.1:

[Look for indicators of metapragmatic awareness (ranging from verba dicendi to sentence adverbs, question tags, hedges, quotations, and reported speech).]

Many of the formal features that have already passed the review rely for their proper interpretation on metapragmatic awareness and thus serve as indicators of such awareness. They include:

- The *positioning of utterer and interpreter* (for instance, by means of certain types of person deixis, as discussed in 2.2.1.1, the appeal to voices [2.2.1.2] and interpreter roles [2.2.1.3], as well as placement in relation to institutional settings [2.2.3], time and space [2.2.4]).
- The use of supporting *graphic features* (see 2.2.5).
- Properties of the *linguistic context* (including choice of *channels* [2.3.1], the establishment of *intertextual links* [2.3.2, including *quotation and reported speech*] and contextual *cohesion* [2.3.4]).
- The definition of the *activity type* (see 3.1, including a treatment of *hedges*, but also the general comments under 3.6 above).
- The choice of *languages, codes, and styles* (see 3.2).
- Choices related to *carriers of information structure* (see 3.3, including quite centrally patterns of word choice and the categorizations they imply, modality and evidentiality, foregrounding and backgrounding, and the establishment of coherence).
- All *carriers of implicit meaning* (see 3.4), as choices at that level depend crucially on an assessment of what an interpreter can be assumed to already know.
- All *interactional features* (see 3.5), as they require awareness of meanings or discourse one interacts with, and hence awareness of what it is one is doing communicatively.

It is not by accident that this list includes just about everything we have already been dealing with. Nor is it, as one might object, trivial to present such a list of non-new information at this stage. It must serve as a reminder that what we are dealing with here is a metalevel, the level of active or potential consciousness, that has every aspect of language use within its scope.

Therefore, looking for indicators of metapragmatic awareness (of which the examples listed in parentheses in the formulation of procedure 3.6.1 are just some of the most typical ones) is a task to be carried out throughout a discourse-analytic exercise. Let me draw attention here to just a few of the more striking types of explicit metacomment that we find in one of our sources, McCarthy (1908):

> Let the bitterest enemy of England write the history of her rule in India, and set down as against her every wrong that was done in her name, from those which Burke denounced to those which the Madras Commission exposed, he will have to say that men, many men, like Henry Lawrence, lived and died devoted to the cause of that rule, and the world will take account of the admission.   (McCarthy 1908, p. 182)

> Lord Dalhousie had shown in many instances a strangely unwise disregard of the principle of adoption [...] [183] [here follows a long explanation of Nana Sahib's missing a princely status as a result] A sense of his [Nana Sahib's] wrongs had eaten him up. It is a painful thing to say, but it is necessary to the truth of this history, that his wrongs were genuine. He had been treated with injustice.   (McCarthy 1908, pp. 183–184)

> It may be said at once, that of the gallant little party who went ashore to attack the enemy, hand to hand, four finally escaped, after adventures so perilous and so extraordinary that a professional story-teller would hardly venture to make them part of a fictitious narrative.
>   (McCarthy 1908, p. 188)

These examples show full reflexive awareness of the British-friendly perspective taken in this, as in other sources, on British history. Extoling the virtues of British commanders is what also enables the author to admit mistakes without loss of face. But quite elaborate, explicitly metapragmatic comment is needed to accomplish that task.

Procedure 3.7: *If possible, try to identify any strategies of meaning generation that may appear from any of the observations based on the foregoing procedural steps. In particular:*

3.7.1:   *Look for potentially strategic ways in which the interplay between the explicit and the implicit is exploited.*

AD 3.7, IN GENERAL:

[If possible, try to identify any strategies of meaning generation that may appear from any of the observations based on the foregoing procedural steps.]

All language use involves strategies, though not all choices at that (or any other) level can be interpreted as fully intentional. Here we must come back once more to the earlier observation that there are hardly any fixed form–function relationships (Caveat 3.1). As was said at that point, the meaningful functioning of language in use allows for near-infinite manipulations of such (often conventional but always negotiable) relationships. As was also suggested, such manipulations or negotiations are not random; rather, principles and strategies can usually be identified. In our history textbook samples, for instance, presupposition-carrying constructions are quite systematically used to convey new information in such a manner that its factuality is underscored by a surface assumption of common ground – the 'typical' prerequisite for the use of presuppositions. And no doubt, for most, if not all, of the authors, there are motivations beyond the mere conveying of academically justifiable knowledge, the 'typical' or conventional function of the chosen activity type; patriotic fervor, for instance, is often quite evident; but since it is usually not the overt goal to instill patriotic zeal in the readers, such an effect may be all the stronger.

Here I will not return to the possible strategic exploitation of all the levels of structure we have already reviewed. This exercise can be performed by every reader by asking on every occasion the following question: What does the choice of this specific form of expression, from among a set of contrasting alternatives, contribute to the meaning that is generated by this text? Rather, I will concentrate only, in the next section, on the fact that communicative strategies often hinge on the way in which explicit and implicit information are made to interact.

AD 3.7.1:

[Look for potentially strategic ways in which the interplay between the explicit and the implicit is exploited.]

To illustrate the strategic interplay between the explicit and the implicit, look at one coherent stretch of text from Parkin (1911), one of the more condensed accounts of the Indian Mutiny.

> [1] We have seen how India was conquered for us largely by the help of natives [sic] troops, or Sepoys. [2] These same Sepoys proved, however, to be a great danger as well as a great assistance. [3] In 1857 occurred the Sepoy Mutiny, when great numbers of the men whom we had drilled and armed so carefully rose in rebellion against our rule. [4] There were frightful massacres of our people. [5] For a short time it seemed probable that British power in India would be overthrown. [6] Had the whole of the people of India joined in the rebellion, this would no doubt have taken place. [7] But they did not do so, and of the Sepoys themselves many regiments remained faithful, and helped us to fight the mutineers. [8] The **Sikhs** of the Punjaub, whom we had conquered shortly before, fought valiantly upon the British side, and rendered great assistance, as did also the princes and people of some of the feudatory native States. [9] The common people of the country went on as usual rendering us those services which are almost necessary for the existence of Europeans in the hot climate of India. [10] Never perhaps did British soldiers display greater courage and endurance than during the Sepoy Mutiny. [11] But it was put down by native aid as well as by the exertions of our own troops. [213] [12] The Mutiny proved that India was not, and probably never will be, a country which can be united to oppose our rule.   (Parkin 1911, pp. 213–214; sentence numbering added)

A schematic presentation of explicit and implicit information in this text, sentence by sentence (but leaving out existential presuppositions), is to be found in Table 8.

Table 8. *Explicit vs. implicit*

	Explicit	Implicit
[1]	- "we": inclusive reference to author + readers - "we have seen": anaphoric reference to earlier text	- "how India was conquered for us largely by the help of native troops, or Sepoys" is presupposed as shared knowledge on the basis of the earlier text which "we have seen" refers to - embedded presupposition: the conquering was done "for us," where "us" refers to the community shared by author + readers - "largely" implies 'not only' - though carried along as presupposed, the equivalence "native troops" = "Sepoys" is spelled out as a reminder
[2]	- "these same Sepoys proved to be a great danger"	- "however" implies a real contrast between a previous proposition (reintroduced after "as well as") and the current one - "proved" presupposes that the "great danger" was not merely a possibility, a risk, but that something already happened; thus this choice of word is a projection toward the following narrative (which is thus expected to clarify the meaning of "a great danger") - the meaning of "a great assistance" is supposed to be known from the preceding discourse
[3]	- "in 1857" - "great numbers of sepoys rose in rebellion against our rule" - this event is called "the Sepoy Mutiny"	- the lengthy redefinition of "sepoys" as "the men whom we had drilled and armed so carefully" presents them by implicature as beneficiaries of "our rule," and hence their rising in rebellion as an act of ingratitude - "great numbers of" implicates 'not all' - the fact that rule in India was "our rule" is presupposed (as a logical consequence of India having been conquered "for us," and again with "our" referring to the community shared by author + readers)
[4]	- "frightful massacres of our people" took place	- "our" – see above - the specific mentioning of "of our people" implicates that no others were victims of "frightful massacres"
[5]	- "British power in India" was in real danger, "for a short time," of being overthrown	- "for a short time" implies "not very long", and hence it anticipates the crushing of the revolt; in combination with "it seemed probable that … would be …" it presupposes that the overthrowing did not happen - the equivalence of "British power in India" with "our rule" is treated as known information

[6]
- the situation was such that, under certain circumstances ("the whole of the people of India" joining the rebellion), "this" (British power in India being overthrown) would have happened

- "had ..., this would no doubt have ..." presupposes again that the overthrowing did not happen

[7]
- "they" (the whole of the people of India) "did not do so" (did not join the rebellion)
- many sepoy regiments "remained faithful," and "helped us to fight the mutineers"

- "but" sets up a contrast between what was implicitly communicated (in [5] and [6]) as not having happened, and introduces an explicit statement of what did happen
- "remained faithful": implicitly 'to us'
- "us" – see above

[8]
- the Sikhs "fought valiantly upon the British side, and rendered great assistance"
- the same is said of "the people and princes of some of the feudatory native States"

- "the Sikhs of the Punjaub" implies "all of them"
- the fact that "we had conquered" the Sikhs "shortly before" is introduced by way of presupposition
- "and rendered great assistance" implies that there were other forms of assistance in addition to fighting with the British
- "some of the feudatory native States" implies "not all"
- "we" – see above
- "rendered great assistance": implicitly "to us"

[9]
- "the common people of the country" continued providing the usual services

- "the common people of the country" sets up an implicit contrast between military and non-military
- "went on as usual" presupposes earlier activity of the type described
- "those services which are almost necessary for the existence of Europeans in the hot climate of India" implies that the hot climate of India is a well-known fact, that this makes life for Europeans difficult, that their life in India can be made more bearable if certain services are rendered by the locals, and it presupposes that readers can be assumed to know what those services are
- "us" – see above

Table 8 *(cont.)*

	Explicit	Implicit
[10]	- perhaps it has never been the case that …	- the complete structure "never perhaps … than during the Sepoy Mutiny" presupposes that the Sepoy Mutiny was an occasion on which British soldiers displayed great courage and endurance, and that it was the occasion on which – though this is modified with "perhaps" – the greatest courage and endurance were displayed - "greater courage and endurance" presupposes that great courage and endurance has also been displayed on other occasions
[11]	- the Mutiny was put down - this was done with native aid and efforts of "our own troops"	- "but" sets up a contrast between British courage and endurance (reintroduced after "as well as") and "native aid" - "native aid" refers back to and presupposes the types of aid described in the preceding discourse (in [7], [8], and [9]) - "our own troops" – see above
[12]	- the Mutiny proved something	- "proved that" presupposes the truth of what follows - "a country which can be united" presupposes that it is not united - "our rule" – see above

Unlike what might be suggested by this tabular presentation, explicit and implicit information are not just juxtaposed and added up. There are interesting forms of interaction, and usually it is not by accident that a bit of information ends up in one column or in the other. The most remarkable property of the meaning generation process that is immediately transparent from Table 8 is the heavy load of implicit information. The explicit seems to function only as a skeleton, and even most of the new information is either implied or carried along in presupposition-carrying constructions. As a communicative strategy, this helps in *building up an interesting narrative*. For instance, that the Mutiny was eventually put down was clear from [5] onwards, but it is not said explicitly until [11], which is an effective way of keeping the reader's attention focused on what the author wants to communicate about circumstances and events leading to this outcome.

Some of the other effects of the use of implicitly communicated content in this text fragment include:

* The *creation of solidarity*: the multiple references to an unquestioned shared community between author and readers, involved in, and clearly situated on one side of, the reported conflict.
* The complete *naturalization* of 'our rule,' culminating in the assessment and corresponding prediction in [12], the truth of which is simply presupposed.
* Aspects of *evaluation*: The combination of explicit statements with implicated meaning casts good vs. bad Indians; the bad, restricted to a group of sepoys in this narrative, are ungrateful beings; since absolutely nothing is said about their reasons for rebelling, except for the suggested ungratefulness, it is implicated that they are rebels without a cause.

Turning all of this into explicit statements would make it more difficult to communicate the same meaning. For one thing, the need would arise to defend and explain. It would take quite an effort, for instance, to argue for the absence of motives; at least reference would have to be made to what the rebelling sepoys regarded as their motives, and then an argument would have to be made for not regarding these professed motives as legitimate. This is the essence of what underlies the strategic interplay of the explicit and the implicit in language use, and laying bare such phenomena is a powerful key to insight into ideological processes.

Guideline 4: For an overall interpretation, ask yourself whether the assembled observations can be seen to represent an identifiable pattern of meaning in relation to issues pertaining to social structures, processes, and relations.

All of the preceding guidelines are pragmatic building blocks for empirical discourse-based ideology research. Since they were only meant as descriptions of tools, all illustrated with reference to the same body of data, they do not in

themselves constitute a full-blown analysis on the basis of which definitive conclusions can be drawn, even in relation to that restricted data set. Yet it is possible
to also illustrate the types of concluding interpretations that research may lead
to. The main thing is to distinguish clearly between the *topical or informational
content* of the discourse of narratives under investigation, and the *involvement or
perspective* that can be identified on the basis of careful analysis. In our sample
data there seems to be a clearly favorable disposition toward the phenomenon of
colonization. Sometimes this is very explicit, most obviously in Lavisse (1902);
sometimes colonial possessions (in this case India) are treated as such completely
natural phenomena that explicit statements of the Lavisse type are not necessary
(e.g., in Synge 1908):

> **6**. Mais la France était alors gouvernée par Louis XV, dont vous connais-
> sez le triste règne. D'ailleurs presque personne ne comprenait que *les col-
> onies sont nécessaires à une nation*. **7**. On dépensait beaucoup d'argent et
> de soldats à des guerres en Allemagne et en Italie, où la France n'avait rien à
> gagner, et on refusait d'envoyer aux colonies 4 ou 5 000 soldats qui auraient
> donné à la France l'*empire du monde*."   (Lavisse 1902, p. 96)

> [**6**. But at the time France was governed by Louis XV, whose sad rule you
> know. Besides, almost no one understood that *colonies are necessary for
> a nation*. **7**. A lot of money and many soldiers were expended on wars in
> Germany and Italy, where France had nothing to gain, and there was a
> refusal to send the 4 or 5,000 soldiers to the colonies that would have given
> to France the *empire of the world*.]

> "There are times in the history of every nation when she must either fight or
> go down."
>   Such a time had come now. Swiftly, silently the blow fell, and heroically,
> alone, without an ally, against odds too great to be counted, England in the
> face of the world set to work to re-conquer India.   (Synge 1908, p. 111)

Given this favorable disposition, it is not surprising that, in the face of conflict,
the colonizer's side or perspective is always taken. That is explicitly the case in
the above quotation from Synge (1908), while it is left implicit in the following:

> Meanwhile the Chinese war was also apparently brought to a satisfactory
> conclusion […].   (Innes 1927, p. 172)

Evaluative terms such as "satisfactory" always imply a perspective. Though in
principle the sentence leaves open whether the conclusion of the war was satisfactory for the Chinese or for the British, there is little doubt as to the 'correct'
interpretation.

Another aspect of the emerging, quite coherent, pattern is the *legitimation*
work that goes into making acceptable what could otherwise be condemned,
such as mingling in the affairs of others, suppression, and even violence. When
such things happen, they are presented as a necessity, rather than a matter of
choice:

> Mais depuis q'on a creusé le *canal de Suez* et que beaucoup de marchands européens se sont établis au Caire et à Alexandrie, les Européens sont forcés de s'occuper des affaires de l'Égypte.   (Lavisse 1902, p. 128)

> [But since the *Suez Canal* was dug and many European merchants have established themselves in Cairo and Alexandria, the Europeans have been forced to occupy themselves with the affairs of Egypt.]

Note that there is a missing link; it is not said why – and hence taken for granted that – the mere presence of European merchants leads to a mingling in Egyptian affairs. Or consider the following:

> Lord Dalhousie was distinguished by a policy of annexation; […] in distinction from the custom, which had hitherto prevailed generally, of maintaining the native rule unless annexation had become a palpable necessity.
>
> (Innes 1927, p. 169)

Though mildly critical of Dalhousie's rash policies (a recurrent attitude in many of the British sources), it is taken for granted that there are – further unspecified – circumstances that necessitate the annexation of (in contrast to mere control over) territory. And when war is involved, as in

> **14**. Mais le gouvernement chinois […] continua à maltraiter les missionnaires* français et les commerçants anglais. **15**. L'Angleterre et la France s'allièrent alors et firent deux expéditions contre 1a [154] Chine (1857 et 1860).   (Lavisse 1902, pp. 154–155)

> [**14**. But the Chinese government […] continued to maltreat the French missionaries and the English merchants. **15**. England and France then formed an alliance and undertook two expeditions against [154] China (1857 and 1860).]

or

> **2**. […] en 1857, quelques missionnaires furent massacrés. **3**. La France envoya une expédition qui prit *Saïgon*.   (Lavisse 1902, p. 157)

> [**2**. […] in 1857, some missionaries were murdered. **3**. France sent an expedition which captured Saigon.]

there is a tendency to present the military "expeditions" as reaction rather than action, the murder or maltreatment of missionaries being an excellent form of legitimation, even though the link is left implicit.

In other types of texts, less concerned than our samples of academic writing with the communication of 'facts,' in addition to legitimation strategies, we may be able to distinguish strategies of *persuasion* or even *propaganda* and *manipulation* (see, e.g., Chilton 2002, 2004). Essentially, the linguistic tools used for these purposes are the same, so that analyses based on the guidelines in this book are appropriate as long as special care is taken with counterscreening steps at all crucial stages of the analysis, especially when claims about intentional misleading are concerned.

Conclusion

If anything is clear from the cursory look at our sample data, which may be subject to further systematic scrutiny by users of this book, it is the patriotic stance taken by both Lavisse and the British sources. This stance did not leave room for fundamental criticism of colonization and its related practices. Specific actions and events were criticized implicitly or explicitly. Thus there is Lavisse's largely implicit critique of the behavior of the Spanish and the British; the French are criticized only for not having their heart in the enterprise of colonization at major moments in history. In the British sources, Dalhousie is presented as daring, but a bit careless in his reforms and annexations; some commanders are presented as insufficiently alert; and others are criticized for their understandable, yet overly pitiless, role in the suppression of the Indian Mutiny. None of this, however, can shake the foundations.

Texts for analysis rarely stand by themselves. Our corpus represents a type of discourse that partly reflects and partly tries to guide what can be assumed to be the dominant mainstream views of the day. It would not be surprising, then, to find reflections of the same views in other contemporary types of discourse. Interesting comparative data could be found in newspaper reports at the turn of the nineteenth into the twentieth century; perhaps more interesting still in political discourse, as we may assume that in the context of a democratic parliamentary system the opposing voices – which were definitely there – could also find expression. A somewhat charming, though at the same time discomforting, observation is the completely coherent faithfulness with which the patriotic stance of our history textbooks can be found in children's books. The British example *par excellence* is Mary Frances Ames' (1899) *An ABC for Baby Patriots* (with 'Mrs. Ernest Ames', after her husband, as author name on the publication) (Figure 3).

Consider the first few letters of the alphabet (Figure 4). The Army, Battles, Colonies, Daring (again on the battlefield), and Empire definitely are good opening concepts for a patriotic way of learning the alphabet. The next letter is of course F (Figure 5). Though an Army, Battles, and Daring arguably serve the cause of freedom, the Flag can also be seen throughout the Empire, including the Colonies. As with Lavisse's (1902) categorization of colonization as a work of peace in spite of the numerous episodes of violence involved, no contradiction is felt here between the taking possession of Colonies or the expansion of the Empire and the freedom symbolized by the Flag. The clue is, of course, that "*You*'re happy and free," i.e., the alphabet-learning baby patriots.

Figure 3. *An ABC for Baby Patriots*, cover

After G for Game and H for Hunting we then get down to a depiction of the role of India (Figure 6). No doubt this is a reflection of the festive, self-congratulatory mood in Britain toward the end of Victoria's reign. This page may also reflect a common perception of what the British were doing in India after they had settled comfortably in the reassurance of a firm colonial grip after the Mutiny. Jules Verne's *La maison à vapeur*, for instance, is mostly a story of the adventures of a hunting party traveling through northern India.

The main conclusion from the pragmatic observations in this book is that details of a story matter less than the way in which it is told and the overall message it carries. This becomes abundantly clear in the process of comparing details of wording. In most of the accounts to be found in Appendix 2, facts are hard to establish even if the manner of presentation is extremely factual. Ideological overtones are relatively easy to identify in the materials I have used for purposes of illustration, simply because at this time in history we no longer share the basic patterns of meaning or frames of interpretation surrounding world politics that were felt to be 'normal' around the end of the nineteenth century.[1] Those meaning patterns and interpretation frames, however, have been replaced by new ones that need to be examined and constantly monitored. If there is talk of neo-colonialism these days, it is because of present-day processes that parallel those from the colonial period. Just like the wars fought in those days, the ones that are raging today require legitimation – which is discursively achieved. 'They' are the beneficiaries of our actions. Victims that fall along the way represent an inevitable side effect, collateral damage. There is a strong awareness of such processes, but even stronger adherence to the mechanisms underlying them – otherwise, what is happening would not be happening. Such adherence finds its expression in dominant forms of discourse in which all possible strategies of persuasion – but also, no doubt, propaganda and manipulation – are mobilized. Underscoring critical

---

[1] This does not mean that present discourses would no longer be affected by the colonial past, as argued so convincingly by Pennycook (1998).

A. a.   *A a.*

A is the Army
That dies for the Queen;
It's the very best Army
That ever was seen.

B b   *B b*

B   stands for Battles
By which England's name
Has for ever been covered
With glory and fame.

C c   *C c*

C   is for Colonies.
Rightly we boast,
That of all the great nations
Great Britain has most.

D d   *D d*

D   is the Daring
We show on the Field
Which makes every enemy
Vanish or yield.

E e   *E e*

E   is our Empire
Where sun never sets;
The larger we make it
The bigger it gets.

Figure 4. *An ABC for Baby Patriots*, letters A to E

Figure 5. *An ABC for Baby Patriots*, letter F

Figure 6. *An ABC for Baby Patriots*, letter I

awareness with tools for analysis can be a major contribution to *an ecology of the public sphere*. That is what this book is aimed at.

Writing about ideology is not itself ideology-free. 'Stance' or perspective is inevitable. Thus it is obvious that my views of colonial relationships depart from those to be found in my illustrations. In the same way, the migrant research I referred to earlier (in Chapters 1 and 2) was clearly based on a view of societal diversity that deviates strongly from what we described as manifested in the types of discourse we investigated. This simple fact does not present a problem for research, as long as researchers know what they are doing when bringing in their own point of view, and as long as they do not try to hide their own involvement. But in order for analyses to be convincing, they require the solid empirical basis this book hopes to contribute to.

Three further remarks are needed by way of conclusion. The first offers a small but important addendum to the research methodology presented. This book, though I have made a few comments on pictorial illustrations (see 2.2.5 in Chapter 3), concentrates almost exclusively on text, i.e., verbal forms of expression. More often than not, and increasingly with new technological developments, language practices occur in a multimodal environment. The interaction between images and texts is an essential ingredient in most forms of situated discourse. This interaction contributes not only to the construction or generation of representational meaning (a process described briefly but convincingly by, e.g., Unsworth and Cléirigh 2009), but also to what Dupret (2011) calls "practices of truth," as well as to multiple layers of connotation and affect. The latter is nicely illustrated by *An ABC for Baby Patriots*. The 'funny' elements (such as the helmeted girl on the wooden horse on wheels, the rather uselessly small parasol held by a kneeling servant, the globe with an old man with a pipe as literal 'face of the earth,' etc.) contribute clearly to the impression of a convivial, almost cosy, and especially innocent imperial rule. This is a powerful tool for 'normalizing' colonial relations. The young patriots' acquired literacy can hardly be expected to go hand in hand with a critical stance toward Britain's role in the world.

Second, what is, after all, the relation between this book and theories of ideology? Clearly, the approach from linguistic pragmatics shares some of the fundamental premises we find in work referred to in the Introduction and in Chapter 1. My emphasis on the essential reflexivity and the necessary contextual embeddedness of relevant phenomena and practices is also shared by social and political scientists such as Flyvbjerg (2001) and Glynos and Howarth (2007). Even more clearly, I certainly do *not* side with talk that has been fashionable since Bell (1960) about 'the end of ideology,' based on the observation that liberalism, socialism, conservatism all had come to accept the common goal of a managed form of market capitalism, nor with Fukuyama's (1992) idea of 'the end of history,' based on an apparently complete triumph of western liberalism. Note Heywood's comment that

> each of these versions of endism has one thing in common: they are conducted within an ongoing framework of ideological thinking. In their different ways, each of them heralds the demise of ideology by highlighting the triumph of a particular ideological tradition, be it welfare capitalism, liberal democracy, postmodernism or scientism. Rather than demonstrating the weakened grasp of ideology, endism in fact shows its remarkable resilience and robustness.   (Heywood 2007 p. 339)

This book unequivocally sides with Heywood (and others who make a plea for taking ideology seriously in a so-called post-ideological age; e.g., Talshir, Humphrey and Freeden [eds.] 2006) while going a step further: because of the everyday nature of the ideology it bears upon (in contrast to Heywood's strictly 'political' ideologies), our subject matter is omnipresent, ubiquitous, immune to extinction as long as humans, as we know them, exist. This is why I see ideology not only in relation to grand political issues, but as much in relation to the working of institutions (cf. Meyer *et al.* eds. 2009) and small-scale 'local' contexts of practice. There are reasons to believe, moreover, that there are paradigms of thinking that provide continuity between the grand or global and the local.

Perhaps the most important theoretical contribution this book can make is an extremely practical one: providing theoretically justified tools for analysis. Remember the origins of structuralism in the humanities and social sciences. Both Marcel Mauss and Claude Lévi-Strauss (see, e.g., Lévi-Strauss 1958, p. 37) credited linguistics – with reference to Saussurean structuralism – with being the most scientifically advanced field in the social sciences, "to which it indisputably belongs," a model to be followed by psychologists, sociologists, and ethnographers alike. The model was indeed followed extensively, all the way into Lacan's psychoanalytic theory, Foucault's and Althusser's philosophies, Barthes' literary criticism. Having moved beyond structuralism (and the tinge of positivism associated with it), and at the risk of sounding overly audacious, linguistic pragmatics may provide the perspective and the tools for further advances in the social sciences, helping them to overcome the fruitless imitation of the natural sciences in attempts to produce cumulative and predictive knowledge by means of large-scale efforts at quantification in value-laden and essentially interpretive domains.

Finally, having dropped the word 'value,' we must return ever so briefly to the wider motivational context of social science research. In the field of ideology, even if we put Thompson's 'meaning in the service of dominance' on the methodological back burner, we cannot avoid the pertinent question of who gains and who loses in the context of the discursive processes and phenomena we investigate. Though, as van Dijk (2001) insists, not all ideologies are negative, counterexamples being antiracism and feminism as ideological alternatives to racism and sexism, and though the categories 'good' and 'bad' do not have analytical relevance as such, a researcher's analysis of ideology in language use must allow for evaluations if we want a social science that really matters. After all, bodily detention finds its match in discursive and ideological imprisonment.[2] Only knowledge and sustained critical awareness provide a way out.

---

[2] For an illustration of how literal such a metaphor can become, see Reetz's (2010) account of Victor Klemperer's (1975) notebooks on the language of the Third Reich.

Appendix 1: Theses, rules, guidelines, procedures, and caveats

Rule 2: Before an aspect of meaning can be seen as an ingredient of   23
ideology, it should emerge coherently from the data, both in terms of
conceptual connectedness with other aspects of meaning and in terms
of patterns of recurrence or of absence.

    Rule 2.1: *Types of data must be varied horizontally and vertically.*   26

    Rule 2.2: *An appropriate amount of data is required.*   28

    Rule 2.3: *Whatever is found throughout a wide corpus should also*   28
    be recoverable in (at least a number of) individual instances of
    discourse.

    Rule 2.4: *The quality of the data must be carefully evaluated in view*   29
    of the precise research goal.

        Preliminary caveat 1: *The following guidelines and procedures may*   53
        be followed step by step. However, actual research will develop cyc-
        lically rather than linearly. Some steps cannot be completed without
        going on to further steps, while sometimes a new step will force you
        to go back to earlier ones. Therefore: Get to know the entire set of
        guidelines and procedures before beginning to apply them.

        Preliminary caveat 2: *The following guidelines and procedures only*   53
        serve the purpose of analyzing collected language use data in view
        of their relationship with ideological patterns and processes. A com-
        plete research project may have to involve other, in particular ethno-
        graphic, stages preceding or coinciding with the analysis stage.

Guideline 1: Get to know your data thoroughly.   54

    Procedure 1.1: *In the case of audio-/video-recorded data: Listen to/*   55
    watch several times; transcribe all the data you want to subject to
    closer investigation.

    Procedure 1.2: *In the case of written text: Read and re-read until*   55
    you are fully familiar with the materials.

Guideline 2: Get to know the context of your data. Ask yourself what   56
it is you need to know in order to interpret the data, i.e., about the
linguistic context, the immediate context of situation, and the wider
context (social, political, historical, geographical, etc.).

    Caveat 2.1: *Context is not a stable 'outside' reality, nor is it finite in*   58
    any sense. Hence it cannot be described exhaustively. Those aspects
    of context may be deemed most relevant – without radically exclud-
    ing others – which are actualized in the discourse (hence the dictum
    that discourse constructs context) and which may thus become recov-
    erable in the analysis.

        Procedure 2.1: *Investigate the wider (social, political, historical,*   63
        geographical, etc.) context, to the extent that it is accessible. In
        particular:

Appendix 2: Sample texts

This Appendix contains all central portions of the texts used for purposes of illustration. For training purposes, they can be used in two ways. Either a student can practice an angle of approach represented in one or more guidelines/procedures by applying it/them to the entire corpus, or a corpus fragment can be used to practice going through the entire set of guidelines/procedures. A searchable pdf version of the corpus is available online to facilitate looking for specific phenomena (www.cambridge.org/verschueren).

Kerr, P. H. and A. C. Kerr   261
1927   *The Growth of the British Empire*. London: Longmans, Green &
        Co. [1st edn. 1911; revised 1921].
Title page + p. 183

Low, Sidney and Lloyd C. Sanders   263
1910   *The History of England During the Reign of Victoria (1837–1901)*
        (part XII of *The Political History of England*, ed. by William
        Hunt and Reginald L. Poole). London: Longmans, Green & Co.
Title page + pp. 132–158

McCarthy, Justin   291
1908   *A Short History of Our Own Times, from the Accession of Queen
        Victoria to the Accession of King Edward VII*. London: Chatto &
        Windus [1st edn., title ending in *[…] to the General Election of
        1880*, published in 1888].
Title page + pp. 170–195

Parkin, George R.   318
1911   *Round the Empire*. London: Cassell & Company [1892, revisions
        in 1898, 1903 and 1911].
Title page + pp. 213–214

Ransome, Cyril   321
1910   *A Short History of England, from the Earliest Times to the Death
        of King Edward VII*. London: Longmans, Green & Co. [12 earlier
        editions, gradually expanded with the course of events; 1st edn.,
        with title ending in *[…] to the Present Day (1890)*, published by
        Rivingtons in 1890].
Title page + pp. 442–443

Richardson, E. M.   324
1924   *The Building of the British Empire*. London: G. Bell & Sons
        [1913, revisions and enlargement 1921, corrections 1924].
Title page + pp. 136–141

Synge, M. B.   331
1908   *The Great Victorian Age*. London: Hodder & Stoughton.
Title page + pp. 111–124

Warner, George Townsend and C.H.K. Marten   346
1912   *The Groundwork of British History*, Part II, *From the Union of
        the Crowns to the Present Day* (by C.H.K. Marten). London:
        Blackie & Son.
Title page + pp. 690–694

Woodward, William Harrison   352
1921   *An Outline History of the British Empire from 1500 to 1920.*
          Cambridge: Cambridge University Press [1901, 2nd edn. 1912, 3rd
          edn. 1921].
Title page + pp. 235–238

HISTOIRE GÉNÉRALE

NOTIONS SOMMAIRES D'HISTOIRE ANCIENNE
DU MOYEN AGE ET DES TEMPS MODERNES

LEÇONS — RÉSUMÉS — RÉFLEXIONS

OUVRAGE CONTENANT

13 cartes — 10 gravures — un Questionnaire — des Devoirs
de rédaction et un Lexique des mots difficiles

A L'USAGE

DES CANDIDATS AU CERTIFICAT D'ÉTUDES PRIMAIRES

ET DES ÉLÈVES DE L'ENSEIGNEMENT SECONDAIRE

PAR

ERNEST LAVISSE

de l'Académie française.

DIX-SEPTIÈME ÉDITION

Ce livre fait suite à **tous les cours** d'Histoire de France

PARIS
LIBRAIRIE ARMAND COLIN
5, RUE DE MÉZIÈRES, 5

1902

PRÉFACE

Une histoire des principaux peuples anciens et modernes doit être enseignée avec *discrétion*, car elle est immense. Il faut se garder de vouloir tout dire, et sacrifier résolument les détails : nous les avons sacrifiés.

Si l'on voulait exposer l'histoire des différents peuples, en les prenant l'un après l'autre, on s'exposerait à des redites, et on se condamnerait à la confusion. Aussi nous sommes-nous efforcé de nous élever au-dessus des histoires particulières, et de considérer l'ensemble de l'histoire universelle. Nous l'avons divisée en quatre périodes : *antiquité, moyen âge, temps modernes, temps contemporains*. Dans chacune, nous avons marqué, par ses grands traits, le caractère des principaux peuples, et mesuré la part qui leur revient dans l'œuvre générale de la civilisation.

Nous avons réservé la plus grande place à l'ère contemporaine, ouverte par la **Révolution française**. Après avoir décrit l'action exercée par la Révolution, nous avons exposé longuement les *grandes affaires* du dix-neuvième siècle : histoire des gouvernements, des réformes et des révolutions ; histoire des guerres politiques et en particulier de la question d'Orient depuis 1815 ; histoire des guerres nationales, qui ont fondé les États nouveaux : **Grèce, Belgique, Italie, Allemagne**. A côté de ces œuvres de la politique et de la guerre, nous avons mis les œuvres de la paix : industrie, commerce, colonisation du monde.

Ces notions d'histoire générale, pourvu qu'elles soient données sobrement, rendront grand service aux écoliers. Elles seront le complément naturel de l'histoire de la France ; car on ne sait pas toute l'histoire de son pays, si l'on n'a point appris quelle place il occupe dans le monde. Elles seront aussi le complément de l'éducation patriotique : nos enfants doivent apprendre, dès l'école, pour y réfléchir ensuite, quels sont les *intérêts* de la France, quels *dangers* la menacent, quelles *espérances* lui sont ouvertes, quels *devoirs* lui sont imposés.

Ernest LAVISSE.

Programme de 1887. — **Histoire.**

(COURS SUPÉRIEUR, DE 11 A 13 ANS.)

Notions *très sommaires* d'**histoire générale**. Pour l'antiquité : l'Egypte, les Juifs, la Grèce, Rome ; — pour le moyen âge et les temps modernes : grands événements étudiés surtout dans leurs **rapports** avec l'histoire de France.

64 INVENTIONS ET DÉCOUVERTES. [*Carte*, p. 66.]

que les armes à feu eurent été inventées, les seigneurs furent moins importants à la guerre. **1.** Les rois, qui avaient beaucoup de canons et beaucoup d'infanterie, devinrent les maîtres dans leur royaume, et ils se firent la guerre les uns aux autres.

99. La boussole. — **2.** La **boussole** est une aiguille aimantée qui *se tourne toujours vers le nord*. **3.** Les Européens la connaissent aussi depuis le xive siècle, et elle a fait *une révolution dans la marine*.

4. Avant d'avoir la boussole, les marins n'osaient pas s'éloigner des côtes. **5.** Avec la boussole, ils ont pu **aller en pleine mer** sans peur de se perdre, puisque la boussole leur indiquait le nord. **6.** Les Espagnols et les Portugais en ont profité pour **découvrir le Nouveau Monde** (carte, p. 66).

100. Découverte de l'Afrique et des Indes. — **7.** Au xve siècle, les Portugais s'étaient avancés le long de l'Afrique occidentale, découvrant peu à peu *Madère*, les *Canaries*, la côte du *Gabon*. **8.** En 1484, un navigateur portugais était arrivé jusqu'au *cap de Bonne-Espérance*.

9. Alors **Vasco de Gama**, parti du Portugal avec quatre navires, tourna le cap de Bonne-Espérance, découvrit la *côte est de l'Afrique* et arriva dans les **Indes** (1498). **10.** Les Portugais y fondèrent des colonies et y firent le commerce.

101. Découverte de l'Amérique. — **11.** Un Italien, **Christophe Colomb**, avait eu l'idée que *la terre était ronde* et qu'en *en faisant le tour* par l'ouest, on arriverait dans l'Inde. **12.** Il parvint enfin à décider le roi d'Espagne à lui donner trois mauvais navires. **13.** Il s'embarqua sur l'océan et, au bout de deux mois, le 11 octobre 1492, il arriva *dans une île* de l'archipel des Lucayes. **14.** *Il avait* **découvert l'Amérique**.

15. En 1520, un autre navigateur au service du roi d'Espagne, **Magellan**, traversa l'océan, *tourna l'Amérique par le sud*, entra dans l'océan Pacifique et découvrit les îles de **l'Océanie**.

---

1. Qu'en résulta-t-il pour les rois? — **2.** Qu'est-ce que la boussole? — **3.** Depuis quand les Européens la connaissent-ils? — **4.** Qu'arrivait-il aux marins avant l'invention de la boussole? — **5.** Qu'ont-ils pu faire avec la boussole? — **6.** Qui en a profité et pourquoi? — **7.** Qu'avaient fait les Portugais au xve siè- cle? — **8.** Où étaient-ils arrivés en 1484? — **9.** Que fit Vasco de Gama? — **10.** Que fondèrent les Portugais? — **11.** Quelle idée avait eue Christophe Colomb? — **12.** Que fit le roi d'Espagne? — **13.** Que fit Christophe Colomb? — **14.** Que découvrit-il? — **15.** Que fit Magellan, et quand?

1. Le navire de Magellan revint en Espagne au bout de trois ans. C'était la première fois qu'on faisait le *tour du monde*.

102. Conquête du Mexique et du Pérou. — 2. L'Amérique était habitée par *des sauvages*. **3.** Mais il y avait *deux grands royaumes* : dans l'Amérique du Nord, le **Mexique**; dans l'Amérique du Sud, le **Pérou**.

4. Le Mexique et le Pérou renferment de *riches mines d'or et d'argent*, et leurs rois avaient amassé des *trésors énormes*. **5.** Les Espagnols le surent et résolurent d'aller les prendre.

Fig. 5. — **Fernand Cortez** au Mexique. — Les Mexicains prirent les hommes blancs pour des fils du Dieu-Soleil, les reçurent avec honneur et les laissèrent entrer à Mexico.

6. En 1519, l'Espagnol **Fernand Cortez** débarquait au Mexique avec 700 soldats, 18 chevaux et 10 canons. **7.** Les Mexicains n'avaient jamais vu ni Européens ni chevaux; ils prirent les *hommes blancs* pour des fils du Dieu-Soleil, les reçurent avec honneur et les laissèrent entrer à Mexico (fig. 5).

8. Les Espagnols en profitèrent pour s'emparer des trésors du roi; les Mexicains se révoltèrent, et plus de 100 000 guerriers vinrent assiéger Cortez, qui pourtant finit par les vaincre. **9.** Le dernier roi fut mis sur des charbons ardents, et le Mexique devint une *colonie espagnole* (1521).

1. Quand revint son navire ? — **2.** Qui habitait l'Amérique ? — **3.** Quels étaient les grands royaumes ? — **4.** Qu'est-ce qui faisait leur richesse ? — **5.** Que résolurent les Espagnols ? — **6.** Que fit Cortez ? — **7.** Pour qui les Mexicains prirent-ils les Espagnols ? — **8.** Que firent les Espagnols ? — **9.** Qu'arriva-t-il au dernier roi et que devint le Mexique ?

66   INVENTIONS ET DÉCOUVERTES.

1. Une autre bande espagnole, commandée par **Pizarre**, entra dans le Pérou et prit le roi (1529). **2.** On le força à payer pour sa rançon* une *chambre pleine d'or*, puis on l'étrangla. **3.** Et le Pérou fut *conquis par les Espagnols*.

103. Empire des Européens. — **4.** Les Portugais et les Espagnols possédèrent alors des *pays immenses hors de l'Europe*.

POSSESSIONS des ESPAGNOLS et des PORTUGAIS au XVIe Siècle.

Madère, Canaries, îles découvertes par les Portugais au XVe siècle. — Cap de Bonne-Espérance, au sud de l'Afrique, tourné par **Vasco de Gama**. — Indes (Asie), colonies fondées par les Portugais. — **Amérique,** découverte par Christophe **Colomb** (1492). — Océanie, plusieurs îles y furent découvertes par **Magellan**. — **Mexique** (Amérique du Nord), conquis par Fernand **Cortez** (1519).

1. Que se passa-t-il au Pérou? — **2.** Que fit-on au roi? — **3.** Que devint le Pérou? — **4.** Que possédaient alors les Portugais et les Espagnols?

INVENTIONS ET DECOUVERTES. 67

1. Les Portugais dominaient **à l'Est**, en Afrique, en Asie et en Océanie. **2.** Ils avaient sur les côtes de l'**Afrique du Sud**, de l'**Inde** et de la **Chine** des *ports* où ils allaient prendre les marchandises de l'Orient, le coton, la soie, l'ivoire, les épices. **3.** Ils possédaient les **îles Moluques** et le **Brésil.**

4. Les Espagnols dominaient **à l'Ouest**, en Amérique.

Pérou, contrée de l'Amérique du Sud conquise par **Pizarre** (1529). — **Moluques**, îles de l'Océanie possédées alors par les Portugais. — **Brésil**, contrée de l'Amérique du Sud conquise par les Portugais. — **Chine** (Asie), où les Portugais avaient des ports. — **Antilles**, îles de l'océan Atlantique, entre l'Amérique du Nord et l'Amérique du Sud. — Iles **Philippines** (Océanie), possessions espagnoles.

1. Où dominaient les Portugais ? | Quels pays possédaient-ils ? — **4.**
— **2.** Où étaient leurs ports ? — **3.** | Où dominaient les Espagnols ?

214

1. Ils possédaient les **Antilles**, le **Mexique**, toute l'**Amérique du Sud**, excepté le Brésil, et en Océanie, les **îles Philippines**.

104. La traite des nègres. — **2.** Les Espagnols qui allaient en Amérique étaient presque tous des *aventuriers* * *féroces*. **3.** Ils voulaient se procurer *de l'argent* et ils *forçaient les habitants du pays* à travailler dans les mines, les tourmentaient, les faisaient chasser par leurs chiens. Les habitants mouraient tous.

4. On envoya alors acheter des nègres en Afrique, on les ramenait en Amérique où on les faisait travailler comme **esclaves**. **5.** Ce commerce inhumain s'appelait la **traite des noirs**. **6.** Les Espagnols l'avaient commencé en 1517; *tous les autres peuples*, Portugais, Français, Anglais ont eu aussi des esclaves noirs.

105. Conséquences des découvertes. — **7.** Jusqu'au xvᵉ siècle, les Européens ne connaissaient qu'un *coin du monde*. Depuis les grandes découvertes, nous connaissons le **monde entier**.

8. Les produits de l'Asie et de l'Amérique, le coton, le poivre, le sucre, la soie étaient très rares et par conséquent *très chers*. **9.** Nous les recevons maintenant en grande quantité. **10.** Les Européens étaient *enfermés en Europe*. Il y en a maintenant dans toute l'*Amérique* et toute l'*Océanie*.

Résumé (*à réciter*).

I. Les découvertes et les inventions de la fin du xvᵉ siècle commencent la période des **temps modernes**.

II. La **poudre**, connue en Europe depuis le xivᵉ siècle, a permis de faire des *canons* et des *arquebuses*, puis des *mousquets*, et a produit une révolution dans l'art de la guerre.

III. La **boussole** a permis de faire de longs voyages **en pleine mer**.

IV. Les Portugais ont découvert toute l'**Afrique** et sont arrivés aux **Indes** par le cap de Bonne-Espérance (1498).

1. Que possédaient-ils? — **2.** Qu'étaient les Espagnols qui allaient en Amérique? — **3.** Que faisaient-ils aux habitants? — **4.** Que fit-on des nègres d'Afrique? — **5** Comment se nommait ce commerce? — **6.** Quels peuples ont eu des esclaves noirs? — **7.** Les Européens connaissaient-ils le monde entier avant le xvᵉ siècle? — **8.** Quels produits étaient très chers? – **9-10.** Le sont-ils encore de nos jours? — Où les Européens se sont-ils répandus après les découvertes du xvᵉ siècle?

V. Les Espagnols ont découvert l'**Amérique** (1492), et fait les premiers le tour du monde (1520).

VI. Le **Mexique**, conquis en 1519 par *Fernand Cortez*, le **Pérou**, conquis en 1529 par *Pizarre*, devinrent des colonies espagnoles.

VII. Les Portugais dominèrent alors à l'est, en Afrique, dans l'Inde, aux îles Moluques et au Brésil. Les Espagnols dominèrent à l'ouest en Amérique.

VIII. Pour cultiver ces colonies, les Espagnols établirent la *traite des noirs* (1517) ; les autres peuples eurent aussi des *esclaves nègres*.

découvertes ont fait connaître le monde entier aux et les ont préparés à en devenir maîtres.

CHAPITRE IX

FORMATION DE L'EMPIRE ANGLAIS

139. Les colonies européennes. — 1. Les Portugais et les Espagnols ont été les premiers peuples européens qui ont découvert le reste du monde. **2.** Ils se sont emparés, en Amérique, en Afrique, en Asie, en Océanie, des pays qui leur convenaient, et ils ont pris *les pays les plus riches*. **3.** Mais comme ils gouvernaient très mal, leurs colonies sont devenues pauvres et faibles.

4. Les *Italiens et les Allemands n'ont pas eu de colonies*, parce qu'ils ne formaient pas une nation et n'avaient pas de gouvernement assez fort pour s'établir au loin.

5. Mais les **Français**, les **Anglais** et les **Hollandais** fondèrent au xviie siècle des colonies considérables. **6.** Les Hollandais s'établirent dans les grandes îles de *Java* et *Sumatra*. **7.** Les Français prirent *tout le nord de l'Amérique*, (Acadie, Canada), le *pays du Mississipi* (Louisiane), et dans les Antilles, la grande île d'*Haïti*. **8.** Les Anglais prirent *toute la côte orientale de l'Amérique du Nord*.

140. Conquête de l'Inde par les Anglais. — 9. Au xviiie siècle, les Anglais et les Français se battirent pour les colonies. **10.** Il y avait alors dans les Indes **deux compagnies de commerce** : l'une, anglaise, à Madras ; l'autre, française, à Pondichéry. **11.** Le directeur de la Compagnie française, **Dupleix**, avait commencé à conquérir les Indes. **12.** Cela n'était pas très difficile, car le pays était partagé

---

1. Quels peuples ont découvert le monde ? — **2.** Quels pays ont-ils pris ? — **3.** Que sont devenues leurs colonies ? — **4.** Pourquoi les Italiens et les Allemands n'ont-ils pas eu de colonies ? — **5.** Qui fonda des colonies au xviie siècle ? — **6.** Dites les colonies des Hollandais. — **7.** Des Français. — **8.** Des Anglais ? — **9.** Que firent les Anglais et les Français au xviiie siècle ? — **10.** Qu'y avait-il alors dans les Indes? — **11.** Que faisait Dupleix ? — **12.** Pourquoi pouvait-on facilement conquérir l'Inde ?

94   FORMATION DE L'EMPIRE ANGLAIS.

entre beaucoup de petits princes qui n'avaient que de très mauvais soldats, et les habitants ne cherchaient pas à se défendre. **1.** C'eût été une **très belle conquête**, car l'Inde a aujourd'hui plus de 200 millions d'habitants, et elle produit en quantité du coton, du riz, du poivre, de la soie.

2. Les Anglais demandèrent au gouvernement français de destituer Dupleix, et le gouvernement le *destitua* (1754).
3. Alors les Auglais commencèrent eux-mêmes à conquérir

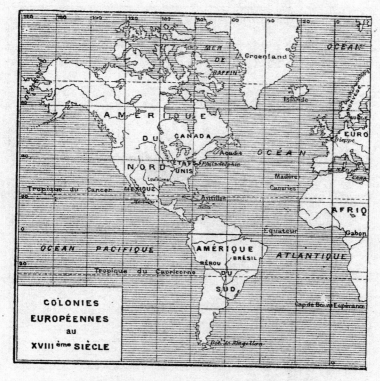

Java, Sumatra, îles où s'établirent les Hollandais. — Canada, Louisiane, pays de l'Amérique du Nord où s'établirent les Français, conquis ensuite par les Anglais. — Pondichéry, ville de l'Inde où se trouvait une compagnie de com-

1. La conquête était-elle belle ? — **2.** Comment se conduisit le gou- | vernement français ? — **3.** Que firent alors les Anglais ?

les Indes. **1.** Une seule bataille, en 1757, leur donna tout l'immense pays du **Bengale. 2.** Puis ils détruisirent les colonies françaises (1763), et ils devinrent les **maîtres de l'Inde.** Ils le sont encore.

141. Conquête de l'Amérique du Nord par les Anglais. — **3.** Ce fut la même chose en Amérique. En 1754, quand la guerre commença entre la France et l'Angleterre, les colons* anglais attaquèrent les colons français

merce française. — **Philadelphie**, réunion du Congrès qui proclama l'indépendance des Etats-Unis (1776). — **Madras**, ville de l'Inde où se trouvait une compagnie de commerce anglaise. — **Bengale**, conquis par les Anglais (1763).

1. Comment acquirent-ils le Bengale? — **2** Que devinrent-ils dans l'Inde? — **3.** Que firent les colons anglais en Amérique?

96   FORMATION DE L'EMPIRE ANGLAIS.   [*Carte*, p. 94.]

du Canada. **1.** Les colons français *résistèrent comme des héros* et furent d'abord *vainqueurs*. **2.** Mais le gouvernement anglais envoya des troupes au secours des colons anglais. **3.** *Le gouvernement français n'envoya personne au secours des colons français.* **4.** Les Canadiens n'avaient que 5 000 hommes contre 40 000, et pas de munitions *. Les Anglais conquirent le Canada, et en 1763 la France céda à l'Angleterre tout ce qui lui restait dans l'Amérique du Nord.

5. Dans toutes ces guerres, les *colons* et les *marins français ont fait leur devoir bravement.* **6.** Mais la France était alors gouvernée par Louis XV, dont vous connaissez le triste règne. D'ailleurs presque personne ne comprenait que *les colonies sont nécessaires à une nation.* **7.** On dépensait beaucoup d'argent et de soldats à des guerres en Allemagne et en Italie, où la France n'avait rien à gagner, et on refusait d'envoyer aux colonies 4 ou 5 000 soldats qui auraient donné à la France l'*empire du monde*.

Résumé (*à réciter*).

I. Les colonies des Espagnols et des Portugais dépérirent par leur mauvais gouvernement. Les Français, les Anglais et les Hollandais fondèrent au xviie siècle de grandes colonies, surtout dans l'Amérique du Nord et aux Indes.

II. Le directeur de la Compagnie française des Indes. **Dupleix**, essaya au xviiie siècle de conquérir l'Inde pour la France. Le gouvernement français le destitua (1754). L'Inde fut alors conquise par les Anglais ; ils commencèrent par le **Bengale** (1757).

III. En Amérique, les colons français du **Canada**, *abandonnés par le gouvernement français*, furent soumis par les Anglais. En 1763, la France renonça à presque toutes ses colonies.

IV. La France a laissé échapper alors, par la faute de son gouvernement, l'*empire du monde;* ce sont les Anglais qui l'ont pris.

1. Comment résistèrent les colons français? — **2.** Que fit le gouvernement anglais ? — **3.** Que fit le gouvernement français ? — **4.** Qu'arriva-t-il en 1763 ? — **5.** Qui a fait alors son devoir ? — **6.** Comprenait-on alors à quoi servent les colonies ? — **7.** Où dépensait-on l'argent et les soldats ?

CHAPITRE X

FONDATION DES ÉTATS-UNIS

142. Soulèvement des colonies d'Amérique. — 1. Les colons anglais de l'Amérique du Nord se gouvernaient eux-mêmes. 2. Car le gouvernement anglais a l'habitude de *ne pas tracasser les colons* anglais, et de ne *pas se mêler de leurs affaires.* 3. Une fois seulement il a manqué à cette habitude, et l'Angleterre y a perdu une de ses plus grandes colonies.

4. En 1770, le gouvernement anglais ayant besoin d'argent, mit un impôt sur les colons *sans les consulter.* 5. Les colons déclarèrent qu'ils ne payeraient pas, se révoltèrent et chassèrent les gouverneurs anglais. 6. Le gouvernement anglais envoya une armée pour les forcer à se soumettre. 7. Les colons de chaque province nommèrent alors des députés qui se réunirent en *congrès** à Philadelphie. 8. Le 4 juillet 1776, ce congrès proclama que les États étaient indépendants* de l'Angleterre et formaient la **République des États-Unis de l'Amérique du Nord.**

143. L'Indépendance des États-Unis. — 9. La guerre entre les Anglais et les États-Unis s'appelle *guerre de l'Indépendance américaine.* 10. Elle dura de 1774 à 1783. 11. Les États-Unis furent vaincus d'abord : ils n'avaient pas d'armée ; le gouvernement anglais au contraire avait *acheté* 20 000 soldats allemands qu'il avait envoyés contre l'Amérique. 12. Mais les *volontaires français* allèrent au secours des Américains, puis le gouvernement français leur envoya une armée, et les Anglais furent vaincus. 13. Ils firent la paix en 1783 et reconnurent la liberté des États-Unis. 14. Le plus grand citoyen des États-Unis fut alors **Washington,** qui s'illustra dans la guerre et le gouvernement.

1. Comment se gouvernaient les colons anglais ? — 2. Quelle est l'habitude du gouvernement anglais ? — 3. Qu'est-il arrivé quand il a manqué à cette habitude ? — 4. Qu'avait fait le gouvernement anglais aux colons ? — 5. Que firent les colons ? — 6. Que fit le gouvernement ? — 7. Où se réunit le congrès ? — 8. Que proclama-t-il et quand ? — 9. Comment se nomme cette guerre ? — 10. Combien dura-t-elle ? — 11. Qui fut vainqueur d'abord ? et pourquoi ? — 12. Qui vint au secours des Américains ? — 13. A quoi les Anglais furent-ils obligés ? — 14. Quel fut le plus grand citoyen des États-Unis ?

98 FONDATION DES ÉTATS-UNIS. [*Carte*, p. 94.]

Résumé (*à réciter*).

I. Les colons anglais de l'Amérique du Nord, habitués à se gouverner eux-mêmes, se révoltent contre le gouvernement anglais, qui a mis un impôt sur eux sans les consulter (1770).

II. Les députés des provinces, réunis au *Congrès de Philadelphie* 1776), proclament l'**indépendance** des États-Unis.

III. Dans la guerre de l'Indépendance américaine (1774-1783), les États-Unis, *avec le secours de la France*, forcent l'Angleterre à reconnaître leur liberté.

IV. Les États-Unis sont gouvernés alors par **Washington**.

Réflexions sur le Livre III.

I. Les *temps modernes* sont annoncés par de grandes inventions et de grandes découvertes.

II. La **boussole** guide les navigateurs, qui découvrent l'Amérique; l'**imprimerie** aide les savants qui répandent dans le monde des connaissances nouvelles; elle aide aussi les hommes qui se révoltent contre l'Église et font la Réforme. L'emploi de la **poudre** à la guerre met aux mains des rois des armes terribles.

III. Ainsi tout se transforme : le monde est agrandi. Les Européens en prennent possession : Espagnols et Portugais d'abord, ensuite Hollandais; les Français fondent de vastes colonies.

IV. Mais l'Europe, au lieu de se donner tout entière à la colonisation*, au commerce, à l'industrie, est troublée par de longues guerres. Les rois de France et d'Espagne, devenus très puissants veulent faire des conquêtes et se disputent l'Italie. Quand Charles-Quint, roi d'Espagne, devient empereur, une grande lutte commence entre les maisons de France et d'Espagne. Les guerres *religieuses* se mêlent partout aux guerres *politiques*.

V. Au milieu du dix-septième siècle la maison d'Espagne est vaincue, et la France prend le premier rang en Europe ; mais elle abuse de sa puissance.

VI. L'Angleterre devient sa plus redoutable ennemie, après avoir fait en 1688 la révolution politique qui lui donne la liberté. Elle nous prend nos **colonies** et fonde un grand empire. — Deux États nouveaux et redoutables apparaissent : la **Russie** et la **Prusse**. — La France ne conduit plus, comme auparavant, les destinées de l'Europe ; mais elle va prendre, par la **Revolution,** la direction de l'humanité.

[**Pour les devoirs** de rédaction sur le Livre III, voir page 166.]

LIVRE IV

LES TEMPS CONTEMPORAINS

CHAPITRE PREMIER

LA RÉVOLUTION FRANÇAISE EN EUROPE

144. Les temps contemporains. — **1.** A la fin du
xviiie siècle, commence une **ère nouvelle** pour la **France**,
pour l'**Europe** et pour le **monde**.

145. Déclaration des Droits de l'homme. —
2. L'Assemblée nationale, réunie en France en 1789, avait
déclaré tous les Français **libres et égaux**. **3.** Mais elle ne
voulait pas avoir travaillé pour les Français seulement. **4.** Elle
voulut proclamer les droits que doivent avoir non seulement
les Français, mais tous les autres peuples, et elle fit la
Déclaration des Droits de l'homme.

146. Principes de 89. — **5.** Dans cette déclaration
sont posées les règles de gouvernement qu'on appelle **principes de 89.** Les voici :

6. 1o Tous les hommes doivent être libres et avoir les
mêmes droits.

2o Chacun est **libre** de faire tout ce qui ne fait de mal à
personne : libre de penser, d'écrire, de pratiquer sa religion,
de publier des livres. Chacun est libre d'aller où il veut, de
s'établir dans la ville qu'il veut, de travailler au métier qu'il
veut. Il ne doit être arrêté que si on le soupçonne d'un
crime, et, dans ce cas, il ne doit être jugé que par ses con-
citoyens réunis en *jury* *.

3o La loi doit être la même pour tous. Tous les citoyens ont
le droit de devenir fonctionnaires ou officiers. On doit tenir
compte seulement de leurs qualités personnelles et non pas

---

1. Qu'est-ce qui commence à la fin
du xviiie siècle ? — **2.** Qu'a déclaré
l'Assemblée nationale ? — **3.** Pour qui
cette déclaration a-t-elle été faite ?

— **4.** Comment s'appelle cette déclaration ? — **5.** Que trouve-t-on dans la
Déclaration des Droits de l'homme ?
— **6.** Quels sont les principes de 89 ?

de leur famille ou de leur fortune. Tous les citoyens doivent
payer les mêmes impôts. Tous sont donc **égaux** devant la loi.

4° Les citoyens se réunissent pour choisir des **représentants**. L'assemblée des représentants a seule le droit de voter
les impôts et de faire les lois. Les ministres doivent obéir
aux représentants, car c'est la **nation qui gouverne**, et non
pas les ministres.

147. État de l'Europe en 89. — **1**. La plupart de
ces règles vous paraissent toutes naturelles. Peut-être ne
vous figurez-vous pas comment on peut vivre dans un pays
où l'on n'est libre ni de travailler, ni de parler, ni de penser;
où le gouvernement peut mettre les gens en prison, leur
prendre leur argent ou les faire pendre à sa fantaisie.
2. Songez pourtant qu'encore aujourd'hui presque tous les
peuples de l'Orient, les Turcs, les Persans, les Égyptiens,
vivent sous un régime arbitraire*. **3**. Avant la Révolution de 89,
l'Espagne, l'Italie, l'Allemagne, la Russie, la France, l'Amérique du Sud étaient, comme la Turquie aujourd'hui, gouvernées par **le bon plaisir** des rois et de leurs ministres.
4. Excepté la Hollande, l'Angleterre, la Suisse et les États-
Unis, aucun peuple ne se gouvernait lui-même. **5**. Il n'y avait
pas de nations, mais seulement des **sujets**.

1. Que pensez-vous de ces principes ? — **2**. Comment sont gouvernés les peuples de l'Orient ? — **3**.
Comment étaient gouvernés les
pays de l'Europe avant 89 ? — **4**.
Quelles exceptions y avait-il ? — **5**.
Y avait-il alors des nations ? — **6**.
Comment étaient gouvernées l'Allemagne et l'Italie ? — **7**. Quel modèle
suivaient les princes ? — **8**. Que faisaient-ils pour ressembler à Louis
XIV ? — **9**. Comment payaient-ils
leurs dépenses ? — **10**. Qui décidait
les affaires ?

168. Soulèvement des colonies espagnoles. —

2. L'Espagne avait en Amérique des colonies immenses (carte, p. 156), et elle ne laissait pas les habitants de ces colonies se gouverner eux-mêmes. **3.** Elle leur envoyait des gouverneurs, et elle ne permettait à aucun colon * d'avoir une place dans le gouvernement. **4.** Elle ne laissait aller dans les colonies que des *navires espagnols*, et, afin de rendre les colons plus ignorants et plus obéissants, elle les empêchait de recevoir *aucun livre ou aucun journal*.

5. En 1811, les Mexicains commencèrent à se soulever ; les premiers qui se révoltèrent furent fusillés. **6.** Mais, en 1821, les soldats entrèrent dans la révolte et le Mexique devint, en 1823, une **république indépendante** qui n'obéit plus à l'Espagne.

7. Toutes les colonies des Espagnols se soulevèrent ainsi l'une après l'autre. **8.** Les insurgés furent battus d'abord parce qu'ils étaient mal organisés ; mais ils reprenaient toujours les armes. **9.** Le célèbre **Bolivar**, surnommé le *libérateur des peuples*, allait avec une petite armée d'un pays à l'autre pour chasser les Espagnols. **10.** Enfin, en 1826, les *colons étaient vainqueurs partout*, et il ne restait plus de soldats espagnols en Amérique.

11. Au lieu d'un seul empire espagnol, il y a depuis lors quinze républiques : le Mexique, les cinq républiques de l'Amérique centrale, le Vénézuela, la Nouvelle-Grenade, la Colombie, le Pérou, la Bolivie, le Chili, la République Argentine, le Paraguay et l'Uruguay.

---

1. Que fit l'armée française en 1823 ? — **2.** Que possédait l'Espagne en Amérique ? — **3.** Que faisait-elle dans ces colonies ? — **4.** Que défendait-elle aux colons ? — **5.** Qu'arrivat-il au Mexique en 1811 ? — **6.** Comment et quand le Mexique devint-il indépendant ? — **7.** Que firent les autres colonies espagnoles ? — **8.** Qu'arriva-t-il aux insurgés ? — **9.** Parlez de Bolivar. — **10.** Quand se termina la guerre et comment ? — **11.** Quels États y a-t-il depuis lors en Amérique ? — **12.** Qui régnait alors en France ? — **13.** Qu'avait fait Louis XVIII ?

122 RÉVOLUTIONS ET RÉFORMES POLITIQUES. [*Carte*, p. 156.]

175. Abolition de l'esclavage des nègres. —
3. En Amérique, depuis le XVIe siècle, on faisait travailler
la terre par des *nègres esclaves* amenés d'Afrique. **4.** Depuis
le XVIIIe siècle, les libéraux réclamaient qu'on rendît la
liberté à ces nègres et qu'on cessât d'en acheter de nouveaux. **5.** Les *Français avaient donné l'exemple* en 1789, en
abolissant l'esclavage. **6.** Mais les colons disaient qu'on ne
pouvait se passer de nègres pour cultiver le coton et le café,
et ils avaient fait rétablir l'esclavage.

7. Les Français l'ont aboli de nouveau en 1848, et tous les
autres Européens les ont imités. **8.** On a défendu aussi la
traite des nègres et les Anglais et les Français ont envoyé
des vaisseaux sur la côte d'Afrique pour prendre les navires
sur lesquels on transportait les noirs. **9.** Les *négriers* (marchands de nègres) sont traités comme des pirates* : quand
on les prend, on les pend au mât de leur navire.

10. Mais dans la République des États-Unis, plusieurs
États du Sud voulaient conserver leurs esclaves. **11.** Ces pays
sont très chauds ; les propriétaires, qu'on appelle **planteurs**,
avaient l'habitude de faire travailler les nègres qui craignent
moins la chaleur, et comme ils n'avaient pas besoin de les
payer, ils étaient devenus très riches. **12.** Dans les États du
Nord, qui sont des pays froids, les propriétaires *n'avaient pas
besoin d'esclaves ;* ils demandèrent qu'on abolît l'esclavage.

13. Les États du Sud refusèrent : ils se séparèrent de la
fédération * et formèrent une *confédération* * à part. **14.** Les
États du Nord leur firent la guerre pour les forcer à rentrer
dans la fédération et à abolir l'esclavage. **15.** La guerre dura
de 1860 à 1865 ; un million d'hommes au moins furent tués.

1. Qu'a fait Alexandre II ? — **2.**
Que sont les paysans russes ? — **3.**
Qui faisait-on travailler en Amérique ? — **4.** Que réclamaient les libéraux ? — **5.** Qui avait donné l'exemple de l'abolition de l'esclavage ? —
6. Pourquoi l'avait-on rétabli ? —
7. Qui l'a aboli de nouveau ? quand ?
— **8.** Qu'a-t-on fait pour empêcher la
traite des nègres ? — **9.** Que fait on
des négriers ? — **10.** Qui voulait conserver des esclaves ? — **11.** Pourquoi ? — **12.** Qui demandait d'abolir
l'esclavage ? — **13.** Que firent les
États du Sud ? — **14.** Et les États du
Nord ? — **15.** Combien dura la guerre ?

1. Pendant ce temps, l'Angleterre et la France ne recevaient plus de coton ; elles faillirent prendre parti pour le Sud. A la fin, les **États du Nord,** beaucoup plus nombreux, furent vainqueurs. **2.** Les **États du Sud** furent ravagés et ruinés ; et *on abolit l'esclavage dans tous les États-Unis* (1865).

3. Aujourd'hui il n'y a plus d'esclaves ni en Europe ni en Amérique. **4.** Les musulmans en ont encore ; les marchands d'esclaves arabes s'en vont au milieu de l'Afrique enlever par force des nègres qu'ils ramènent à coups de bâton et qu'ils vendent en Égypte ou en Turquie.

Résumé (*à réciter*).

I. Depuis la Révolution française, tous les pays d'Europe sont divisés entre deux partis : les **absolutistes,** qui veulent le gouvernement *du bon plaisir*, et les **libéraux,** qui veulent établir le gouvernement de la nation par elle-même.

II. Les absolutistes étaient les plus forts en 1815 ; les rois alliés contre Napoléon formèrent la **Sainte-Alliance,** et s'engagèrent à se soutenir les uns les autres contre leurs peuples.

III. Les libéraux d'Italie et d'Espagne se soulevèrent en 1820, et forcèrent les princes à donner des constitutions à leurs pays. Mais ils furent vaincus : en Italie, par les armées de l'empereur d'Autriche ; en Espagne, par l'armée du roi de France (1823).

IV. Les colons des **colonies espagnoles** d'Amérique, opprimés par le gouvernement, se soulevèrent contre l'Espagne. Après des guerres qui durèrent plus de dix ans, et où Bolivar se distingua, ils se déclarèrent indépendants, et formèrent **quinze républiques.**

V. La **Révolution de 1830,** faite par les Français contre le roi Charles X, fut suivie d'agitations dans tous les pays de l'Europe. L'Angleterre fit en 1832 une **réforme électorale.** Le tzar de Russie, Nicolas Ier, maintint par la force le gouvernement despotique.

VI. La **Révolution de 1848,** qui établit le suffrage universel, amena des soulèvements dans toute l'Europe. Les libéraux furent d'abord vainqueurs en Autriche, en Prusse, en Italie. Mais les souverains s'aidèrent les uns les autres. Les libéraux furent vaincus en Hongrie par l'armée russe, en Allemagne par l'armée prussienne, en Italie par l'armée autrichienne. Après le coup

1. Quelle fut la conséquence de cette guerre pour l'Angleterre et la France ? — **2.** Qui resta vainqueur ? Qu'en résulta-t-il ? — **3.** Où n'y a-t-il plus d'esclaves ? — **4.** Qui en a encore ? comment se les procure-t-on ?

124   GUERRES POLITIQUES EN ORIENT. [*Carte*, p. 126.]

d'État de Napoléon III (1851), il ne resta presque plus que des gouvernements absolus.

VII. Les libéraux sont redevenus les plus forts depuis 1860. L'Autriche a reçu une constitution en 1861, la Hongrie en 1867, l'Italie en 1861 ; l'Espagne a chassé la reine Isabelle (1868) et repoussé les *Carlistes* (1876).

VIII. Les **représentants des pays** gouvernent aujourd'hui tous les États de l'Europe, excepté l'Allemagne, où le roi de Prusse force le *Reichstag* à lui obéir, et la Russie, où le tzar gouverne seul, toujours menacé d'être assassiné par les *nihilistes*.

IX. Dans la plupart des pays, tous les habitants ne sont pas électeurs. Le **suffrage universel** n'est établi qu'en France, en Suisse, aux États-Unis et, depuis 1868, en Allemagne.

X. Les paysans esclaves de Russie ont été **affranchis** en 1863 par un décret du tzar Alexandre II.

XI. L'**esclavage des nègres**, aboli d'abord par la France en 1789, puis rétabli, a été aboli définitivement par la France en 1848, puis par les autres pays d'Europe, et on a défendu la traite* des nègres.

XII. Les États du Sud, dans la république des États-Unis, ayant voulu conserver leurs esclaves et se séparer de l'Union, les États du Nord leur ont fait la guerre (1860-1865), et les ont forcés à abolir l'esclavage.

XIII. Il reste encore des esclaves dans les pays **musulmans**.

----

1. Quelles sortes de guerres y a-t-il eu depuis 1815 ? — **2.** Qu'est-ce que les guerres politiques ? — **3.** Qu'est-ce que les guerres nationales ? — **4.** Que pensez-vous de ces guerres ?

128   GUERRES POLITIQUES EN ORIENT.   [*Carte*, p. 126.]

182. Affaires d'Égypte. — **11**. L'Egypte est un pays musulman, qui relève de la Turquie, mais qui est à peu près indépendant et gouverné par un **khédive**. **12**. Mais depuis qu'on a creusé le *canal de Suez* et que beaucoup de marchands européens se sont établis au Caire et à Alexandrie, les Européens sont forcés de s'occuper des affaires de l'Égypte. **13**. Ils ont établi un tribunal composé de *juges européens*, parce que les juges musulmans, dans les procès entre un musulman et un chrétien, donnaient toujours tort au chrétien. **14**. Ils ont envoyé des *ministres anglais et français*, parce que le khédive ne savait pas gouverner ses finances*.

15. Les soldats égyptiens se sont révoltés contre le khédive ; les Anglais ont envoyé une *armée anglaise* qui a vaincu les révoltés et pris leur chef, Arabi-Pacha. **16**. Les Anglais

---

1. Où fut signée la paix ? — **2**. Qu'est-ce que le congrès de Berlin ? — **3**. Que sont devenus les peuples chrétiens de Turquie ? — **4**. Quels sont les pays indépendants ? — **5**. Quels peuples payent encore un tribut ? — **6**. Qu'a pris l'Autriche ? — **7**. La Russie ? — **8**. L'Angleterre ? — **9**. La Grèce ? — **10**. Que reste-t-il au sultan ? — **11**. Qui gouverne l'Egypte ? — **12**. Qu'est-il arrivé depuis qu'on a creusé le canal de Suez ? — **13**. Qu'ont établi les Européens ? pourquoi ? — **14**. Qui ont-ils envoyé en Egypte ? pourquoi ? — **15**. Qu'ont fait les Anglais ? — **16**. Qui occupe l'Egypte ?

occupent aujourd'hui l'Égypte, et cette occupation leur cause les plus grands embarras.

Résumé (*à réciter*).

I. Il y a eu, depuis 1815, des **guerres politiques**, faites par des souverains pour agrandir leurs domaines, et des **guerres nationales**, faites par des peuples qui voulaient devenir libres.

II. **L'empire turc**, où se sont faites les guerres politiques, était grand mais *très faible;* il avait perdu l'Égypte (1808), la Serbie (1817), la Grèce (1828).

III. Depuis ce temps, les Russes désirent *prendre Constantinople*, et les Anglais veulent les en empêcher en maintenant l'empire Turc. La **question d'Orient** donna lieu, en 1840, à une guerre faite par les Anglais au vice-roi d'Égypte Méhémet-Ali.

IV. Elle a donné lieu, en 1854, à la **guerre de Crimée**. Pour sauver les Turcs attaqués par les Russes, l'Angleterre et la France assiégèrent et prirent Sébastopol (1855), et le **congrès de Paris** imposa la paix à la Russie.

V. En 1877, le Monténégro et la Serbie étant vaincus par les Turcs, les Russes envahissent la Turquie, et après le long siège de Plewna, arrivèrent jusque près de Constantinople.

VI. Le traité de San-Stefano, corrigé par le **congrès de Berlin**, a réglé, en 1878, les affaires de Turquie. L'empire turc subsiste, mais on lui a pris une partie de ses provinces.

VII. Les Européens ont été obligés de s'occuper des affaires de l'Égypte, où résidaient beaucoup de marchands européens. L'Égypte a reçu des juges européens, des ministres des finances européens, et enfin une armée anglaise qui l'occupe.

CHAPITRE VIII

LES EUROPÉENS HORS D'EUROPE

214. Les Anglais dans l'Inde. — **1.** L'Inde était divisée en plusieurs royaumes ; les Anglais les ont conquis l'un après l'autre en cent ans (de 1757 à 1856). **2.** Ils sont devenus maîtres d'un empire de 240 millions de sujets.

3. Le pays est très chaud et très malsain (c'est de l'Inde que nous vient le choléra). Les Européens ont de la peine

1. Qu'ont fait les Anglais dans l'Inde ? — **2.** Combien ont-ils de sujets dans l'Inde ? — **3.** Quel est le climat de l'Inde ?

à y vivre. **1.** Aussi les Anglais ne vont-ils pas dans les Indes comme ils vont en Amérique, pour s'y établir. Ils n'y vont que pour faire le commerce, gouverner les Hindous, et commander les troupes.

2. Pour faire leurs conquêtes, les Anglais n'auraient pas eu assez de soldats anglais ; ils ont pris pour soldats des habitants de l'Inde. **3.** Ils en ont fait des régiments de *Cipayes*, qui sont commandés par des officiers anglais.

4. Il y avait dans l'Inde, en 1857, 290 000 soldats; 240 000 étaient des Cipayes, c'est-à-dire des Hindous. **5.** Ils avaient encore la vieille religion de l'Inde ; ils croyaient que la vache est un animal sacré. **6.** Les officiers anglais voulurent leur faire tirer des cartouches enduites de graisse de vache. Les Cipayes se révoltèrent. **7.** Ce fut une **révolte générale.** Le chef des révoltés, Nana-Sahib, massacrait les Anglais, les femmes comme les hommes, et faisait jeter les enfants au feu.

8. Les soldats anglais marchèrent contre les Cipayes révoltés, reprirent la ville de Delhi, et attachèrent les prisonniers hindous à la gueule des canons (fig. 10). **9.** Ils réussirent à reprendre l'Inde ; depuis il n'y a plus eu de révolte, et les Hindous commencent à parler anglais et à adopter les usages des Anglais.

10. En 1876, la reine d'Angleterre a été proclamée, par le Parlement anglais, **impératrice des Indes.**

212. Les Russes en Asie. — **11.** La Russie s'arrête aux montagnes du Caucase, l'Inde s'arrête aux monts Himalaya. **12.** Les Russes et les Anglais étaient donc séparés par des pays immenses, l'Arménie, la Perse, l'Afghanistan, le Turkestan. **13.** Mais les Russes ont commencé, en 1799, à conquérir ces pays. **14. Ils s'avancent du côté de l'Inde,** comme ils s'avancent en Turquie du côté de Constantinople. **15.** Les

1. Les Anglais s'établissent-ils aux Indes? Qu'y vont-ils faire? — **2.** Comment les Anglais ont-ils fait leurs conquêtes? — **3.** Qu'est-ce que les Cipayes? — **4.** Comment était composée l'armée anglaise en 1857? — **5.** Quelle religion avaient les Cipayes? — **6.** Pourquoi se révoltèrent-ils? — **7.** Que faisait Nana-Sahib? — **8.** Que firent les Anglais aux Cipayes révoltés? — **9.** Quel est l'état actuel de l'Inde? — **10.** Quel titre a pris la reine d'Angleterre? — **11.** Où s'arrêtent la Russie et l'Inde? — **12.** Quels pays séparaient les Russes des Anglais? — **13.** Qu'ont commencé à faire les Russes? — **14.** De quel côté s'avancent-ils? — **15.** Que cherchent à faire les Anglais?

Anglais cherchent à empêcher les Russes d'arriver jusqu'à l'Inde, comme ils cherchent à les empêcher de prendre Constantinople.

Fig. 10. — **Exécution des Cipayes.** Les soldats anglais marchèrent contre les Cipayes révoltés, reprirent la ville de Delhi et attachèrent les prisonniers hindous à la gueule des canons.

1. Mais les Russes ont des armées de *Cosaques* établies à la frontière et qui avancent toujours. **2.** En 1804, ils ont conquis les pays du Caucase; en 1828, l'Arménie. **3.** En 1838, ils aidaient le roi de Perse à assiéger Hérat. **4.** Les Anglais forcèrent le roi de Perse à se retirer, puis ils envoyèrent une armée dans l'Afghanistan. **5.** Les Afghans, soumis d'abord, se révoltèrent en 1842. Toute l'armée anglaise fut massacrée, excepté un seul officier. **6.** Pourtant les Anglais se réconcilièrent avec le roi des Afghans et, en 1863, ils l'aidèrent à prendre Hérat.

7. Les Russes, arrêtés de ce côté, se sont avancés par le Nord. **8.** L'armée qu'ils envoyèrent en 1841 périt tout entière dans la neige; mais depuis, ils ont conquis peu à peu

1. Comment les Russes avancent-ils? — **2.** Qu'ont-ils conquis d'abord, quand? — **3.** Qu'ont-ils fait pour le roi de Perse en 1838? — **4.** Que firent les Anglais? — **5.** Qu'arriva-t-il en Afghanistan? — **6.** Qui a pris Hérat? quand? — **7.** Qu'ont fait alors les Russes? — **8.** Qu'arriva-t-il à l'armée russe en 1841? Qu'ont-ils conquis depuis?

tout le Turkestan (de 1860 à 1867), le pays de Khiva en 1873 et le pays de Merv en 1884. **1.** Ils ne sont plus maintenant bien loin de l'Inde et ils ont déjà fait des chemins de fer dans le Turkestan. **2.** S'ils prolongent leur chemin de fer jusqu'à l'Inde, ce sera le chemin le plus court pour aller de France ou d'Angleterre dans l'Inde; on pourrait faire ce trajet en 11 jours.

3. Les Russes se sont avancés aussi au sud de la Sibérie. **4.** En 1858 ils ont pris à la Chine la vallée du fleuve Amour, un pays quatre fois grand comme la France, tout couvert encore de forêts, mais qui pourra être cultivé.

213. Guerres de Chine. — **5.** La **Chine** est un pays très riche et très peuplé. **6.** Elle a au moins **400 millions d'habitants,** plus que toute l'Europe réunie. **7.** Les Chinois produisent beaucoup de riz, de thé, de coton; ils fabriquent de la porcelaine et de la soie. **8.** On pourrait faire avec eux un grand commerce. **9.** Mais le gouvernement chinois *n'aime pas les étrangers*, et il ne voulait pas laisser les Européens entrer en Chine.

10. Beaucoup de Chinois ont l'habitude de fumer de **l'opium. 11.** Ceux qui en fument deviennent fous ou meurent, car l'opium est un poison. **12.** Les Anglais vendent beaucoup d'opium en Chine. Le gouvernement chinois défendit d'en acheter, et en 1839, il fit jeter à la mer 22 000 caisses d'opium apportées par des navires anglais. **13.** Les Anglais firent la guerre à la Chine et, en 1842, forcèrent les Chinois à ouvrir cinq ports, dans lesquels les Européens auraient le droit de débarquer et de vendre leurs marchandises.

14. Mais le gouvernement chinois n'avait accepté ce traité que par force, et il continua à maltraiter les missionnaires * français et les commerçants anglais. **15.** L'Angleterre et la France s'allièrent alors et firent deux expéditions contre la

---

1. Qu'ont-ils fait en Turkestan? — **2.** A quoi pourraient servir les chemins de fer russes? — **3.** Qu'ont fait les Russes au sud de la Sibérie? — **4.** Quel pays ont-ils acquis? quand? sur quel peuple? — **5.** Qu'est-ce que la Chine? — **6.** Combien a-t-elle d'habitants? — **7.** Que produit la Chine? — **8.** Que pouvait-on faire avec la Chine? — **9.** Que faisait le gouvernement chinois envers les Européens? — **10.** Que fument les Chinois? — **11.** Qu'arrive-t-il aux fumeurs d'opium? — **12.** Que se passa-t-il en 1837 au sujet de l'opium? — **13.** A quoi furent forcés les Chinois? — **14.** Que fit le gouvernement chinois contre les Anglais et les Français? — **15.** Quels pays s'allièrent contre la Chine?

Chine (1857 et 1860). **1.** Une petite armée de 12 000 Français battit à Palikao 40 000 cavaliers tartares, et entra dans **Pékin**, capitale de la Chine (1860). **2.** Le gouvernement chinois signa un traité qui permet aux Européens de faire le commerce avec la Chine dans certains ports.

3. Il est pourtant très dangereux encore pour un Européen d'aller seul dans l'intérieur de la Chine ; il risquerait d'y être massacré. **4.** Les *Mandarins** qui gouvernent la Chine méprisent et détestent les Européens, qu'ils appellent les *barbares*. **5.** On avait établi un petit chemin de fer en Chine. Le gouvernement chinois *l'a fait détruire*, pour ne pas changer les vieux usages.

214. L'émigration chinoise. — 6. Les Chinois ont beaucoup d'enfants et la Chine n'est plus assez grande pour les nourrir tous. Beaucoup de Chinois, ouvriers, marchands et paysans s'en vont hors de leur pays. **7.** Ceux du nord s'établissent dans le pays des Tartares, ceux du sud partent sur des navires pour l'Océanie, les États-Unis, le Pérou.

8. Les Chinois mangent peu, supportent bien le froid et la chaleur, et sont très économes ; ils peuvent donc travailler partout à bien meilleur marché que les ouvriers Européens. Ce sont les Chinois qui ont construit les chemins de fer de l'Amérique ; ce sont les Chinois qui font le commerce dans toutes les îles de l'Océanie. **9.** Ils augmentent sans cesse et on ne sait si un jour les Chinois n'occuperont pas l'Océanie et la moitié de l'Amérique.

215. Les Européens au Japon. — 10. Le **Japon** était autrefois *fermé aux Européens* comme la Chine ; les Hollandais seuls y avaient un port. **11.** En 1858, le gouverneur japonais de Yédo signa avec les États-Unis, la Russie, la France et l'Angleterre le traité de Yédo, qui permettait aux Européens de vendre leurs marchandises *dans trois ports japonais*.

1. Que fit l'armée française ? — **2.** Quel traité signa la Chine ? — **3.** Les Européens peuvent-ils aller dans l'intérieur de la Chine ? — **4.** Comment les mandarins nomment-ils les Européens ? — **5.** Comment a-t-on reçu en Chine les chemins de fer ? — **6.** Pourquoi les Chinois sortent-ils de leur pays ? — **7.** Où vont-ils ? — **8.** Quelles sont les qualités des Chinois ? Dans quels pays travaillent-ils ? — **9.** Que peut-on prévoir sur l'avenir des Chinois ? — **10.** Qu'était autrefois le Japon ? — **11.** Quand et comment s'est-il ouvert aux Européens ?

1. Depuis ce temps, les Japonais ont fait connaissance avec les Européens, et au lieu de nous mépriser, comme les Chinois, ils se sont mis à **nous imiter. 2.** Ils ont construit des chemins de fer, fondé des écoles, établi des télégraphes et des usines à gaz. **3.** Il vient beaucoup de jeunes Japonais en France et en Angleterre, et ils cherchent à introduire au Japon toutes nos inventions.

LES EUROPÉENS DANS LE MONDE au XIXᵉᵐᵉ SIÈCLE

Hérat, assiégé par le roi de Perse aidé des Russes (1838). — **Turkestan,** conquis par les Russes (1838). — **Pays de Khiva,** conquis par les Russes (1873). — **Pays de Merv,** conquis par les Russes (1884). — **Yédo,** où furent signés les traités entre le **Japon** et les Européens (1858).

1. Que pensent les Japonais de nos usages? — **2.** Qu'ont-ils fait dans leur pays? — **3.** Que font les jeunes **Japonais?**

236

LES EUROPÉENS HORS D'EUROPE.   157

216. Les Français en Indo-Chine. — **1.** L'Indo-Chine est, comme l'Inde, un *pays très riche;* elle est partagée entre plusieurs rois qui ont de mauvaises armées.

2. Les Anglais avaient conquis en 1824 une partie de la Birmanie; les Français n'avaient envoyé que des missionnaires; en 1857, quelques missionnaires furent massacrés. **3.** La France envoya une expédition qui prit *Saïgon.* **4.** Puis

Birmanie, conquise par les Anglais (1824). — Saïgon, prise par les Français (1857). — Tien-tsin, traité avec la Chine (1884). — Cambodge, Annam, sous le protectorat français. — Nouvelle-Calédonie, à la France (1853). — Ile Taïti et îles de la Société, à la France (1879). — Nouvelle-Zélande, à l'Angleterre.

1. Qu'est-ce que l'Indo-Chine? à qui appartient-elle? — **2.** Qu'avaient fait les Anglais et les Français dans ce pays? — **3.** Que fit la France après 1857? — **4.** Comment a été formée la Cochinchine française?

elle se fit céder trois provinces en 1862, et trois autres en 1867, et elle en fit la **Cochinchine française.** 1. Ce sont des pays riches, mais très malsains.

2. Le **Tonkin** est au nord de l'Indo-Chine. 3. Des marins et des soldats français, envoyés en expédition en 1873, avaient trouvé le Tonkin si mal défendu qu'ils l'avaient conquis presque sans combattre. 4. Un officier de marine et quatre matelots avaient pris à eux seuls une forteresse gardée par 1800 soldats. 5. Mais le gouvernement français avait rendu cette conquête.

6. La France a recommencé la guerre en 1883. 7. Cette fois on a eu à combattre des *troupes chinoises*, parce que les Chinois ne voulaient pas laisser la France s'établir si près d'eux. 8. Les Chinois ont enfin traité à Tien-tsin (1884).

9. Aujourd'hui la Cochinchine et le Tonkin appartiennent à la France. 10. Le Cambodge et l'Annam sont sous le *protectorat* français, c'est-à-dire qu'ils obéissent à des gouverneurs français. Les Français pourront bientôt, s'ils veulent, être **maîtres de l'Indo-Chine**, comme les Anglais sont maîtres de l'Inde.

217. Les Français en Océanie. 11. La France a occupé, en 1853, la **Nouvelle-Calédonie.** 12. C'est une grande île presque déserte, mais le climat y est bon et les Européens peuvent s'y établir. 13. On y a fondé la ville de Nouméa et on y envoie tous les condamnés.

14. En 1879, la France a annexé l'île de **Taïti** et les îles de la Société. 15. C'est un pays charmant où les plantes viennent sans culture, et où le climat est si doux qu'on peut coucher la nuit en plein air. 16. Les sauvages qui habitaient l'île disparaissent, il en meurt plus qu'il n'en naît; les Français les remplaceront.

218. Les Anglais en Australie. — 17. Il y a cent ans,

1. Que sont ces pays? — 2. Où est le Tonkin? — 3. Qu'avait fait l'expédition française de 1873? — 4. Combien avait-il fallu d'hommes pour prendre une forteresse? — 5. Qu'était devenue cette conquête? — 6. Quand a recommencé la guerre? — 7. Qui a-t-il fallu combattre? — 8. Comment s'est terminée la guerre? — 9. Que possède la France en Indo-Chine? — 10. Quels pays sont sous son protectorat? — 11. A quelle époque la France a-t-elle occupé la Nouvelle-Calédonie? —12. Qu'est-ce que la Nouvelle-Calédonie? — 13. Qu'y envoie-t-on? — 14. Qu'a annexé la France en 1879? — 15. Quel pays est Taïti? — 16. Que deviennent les sauvages? — 17. Par qui était habitée autrefois l'Australie?

l'Australie n'était encore habitée que par des sauvages stupides et misérables, qui n'avaient ni maisons ni troupeaux, et parcouraient les déserts, n'ayant souvent à manger que des insectes et des bêtes mortes.

1. En 1788, les Anglais débarquèrent, sur la côte est de l'Australie, quelques centaines de condamnés gardés par des soldats et, avec eux, quelques vaches et quelques moutons. Cette colonie s'établit à Sydney.

2. Le milieu de l'Australie est un désert de sable ; mais, dans toute la région voisine des côtes, il y a **d'immenses prairies**. **3.** Les Anglais eurent bientôt de grands troupeaux, ils purent vendre les *peaux* de leurs bœufs et la *laine* de leurs moutons. **4.** Comme le pays est sain et fertile, il y vint des Anglais. **5.** Pendant 50 ans, le gouvernement continua à envoyer en Australie tous les condamnés ; l'Australie en reçut 150 000.

6. En 1851, on découvrit de riches **mines d'or** dans la province de Victoria. **7.** Les mineurs y arrivèrent de tous côtés ; on trouva en quatre ans pour plus d'un milliard* d'or. La ville de Victoria, qui avait 170 000 habitants, en a aujourd'hui 900 000.

8. Depuis 1840, les colons australiens n'ont plus voulu qu'on leur envoyât de condamnés. **9.** Mais il part chaque année d'Angleterre environ 40 000 émigrants* qui viennent s'établir en Australie, les uns pour chercher de l'or, les autres pour élever du bétail. **10.** Il y a plus de 2 000 000 d'habitants, divisés en 6 États. **11.** Le pays pourrait en nourrir bien davantage, et chaque année leur nombre augmente.

12. La **Nouvelle-Zélande** est un *beau pays* de montagnes et de rivières. **13.** Elle n'était pas encore occupée en 1842. **14.** Quelques Français vinrent alors s'y établir, mais il y vint beaucoup plus d'Anglais, et ce fut l'Angleterre qui annexa la Nouvelle-Zélande. **15.** Elle a aujourd'hui 400 000 habitants.

---

1. Comment les Anglais ont-ils fondé la colonie de Sidney ? — **2.** De quelle nature est le sol de l'Australie ? — **3.** Comment les Anglais établis en Australie devinrent-ils riches ? — **4.** Pourquoi le pays se peupla-t-il? — **5.** Combien l'Australie a-t-elle reçu de condamnés ? — **6.** Que découvrit-on en 1851 dans ce pays ? — **7.** Combien d'or trouva-t-on en 4 ans ? — **8.** Quel changement s'est fait en Australie ? — **9.** Comment le pays se peupla-t-il ? — **10.** Combien a-t-il d'habitants ? — **11.** Leur nombre augmente-t-il ? — **12.** Qu'est-ce que la Nouvelle-Zélande ? — **13.** Est-elle occupée depuis longtemps ? — **14.** Comment l'Angleterre l'a-t-elle annexée ? — **15.** Combien a-t-elle d'habitants ?

160   LES EUROPÉENS   *[Carte, p. 156.]*

Résumé (*à réciter*).

I. Les Anglais ont conquis **l'Inde** de 1757 à 1856. Ils ont eu à combattre, en 1857, la grande *révolte des Cipayes*, c'est-à-dire des soldats hindous au service de l'Angleterre, et ils sont restés les maîtres.

II. Les Russes, établis en Asie depuis 1799, **s'avancent du côté de l'Inde** malgré les Anglais. Ils n'ont pu faire prendre Hérat par le roi de Perse ; mais ils ont conquis le Turkestan (1867), le pays de Khiva (1873) et le pays de Merv (1884). Ils ont enlevé à la Chine (1858) la grande vallée du fleuve Amour.

III. La **Chine**, qui a plus de 400 millions d'habitants, refusait de laisser entrer les Européens. L'Angleterre lui a fait la guerre au sujet de l'opium (1839-1842). La France et l'Angleterre réunies lui ont fait la guerre, et l'armée française, après la victoire de Palikao, est entrée dans Pékin (1868). La Chine a été forcée d'ouvrir ses ports au commerce, mais elle continue à détester les Européens.

IV. Les Chinois **émigrent** en grand nombre comme ouvriers et comme marchands, et s'établissent en Amérique et en Océanie.

V. Le **Japon**, longtemps fermé aux Européens, s'est ouvert en 1858, et les Japonais ont commencé à imiter les Européens.

VI. La France a conquis la **Cochinchine française** (1862-1867) et le **Tonkin** (1873-1883) ; elle a mis sous son protectorat* l'Annam et le Cambodge, et pourra être bientôt **maîtresse de l'Indo-Chine**.

VII. La France a occupé en 1853 la **Nouvelle-Calédonie**, où elle transporte les condamnés, et en 1879, l'île de **Taïti**.

VIII. L'Angleterre a fondé en 1788, en Australie, une colonie qui est devenue très riche par les *troupeaux* et les *mines d'or*. La population, formée de condamnés jusqu'en 1840, se recrute maintenant avec des émigrants anglais, et elle augmente rapidement. Il y a plus de 2 millions d'habitants.

IX. L'Angleterre a colonisé, depuis 1842, la **Nouvelle-Zélande**, qui a maintenant 400 000 habitants.

CHAPITRE IX

LES EUROPÉENS EN AFRIQUE ET EN AMÉRIQUE

219. Les Français en Afrique. — 1. En 1830, les Français prirent Alger, ils ont conquis ensuite toute

---

1. Quand les Français ont-ils pris Alger ?

l'**Algérie**. **1.** Elle était habitée par les *Kabyles* qui cultivaient, et par les *Arabes* qui faisaient la guerre. **2.** Beaucoup de Français sont allés s'y établir ; ils ont semé du blé, planté des vignes, bâti des villes, et l'Algérie est devenue un **pays français.**

3. La France a fondé, de 1855 à 1860, la colonie du **Sénégal.** Le pays est très chaud et très malsain ; les Français ne peuvent pas y vivre. **4.** Mais il y va quelques marchands, qui font de bonnes affaires, car le pays est riche.

5. En 1882, la France a conquis la **Tunisie**, qui touche à l'Algérie. **6.** Elle ne l'a pas annexée*, mais elle y a établi un gouvernement français, et la Tunisie sera bientôt habitée par des colons français.

7. Entre le Sénégal et l'Algérie, s'étend le grand désert de sable, le Sahara. **8.** On a pensé à construire un chemin de fer à travers le Sahara, par lequel on pourrait faire le commerce avec les nègres de l'Afrique.

9. En 1881, le gouvernement français a envoyé une mission commandée par le colonel Flatters, pour étudier le terrain. La mission a été massacrée par les brigands du désert.

10. Un Français, M. de Lesseps, a fait creuser le **canal de Suez**, par lequel on va directement aux Indes et en Chine, sans faire le tour de l'Afrique.

220. Les Anglais en Afrique. — 11. Les Anglais ont pris aux Hollandais la colonie du **Cap** et l'ont gardée depuis 1815. **12.** Ils se sont établis sur la côte de **Guinée** et à **Aden**, près de l'entrée de la mer Rouge. **13.** Ils ont eu à faire plusieurs guerres : en 1868, au roi d'*Abyssinie ;* en 1873, au roi des *Ashantis ;* en 1878, aux *Zoulous.*

221. Explorations en Afrique. — 14. L'intérieur de l'Afrique était autrefois complètement inconnu. **15.** Des

---

1. Qui habitait l'Algérie en 1830 ? — **2.** Comment est-elle devenue un pays français ? — **3.** Quand a été fondé le Sénégal ? — **4.** Que vont y faire les Français ? — **5.** Qu'a conquis la France en 1882 ? — **6.** Comment est gouvernée la Tunisie ? — **7.** Où s'étend le Sahara ? — **8.** Qu'a-t-on voulu établir dans le Sahara ? — **9.** Qu'est-il arrivé à la mission Flatters ? — **10.** Qu'est-ce que le canal de Suez ? Qui l'a fait creuser ? — **11.** Qu'ont pris les Anglais aux Hollandais ? — **12.** Où se sont-ils établis en 1815 ? — **13.** Quelles guerres ont-ils faites ? — **14.** Que savait-on de l'intérieur de l'Afrique ? — **15.** Qu'ont fait les explorateurs ?

explorateurs* européens ont cherché à y pénétrer. **1.** La plupart sont morts de la fièvre ou ont été tués par les sauvages. **2.** Mais plusieurs ont réussi à revenir, et nous ont fait connaître le pays.

3. Ils ont découvert que le centre de l'Afrique est beaucoup *plus sain* que la côte. **4.** C'est un pays fertile, arrosé par de *grands fleuves.* **5.** Les nègres qui l'habitent feraient volontiers le commerce avec les Européens ; ils achèteraient des étoffes de coton, des colliers de verre, des fusils ; ils donneraient en échange de la gomme, de l'ivoire, de la poudre d'or. **6.** Aussi, les Anglais, les Français et les Allemands cherchent-ils à établir en Afrique des *postes* de commerce.* **7.** Une expédition française est partie, commandée par M. Savorgnan de Brazza, pour établir des postes français.

222. Les États-Unis. — **8.** Les **États-Unis** sont une grande république formée de plusieurs États. **9.** En 1783, il n'y avait encore que 13 États et 3 millions d'habitants. **10.** Tout le pays, entre le Mississipi et l'océan Pacifique, était un désert couvert de grandes prairies que parcouraient des troupeaux de bisons* et des bandes de sauvages.

11. Comme ces pays étaient fertiles, les colons sont venus s'y établir, et il s'y est fondé de grandes villes en moins de cinquante ans.

12. En 1848, on a découvert des mines d'or dans la **Nouvelle-Californie. 13.** C'était un pays presque désert. **14.** Les chercheurs d'or y accoururent, et la Nouvelle-Californie est devenue un État de 500 000 habitants. **15.** On a construit le grand *chemin de fer du Pacifique* qui traverse toute l'Amérique du Nord, et avec lequel on va de New-York (sur l'Océan) à San-Francisco (sur le Pacifique) en sept jours.

16. En 1866, les États-Unis ont acheté à la Russie l'*Amérique russe.*

17. Ils comptent aujourd'hui 38 États et près de 50 millions

1. Que leur est-il arrivé ? — **2.** Qu'ont fait ceux qui ont réussi ? — **3.** Qu'ont-ils découvert ? — **4.** Comment est le pays au centre de l'Afrique ? — **5.** Que pourrait-on y faire ? — **6.** Que cherchent à faire les Européens ? — **7.** Qu'a envoyé la France ? — **8.** Qu'est-ce que les Etats-Unis ? — **9.** Combien y avait-il d'habitants en 1783 ? Combien d'Etats ? — **10.** Qu'était alors le pays entre le Mississipi et l'océan Pacifique ? — **11.** Qu'a-t-on fait dans ces pays ? — **12.** Qu'a-t-on découvert dans la Nouvelle-Californie ? — **13.** Qu'était alors ce pays ? — **14.** Qu'est-il devenu ? — **15.** Qu'est-ce que le chemin de fer du Pacifique ? — **16.** Qu'ont acheté les Etats-Unis à la Russie ? — **17.** Combien y a-t-il aujourd'hui d'Etats ? et d'habitants ?

d'habitants. **1.** Chaque année, il y en a 1 million de plus ; car les familles sont nombreuses, et de plus, il arrive chaque année beaucoup d'Européens qui **émigrent** en Amérique. Rien qu'en 1867, il en est venu 390 000. **2.** Depuis 1820, il en est entré environ 10 millions.

3. La plupart des émigrants sont des Irlandais (depuis 1847 il en est venu plus de 3 millions) et des Allemands (il part souvent 150 000 Allemands par an pour l'Amérique). **4.** Mais dès qu'ils sont établis aux États-Unis, ils se mettent à parler anglais.

5. Depuis quelques années, il part moins d'émigrants pour les États-Unis, parce qu'il n'est plus aussi facile qu'autrefois d'y faire fortune. **6.** Pourtant les États-Unis sont grands dix-sept fois comme la France, et il y reste encore bien de la place.

7. Les États-Unis, qui n'ont pas de voisins à redouter, n'ont pas besoin d'une armée. Aussi ont-ils beaucoup d'argent. **8.** Après la grande guerre civile de 1865, ils avaient une dette de 20 milliards, qu'ils sont arrivés à payer.

223. Le Canada. — **9.** Le **Canada** a été conquis par l'Angleterre, en 1763. **10.** Il était alors habité par 60 000 Français seulement. **11.** Ils ont si bien multiplié qu'il y en a aujourd'hui *un million*. **12.** Tout le bas Canada est habité par ces Canadiens-Français, qui sont restés catholiques et ont continué à *parler français*.

13. Il y a aussi, en Acadie, 100 000 Français qui descendent des colons français venus il y a deux cents ans.

14. Aux États-Unis et dans l'Amérique anglaise, il ne reste presque plus de sauvages ; les Anglais en ont massacré beaucoup, les autres ont été tués par l'eau-de-vie ou les maladies.

224. Le Mexique. — **15.** Tous les habitants du **Mexique** sont catholiques et parlent espagnol. **16.** Mais il n'y a guère

---

1. Pourquoi la population augmente-t-elle ? — **2.** Combien est-il venu d'émigrants depuis 1820 ? — **3.** De quels pays viennent les émigrants ? — **4.** Que deviennent-ils aux Etats-Unis ? — **5.** Pourquoi part-il moins d'émigrants depuis quelques années ? — **6.** Comment sont grands les Etats-Unis ? — **7.** Pourquoi les tats-Unis ont-ils beaucoup d'argent ? — **8.** Quelle somme ont-ils payée depuis 1865 ? — **9.** Depuis quand le Canada appartient-il à l'Angleterre ? — **10.** Combien y avait-t-il d'habitants français ? — **11.** Combien y en a-t-il aujourd'hui ? — **12.** Qui habite le bas Canada ? — **13.** Où y a-t il encore des Français ? — combien ? — **14.** Que sont devenus les sauvages ? — **15.** Quelle est la langue et la religion des Mexicains ? — **16.** Descendent-ils des Espagnols ?

que 800 000 descendants d'Espagnols. **1.** La plupart des Mexicains ne sont que les descendants des *anciens Indiens.* **2.** Ces sauvages, mal civilisés, ne savent ni travailler ni se gouverner. **3.** Aussi le Mexique a-t-il été déchiré par les *guerres civiles.*

4. En 1863, Napoléon III avait conquis le Mexique et l'avait donné à un prince autrichien, Maximilien, qui était devenu *Empereur du Mexique.* **5.** Mais quand on a fait revenir les soldats français, Maximilien a été pris et fusillé (1867), et les Mexicains ont rétabli leur République.

225. République argentine. — **6.** La **République argentine** est un pays de grandes plaines ; elle est encore couverte de prairies qu'on appelle les **Pampas,** et où l'on élève de grands troupeaux de bœufs. Mais la terre est profonde et peut donner *d'excellentes récoltes.*

7. Les habitants sont catholiques et parlent espagnol. **8.** Ils descendent des anciens colons d'Espagne. **9.** Mais il y arrive beaucoup d'Européens ; depuis dix ans, il en vient au moins 80 000 chaque année. **10.** La moitié sont des **Italiens ;** il y a aussi beaucoup de Français, surtout des **Basques*.**

11. La République argentine a aujourd'hui 2 millions d'habitants ; et elle peut en avoir plus de 100 millions.

Résumé (*à réciter*).

I. La France a conquis, depuis 1830, l'**Algérie** qui est devenue un pays français ; de 1855 à 1860, le **Sénégal,** pays riche mais malsain ; en 1882, la **Tunisie.** Elle cherche à établir un chemin de fer à travers le Sahara.

II. L'Angleterre a occupé, depuis 1815, le **Cap,** la côte de **Guinée** et **Aden ;** elle a fait la guerre aux rois d'Abyssinie, aux Ashantis et aux Zoulous.

III. Les **explorateurs** européens ont pénétré jusqu'au **centre de l'Afrique,** et ont découvert des pays fertiles avec lesquels on cherche à faire le commerce.

IV. Les **États-Unis,** qui n'avaient encore, en 1783, que treize Etats et 3 millions d'habitants, ont aujourd'hui trente huit États et

1. De qui descendent-ils ? — **2.** Le Mexique est-il bien gouverné ? — **3.** Par qui a-t-il été déchiré ? — **4.** Qu'avait fait Napoléon III au Mexique ? quand ? — **5.** Qu'est-il arrivé quand les soldats français se sont retirés ? — **6.** Qu'est-ce que la République argentine ? — **7.** Que sont les habitants ? — **8.** De qui descendent-ils ? — **9.** Qui vient s'y établir ? — **10.** De quels pays viennent les émigrants ? — **11.** Combien y a-t-il d'habitants ?

50 millions d'habitants. Toute la plaine du Mississipi s'est peuplée ; on a découvert des *mines d'or* en Nouvelle-Californie et construit le *chemin de fer du Pacifique* qui traverse toute l'Amérique du Nord. Il arrive aux États-Unis beaucoup d'**émigrants** européens, surtout des *Irlandais* et des *Allemands*.

V. Le **Canada**, habité en 1763 par 60 000 Français, a aujourd'hui un million d'habitants, *restés Français de cœur* sous le gouvernement de l'Angleterre.

VI. Dans l'Amérique du Nord, les sauvages ont été presque tous exterminés. Le **Mexique** est habité surtout par les descendants des anciens Indiens, qui sont catholiques et *parlent espagnol;* après de longues guerres civiles, le Mexique, conquis par Napoléon III (**1863**), était devenu un empire ; depuis 1867, il est redevenu une République.

VII. La **République Argentine**, pays en partie désert mais très fertile, est habitée par des Espagnols ; mais il y vient beaucoup d'émigrants *italiens* et *français*.

Réflexions sur le Livre IV.

I. Il s'est fait, au XIXᵉ siècle, plus de choses importantes que dans aucun autre.

II. La **science** a donné le moyen de **produire** beaucoup plus qu'autrefois, et de **transporter** les produits d'un bout à l'autre du monde. Tous les pays sont devenus **plus riches**; les habitants sont mieux logés, mieux vêtus, mieux nourris et plus instruits. Il s'est formé des **peuples nouveaux** en Amérique et en Australie. Ailleurs, les Européens sont devenus les maîtres. Dans les anciens pays, la population a doublé.

III. Les peuples sont devenus **plus libres ;** les anciens gouvernements absolus* ont été supprimés. Excepté la Russie et l'Allemagne, tous les peuples d'Europe et d'Amérique se gouvernent eux-mêmes.

IV. Plusieurs **nations** nouvelles se sont formées.

V. Malheureusement, il s'est formé en même temps de grandes armées. Plusieurs peuples sont encore mécontents, parce qu'ils sont encore soumis à un peuple étranger. La Prusse a *violé la liberté des nations* en **annexant, malgré eux, les Hanovriens, les Danois du Sleswig et les Alsaciens-Lorrains.** On ne peut donc pas encore espérer une *paix définitive* en Europe, et bien qu'on trouve la guerre horrible, le devoir de chacun est de se préparer à la guerre, jusqu'au moment où chaque nation se gouvernera en paix sans chercher à annexer les pays voisins.

VI. Mais l'Europe n'est qu'une **petite partie du monde**. Il y a en Asie, en Australie, en Amérique, en Afrique, des pays **plus grands et plus fertiles**. Le **tort des Français** a été de ne pas penser assez à ces pays. Ils ont laissé prendre les *meilleures places*. L'Amérique du Sud est

166   RÉFLEXIONS SUR LE LIVRE IV.

espagnole ; l'Amérique du Nord, l'Australie, l'Inde sont **anglaises**. Aussi l'Angleterre, qui est plus petite que la France, tient-elle une bien plus grande place dans le monde.

VII. Mais il n'est pas trop tard. Il reste encore bien des *pays à occuper*, et dans les pays occupés bien de la *place vide*. Ceux qui ne trouveront pas en France à gagner leur vie et qui n'ont pas peur de travailler, feront bien de penser à tous ces pays, où l'on a besoin de travailleurs.

VIII. Souvenez-vous que si on sert bien la France en combattant pour elle, on la sert aussi en allant au loin fonder une famille française, qui répandra notre langue, nos idées, nos habitudes, et qui fera respecter et aimer la France dans le monde entier.

DEVOIRS DE RÉDACTION SUR LE LIVRE III. (*Voir page* 63.)

1. Inventions du xvᵉ siècle : poudre, boussole, imprimerie.

2. Découvertes du xvᵉ siècle : les Portugais en Afrique et aux Indes ; Christophe Colomb en Amérique ; conquêtes de Cortez et de Pizarre.

3. Renaissance des lettres et des arts.

4. La réforme en Europe.

5. Les guerres de religion.

6. Les guerres d'Italie.

7. La guerre de Trente ans : traités de Westphalie et des Pyrénées.

8. L'Angleterre : guerre civile ; le parlement et le roi, Cromwell.

9. La révolution de 1688 en Angleterre ; le régime parlementaire.

10. L'Europe coalisée contre Louis XIV.

11. La Russie au xviiᵉ siècle : Pierre le Grand, conquêtes des Russes ; partage de la Pologne.

12. La Prusse : Frédéric II ; la guerre de Sept ans.

13. Les Anglais dans l'Inde : Dupleix ; perte du Canada.

14. Les Anglais en Amérique : soulèvement contre les Anglais ; indépendance des États-Unis.

DEVOIRS DE RÉDACTION SUR LE LIVRE IV.

1. La Révolution de 1789.

2. Coalition contre la Révolution ; guerres de 1792 et de 1793 ; annexions à la France.

3. L'Empire : victoires et conquêtes.

4. Blocus continental : soulèvements en Espagne, en Autriche.

5. Campagne de Russie : soulèvements de 1813.

6. Les alliés en France : Waterloo ; conséquences des guerres de l'Empire.

7. Les absolutistes et les libéraux.

8. La révolution de 1830 : mouvements en Europe.

9. La révolution de 1848 : ses conséquences en Europe ; victoire des libéraux.

10. État politique des divers pays d'Europe depuis 1860.

11. Abolition de l'esclavage des nègres.

12. La question d'Orient : guerres auxquelles elle a donné lieu.

13. L'unité italienne.

14. L'unité allemande.

15. Guerre de 1870, entre la France et l'Allemagne.

16. État actuel des divers pays d'Europe : les armées, le devoir national.

17. Découvertes scientifiques du xixᵉ siècle : applications à l'industrie.

18. Le système de la protection et le système du libre-échange.

19. Les Anglais dans l'Inde.

20. Les Russes en Asie.

21. La Chine : guerres avec l'Angleterre et la France.

22. Expéditions françaises dans l'extrême Orient.

23. La France en Afrique.

24. Les explorations en Afrique.

25. Principaux États d'Amérique.

CASSELL'S
Concise History
OF
ENGLAND

For School and Home Use.

BEING

THE GROWTH AND EXPANSION OF THE
BRITISH EMPIRE

FROM THE

ROMAN INVASION TO THE

DIAMOND JUBILEE.

(ILLUSTRATED.)

CASSELL AND COMPANY, LIMITED, PUBLISHERS,
376 LITTLE COLLINS STREET, MELBOURNE.

AND

London, Paris, New York & Sydney.

124

devoted services, which sum was, at her request, expended on the Nightingale Home for training nurses in London.

1857. The Indian Mutiny, a rising of native Indian troops, broke out this year. It had been long maturing, but the reason put forward by the mutineers was, that the cartridges served out to them were greased with cow's fat. Now a true Hindoo will not kill a cow, nor allow the meat of it to touch his lips. Before putting the cartridge into the gun it was necessary to bite off the end of it. The Hindoos objected to do this and mutinied. Leaders had for a long time past been instilling feelings of dissatisfaction in the minds of the men, and this pretext was advanced to start the rebellion.

The mutiny commenced at Meerut. Regiments of soldiers refused to obey their officers, who in many instances they murdered. They then marched to and took possession of Delhi. General Havelock proceeded to the relief of Lucknow, which was besieged by the rebels. General Outram (Havelock's superior officer) very generously served under Havelock as a volunteer in the relief of Lucknow, to allow the latter the honour of relieving the city. Havelock succeeded with his troops in getting through the rebel lines into the city, but was not strong enough to attack the enemy. He was therefore compelled to remain within the walls with the besieged. Sir Colin Campbell arrived later on with an army, which fought its way through the streets of Lucknow to the fort. This was entered, and then the combined forces of Sir Colin Campbell and General Havelock marched against the enemy, dispersed them, and raised the siege.

At Cawnpore, a short distance from Lucknow, a British garrison held out for 21 days against Nana Sahib, the rebel leader. Being out of food and ammunition, they surrendered to that chief on the promise that their lives should be spared. The promise was broken; all except four, who escaped, were foully massacred, and their bodies thrown into a well. Sir John Lawrence, the Governor of the Punjaub, who had, by his humane treatment of the Sikhs, endeared those natives to him, now marched in command of a united British and Sikh force to Delhi, the rebel stronghold. This place was taken after a prolonged siege, and from that day the mutiny was at an end. The East India Company, which till then had ruled India, transferred its rights over that country to the Crown of England, and a proclamation was issued by the British Government taking over the administration of the country. Since then India has been ruled by a Viceroy, or Governor-General and Council, on behalf of the Sovereign of Great Britain and Ireland.

1858. Lord Palmerston, the Prime Minister, brought in a Bill providing for the admission of Jews into Parliament; till that time they had been excluded. Baron Rothschild was then elected as a member for London.

1861. Prince Albert, the Queen's husband, died from fever. His death was a great blow to the Queen and a serious loss to the nation. By his wise counsels, he assisted in the development of our commerce and stimulated interest in the arts and sciences.

1863. The Prince of Wales was married to the Princess Alexandra, of Denmark, amid great rejoicings of the British people.

1866. The first submarine cable was successfully laid between Ireland and America by means of the Great Eastern steamship

125

the largest afloat till that time. Congratulatory messages were flashed from both ends of the cable, and time has proved that the

MEETING OF SIR COLIN CAMPBELL AND GENERAL HAVELOCK.

wire then laid has not only developed trade between the countries of Great Britain and America, but has, by making the people of the two countries better known to each other, promoted a friendly feeling between those nations.

MATRICULATION
MODERN HISTORY

BEING ENGLISH HISTORY FROM 1485 TO 1901, WITH
SOME REFERENCE TO THE CONTEMPORARY HISTORY
OF EUROPE AND COLONIAL DEVELOPMENTS

BY

C. S. FEARENSIDE, M.A. Oxon.

AUTHOR OF "THE INTERMEDIATE TEXT-BOOK OF ENGLISH HISTORY"
"THE TUTORIAL HISTORY OF ENGLAND," ETC.

Second Edition (Eleventh Impression)

LONDON : W. B. CLIVE

University Tutorial Press Ld.

HIGH ST., NEW OXFORD ST., W.C.

1922

537. Causes of the Indian Mutiny, 1857.—One reason why the Second Chinese War dragged on so long was the preoccupation of British forces in India. There Dalhousie's annexations had caused considerable anxiety and vexation among the native princes; recent land settlements had annoyed the larger landowners, especially in Oudh, by favouring the actual cultivators of the soil; and religious prejudices had been offended by the equipment of the native sepoys with rifles which required greased cartridges. Those who cherished these and other grievances thought that they had a good opportunity for vengeance in the fact that the British troops in India were few and scattered. The discontent was most widespread in the native regiments in the North-West Provinces; and in May 1857 some of these, stationed at Meerut, broke out in open mutiny, shot their officers, and stirred up similar mutinies in the neighbouring camps. Bengal and the greater part of the Madras and Bombay Presidencies kept quiet; and the Sikhs of the Punjab had been so well used by Sir John Lawrence that they helped the British.

The main incidents in the struggle were the massacre of Cawnpore and the sieges of Delhi and Lucknow. The Europeans at Cawnpore surrendered in June, after a month's siege, and were butchered. At Delhi, where a descendant of the Moguls had been set up as Emperor, the mutineers themselves were besieged from May to September by troops from the Punjab under John Nicholson. At Lucknow a handful of British troops under Sir Henry Lawrence held the ill-fortified Residency from May till September, when they were relieved by Sir Henry Havelock, and again on till November, when they were brought away by Lord Clyde, the Sir Colin Campbell of Crimea fame. Clyde reoccupied Lucknow in March 1858, and in June the Mutiny was finally crushed by the capture of Gwalior.

538. Results of the Indian Mutiny, 1858.—The rising failed partly because it was, for the most part, a military, not a national movement; partly because it did not spread all over India; partly because the Hindus and the Muhammadans did not work well together; but above all because nearly all the British officers displayed a resourcefulness which matched the courage and endurance of the troops and civilians under their care.   The most enduring results of the Mutiny were the re-organisation of the Indian army and the transfer of Indian administration from the Company to the Crown.   Preparations for such a transfer had been made when the Company's Charter had been renewed in 1853—not for twenty years, as heretofore, but simply until Parliament should determine otherwise.   The *Indian Government Act* of 1858 placed the control of British India in the hands of a new Secretary of State, responsible to Parliament, and represented in India by a Governor-General.   George Canning's son, Lord Canning, who had succeeded Dalhousie, was continued in office and was thus the first Governor-General in India who can be called " Viceroy."

A FIRST BOOK OF
ENGLISH HISTORY

BY

F. J. C. HEARNSHAW, M.A., LL.D.

PROFESSOR OF HISTORY IN KING'S COLLEGE, UNIVERSITY OF LONDON

WITH EPILOGUE
A.D. 1913-1927

MACMILLAN AND CO., LIMITED
ST. MARTIN'S STREET, LONDON
1930

108. The Indian Mutiny.—The Crimean War was one of the causes of the Indian Mutiny which broke out in 1857. On the one hand, the war had drawn away a large part of the British garrison in India ; on the other hand, it had excited the religious passions of the Mohammedan peoples of the peninsula. Other causes, however, were more potent. The Afghan disaster of 1842 had lowered British prestige. At the same time, the East India Company had been rapidly extending its dominions and its protectorates. Early in the nineteenth century many of the Central States had been brought under control ; in 1843 Sindh had been forcibly annexed ; in 1849 the Sikhs had been reduced and the Punjab incorporated ; finally, in 1856, Lord Dalhousie had acquired the great province of Oudh. The Indian peoples seemed to be threatened by a complete loss of independence. Finally, the introduction of European education, the suppression of some cruel and obnoxious native religious customs, the zealous labours of Christian missionaries, the development of railways and other Western devices, appeared to forebode the total suppression of Eastern civilisation and the destruction of oriental faiths.

Hence in May, 1857, at Meerut the native " sepoys," suddenly excited over a trivial dispute concerning greased cartridges, revolted and murdered their officers. The revolt rapidly spread throughout Upper Bengal and Oudh ; but fortunately it did not extend beyond the Ganges valley. The native troops both in the west and in the south remained faithful. Horrible barbarities and fierce fights were witnessed at Delhi, Lucknow, and Cawnpore. The British government (immensely aided by the electric telegraph, a new invention which had recently been installed) hurried reinforcements to India, and within twelve months of the original outbreak complete order had been restored.

The effects of the mutiny were, first, that the British forces in India were strengthened ; secondly, that the

East India Company was abolished and its functions transferred to the Crown; and, thirdly, that British methods of governing India were thoroughly revised and remodelled.

HISTORY OF ENGLAND

FOR USE IN SCHOOLS

BY

ARTHUR D. INNES, M.A.

FORMERLY SCHOLAR OF ORIEL COLLEGE, OXFORD

PART III. 1689—1918

CAMBRIDGE:

AT THE UNIVERSITY PRESS

1927

§ 2. *India and the Great Mutiny*, 1856—1858.

We have already noted that in India the Governor-Generalship of Lord Dalhousie was distinguished by a policy of annexation; broadly speaking, of bringing under direct British dominion any territories which could be claimed as lapsing to us under the law of succession, in distinction from the custom, which had hitherto prevailed generally, of maintaining the native rule unless annexation had become a palpable necessity. On the east half Burma, and on the west the Panjab, had been conquered. Satara on the borders of Bombay, Jhansi on the borders of the "North-West Provinces," Nagpur a great Central Indian principality, and several minor states, were absorbed, through the refusal to recognise heirs by adoption. Finally, in 1856, the Mohammedan kingdom of Oude, on the Ganges above Bengal, was annexed on the plain ground of the persistent misrule of its kings, who had been warned over and over again that, if they did not amend their ways, their dynasty would be deposed. These events created general alarm among all the remaining native princes.

Dalhousie's policy.

Again Dalhousie did everything in his power to extend railways, to introduce the telegraph—a recent invention—and to bring in innumerable improvements. But the improvements, in the eyes of large classes of natives, were only insidious methods of tightening the grip of the "sahibs" on India; besides savouring of sorcery. Moreover, the strong hand of government had deprived the lawless sections of society of their old license; and both Mohammedans and Hindus were filled with suspicions that the British intended to convert them forcibly to Christianity. With all these elements of danger, the British position had been weakened in a military point of view; by the multiplication of sepoys or native soldiers, necessitated by the annexations; by the actual reduction in the number of white troops, owing to the recall of some regiments for service in the Crimea; and by the absorption of a large proportion of the rest in the new provinces, especially in the Panjab.

Sources of unrest.

In 1856 Dalhousie was replaced by Lord Canning, who, under ill advice, issued an Act under which all recruits in the Bengal army would in future be liable for service abroad. But the bulk of the recruits came from high-caste families who would lose caste if they crossed the sea. The Hindu believes that his life beyond the grave is affected by caste; to preserve caste he will suffer anything. The military class found themselves threatened

The Caste panic.

with the loss either of caste or of the career they had counted on adopting. On the other hand, there was an extensive Mohammedan conspiracy afoot for restoring the Mogul dynasty and the Mohammedan ascendency. For their own ends, the conspirators fomented the alarm among the Hindus. And then came the report that Hindus and Mohammedans alike would suffer contamination by the use of the new rifles and cartridges just issued to the troops; since the cartridges were said to be greased with the fat of pigs which the Mohammedan reckons unclean, and of cows which the Hindu accounts sacred. Lastly, there was a prophecy current among the natives that the British Raj was to last a hundred years and no more; and the British Raj had begun with Clive's victories in 1757.

Yet, with hardly an exception, the authorities in India were perfectly unsuspicious. Lower Bengal, from Patna to the coast, was fairly well supplied with white troops. But between Patna and the Panjab frontier there were only five white regiments and some batteries of artillery; while the whole great district was full of sepoys. Some mutinous outbreaks in connexion with the cartridges were readily suppressed. Then suddenly, on May 10th, 1857, the sepoys at Mirat rose, massacred every European they could lay hands on, and marched to Delhi, where the Mogul still lived. There the natives at once rose, massacred the Europeans, and proclaimed the restoration of the Mogul Empire. Yet the telegraph operator had first managed to flash half his warning message through to the Panjab; and the Europeans had succeeded in blowing up the arsenal. A month later a small British force had occupied the Ridge in front of Delhi; Henry Lawrence in Lucknow, the capital of Oude, had brought the Residency into a state of defence; the tiny garrison at Cawnpore had begun its desperate resistance to the overwhelming forces led by the Maratha, Nana Sahib; and all the sepoys in the Ganges districts above Patna were in revolt. By the end of June, the force in front of Delhi had much ado to hold its own; the Cawnpore garrison had been shot down when withdrawing under a safe-conduct, though the women and children were kept prisoners—as yet; and the Lucknow garrison was shut up in the Residency, where Henry Lawrence was mortally wounded two days later. But Henry Havelock was beginning to advance from Allahabad.

1857.
The Mogul proclaimed (May).

June.

Outside the Ganges basin, the sepoys in the districts to the south and south-west of Agra also revolted; though the Maratha prince, Sindhia himself, at Gwalior, remained loyal. In fact, the native princes all held aloof from the revolt—partly, it may

Limits of the Revolt.

be, because they had no desire for the restoration of a Mohammedan Empire. But the general effect was that the rising was confined to Northern India; excluding lower Bengal on the east and the Panjab on the north-west, where any tendency to mutiny had been promptly mastered. And presently troops were on the march from the Panjab to join the force at Delhi, as well as from Allahabad to relieve Lucknow.

It was not, however, till September that the force on the Delhi Ridge had been sufficiently strengthened to make an attack on the city. On the 14th the outer defences were successfully stormed, John Nicholson losing his life at the head of one of the columns of attack. Even then it was not till the 21st that the whole city—with the Mogul himself—was in the hands of the British, and the rebels were in full retreat to join their associates at Lucknow.

Delhi
captured,
Sept.

Here a stubborn defence had been maintained, with a success chiefly due to the unceasing vigilance and energy of the Engineer department, whose counter-mines frustrated no fewer than twenty-five of the enemy's mines. Only once did the rebels explode a mine successfully, and then the damage was repaired before they attempted to take advantage of it. But the loyal sepoys were beginning to lose heart, in the belief that the defence was hopeless; and, if no relief had arrived before the end of the month, they would probably have marched out. But relief came. Havelock, with his little force, advanced with sharp fighting to Cawnpore, only to find that Nana Sahib had butchered the women and children in cold blood before his arrival. Then he marched towards Lucknow, but was forced to fall back. In the middle of September he was joined by Outram with fresh forces. On the 23rd the troops were four miles from Lucknow; on the 25th they fought their way in. With its garrison thus reinforced, there was no more fear that the Residency would be captured.

Lucknow
(June—
Sept.).

By this time Sir Colin Campbell had come out to Calcutta to organise a campaign of conquest; troops had arrived; others, on the way to the China War, had been diverted to help in the much more serious emergency in India. In November Campbell relieved the Lucknow Residency, withdrawing the non-combatants and leaving a garrison under Outram. In March (1858) the mutineer army was in its turn besieged in Lucknow, and shattered; Sir Hugh Rose, advancing from the west, overcame the forces which opposed him and captured Jhansi. But it was not till the end of the year that the last embers of the great revolt were finally stamped out.

Sir Colin
Campbell,
1857—8.

One main result of the Mutiny was that the curious system, under
India   which a mercantile company had for a century been the
transferred   dominant Power in India, was brought to an end. It was
to the   resolved that the Company's control should cease, and the
Crown,   government of India should be transferred to the Crown.
1858.
To this end, Palmerston brought in a Bill in February, 1858; but
other events causing his resignation at this time, a very similar Act
was passed in August by the ministry of Lord Derby, who succeeded
him. The Company's Governor-General became the British Viceroy;
the Board of Control became the India Office; and the Company
vanished.

Meanwhile the Chinese war was also apparently brought to a
satisfactory conclusion by the Treaty of Tien Tsin (June). It broke
out again, however, in the next year, and was not really ended till
Pekin was captured in 1860.

THE GROWTH OF THE BRITISH EMPIRE

BY

P. H. AND A. C. KERR

*WITH 4 COLOURED ILLUSTRATIONS, 4 COLOURED MAPS
AND 58 MAPS AND OTHER ILLUSTRATIONS*

NEW IMPRESSION

LONGMANS, GREEN AND CO. LTD.
39 PATERNOSTER ROW, LONDON, E.C. 4
NEW YORK, TORONTO
BOMBAY, CALCUTTA, AND MADRAS
1927

4. Inside India, British rule has only once been in real danger, and that was in the year 1857. For some time there had been a growing restlessness in the northern parts of the country, round Delhi and Lucknow. The native princes were jealous of the power of England, and the people thought that the British were going to interfere with their religion. This discontent soon spread to the Sepoys, as the native soldiers in the Indian army were called. There were only 50,000 British troops in the whole country, while the Sepoys numbered over 250,000. When the Sepoys realised their strength, a great number of them rose suddenly without warning. They murdered their officers, and then marched off to Delhi and set up a feeble old man, who was descended from their Mughal Emperors, as Lord of India. The story is too long to tell here. But if you want to know how first Sir Henry Havelock, and then Sir Colin Campbell and his Highlanders, rescued the heroic defenders of Lucknow; how 8000 British besieged 30,000 Indian troops in Delhi all through the long, hot summer months, and how at last they took the city, you must read the story in another book. In the end the Mutiny was put down, and the British dominion was set up more strongly than before.

THE

HISTORY OF ENGLAND

DURING THE REIGN OF
VICTORIA

(1837-1901)

BY

SIDNEY LOW, M.A.

FELLOW OF KING'S COLLEGE, LONDON
FORMERLY SCHOLAR OF BALLIOL COLLEGE, OXFORD

AND

LLOYD C. SANDERS, B.A.

SECOND EDITION

LONGMANS, GREEN, AND CO.
39 PATERNOSTER ROW, LONDON
NEW YORK, BOMBAY, AND CALCUTTA
1910

CHAPTER VII.

THE INDIAN MUTINY.

THE news that the Indian native army had broken out into
revolt in the late spring of 1857 came upon England like a
thunder-clap. There had been mutterings of the storm for
some months past, and all through the earlier part of the year
disaffection was rife at some of the Indian military stations,
where mutinous demonstrations had occurred. But the true
character of the danger was quite unknown at home and
scarcely suspected in India itself.

Yet the state of affairs in the Asiatic empire might well
have justified uneasiness. During the preceding few years
India had been the scene of important events and critical
changes ; and new territories of large extent had been incorporated with the British dominions. After the dramatic close
of the Afghan war Lord Ellenborough had turned to further conquests.[1] In 1843 the amírs of Sind were called upon to surrender their independent rule. On their refusal to comply,
their country was annexed, after a successful campaign under
Sir Charles Napier, and a brilliant victory against overwhelming numerical odds at Miáni. The seizure of Sind, which
Napier described as " a very advantageous, useful and humane piece of rascality," was followed by intervention in
the affairs of Gwalior. The internal politics of the Marátha
principality were in disorder, and the maharaja was at the
mercy of a large and insubordinate native army. This force
was defeated in two engagements and partly disbanded, and a
body of native troops under British command, destined to play
its part in history as the Gwalior contingent, was placed in
cantonments near Sindhia's capital.

[1] *Supra*, p. 40.

132

The next year the court of directors, alarmed by Ellenborough's adventurous policy, recalled him, and appointed as his successor General Sir Henry (afterwards Viscount) Hardinge, who held office from 1844 to 1848. The administration of this veteran soldier was no more peaceful than that of his predecessor; and the Indian government soon found itself involved in hostilities with the great Sikh confederacy of the Punjab. The Sikhs were a military and religious Hindu sect which had gradually become the strongest power in North-Western India. Under Ranjít Singh they established a kingdom which extended from Pesháwar on the west to the Sutlej on the east. On his death, the khálsa, or military council of the Sikh army, dominated the Punjab, and sought to extend its influence to British territory. Organised on a democratic basis, inspired by religious enthusiasm, and trained by capable European officers, whom Ranjít Singh had attracted to his service, this Sikh host proved the most formidable body of adversaries Britain has ever had to encounter in Asia. In December, 1845, the khálsa army, 60,000 strong, with a fine and powerful artillery, crossed the Sutlej, and the first Sikh war began. The invaders were opposed by Sir Hugh Gough, the commander-in-chief, and desperate and obstinately contested battles were fought at Múdki on December 18, Firozshah on December 21, and Aliwál on January 28, 1846. At Sobráon on February 10 Gough and Hardinge attacked the Sikhs strongly entrenched upon the banks of the Sutlej, and drove them from their position with great slaughter and the loss of sixty-seven of their guns. The Sikhs were defeated in what Hardinge described as a "series of the most triumphant successes ever recorded in the military history of India,"[1] a description scarcely justified by the facts; for the hard-won British victories, except the last, were by no means decisive and were far from impressing the enemy with a conviction of their military inferiority. They agreed, however, to modify their warlike organisation, and to receive a British resident at Lahore.

So little were the Sikhs discouraged by the campaign, that Hardinge's successor, the Earl (afterwards Marquis) of Dalhousie (1848-56), was compelled to resume operations against

[1] Governor-General's Proclamation, Lahore, Febr. 22, 1846.

them. The second Sikh war began with local disturbances and an outbreak at Múltán; and presently the khálsa army came together again, and once more engaged the British. An indecisive battle was fought at Chiliánwála on January 13, 1849, in which both sides lost heavily. Gough was angrily attacked in England, and Sir Charles Napier was ordered out in haste to supersede him; but before he could arrive the commander-in-chief had retrieved his reputation and ended the campaign at Gujrát on February 21, where the Sikhs were completely defeated. Using his artillery with great skill and effectiveness, Gough was able to win this crushing victory with very little loss on his own side. The Sikh army was almost annihilated in the battle and the subsequent pursuit. The Punjab was annexed by a proclamation issued March 29, 1849, and placed under a commission of able officers, who not only disarmed and pacified the Sikhs, but contrived in the course of a few years to turn them into the most loyal and contented subjects of the British ráj in Asia.

Dalhousie was a vigorous and able ruler, who devoted himself with unsparing zeal to the interests, as he understood them, of the Indian people. His viceroyalty was one of annexation and energetic assertiveness; for he was impatient of the abuses of native rule, and he believed that the happiness of the subject populations could best be secured by placing them under direct British control. One of his important additions to the empire was that of Lower Burma in 1852. The country was badly governed by the King of Ava; European merchants were ill-treated, and the British remonstrances were contemptuously ignored. The province of Pegu was annexed by proclamation on December 20 to Aracán and Tenasserim, the conquests of the first Burmese war. An irregular campaign followed, which ended in June, 1853, with the concession by the king of freedom of navigation on the Irawády. Rangoon became the capital of British Burma, and began to make a rapid advance towards its present standard of population and prosperity.

Another annexation which attracted more attention at the time was that of Oudh. The Mohammedan wazírs or kings of this country, originally feudatories of the Delhi emperors, had for several generations displayed the worst vices of Oriental sovereignty. Their government was abominably oppressive and corrupt, and at the same time so feeble that they would certainly have fallen before external attack or domestic rebellion, but for the support of the English. Their fertile and populous territory was in a state of chronic disorder and a prey to rapine, brigandage, and violent anarchy.[1] Dalhousie, somewhat against his own will, but pressed by the representations of the board of control and the directors of the East India Company, decided to assume the administration of the country. Colonel Outram, the resident at Lucknow, was instructed to inform the King of Oudh of the revocation of the treaty of 1801, which guaranteed him British protection, and to submit for his signature a new treaty of a more limited character. On the refusal of the king to accept this instrument, a proclamation was issued on February 13, 1856, declaring that "the government of the territories of Oudh is henceforth vested exclusively and for ever in the Honourable East India Company". The revenues of the country were thus at the disposal of the company, with the exception of an ample pension assigned to the deposed royal family; and Oudh passed under British administration to be subsequently incorporated with Agra in the lieutenant-governorship of the North-west Provinces.

Necessary and justifiable as these proceedings were, they roused considerable alarm among the Indian princes and great landowners. The Lucknow wazírs had given the deepest cause of complaint to their own maltreated subjects, but they had always been steadily loyal to the English, and many of the chiefs were alarmed and disturbed by the dispossession of these faithful allies of the paramount power. In the years that preceded the annexation of Oudh grave uneasiness had been caused by other developments of Dalhousie's policy. Anxious to lose no opportunity of transferring native territory to the company, and so extending the area of just and sound administration, the governor-general had made it known that he would regard a state as "lapsed" when there was a failure of natural heirs. This was entirely contrary to Indian law and practice, which gave the fullest recognition to the custom of adoption. In pursuance of his policy, the governor-general seized the territories of several of the Marátha states, including those of Satára

CHAP.
VII.

---

[1] Sleeman, *A Journey through the Kingdom of Oudh in 1849-50, passim.*

CHAP.
VII.

in 1849, and Jhánsi in 1853. By an extension or application of the same principle the adopted son of Bájí Ráo, the ex-peishwa, subsequently destined to an immortality of infamy as the Nana Sahib,[1] was deprived of the large pension which had been paid to the dethroned potentate from his deposition in 1818 to his death in 1853. Moreover, Bahádur Sháh, the representative of the Mughals, was informed that his successor would not be allowed to retain the titular dignities and the shadowy sovereignty in Delhi, which were still enjoyed by the head of the house of Timúr.

Thus some of the leading princely houses of Northern India, Hindu and Mohammedan alike, were smarting under a sense of wrong, and their agents were active in promoting discontent. Other causes contributed to the feeling of unrest, which was gathering strength, when Charles John, Viscount Canning, son of George Canning, succeeded Lord Dalhousie as governor-general in February, 1856. Recent western innovations, and more particularly the introduction of railways and the telegraph, had shocked and alarmed the natives, who were encouraged by the Bráhmans to see in these inventions an attack upon their religion. The fanaticism of the people and the priestly caste had been roused by the prohibition of *sati*, or widow-burning, the efforts to check female infanticide, the removal of legal obstacles to the remarriage of widows, the spread of European education, and the execution of Bráhmans guilty of capital offences.[2] Military officers in the British Indian service, inspired by an ill-timed zeal, had given much assistance to missionary enterprise, and had themselves endeavoured to make proselytes, going about " with the order-book in one hand and the Bible in the other ".[3] Rumours were circulated that the government intended to compel the people to embrace Christianity by force or artifice, and to bring about the destruction of the entire social and religious fabric of Hindu society. To all this must be added that the English had suffered con-

[1] Properly Dandhu Panth Nana. For his memorial to the East India directors, asking that the decision of the governor-general should be reconsidered, see Kaye and Malleson, *History of the Indian Mutiny* (ed. 1888), i., 74.

[2] Lord Roberts, *Forty-one Years in India*, i., 414 *seq.*

[3] Kaye and Malleson, *Indian Mutiny*, i., 352.

siderable loss of prestige through the Afghan disasters of 1841-42, and subsequently through the Russian war, of which very misleading accounts had been circulated. In the early part of 1857 *chupättis,* or flat cakes of flour, were passed on from village to village in Northern India, perhaps as a sign of preparation for a rising, perhaps only to sow vague suspicion in the minds of the people.

     The ferment among the civil population would have been powerless for injury, if it had not extended to the contingents of trained native troops, on which British dominion in India mainly rested. The sepoy[1] armies had been increased in consequence of the recent annexations, and the European regiments diminished owing to the exigencies of the Crimean and China wars. At the beginning of 1857 the native troops amounted to 257,000 men, while there were only about 45,000 effective European soldiers of all arms in the whole of India. The disaffection was most acute in the Bengal army, which had for several years been in an unsatisfactory state of discipline. It was partly composed of Bráhmans and other high-caste men, who declined to render due subordination to their native officers if they were of inferior standing in the social scale. Nor were the British officers of this force always equal to their critical duties. Promoted by seniority, many of them were enfeebled by age and long residence in a trying climate; there were generals getting on for eighty, sexagenarian colonels, captains well over fifty. These elderly warriors, as events sadly proved, often broke down under the strain of sudden emergency. Some of the most capable of the younger men, like John Nicholson and Herbert Edwardes, had left their regiments to accept civil posts in the newly annexed provinces, or commissions in the irregular corps recruited for the frontier districts. If India was saved for the empire, it was largely through the genius and the daring energy of this band of officers and officials, trained and inspired by the two great Lawrences, Henry, chief commissioner of Oudh, and his younger brother John, head of the commission of the Punjab. Almost alone among the lead-

---

[1] The word should be written *sipáhi* according to the rules of orthography now officially recognised in the transliteration of Indian names; but in this, as in some other cases, the spelling consecrated by tradition and usage has been retained.

CHAP.
VII.

ing administrators of India, Sir Henry Lawrence foresaw the approach of the revolt, and warned the government to prepare for it.[1]

The Bengal sepoys were much agitated by the events of the first year of Canning's rule. The annexation of Oudh had been followed by a land settlement, carried out with the customary legal pedantry which insisted on assimilating the Indian system of tenure to that of Great Britain. Many of the *tálukdárs*, or revenue collectors, who exercised ownership rights over the villages, were dispossessed. There was a general sense of insecurity, which reacted upon the Bengal regiments, largely recruited from Oudh. The sepoys were further perturbed by efforts to induce them to serve on the frontier, in Burma, and in other regions remote from their own homes, culminating in Canning's enlistment order of September 1, 1856, which prescribed that all native recruits should undertake to serve beyond the sea, "whether within or beyond the company's territories". This was regarded as another of the measures intended to break the caste of the Indian troops, and bring about their conversion to Christianity. The soldiers were rapidly drifting into that state of panic which is capable of driving Orientals to frenzy. Stories were circulated that the dust of human bones was deliberately mixed with the grain sold to the army by government contractors. And then came a rumour, more alarming than any other, which ran like wild-fire through the sepoy lines in the late autumn. The old Brown Bess musket was being replaced by the Enfield rifle, and then ew cartridges were lubricated in order to fit the grooves of the barrel. It was universally believed that these cartridges, which the men had to bite with their teeth, were greased with a mixture of cow's fat and pig's lard. Thus the soldiers of both religions were outraged by the thought of touching with their lips the fat either of the unclean pig or the sacred cow.[2] The government tried to allay the excite-

---

[1] Edwardes and Merivale, *Life of Sir Henry Lawrence*, pp. 564-65, 568.

[2] It seems that some cartridges lubricated with the objectionable composition had actually passed into the hands of the troops before the issue was checked by the authorities. The evidence is however conflicting. See G. W. Forrest, *Selections from State Papers in the Military Department of the Government of India*, i., 7, 8, etc. Kaye and Malleson, i., 359 *seq.*; and T. Rice Holmes, *History of the Indian Mutiny* (5th ed.), appendix W.

ment by publishing a chemical analysis of the cartridge-grease, and instructing the officers to assure the troops on parade that the defiling ingredients were not employed. But the sepoys were filled with terror and suspicion, and fit for any violence. Even then Canning and his council and the commander-in-chief, General Anson, saw no occasion for special anxiety. Stranger still, their blind indifference to the portents about them was shared by many of the officers commanding the native regiments, who retained (sometimes to the tragic close of their own lives) their pathetic confidence in the loyalty of their men.

Yet in that fateful spring of 1857 the danger signs were blowing thickly over the lowering skies of Northern India. The sepoys in many stations had refused to receive the new cartridges, and at Berhampur on February 25 there was an outbreak of open insubordination. The rulers of India were at length alarmed, as well they might be, for Bengal lay at the mercy of the native soldiers. Between Calcutta and Allahábád, 600 miles up the Ganges, there were no bayonets in English hands save only those of a single regiment at Dinapur. Another British regiment was hastily ordered back from Burma. By the time it arrived events were moving fast. At Barrackpur, the cantonment near the capital, the 34th Native Infantry were on parade, when a sepoy attacked the adjutant, while his comrades looked on and some even assisted him. General Hearsey, the commandant, acted with prompt resolution, and the mutinous corps seemed for the moment cowed. But the disorder spread; incendiary fires occurred in various cantonments; officers were insulted by their men; there were serious disturbances at Ambála; and one of the Oudh regiments in Lucknow made a mutinous demonstration, only to be at once disarmed by the commissioner and disbanded. Henry Lawrence had by this time fully grasped the situation; but the commander-in-chief made no effectual preparations to cope with it. The military revolt was imminent; but even then, if vigour and energy had been displayed, it might have been quelled at the outset.

Such qualities were conspicuously wanting when the disaffection first blazed into a flame of violent rebellion early in May, 1857, at Meerut, forty miles from Delhi. At this large

CHAP.
VII.
station there were two native regiments of infantry and one of cavalry; but there were also a battalion of the 60th Rifles, a regiment of dragoons, and several batteries of European artillery. Unhappily the command of the district was held by General Hewitt, a hesitating veteran, painfully unfit to cope with the emergency which he now had to face. Eighty-five troopers of the 3rd Native Cavalry had refused to receive their cartridges on parade. They were tried by court-martial and ordered to be imprisoned Publicly degraded and stripped of their uniforms, in the presence of the whole garrison, they were then marched off to jail. This was on May 9, a Saturday. European Meerut, unconscious to the last, spent the following Sunday as usual; and as the hot afternoon waned towards the brief Indian twilight, the design which had been brooding in the hearts of the sepoys took shape. With arms in their hands they assembled in an excited mass before their huts. Some of the English officers, observing the commotion, rode across to the lines, and were shot down. Then began a night of terror and massacre. The sowars of the 3rd Cavalry dashed to the jail and set free their imprisoned comrades. The sepoys rushed across to the European quarter, and were joined by all the rabble of the native city. Officers, civilians, women, and children were assaulted and murdered, the defenceless bungalows were attacked, and the ruffians of the bazaar kept up the orgy of bloodshed and plunder till morning.

The mutineers went back to the lines, eager to make their escape from the scene of their crime. With deplorable weakness they were suffered to depart without a blow struck against them. The British troops were held inactive while the mutineers hastened through the night to Delhi; and the next morning their cavalry rode into that city, with the infantry following. They had marched on the wings of fear, never doubting that the tramp of English horse and the rumble of English cannon would speedily be heard behind them. But there was no one to do with the cavalry and horse artillery at Meerut what Gillespie had done with the dragoons and galloper-guns at Vellore half a century earlier. Hewitt was incapable of giving a decisive order; Archdale Wilson, his brigadier, was weighed down by the responsibility of protecting the stores and residents of Meerut, and he too kept the troops inactive. The

delay was calamitous. For though the conspiracy had been CHAP.
long preparing, it was without cohesion or unity. It is possible VII.
that if the Meerut rebels had been followed up at once and
destroyed by the strong force in the European cantonments,
the incipient rising might have been checked. At least it
would not have found a centre in the old Mughal capital, which
became a rallying place for many of the regiments of the Bengal
army, as in swift succession they rose against their officers, and
hastened to join their comrades in the imperial city.[1]

The revolt spread rapidly through all the north-western
provinces and Oudh, into Lower Bengal and Central India.
Its most conspicuous figures were the Mughal princes at Delhi;
Nana Sahib at Cawnpore; his counsellor and coadjutor, Tántia
Topí; the Rání of Jhánsi, widow of the deceased maharaja of
that state, who was deeply incensed because her adopted son
had been deprived of the right of succession; and Kunwar
Singh, a Rájput chief and landowner, who directed the trouble-
some guerilla warfare in Upper Bengal. Except at Delhi and
Cawnpore, the rebels were not joined by the representatives
of the older dynasties, or by the more important native rulers.
The Nizám at Hyderabad stood by the English; so did the
greater princes of Rájputána and Central India. Sindhia,
the most powerful of the Marátha potentates, remained loyal,
against the pressure of his own troops and subjects, through
the influence of his prime minister, Dinkar Ráo, and Charters
Macpherson, the political agent at Gwalior. The rebellion
scarcely touched Southern India, and the Madras army was
able to spare some useful regiments, and its best officer, Colonel
James Neill, for the campaign in the north.

But in the vast disturbed area, which extended from the
alluvial plains of the Ganges delta to the north-west frontier,
there were outbreaks and attacks upon Europeans everywhere,
riots and disorders in the larger towns, and small sieges of
isolated posts in which the English had sought refuge. Such
was that of Arrah in Bengal, where a few residents with a
handful of Sikh troops defended themselves in a billiard-room

[1] Lord Roberts suggests that Hewitt and Wilson had some excuse for not
pursuing the mutineers, since their available cavalry, the Carabineers, were few
in number, and largely consisted of recruits with unbroken horses (*Forty-one
Years in India*, i., 90).

CHAP.
VII.

against 3,000 irregulars under Kunwar Singh, who entrapped and nearly destroyed a rescuing force of 400 British and Sikh soldiers sent from Dinapur, but was himself completely routed and driven off by a much smaller body under Major Vincent Eyre on August 2. There were six main theatres of operations: Delhi; Cawnpore and Lucknow; the Punjab; Central India; the rural districts of Oudh and Rohilkhand; and parts of Upper Bengal and Behar extending to the Nipál frontier. The dramatic interest of the events connected with the sieges and reliefs of the great cities have thrown into the background the other episodes of the war; but the operations in the Marátha countries were scarcely less important, and the guerilla campaigns in Oudh, Rohilkhand, and Behar were extremely prolonged and trying.

At first, however, Delhi was the critical point. When the Meerut mutineers dashed into the city, they made at once for the palace, that maze of rose-red courts and marble halls overlooking the shining reaches of the Jumna, where the princes of the house of Timúr kept up a phantom royalty with a vast retinue of retainers and disorderly dependants. Bahádur Sháh, the octogenarian king, was proclaimed emperor; the rabble of the city was roused; the commissioner, the commandant of the palace guards, and nearly all the other British officials and residents, male and female, were massacred, or made prisoners to be put to death a few days later. The native troops from the cantonments on the Ridge, outside the city, were marched down to the gates; but they too mutinied, and joined the rebels. Lieutenant Willoughby, with eight companions, held the powder magazine against a swarm of assailants, and then with splendid self-devotion blew it up and 2,000 rebels with it. Delhi was completely in the hands of the insurgents; and the revolted sepoys, many of them Hindus, were supporting the revived Mughal monarchy in the person of the feeble old "emperor," and his ambitious eldest son.

The governor-general, however little he may have perceived the danger while it was developing, acted with promptitude and vigour when he at length grasped its character and magnitude. He asked for large reinforcements from England, and 30,000 troops were got ready for embarkation at once; he summoned reinforcements to Bengal from Ceylon, Burma, and the southern presidencies; he ordered back to Calcutta, as rapidly as possible, the troops under Outram set free by the successful close of the Persian war; and he took upon himself the responsibility of requesting Lord Elgin to land in India the regiments then on their way to China. "Yeh," he wrote, "may wait; but Bengal with its stretch of seven hundred and fifty miles, from Barrack-pore to Agra, guarded by nothing but the 10th Queen's, cannot wait, if the flame should spread."[1] He retained his sense of justice even in the excitement produced by the outbreak; and he deprecated undue and excessive reprisals with the calmness that earned him the sobriquet of "Clemency Canning" from some less able than himself to temper with mercy the uncontrolled and natural resentment kindled in English hearts by the news of the first massacres. "I will not govern in anger," said Canning. On July 31 he issued an order, intended to check the summary executions of sepoys suspected of mutiny or of complicity in the murder of their officers.[2]

The commander-in-chief received urgent instructions to hurry all available troops to Delhi and the other threatened cities. But there were great difficulties. Transport was defective, roads were bad, and the only railway was a short line of 120 miles from Calcutta to Raniganj. The troops sent up from the coast just managed to secure Benares and Allahábád, Neill with his regiment of the 1st Madras Fusiliers rescuing the European residents and inflicting stern vengeance on the rebels. Anson collected between 3,000 and 4,000 troops at Ambála and marched upon Delhi, but died on the way on May 27. He was succeeded in the command by General Barnard, who reached Badli-ki-sarai, six miles from Delhi, on June 8, and found 30,000 of the rebels, strongly entrenched, to dispute his passage. The insurgents were defeated with the loss of twenty-six of their guns. Barnard's force, however, was unable to attempt the assault of the great city, with its vast circuit of massive walls and fortified gates, defended by a powerful artillery, and by many thousands of the trained sepoys, who were

---

[1] Lord Elgin deserves all credit for so promptly diverting to India the Chinese regiments; but it was Canning who suggested the transfer. See MS. Correspondence of Lord Canning, quoted by Kaye and Malleson, i., 441; and R. Garnett's paper in *Engl. Hist. Review*, xvi. (1891), 739.

[2] *Parliamentary Papers*, 1857-58, p. 94 *seq.*

CHAP.
VII.

daily receiving accessions to their numbers. The British could only entrench themselves on the Ridge, and await reinforcements either from Bengal or the Punjab. On July 5, General Barnard died : he was succeeded by General Reed, and he, owing to ill-health, handed over the command to Archdale Wilson a fortnight later. Some further additions of native and European troops brought Wilson's force up to about 6,500 men. But it was still far too weak to attack the city, and could only cling grimly to the long, low, natural mound that lies just beyond the ramparts of Delhi, itself besieged rather than besieging, preyed upon by sickness and the fierce Indian summer, and constantly engaged in beating back the attacks of the rebels who swarmed out of the city against the little garrison of the Ridge.

Elsewhere the English were struggling against terrible odds. At Cawnpore the command was held by Sir Hugh Wheeler, a general of seventy-five. Believing in the fidelity of his sepoys and the loyalty of the Nana Sahib, who kept a kind of court at Bithúr, a few miles distant, Wheeler had been in no hurry to take adequate precautions for defence. When he did prepare to make a stand, he chose the wrong position. Instead of selecting the magazine near the river bank, a building easily fortified, he withdrew the European troops and residents to a rude and hasty entrenchment constructed near the barracks. It was a flat open field, with a low mud wall round it, and a few bungalows and other buildings inside. In this miserable enclosure nearly 900 persons, of whom 400 were women and children, were besieged on June 5 by several thousand mutineers and other armed natives, commanded by Tántia Topí under the Nana Sahib's direction. The defence, hopeless from the first, was maintained with desperate tenacity for three weeks: the women behaved as heroically as the men ; and every attempt of the besiegers to carry the place by assault was baffled. But the garrison was wearing away under exhaustion, thirst, the heat of the sun, and the hail of bullets that swept over the low wall. On the 27th they entered into a capitulation with the Nana Sahib, who agreed to send them down the river under safe conduct to Allahábád. Deeds of treachery and bloodshed, almost unparalleled in their infamy and horror, were the sequel to this agreement. When the English reached the place of embarkation they were fired upon

by the Nana's troops, and many were killed as they endea- CHAP.
voured to push off into the stream.   The male survivors, except   VII.
two officers and two soldiers, who escaped to tell the tale of
the siege, were brought back to the town and shot; the women
and children were thrust into a small ill-kept prison-house, the
Bibigarh, and spent eighteen days of terrible privation and
suffering before the end came.   On the night of July 15, when
the relieving force was approaching, the armed ruffians of the
Nana, his sepoys refusing to do the work, were sent among
these women and children and hacked them to pieces.   In the
morning the doors of the slaughter-house were opened, and the
bodies were thrown, " the dying with the dead," [1] down a well
near by.

The despairing garrison of Cawnpore had in vain sought
help from Lucknow, for there also the English were themselves
in dire extremity.   Sir Henry Lawrence, who had long foreseen
the rising, was prepared for it; and he knew that if no other
place were attacked the old capital of the kings of Oudh was
certain to become a core of the rebellion.   The residency, a
substantial building of brick and stone, with its outlying tene-
ments, was entrenched and fortified.   At the end of May the
Oudh regiments revolted, and all the outlying stations passed
into the hands of the enemy.   Lawrence, with the English
residents and troops to the number of about a thousand, and
some 700 faithful sepoys and native pensioners, after fighting
an unsuccessful action at Chinhat, retired into the residency on
June 30.   Two days afterwards Henry Lawrence, the statesman,
soldier, and saint, who asked only that it should be recorded of
him that he had " tried to do his duty," was mortally wounded
by a shell.   The command passed to General Inglis, who maintained the defence in the spirit of his predecessor.   For eighty-
seven days the garrison held out against a host of besiegers, at
one time computed at 60,000 men.   The area of the enclosure
was small, and the bazaar of the city came close up to its
walls, so that the assailants were able to fire right down into
the residency grounds from the roofs and upper rooms of the
native houses. They were well supplied with cannon, and
their batteries were worked at the shortest range by trained

[1] Inscription on the Memorial at Cawnpore.

CHAP.
VII.

sepoy artillerymen, while skilled engineers drove covered ways close to the defences and mines under them. But all the assaults were repelled by the garrison, which never faltered or lost courage, weakened though it was by the enemy's fusillade and by the ravages of disease. They had counted on being relieved by the end of July; but it was not till September 25 that a British force appeared in Lucknow, and when it did come it was not strong enough to raise the siege.

The relieving column was commanded by Henry Havelock, a fine soldier, who in forty-two years of varied service had never yet found full opportunity for displaying his powers as a strategist and a leader of men. Recalled from Persia, he landed at Calcutta on June 17, and was immediately sent up the country in command of the column designed to relieve the cities of Hindustan. On the 30th he reached Allahábád, and a week later he started for Cawnpore with a body of 1,500 European infantry and some volunteer cavalry, which had been preceded, a week earlier, by an advance detachment under Major Renaud, with 300 Sikhs and 400 of the 84th and Neill's Madras Fusiliers. The march in the hot season with inadequate transport was toilsome and costly. On July 13 Havelock's first battle was won at Fatehpur, where the rebels were scattered, losing eleven of their guns; and they were again defeated in two actions on the 15th. Havelock pressed on, and wearied as his soldiers were they marched fourteen miles that night, and the next day encountered the Nana, with over 5,000 men and eight guns, drawn up to dispute the entrance to Cawnpore. Havelock had no more than 1,100 infantry, 300 Sikhs, and a handful of the cavalry volunteers. His troops were fainting with fatigue, and some of them died of sunstroke and exhaustion on the field of battle. But the British soldiers had heard rumours of the Cawnpore butcheries, and nothing could stop them. They carried the enemy's guns and drove the sepoys before them in a furious rush. The Nana fled; and Havelock's wearied followers tottered into Cawnpore, to look down into the well where the still uncovered bodies of the 200 murdered women and children met their gaze. It was too late to save them—not too late for signal vengeance. Some of those who had taken a prominent part in the massacres, high-caste Bráhmans and Mohammedan officers, were forced by Neill under the lash to clean the blood from the walls and floors of the Bibigarh, and then CHAP. executed. VII.

But there was little time to linger in Cawnpore either for revenge or for repose. On the 20th, Havelock, with twelve guns and 1,500 men, of whom 1,200 were Europeans, marched out towards Lucknow. He defeated the rebels in two engagements, but his small force, weakened by cholera and dysentery, had to fall back without getting into touch with the beleaguered residency. Further unsuccessful attempts were made on August 4 and 11, and on the 16th at Bithúr, 4,000 of the sepoys, whom the Nana Sahib had rallied, were routed. On the 29th, however, the exhausted garrison had to receive a letter from Havelock telling them that he had no hope of reaching them for another twenty-five days, and advising them to perish sword in hand rather than negotiate.[1] In great depression, and suffering much from the miseries of the siege, sickness and hunger,[2] the garrison yet held out for another month. On September 15 Sir James Outram arrived in Cawnpore with orders to take over the command from Havelock; for the government of India, if it could not support its officers, knew how to supersede them.[3] The supersession was unaccompanied by one word of acknowledgment for the heroic energy with which Havelock and his minute army had fought against the marauders of Oudh, the rebel sepoys, fever, cholera and the sun. Outram, "the Bayard of India," was more generous than his employers. He issued a divisional order the day after his arrival at Cawnpore, in which he waived his superior rank, left to Havelock the command of the column for the relief of Lucknow,[4] and intimated his own intention of accompanying the force in his civil capacity as chief commissioner of Oudh, tendering his military services to Havelock as a volunteer.

Havelock's and Outram's army, reinforced by two British regiments and two batteries of artillery, was 3,179 strong

[1] Marshman, *Memoirs of Sir H. Havelock*, p. 383.

[2] Rations had been reduced, though there was in fact a sufficient supply of grain, unknown to Inglis, to sustain the garrison for months. See General Innes, *Lucknow and Oudh in the Mutiny*, pp. 146-49, etc., and Innes's personal statement to Mr. T. Rice Holmes given by the latter in his *Indian Mutiny* (5th ed.), p. 279.

[3] Kaye and Malleson, iii., 345; but see also Forrest, *Indian Mutiny*, ii., 5.

[4] Sir F. J. Goldsmid, *Life of James Outram*, ii., 221, 222

CHAP.
VII

when on September 20 it again crossed the Ganges and marched along the familiar northward road through Oudh. On the 23rd the relievers were in the suburbs of Lucknow. It took two more days of hard fighting, and much loss of life, including that of General Neill, before they could force their way through the swarming streets of the great city to the bailey guard of the residency, see the shot-riven banner of England still waving from the tower, and amid a scene of tumultuous emotion at length enter the enclosure. But the relieving force, diminished by the loss of 700 men since it left Cawnpore, was unable to bring away the women and children through the city and suburbs, still held by a horde of rebels and mutineers, directed by the fanatical Mohammedan maulvi of Faizábád, who showed considerable military skill. The investment continued, but the reinforced garrison was now able to occupy a much larger extent of ground adjacent to the residency; and though constantly attacked by sap and mine, it was well able to hold its own until finally relieved by Sir Colin Campbell nearly two months later. Outram was content to remain quiescent, knowing when he entered Lucknow that Delhi, the heart and centre of the rebellion, had already fallen.

Through the long summer the British troops outside the Mughal capital held their position on the Ridge. Too weak at first to do more than beat back the sorties from the city, they were gradually reinforced. The most valuable assistance came to them, not from Calcutta but from the north. The Punjab, newly annexed and inhabited by a warlike population and half-tamed tribesmen, was administered and defended by the ablest body of officers and civilians in the British Indian service, with John Lawrence at their head. There was great danger of a Sikh rising, and of an attack from the frontier clans and the Afghans. Even Lawrence hesitated for a moment, and was disposed to hand over Pesháwar to the Amír Dost Muhammad in return for his assistance, withdraw the British frontier to the Indus, and send down every available bayonet and sabre to the relief of Delhi. But Herbert Edwardes, John Nicholson, Neville Chamberlain, Montgomery, and Sydney Cotton, the ardent and daring spirits of the border province, argued for a bolder policy, and they were encouraged by the governor-general, who bade Lawrence "hold on to Pesháwar to the last". The plan of action, settled in council, two days CHAP.
VII. after the receipt of the news of the Meerut outbreak, was carried into effect.[1] The Punjab was strongly held; the mutinies of the sepoys at the principal military cantonments were energetically suppressed; the arsenals at Phillaur and Ferozepur were secured; help was accepted from the loyal Rajas of Patiala, Jhind, and Nabha, who put their Sikh troops at the disposal of the government; and Nicholson, whose commanding personality exerted a magnetic influence over the natives, swept through the country at the head of a movable column, sternly suppressing disorder. The first of the Punjab reinforcements, the Guides, a fine corps of frontiersmen, left Mardan three days after the Meerut mutiny, and entered the camp before Delhi on June 9, having marched at the rate of twenty-seven miles a day for three weeks.

On August 14, Nicholson at the head of a strong body of the Punjab troops arrived on the Ridge. The operations there had gone on slowly; men and officers suffered severely from sickness, and General Wilson had seriously thought of abandoning the siege altogether. Nicholson infused fresh energy into the besiegers. Their force now amounted to about 8,000 effectives (there were 3,000 in hospital), of whom 3,700 were British. Preparations for the assault were pushed on with some vigour, though still too slowly for the impatient spirit of Nicholson, who chafed at Wilson's dilatoriness and was "quite prepared," as he avowed, if the general still hesitated, "to appeal to the army to set him aside and elect a successor".[2] The long-delayed assault took place at dawn on September 14. The attacking parties were sent forward in four columns. The first led by Nicholson, stormed the breach which had been made by the cannon at a strong angle of the walls called the Kashmír bastion; the second attacked another breach at the water bastion; the third passed through the Kashmír gate which was daringly blown in by a small party of engineers under Lieutenants Home and Salkeld; and the fourth was to enter the city by the Lahore gate on the western side. This

[1] See Roberts, *Forty-one Years in India*, i., 66 *seq.*; L. J. Trotter, *Life of John Nicholson*, ch. xvii.; Bosworth Smith, *Lord Lawrence*, ii., 9, 44, etc.

[2] See Nicholson's letter to Lawrence of September 11 printed in Bosworth Smith's *Lord Lawrence*, and in Trotter's *John Nicholson*, ch. xxii.

CHAP.   detachment was repulsed, but the others forced their way inside
VII.   the line of ramparts.   Nicholson determined that the Lahore
gate must be captured from within, though the only approach
to it was by a narrow lane, with sharpshooters firing down
upon it from the windows of the houses and the parapet of the
city wall.   And here Nicholson himself was mortally wounded
as he led his men to an unsuccessful attack on the gun which
commanded the passage.

It was not till five days after the original assault that the
Lahore gate was taken.   Fighting their way through the streets,
the assailants reached the palace and gradually mastered the
city, though not before 1,145 officers and men had been slain
in the process of capture.   Bahádur Sháh, the puppet emperor,
fled with his sons to the tomb of his ancestor, Humayun, six
miles beyond the southern gate of Delhi.   From this refuge he
was taken, with a promise that his life should be spared, by
William Hodson, a Punjab officer of reckless daring, who had
done good service with a corps of irregular cavalry.   The
emperor was subsequently tried by court-martial for treason
and complicity in murder, and deported as a state prisoner to
Rangoon, where he died on November 7, 1862.   On the day
after his surrender, Hodson dragged out the Mughal princes
from Humayun's tomb and was escorting them to the city
when, fearing as he alleged that they would be rescued by the
turbulent crowd of armed Mohammedan spectators, he caused
them to descend from their palanquins and shot them dead
with his own hand.[1]   It was but one of many deeds of blood
which conquered Delhi witnessed ; for heavy indeed was the
retribution that fell on the guilty city, and martial law, not
always discriminating in its wrath, hurried hundreds of its
citizens from their wrecked and pillaged homes to the gallows.
Even Outram suggested that the rebel capital should be destroyed and left to desolation like the ruined Hindu cities
beyond its walls.

The capture of Delhi and the first relief of Lucknow were

---

[1] G. H. Hodson, *Hodson of Hodson's Horse*, pp. xvi and xvii, and 224.
Hodson's statement that the slaughter of the princes was justified by his situation was not accepted at the time or afterwards by those best competent to
judge.   See Bosworth Smith, *Lord Lawrence*, ii., 507; Roberts, *Forty-one Years
in India*, i., 250.

the turning points of the mutiny war. After September the tide turned steadily. Reinforcements were pouring in, and the English gradually re-established their authority through one after another of the wide tracts of territory in which it had been shaken or destroyed. Much, however, still remained to be done, and there was hard fighting in store for the local troops and the regiments coming in from England and the foreign stations. The operations were now directed by a single mind. Early in July Sir Colin Campbell had been appointed commander-in-chief in India. He was an officer of sixty-five, who had seen much active service, and had distinguished himself in command of the Highland Brigade in the Crimea— a good soldier, methodical and judicious, if a little slow and at times overcareful. He reached Calcutta on August 17, and busied himself with the preparation of reinforcements for the north-west districts. Transport was still difficult, and it was not till November 1 that he was able to move from Allahábád towards the Oudh capitals.

On the 3rd the commander-in-chief arrived at Cawnpore. He had at his disposal about 5,000 men and thirty guns, including a naval brigade, under Captain Peel of the *Shannon*, and a column 2,500 strong, which had marched down from Delhi under General Hope Grant and dispersed the rebels at Agra. But other enemies were gathering from the south. The Gwalior contingent, the drilled force of native troops nominally in the service of Sindhia, had revolted, and were now under the command of Tántia Topí, the Nana's former minister, and the most able military leader on the rebel side during the entire campaign.[1] Campbell left a detached force to hold the bridge across the Ganges against the advancing Gwalior insurgents, and pressed on for Lucknow, believing, erroneously,[2] that Havelock and Outram were in much worse straits for supplies than was actually the case. On the 12th he arrived at the Alambagh, the outlying fort which had been held by Outram's detached corps since the first relief. But the progress of his force through the suburbs and the devious streets was slow

---

[1] With the possible exceptions of the Oudh maulvi and the Ráni of Jhánsi. Sir Hugh Rose thought that the Maráthá princess was "the best and bravest military leader of the rebels".

[2] See *supra*, p. 147, note 2.

CHAP.
VII.
and difficult. The city was full of palaces, mosques, public buildings, and enclosed gardens, which were strongly fortified and had to be captured in detail. On the 17th the residency was reached, and by the 22nd the women and children had been removed, and the garrison withdrawn, with the exception of a force left behind to hold the Alambagh under Outram. Havelock died just as the withdrawal was accomplished on the 24th. No one of the heroes of the mutiny left a deeper impression upon the minds of his countrymen than this puritan soldier of sixty-two, who had prepared himself by a life of strenuous action, of profound study, and of religious meditation, for the opportunity which only came to him just before the close.

The commander-in-chief, with his convoy of women and children, and invalids, marched back towards Cawnpore, where he was badly needed. In his absence, General Windham, whom he had left in charge of the town, had been worsted in an engagement with the Gwalior mutineers; and an army of 25,000 men under Tántia Topí and the Nana now lay across the road from Lucknow. Campbell sent his sick and wounded and the women and children to Allahábád. On December 6, by which date his force, strengthened by reinforcements from England, reached a total of 5,000 infantry, 600 cavalry, and thirty-five guns, he attacked and completely defeated the rebels, scattered the whole Gwalior contingent in disorderly flight, and pursued them for miles from the scene of the engagement. Nana Sahib himself managed to escape; but his guns and baggage were taken, and many of his followers were driven into the river or cut to pieces in the pursuit. With Cawnpore once more in the hands of the British, the reconquest of the Doab was undertaken by Sir Colin and his lieutenants, and in the early days of January, 1858, the rebels were beaten in two engagements in this region, and the commander-in-chief was free to proceed in earnest to the pacification of Oudh, and the re-capture of Lucknow.

Upon that city the Oudh rebels were being gradually pressed back. Outram, who had held out against all their attacks in the Alambagh, was on their flank and rear; a Ghúrka army of 9,000 men, under Jang Bahádur, the staunch ally of the English in Nipál, was marching down upon them from the north: and General Franks, with a force of 3,000 Ghúrkas and

2,300 Europeans, was approaching from the east, after clearing CHAP
the Benares division, and re-establishing British authority in VII.
the country north of Allahábád. On February 28, Sir Colin
himself advanced from Cawnpore at the head of a powerful
army which had been swelled by numerous drafts from Calcutta to 19,000 men and 134 guns. With Jang Bahádur's and
Franks' contingents Campbell could dispose of over 30,000
troops; but his forces were none too large for the work before
them. There were computed to be 150,000 fighting men in
and about Lucknow, of whom nearly two-thirds were trained
soldiers. The city was strongly fortified, barricades and bas-
tions were erected in the main streets, and many of the houses
were loopholed and equipped for defence. The series of
assaults began on March 3, and was conducted along several
different lines of advance. After the outer ring of works had
been broken down, there was severe fighting in the streets,
which continued for several days, while the fortified buildings
were gradually battered in or carried at the point of the bayonet.
Not till the 21st was the entire city with the citadel securely
occupied.

The capture of Lucknow, though it did much to re-establish
British prestige, did not put an end to the disturbances in
Oudh. By an unfortunate error, the best troops of the in-
surgent host had been allowed to escape from Lucknow with
arms in their hands and so were enabled to resume hostilities
in the rural districts. A miscalculation, even more serious
in its results, was the publication during the last days of
the siege of a proclamation by the governor-general on March
20 confiscating all the lands of the province, with the exception
of those belonging to persons who immediately surrendered and
could prove that they had not "murderously shed" English
blood. This wholesale measure of sequestration, which exas-
perated the entire land-owning population, was gravely condemned by Outram and by John Lawrence, who urged that the
time had now come for amnesty and lenient treatment. "No
mutineer," said Lawrence, "ever surrenders; for directly he is
caught he is shot or hanged." At home, too, Canning's proclamation was severely criticised. Lord Ellenborough, who
had become president of the board of control, commented upon
it in an angry and intemperate despatch which he sent out at

CHAP.
VII.

once to the governor-general, and then allowed to be published. That the proclamation was a mistake was also the view of the new Derby cabinet, and Disraeli announced in the house of commons that its policy did not meet with the approval of her majesty's government, an opinion which after acrimonious discussion [1] was ultimately endorsed by the house of commons. Canning, however, though much mortified by this treatment, was neither compelled nor expected to resign. The directors of the East India Company passed a resolution of confidence in him, and Ellenborough retired from the board of control.

The hostile comments on the confiscation order seemed to be justified by its immediate consequences. Disregarding its limitations and concessions, the talukdars and barons of Oudh, and the chiefs of Rohilkhand and the neighbouring provinces, including many who had previously refrained from active participation in the revolt, now joined in the sporadic warfare which was maintained for several months after the fall of Lucknow. Scattered bands of the mutinous soldiery, armed clansmen, feudal retainers, and the *budmashes* or disorderly characters of the towns and villages, gathered round the Nana and other local leaders, and had to be followed up and dispersed in detail. In Behar a separate campaign was undertaken against the Rájput chieftain, Kunwar Singh, who gathered a large force about him, and gained several successes against British detachments. After his death on April 23, 1858, his followers kept up a harassing guerilla war, baffling the slow British columns by · the swiftness with which they moved through the jungles. At the suggestion of young Sir Henry Havelock, who received the baronetcy his father did not live to enjoy, detachments of mounted infantry were organised to pursue the elusive bands, which were eventually hunted down and dispersed.

In Rohilkhand, where the Faizábád maulvi organised and led the defence with energy and determination, the commander-in-chief carried on operations on an extensive scale through the spring of 1858. On May 5, at the head of an army of 7,600 men, he defeated the rebels in a hard fought battle at Bareilly. A month later the maulvi was killed in an attack on a loyalist raja, and Campbell leaving Rohilkhand quiescent, was able

---

[1] For the debates in parliament on the Oudh proclamation and Lord Ellenborough's despatch, see *infra*, p. 167.

to set about the final pacification of Oudh. The task was long and arduous. The whole province was covered with fortified castles and strongholds, and was pervaded by detached bands of insurgents, amounting in the aggregate to over 100,000, with 30,000 or 40,000 of the drilled sepoys among them. Sir Colin went to work with systematic method, though with perhaps an excess of caution, and a neglect of those expedients by which alone it is possible for regular troops to cope effectually with a scattered and mobile enemy in a difficult country. The problem was not wholly dissimilar from that which the British army had to face, forty-three years afterwards, in South Africa. A series of "drives," to use the term current later, was arranged, and the province was swept by a number of converging columns acting in unison, which gradually cornered the rebels on the northern frontier. Many of them surrendered ; others were driven into the pestilential jungles of the Terai or perished among the mountains of Nipál, where the inhabitants assisted the British troops to hunt them down. The Nana Sahib was among the last of the fugitives, and the English missed the satisfaction of sending this bloodthirsty and perfidious scoundrel to the gallows. He is commonly thought to have died of fever in the jungle, though it was long rumoured that he had escaped to Tibet, or was hiding in India.[1]

The operations in the north-west provinces employed Sir Colin Campbell (now raised to the peerage as Lord Clyde), with the largest European force in India, during the whole of 1858, and it was not till the early part of the following year that he was able to leave Hope Grant to complete the pacification of Oudh. Meanwhile a more exciting campaign had been carried on in the region south of the Jumna, under the leadership of Sir Hugh Rose (afterwards Lord Strathnairn), a general whose activity of movement and tactical daring were as conspicuous as the commander-in-chief's calculating caution. From the beginning of the mutiny there was great unrest in the Marátha principalities. At Indore, though the Maharaja Holkar was himself loyal, like most of the greater chiefs, his troops mutinied

---

[1] See Holmes, *Indian Mutiny*, p. 534 n. Mr. Perceval Landon in *Under the Sun* (1906) gives reasons for believing that Nana Sahib, by the connivance of Jang Bahádur, was allowed to live in concealment in Nipál, and that he may have been alive in 1885, or perhaps even later.

CHAP.
VII.

in July, 1857, and murdered the European and Eurasian inhabitants. The resident, Colonel Durand, marched through
Malwa with a small column, inflicted several defeats upon the
rebels, and succeeded in maintaining the English foothold at
Mhow, through the autumn and winter. More formidable
was the rising in Bandelkhand. At the western extremity
of this district, Ganga Bhai, the Ráni of Jhánsi, in the weeks
immediately succeeding the outbreak at Meerut, induced the
sepoy troops and populace to rebel, seized the fort, put to death
the Europeans, and caused herself to be proclaimed ruler of the
territory which under Dalhousie had "lapsed" to the company.
Stirred by the example of the fiery Marátha princess, most of
the chiefs of Bandelkhand declared against the English, and the
whole province was in great disorder. There were mutinies of
the sepoys at Ságar and Jabalpúr; the disturbance extended
into the Deccan, and only the firmness and swift resolution of
Major Davidson, the British resident at the court of the Nizám,
aided by the loyal co-operation of the minister, Sálar Jang,
kept the great city of Hyderabad, with its hordes of armed
Mussulmans, from joining the insurrection. There was one
critical moment on July 17, 1857, when a violent mob assembled
to attack the residency; but the Madras regiments stood firm,
and a volley of grape from the guns of their artillery saved
Southern India from sharing in the revolt.

   To subdue the Central Indian rebels it was decided that a
column of Madras troops should march from Jabalpúr across
Bandelkhand to Bandu; and that a Bombay force should
simultaneously advance from Mhow through Jhánsi to Kalpi
on the Jumna, to which place Tántia Topí's levies and the
remnants of the Gwalior contingent had withdrawn after their
defeat at Cawnpore. Sir Hugh Rose arrived at Indore to
take command of the Bombay column on December 16, 1857.
Two regiments of European infantry, and one of European
cavalry were included in a command which all told was well
under 5,000 men. On March 21, 1858, the column arrived
before Jhánsi, where, behind the precipitous rocks and frowning
granite walls of the fort, Ganga Bhai had established herself
with nearly 11,000 armed followers. The fort was fiercely
bombarded for several days. When the ramparts had been
sufficiently battered, Rose determined to assault. But on the

31st Tántia Topí, with 22,000 mutineers and rebels, appeared a few miles in the rear of the besiegers. Leaving a part of his force to hold the garrison of the fort in check, Rose turned swiftly upon the new assailant, and in a dashing battle at Betwa, in which he made brilliant use of his cavalry, completely defeated him. Two days afterwards Jhánsi was carried by assault, and the Rání, with a few attendants, rode away to join Tántia Topí at Kalpi. Directing his march upon that place, Rose again came upon the rebel leader and on May 1 inflicted a second severe defeat upon him at Kunch, and shattered as his troops were from marching and fighting in the sun, he followed the retreating enemy close and pressed on to Kalpi. Tántia Topí marched out to meet him; and on the 22nd there was another severe battle. The skilful use of his cavalry and guns again gave Rose the victory. Kalpi was occupied, and both Rose and the commander-in-chief believed that this phase of the campaign was at an end.

But the undaunted Rání had an audacious scheme in reserve. She persuaded Tántia Topí to retire to Gwalior, where, as she knew, the disaffected population and the Marátha leaders were with difficulty kept by Sindhia and his minister from joining the insurrection. The loyal maharaja marched out to oppose Tántia Topí, but his army went over to the rebels; he himself had to flee to Agra; and Tántia Topí and the Rání entered his capital, seized the fortress, the treasury and the arsenal, and proclaimed the Nana Sahib as peishwa amid the acclamation of the populace. Rose, reinforced by some troops from the south and east, marched, as rapidly as the heat and the condition of his soldiers would permit, into Sindhia's country. On June the 17th, one of his detached columns under Brigadier-General Smith appeared to the south of Gwalior, and beat back a fierce sally by the garrison. In this engagement the young Marátha heroine, whose fertile brain and valiant heart had cost the English so many lives, lost her own. Dressed like a man, the Rání of Jhánsi charged with the cavalry of the Gwalior contingent, and was killed in the rout by a sword-stroke from a trooper of the 8th Hussars. Two days afterwards Rose won another battle and then entered the city, and his troops stormed their way up the steep and rugged cliffs from which the mighty fort towers above the plain. Tántia Topí, with the Ráo Sahib,

CHAP.
VII.

CHAP.
VII.

the brother of the Nana, and the bravest of his followers some thousands strong, with thirty guns, fled towards the deserts of Rájputána, hotly pursued by the British. The chase was long; for Tántia Topí, with a constantly diminishing company of followers, doubled and twisted in front of the pursuing columns, and he was not captured till April, 1859. He was tried by court-martial, and hanged on the 18th; for his courage and indomitable resolution could not save him from the doom he had earned by his participation in the infamies of Cawnpore.[1]

The war was over; but there was much to be done and many marauding bands to be followed up and dispersed before order was restored, and civil government and public security gradually re-established in the disturbed districts. The process was not complete till the close of the year 1859, and by that time the government of India had undergone a sweeping change. According to the popular rumour current in the bazaars before the mutiny the rule of the company was destined to end on the hundredth anniversary of the battle of Plassey, June 23, 1757. As a fact it lasted a little more than a year longer. On August 3, 1858, the India bill of the Derby cabinet was passed, and the East India Company ceased to be the body nominally responsible for the government and the protection of 200,000,000 of Asiatics.[2] And on November 1, 1858, the queen's proclamation announced to the people of India that the territories, possessions, and executive powers of the company had been transferred to the crown. The proclamation declared that the government would henceforth be carried on by the viceroy in the name of the queen; that all treaties and engagements made by or under the authority of the East India Company would be observed; that "no extensions of our present territorial dominions" would be sought; that the rights, dignity, and honour of the native princes would be respected; that full religious toleration would be maintained; and that neither race, creed, nor colour would impose any legal disability upon the queen's Indian subjects, nor debar them from opportunities of suitable employment in the public service of the empire.

[1] For the closing stage of Tántia Topí's career, see Holmes, *Indian Mutiny*, p. 551, where some points are given from the unpublished papers of Sir Richard Meade; and Kaye and Malleson, v., 250 *seq*.

[2] For the provisions of the bill and the transactions in parliament which preceded it, see *infra*, p. 167.

A SHORT HISTORY

OF

OUR OWN TIMES

FROM

THE ACCESSION OF QUEEN VICTORIA

TO

THE ACCESSION OF KING EDWARD VII

BY

JUSTIN McCARTHY

A NEW EDITION

REVISED AND ENLARGED

LONDON

CHATTO & WINDUS

1908

CHAPTER XIII

THE INDIAN MUTINY

IN May 1857 the great Indian Mutiny shook to its foundations the whole fabric of British rule in Hindostan. Throughout the greater part of the north and north-west of the great Indian peninsula there was a rebellion of the native races against English power. It was not by any means a merely military mutiny. It was a combination of military grievance, national hatred and religious fanaticism, against the English occupiers of India. The native princes and the native soldiers were in it. The Mohammedan and the Hindoo forgot their own religious antipathies to join against the Christian. Let us first see what were the actual facts of the outbreak. When the improved (Enfield) rifle was introduced into the Indian army in 1856, the idea got abroad that the cartridges were made up in paper greased with a mixture of cow's fat and hog's lard. It appears that the paper was actually greased, but not with any such material as that which religious alarm suggested to the native troops. Now a mixture of cow's fat and hog's lard would have been, above all things, unsuitable for use in cartridges to be distributed among our Sepoys; for the Hindoo regards the cow with religious veneration, and the Mohammedan looks upon the hog with utter loathing. In the mind of the former something sacred to him was profaned; in that of the latter something unclean and abominaable was forced upon his daily use. Various efforts were made to allay the panic among the native troops. The use of the cartridges complained of was discontinued by orders issued in January 1857. The Governor-General sent out a proclamation in the following May, assuring the army of Bengal that the tales told to them of offence to their religion or injury to their caste being meditated by the Government of India were all malicious inventions and falsehoods. Still the idea was strong among the troops that some design against their religion was meditated. A mutinous spirit began to spread itself abroad. In March some of the native regiments had to be disbanded. In April some executions of Sepoys took place for gross and open mutiny. In the same month several of the native Bengal cavalry in Meerut refused to use the cartridges served out to them, although they had been authoritatively assured that the paper in which the cartridges were wrapped had never been touched by any offensive material. On May 9 these men were sent to the gaol. They had been tried by court-martial, and were sentenced, eighty of them, to imprisonment and hard labour for ten years, the remaining five to a similar punishment for six years. They had chains put on them in the presence of their comrades, who no doubt regarded them as martyrs to their religious faith, and they were thus publicly marched off to the common gaol. The guard placed over the gaol actually consisted of Sepoys.

The following day, Sunday, May 10, was memorable. The native troops in Meerut broke into open mutiny. They fired upon their officers, killed a colonel and others, broke into the gaol, released their comrades, and massacred several of the European inhabitants. The European troops rallied and drove them from their cantonments or barracks. Then came the momentous event, the turning point of the mutiny: the act that marked out its character, and made it what it afterwards became. Meerut is an important military station between the Ganges and the Jumna, thirty-eight miles north east from Delhi. In the vast palace of Delhi, almost a city in itself, lived the aged King of Delhi, as he was called; the disestablished, but not wholly disendowed, sovereign, the descendant of the great Timour, the last representative of the Grand Mogul. The mutineers fled along the road to Delhi; and some evil fate directed that they were not to be pursued or stopped on their way. Unchecked, unpursued, they burst into Delhi, and swarmed into the precincts of the palace of the king. They claimed his protection; they insisted upon his accepting their cause and themselves. They proclaimed him Emperor of India, and planted the standard of rebellion against English rule on the battlements of his palace. They had found in one moment a leader, a flag and a cause, and the Mutiny was transfigured into a revolutionary war. The Sepoy troops, in the city and the cantonments on the Delhi ridge, two miles off, and overlooking the city, at once began to cast in their lot with the mutineers. The poor old puppet whom they set up as their emperor was a feeble creature some eighty years of age. He had long been merely a pensioner of the East India Company. But he was the representative of the great dynasty whose name and effigies had been borne by all the coin of India until some twenty years before. He stood for legitimacy and divine right; and he supplied all the various factions and sects of which the mutiny was composed, or was to be composed, with a visible and acceptable head. If the mutineers flying from Meerut had been promptly pursued and dispersed, or captured, before they reached Delhi, the tale we have to tell might have been shorter and very different. But when they reached, unchecked, the Jumna glittering in the morning light, when they swarmed across the bridge of boats that spanned it, and when at length they clamoured under the windows of the palace that they had come to restore the rule of the Delhi dynasty, they had all unconsciously seized one of the great critical moments of history, and converted a military mutiny into a national and religious war.

This is the manner in which the Indian Rebellion began and assumed its distinct character. Mutinies were not novelties in India. There had been some very serious outbreaks before the time of the greased cartridges. But there was a combination of circumstances at work to bring about this revolt which affected variously but at once the army, the princes, and the population of India.   Let us speak first of the army.   The Bengal army was very different in its constitution and conditions from that of Bombay or Madras, the other great divisions of Indian Government at that time.   In the Bengal army, the Hindoo Sepoys were far more numerous than the Mohammedans, and were chiefly Brahmins of high caste; while in Madras and Bombay the army was made up, as the Bengal regiments are now, of men of all sects and races without discrimination.   Until the very year before the Mutiny the Bengal soldier was only enlisted for service in India, and was exempted from any liability to be sent across the seas; across the black water which the Sepoy dreaded and hated to have to cross.   No such exemption was allowed to the soldiers of Bombay or Madras; and in July 1856 an order was issued by the military authorities to the effect that future enlistments in Bengal should be for service anywhere without limitation.   Thus the Bengal Sepoy had not only been put in the position of a privileged and pampered favourite but he had been subjected to the indignity and disappointment of seeing his privileges taken away from him.

But we must above all other things take into account, when considering the position of the Hindoo Sepoy, the influence of the tremendous institution of caste.   An Englishman or European of any country will have to call his imaginative faculties somewhat vigorously to his aid in order to get even an idea of the power of this monstrous superstition.   The man who by the merest accident, by the slightest contact with anything that defiled, had lost caste, was excommunicated from among the living, and was held to be for evermore accurst of God.   His dearest friend, his nearest relation shrank back from him in alarm and abhorrence.   Now, it had become from various causes a strong suspicion in the mind of the Sepoy that there was a deliberate purpose in the minds of the English rulers of the country to defile the Hindoos, and to bring them all to the dead level of one caste or no caste.   No doubt there was in many instances a lack of consideration shown for the Hindoo's peculiar and very perplexing tenets.   To many a man fresh from the ways of England, the Hindoo doctrines and practices appeared so ineffably absurd that he could not believe any human beings were serious in their devotion to them, and he took no pains to conceal his opinion as to the absurdity of the creed, and the hypocrisy of those who professed it.   Some of the elder officers and civilians were imbued very strongly with a conviction that the work of open proselytism was part of their duty; and in the best faith and with the purest intentions they thus strengthened the growing suspicion that the mind of the authorities was set on the defilement of the Hindoos. Nor was it among the Hindoos alone that the alarm began to be spread abroad. It was the conviction of the Mohammedans that their faith and their rites were to be tampered with as well. It was whispered among them everywhere that the peculiar baptismal custom of the Mohammedans was to be suppressed by law, and Mohammedan women were to be compelled to go unveiled in public. The slightest alterations in any system gave fresh confirmation to the suspicions that were afloat among the Hindoos and Mussulmans. When a change was made in the arrangements of the prisons, and the native prisoners were no longer allowed to cook for themselves, a murmur went abroad that this was the first overt act in the conspiracy to destroy the caste, and with it the bodies and souls of the Hindoos. Another change must be noticed too. At one time it was intended that the native troops should be commanded for the most part by native officers. The men would, therefore, have had something like sufficient security that their religious scruples were regarded and respected. But by degrees the natives were shouldered out of the high positions, until at length it became practically an army of native rank and file commanded by Englishmen. If we remember that a Hindoo sergeant of lower caste would, when off parade, often abase himself with his forehead in the dust before a Sepoy private who belonged to the Brahmin order, we shall have some idea of the perpetual collision between military discipline and religious principle which affected the Hindoo members of an army almost exclusively commanded by Europeans and Christians.

We have spoken of the army and of its religious scruples; we must now speak of the territorial and political influences which affected the princes and the populations of India. Lord Dalhousie had not long left India on the appointment of Lord Canning to the Governor-Generalship when the Mutiny broke out. Lord Dalhousie was a man of commanding energy, of indomitable courage, with the intellect of a ruler of men, and the spirit of a conqueror. He was undoubtedly a great man. He had had some Parliamentary experience in England and in both Houses; and he had been Vice-President and subsequently President of the Board of Trade under Sir Robert Peel. He had taken great interest in the framing of

regulations for the railway legislation of the mania season of
1844 and 1845.   Towards the close of 1847 Lord Dalhousie
was sent out to India.   Never was there in any country an administration of more successful activity than that of Lord Dalhousie.   He introduced cheap postage into India ; he made railways ; he set up lines of electric telegraph.   He devoted much
of his attention to irrigation, to the making of great roads, to
the work of the Ganges Canal.   He was the founder of a com-
prehensive system of native education.   He put down infanticide, the Thug system, and he carried out with vigour Lord
William Bentinck's Act for the suppression of the Suttee or
burning of widows on the funeral pile of their husbands.   But
Lord Dalhousie was not wholly engaged in such works as these.
During his few years of office he annexed the Punjaub ; he
incorporated part of the Burmese territory in our dominions ;
he annexed Nagpore, Sattara, Jhansi, Berar and Oudh.   In the
Punjaub the annexation was provoked by the murder of some
of our officers, sanctioned, if not actually ordered, by a native
prince.   Lord Dalhousie marched a force into the Punjaub.
This land, the 'land of the five waters,' lies at the gateway of
Hindostan, and was p eopled by Mussulmans, Hindoos, and
Sikhs, the latter a new sect of reformed Hindoos.   We found
arrayed against us not only the Sikhs but our old enemies the
Afghans.   Lord Gough was in command of our forces.   He
fought rashly and disas trously the famous battle of Chillian-
wallah : he was defeated.   But he wholly recovered his position
by the complete defeat which he inflicted upon the enemy at
Goojrat.   Never was a victory more complete in itself or more
promptly and effectively followed up.   The Sikhs were crushed ;
the Afghans were driven in wild rout back across their savage
passes ; and Lord Dalhousie annexed the Punjaub.   He presented as one token of his conquest the famous diamond, the
Koh-i-noor, surrendered in evidence of submission by the
Maharajah of Lahore, to the Crown of England.

Lord Dalhousie annexed Oudh on the ground that the
East India Company had bound themselves to defend the
sovereigns of Oudh against foreign and domestic enemies on
condition that the State should be governed in such a manner
as to render the lives and property of its population safe ; and
that while the Company performed their part of the contract,
the King of Oudh so governed his dominions as to make his rule
a curse to his own people, and to all neighbouring territories.
Other excuses or justifications there were of course in the case

of each other annexation ; and we shall yet hear some more of what came of the annexation of Sattara and Jhansi. If, however, each of these acts of policy were not only justifiable but actually inevitable, none the less must a succession of such acts produce a profound emotion among the races in whose midst they were accomplished. The populations of India became stricken with alarm as they saw their native princes thus successively dethroned. The subversion of thrones, the annexation of states, seemed to them naturally enough to form part of that vast scheme for rooting out all the religions and systems of India, concerning which so many vague forebodings had darkly warned the land. Many of our Sepoys came from Oudh and other annexed territories, and little reason as they might have had for any personal attachment to the subverted dynasties, they yet felt that national resentment which any manner of foreign intervention is almost certain to provoke.

There were peculiar reasons too why, if religious and political distrust did prevail, the moment of Lord Canning's accession to the supreme authority in India should seem inviting and favourable for schemes of sedition. The Afghan war had told the Sepoy that British troops are not absolutely invincible in battle. The impression produced almost everywhere in India by the Crimean war was a conviction that the strength of England was on the wane. The Sepoy saw that the English force in Northern India was very small ; and he really believed that it was small because England had no more men to send there. In his mind Russia was the great rising and conquering country ; England was sinking into decay ; her star waning before the strong glare of the portentous northern light. Moreover Lord Canning had hardly assumed office as Governor-General of India, when the dispute occurred between the British and Chinese authorities at Canton, and almost at the same moment war was declared against Persia by proclamation of the Governor-General at Calcutta, in consequence of the Shah having marched an army into Herat and besieged it, in violation of a treaty with Great Britain made in 1853. A body of troops was sent from Bombay to the Persian Gulf, and shortly after General Outram left Bombay with additional troops, as Commander-in-Chief of the field force in Persia. Therefore in the opening days of 1857, it was known among the native populations of India that the East India Company was at war with Persia and that England had on her hands a

quarrel with China.   The native army of the three Presidencies
taken together was nearly three hundred thousand, while the
Europeans were but forty-three thousand, of whom some five
thousand had just been told off for duty in Persia.   It must
be owned that, given the existence of a seditious spirit, it
would have been hardly possible for it to find conditions more
seemingly favourable and tempting.   There can be no doubt
that a conspiracy for the subversion of the English government in India was afoot during the early days of 1857, and
possibly for long before.   The story of the mysterious
chupatties is well known.   The chupatties are small cakes
of unleavened bread, and they were found to be distributed
with amazing rapidity and precision of system at one time
throughout the native villages of the north and north-west.
In no instance were they distributed among the populations
of still-existing native States.   They were only sent among
the villages over which English rule extended.   A native
messenger brought two of these mysterious cakes to the
watchman or headman of a village, and bade him to have
others prepared like them, and to pass them on to another
place.   There could be no doubt that the chupatties conveyed
a warning to all who received them that something strange
was about to happen, and bade them to be prepared for whatever might befall.

The news of the outbreak at Meerut, and the proclamation
in Delhi, broke upon Calcutta with the shock of a thunder
clap.   For one or two days Calcutta was a prey to mere panic.
The alarm was greatly increased by the fact that the dethroned
King of Oudh was living near to the city, at Garden Reach, a
few miles down the Hooghly.   The inhabitants of Calcutta,
when the news of the Mutiny came, were convinced that the
palace of the King of Oudh was the headquarters of rebellion,
and were expecting the moment when, from the residence at
Garden Reach, an organised army of murderers was to be
sent forth to capture and destroy the ill-fated city, and to
make its streets run with the blood of its massacred inhabitants.   Lord Canning took the prudent course of having the
king with his prime minister removed to the Governor-General's
own residence within the precincts of Fort William.   If ever
the crisis found the man, Lord Canning was the man called
for by that crisis in India.   He had all the divining genius
of the true statesman ; the man who can rise to the height of
some unexpected and new emergency ; and he had the cool

N

courage of a practised conqueror. Among all the distracting counsels and wild stories poured in upon him from every side, he kept his mind clear. He never gave way either to anger or to alarm. If he ever showed a little impatience, it was only where panic would too openly have proclaimed itself by counsels of wholesale cruelty. He could not, perhaps, always conceal from frightened people the fact that he rather despised their terrors. Throughout the whole of that excited period there were few names, even among the chiefs of rebellion, on which fiercer denunciation was showered by Englishmen than the name of Lord Canning. Because he would not listen to the bloodthirsty clamours of mere frenzy, he was nicknamed ' Clemency Canning,' as if clemency were an attribute of which a man ought to be ashamed. Indeed, for some time people wrote and spoke, not merely in India but in England, as if clemency were a thing to be reprobated, like treason or crime. For a while it seemed a question of patriotism which would propose the most savage and sanguinary measures of revenge. Mr. Disraeli, to do him justice, raised his voice in remonstrance against the wild passions of the hour, even when these passions were strongest and most general. He declared that if such a temper were encouraged we ought to take down from our altars the image of Christ and raise the statue of Moloch there. If people were so carried away in England, where the danger was far remote, we can easily imagine what were the fears and passions roused in India, where the terror was or might be at the door of everyone. Lord Canning was gravely embarrassed by the wild urgencies and counsels of distracted Englishmen, who were furious with him because he even thought of distinguishing friend from foe where native races were concerned. But he bore himself with perfect calmness. He was greatly assisted and encouraged in his counsels by his brave and noble wife, who proved herself in every way worthy to be the helpmate of such a man at such a crisis. He did not for a moment under-estimate the danger ; but neither did he exaggerate its importance. He never allowed it to master him. He looked upon it with the quiet, resolute eye of one who is determined to be the conqueror in the struggle.

Lord Canning saw that the one important thing was to strike at Delhi, which had proclaimed itself the head-quarters of the rebellion. He knew that English troops were on their way to China for the purpose of wreaking the wrongs of

English subjects there, and he took on his own responsibility
the bold step of intercepting them, and calling them to the
work of helping to put down the Mutiny in India. The dispute with China he thought could well afford to wait, but
with the Mutiny it must be now or never. India could not
wait for reinforcements brought all the way from England.
Lord Canning knew well enough, as well as the wildest alarmist
could know, that the rebel flag must be forced to fly from
the field before that help came, or it would fly over the dead
bodies of those who then represented English authority in
India. He had, therefore, no hesitation in appealing to Lord
Elgin, the Envoy in charge of the Chinese expedition, to stop
the troops that were on their way to China, and lend them to
the service of India at such a need. Lord Elgin had the
courage and the wisdom to assent to the appeal at once.
Fortune, too, was favourable to Canning in more ways than
one. The Persian war was of short duration. Sir James
Outram was soon victorious, and Outram, therefore, and his
gallant companions, Colonel Jacob and Colonel Havelock,
were able to lend their invaluable services to the Governor-
General of India. Most important for Lord Canning's purposes was the manner in which the affairs of the Punjaub
were managed at this crisis. The Punjaub was under the
administration of one of the ablest public servants India has
ever had—Sir John, afterwards Lord Lawrence. John
Lawrence had from his youth been in the Civil Service of
the East India Company ; and when Lord Dalhousie annexed
the Punjaub, he made Lawrence and his soldier-brother—the
gallant Sir Henry Lawrence—two out of a board of three for
the administration of the affairs of the newly-acquired province. Afterwards Sir John Lawrence was named the Chief
Commissioner of the Punjaub, and by the promptitude and
energy of himself and his subordinates, the province was
completely saved for English rule at the outbreak of the
Mutiny. Fortunately, the electric telegraph extended from
Calcutta to Lahore, the chief city of the Punjaub. On
May 11 the news of the outbreak at Meerut was brought to
the authorities at Lahore. As it happened, Sir John Lawrence
was then away at Rawul Pindee, in the Upper Punjaub ; but
Mr. Robert Montgomery, the Judicial Commissioner at Lahore,
was invested with plenary power, and he showed that he could
use it to advantage. Meean Meer is a large military cantonment five or six miles from Lahore, and there were then some

four thousand native troops there, with only about thirteen hundred Europeans of the Queen's and the Company's service. There was no time to be lost. While the Punjaub held firm it was like a barrier raised at one side of the rebellious movement, not merely preventing it from going any farther in that direction, but keeping it pent up until the moment came when the blow from the other direction could fall upon it. The first thing to be done to strike effectively at the rebellion was to make an attack on Delhi ; and the possession of the Punjaub was of inestimable advantage to the authorities for that purpose. There was no actual reason to assume that the Sepoys in Meean Meer intended to join the rebellion. There would be a certain danger of converting them into rebels if any rash movement were to be made for the purpose of guarding against treachery on their part. Either way was a serious responsibility, a momentous risk. The authorities soon made up their minds. Any risk would be better than that of leaving it in the power of the native troops to join the rebellion. A ball and supper were to be given at Lahore that night. To avoid creating any alarm it was arranged that the entertainments should take place. During the dancing and feasting Mr. Montgomery held a council of the leading officials of Lahore, civil and military, and it was resolved at once to disarm the native troops. A parade was ordered for daybreak at Meean Meer ; and on the parade ground an order was given for a military movement which brought the heads of four columns of the native troops in front of twelve guns charged with grape, the artillerymen with their port-fires lighted, and the soldiers of one of the Queen's regiments standing behind with loaded muskets. A command was given to the Sepoys to pile arms. They had immediate death before them if they disobeyed. They stood literally at the cannon's mouth. They piled their arms, which were borne away at once in carts by European soldiers, and all chances of a rebellious movement were over in that province, and the Punjaub was saved. Something of the same kind was done at Mooltan, in the Lower Punjaub, later on ; and the province, thus assured to English civil and military authority, became a basis for some of the most important operations by which the Mutiny was crushed, and the sceptre of India restored to the Queen.

Within little more than a fortnight from the occupation of Delhi by the rebels, the British forces under General Anson, the Commander-in-Chief, were advancing on that city. The commander did not live to conduct any of the operations. He died of cholera almost at the beginning of the march. The siege of Delhi proved long and difficult. Another general died, another had to give up his command, before the city was recaptured. It was justly considered by Lord Canning and by all the authorities as of the utmost importance that Delhi should be taken before the arrival of great reinforcements from home. Meanwhile the rebellion was breaking out at new points almost everywhere in these northern and north-western regions. On May 30 the Mutiny declared itself at Lucknow. Sir Henry Lawrence was governor of Oudh. He endeavoured to drive the rebels from the place, but the numbers of the mutineers were overwhelming. He had under his command, too, a force partly made up of native troops, and some of these deserted him in the battle. He had to retreat and to fortify the Residency at Lucknow, and remove all the Europeans, men, women, and children thither, and patiently stand a siege. Lawrence himself had not long to endure the siege. On July 2 he had been up with the dawn, and after a great amount of work he lay on the sofa, not, as it has been well said, to rest, but to transact business in a recumbent position. His nephew and another officer were with him. Suddenly a great crash was heard, and the room was filled with smoke and dust. One of his companions was flung to the ground. A shell had burst. When there was silence the officer who had been flung down called out, ' Sir Henry, are you hurt ? ' ' I am killed,' was the answer that came faintly but firmly from Sir Henry Lawrence's lips. The shell had wounded him in the thigh so fearfully as to leave surgery no chance of doing anything for his relief. On the morning of July 4 he died calmly and in perfect submission to the will of Providence. He had made all possible arrangements for his successor, and for the work to be done. He desired that on his tomb should be engraven merely the words, ' Here lies Henry Lawrence, who tried to do his duty.' The epitaph was a simple truthful summing up of a simple truthful career. The man, however, was greater than the career. Lawrence had not opportunity to show in actual result the greatness of spirit that was in him. The immense influence he exercised over all who came within his reach bears testimony to his strength and nobleness of character better than any of the mere successes which his biographer can record. He was full of sympathy. His soul was alive to the noblest and purest aspirations. ' It

304

182 A SHORT HISTORY OF OUR OWN TIMES CH. XIII

is the due admixture of romance and reality,' he was himself
accustomed to say, ' that best carries a man through life.' No
professional teacher or philosopher ever spoke a truer sentence.
As one of his many admirers says of him—' what he said and
wrote, he did, or rather he was.' Let the bitterest enemy of
England write the history of her rule in India, and set down
as against her every wrong that was done in her name, from
those which Burke denounced to those which the Madras
Commission exposed, he will have to say that men, many men,
like Henry Lawrence, lived and died devoted to the cause of
that rule, and the world will take account of the admission.

The later days of Sir Henry Lawrence's life had another
trouble added to them by the appeals that were made to
him from Cawnpore for a help which he could not give. The
city of Cawnpore stands in the Doab, a peninsula between the
Ganges and the Jumna, and is built on the south bank of the
Ganges, there nearly a quarter of a mile broad in the dry
season, and more than a mile across when swelled by the rains.
In 1801, the territory lapsed into the possession of the Company.
From that time it took rank as one of our first-class military
stations. The city commanded the bridge over which passed
the high road to Lucknow, the capital of our new province.
The distance from Cawnpore to Lucknow is about fifty miles
as the bird flies. At the time when the Mutiny broke out
in Meerut there were some three thousand native soldiers
in Cawnpore, consisting of two regiments of infantry, one
of cavalry, and a company of artillerymen. There were
about three hundred officers and soldiers of English birth.
The European or Eurasian population, including women
and children, numbered about one thousand. These consisted of the officials, the railway people, some merchants
and shopkeepers and their families. The native town had
about sixty thousand inhabitants. The garrison was under
the command of Sir Hugh Wheeler, a man of some seventy-
five years of age, among the oldest of an old school of Bengal
officers. The revolt was looked for at Cawnpore from the
moment when the news came of the rising at Meerut; and
it was not long expected before it came. Sir Hugh Wheeler
applied to Sir Henry Lawrence for help; Lawrence of course
could not spare a man. Then Sir Hugh Wheeler remembered
that he had a neighbour whom he believed to be friendly,
despite of very recent warnings from Sir Henry Lawrence
and others to the contrary. He called this neighbour to

his assistance, and his invitation was promptly answered.
The Nana Sahib came with two guns and some three hundred
men to lend a helping hand to the English commander.

The Nana Sahib resided at Bithoor, a small town twelve
miles up the river from Cawnpore. He represented a grievance. Bajee Rao, Peishwa of Poonah, was the last prince of
one of the great Mahratta dynasties. The East India Company believed him guilty of treachery against them, of bad
government of his dominions, and so forth ; and they found
a reason for dethroning him. He was assigned, however,
a residence in Bithoor, and a large pension. He had no children, and he adopted as his heir Seereek Dhoondoo Punth,
the man who will be known to all time by the infamous name
of Nana Sahib. According to Hindoo belief it is needful for
a man's eternal welfare that he leave a son behind him to
perform duly his funeral rites ; and the adoption of a son
is recognised as in every sense conferring on the adopted all
the rights that a child of the blood could have. Bajee died
in 1851, and Nana Sahib claimed to succeed to all his possessions. Lord Dalhousie had shown in many instances a strangely
unwise disregard of the principle of adoption. The claim of the
Nana to the pension was disallowed. Nana Sahib sent a con-
fidential agent to London to push his claim there. This
man was a clever and handsome young Mohammedan who had
at one time been a servant in an Anglo-Indian family, and had
picked up a knowledge of French and English. His name
was Azimoolah Khan. This emissary visited London in 1854,
and became a lion of the fashionable season. He did not succeed in winning over the Government to take any notice of the
claims of his master, but being very handsome and of sleek
and alluring manners, he became a favourite in the drawing-
rooms of the metropolis, and was under the impression that an
unlimited number of Englishwomen of rank were dying with
love for him. On his way home he visited Constantinople and
the Crimea. It was then a dark hour for the fortunes of England in the Crimea, and Azimoolah Khan swallowed with glad
and greedy ear all the alarmist rumours that were afloat in
Stamboul about the decay of England's strength and the impending domination of Russian power over Europe and Asia.
The Western visit of this man was not an event without
important consequences. He doubtless reported to his master
that the strength of England was on the wane ; and while
stimulating his hatred and revenge, stimulated also his

confidence in the chances of an effort to gratify both. With Azimoolah Khan's mission and its results ended the hopes of Nana Sahib for the success of his claims, and began, we may presume, his resolve to be revenged.

Nana Sahib, although his claim on the English Government was not allowed, was still rich. He had the large private property of the man who had adopted him, and he had the residence at Bithoor. He kept up a sort of princely state. He never visited Cawnpore; the reason being, it is believed, that he would not have been received there with princely honours. But he was especially lavish of his attentions to English visitors, and his invitations went far and wide among the military and civil servants of the Crown and the Company. He cultivated the society of English men and women; he showered his civilities upon them. He did not speak or even understand English, but he took a great interest in English history, customs, and literature. He was luxurious in the most thoroughly Oriental fashion; and Oriental luxury implies a great deal more than any experience of Western luxury would suggest. At the time with which we are dealing he was only about thirty-six years of age, but he was prematurely heavy and fat, and seemed to be as incapable of active exertion as of unkindly feeling. There can be little doubt that all this time he was a dissembler of more than common Eastern dissimulation. It appears almost certain that while he was lavishing his courtesies and kindnesses upon Englishmen without discrimination, his heart was burning with a hatred to the whole British race. A sense of his wrongs had eaten him up. It is a painful thing to say, but it is necessary to the truth of this history, that his wrongs were genuine. He had been treated with injustice. According to all the recognised usages of his race and his religion, he had a claim indefeasible in justice to the succession which had been unfairly and unwisely denied to him. It was to Nana Sahib, then, that poor old Sir Hugh Wheeler in the hour of his distress applied for assistance. Most gladly, we can well believe, did the Nana come. He established himself in Cawnpore with his guns and his soldiers. Sir Hugh Wheeler had taken refuge, when the Mutiny broke out, in an old military hospital with mud walls, scarcely four feet high, hastily thrown up around it, and a few guns of various calibre placed in position on the so-called entrenchments. Within these almost shadowy and certainly crumbling entrenchments were gathered about a thousand persons, of whom 465 were men of every age and profession. The married women and grown daughters were about 280; the children about the same number. Of the men there were probably 400 who could fight.

As soon as Nana Sahib's presence became known in Cawnpore he was surrounded by the mutineers, who insisted that he must make common cause with them and become one of their leaders. He put himself at their disposal. He gave notice to Sir Hugh Wheeler that if the entrenchments were not surrendered, they would be instantly attacked. They were attacked. A general assault was made upon the miserable mud walls on June 12, but the resistance was heroic and the assault failed. It was after that assault that the garrison succeeded in sending a message to Sir Henry Lawrence at Lucknow, craving for the aid which it was absolutely impossible for him to give. From that time the fire of the mutineer army on the English entrenchments never ceased. Whenever a regular attack was made the assailants invariably came to grief. The little garrison, thinning in numbers every day and almost every hour, held out with splendid obstinacy, and always sent those who assailed it scampering back—except of course for such assailants as perforce kept their ground by the persuasion of the English bullets. The little population of women and children behind the entrenchments had no roof to shelter them from the fierce Indian sun. They cowered under the scanty shadow of the low walls often at the imminent peril of the unceasing Sepoy bullets. The only water for their drinking was to be had from a single well, at which the guns of the assailants were unceasingly levelled. To go to the well and draw water became the task of self-sacrificing heroes, who might with better chances of safety have led a forlorn hope. The water which the fainting women and children drank might have seemed to be reddened by blood; for only at the price of blood was it ever obtained. It may seem a trivial detail, but it will count for much in a history of the sufferings of delicately nurtured English women, that from the beginning of the siege of the Cawnpore entrenchments to its tragic end, there was not one spongeful of water to be had for the purposes of personal cleanliness. The inmates of that ghastly garrison were dying like flies. One does not know which to call the greater; the suffering of the women or the bravery of the men.

A conviction began to spread among the mutineers that it was of no use attempting to conquer these terrible British sahibs ; that so long as one of them was alive he would be as formidable as a wild beast in its lair. The Sepoys became unwilling to come too near the low crumbling walls of the entrenchment. Those walls might have been leaped over as easily as that of Romulus ; but of what avail to know that, when from behind them always came the fatal fire of the Englishmen ? It was no longer easy to get the mutineers to attempt anything like an assault. The English themselves began to show a perplexing kind of aggressive enterprise, and took to making little sallies in small numbers indeed, but with astonishing effect, on any bodies of Sepoys who happened to be anywhere near. Utterly, overwhelmingly, preposterously outnumbered as the Englishmen were, there were moments when it began to seem almost possible that they might actually keep back their assailants until some English army could come to their assistance and take a terrible vengeance upon Cawnpore. Nana Sahib began to find that he could not take by assault those wretched entrenchments ; and he could not wait to starve the garrison out. He therefore resolved to treat with the English. The terms, it is believed, were arranged by the advice and assistance of Tantia Topee, his lieutenant, and Azimoolah Khan, the favourite of English drawing-rooms. An offer was sent to the entrenchments, the terms of which are worthy of notice. ' All those,' it said, ' who are in no way connected with the acts of Lord Dalhousie, and who are willing to lay down their arms, shall receive a safe passage to Allahabad.' The terms had to be accepted. There was nothing else to be done. The English people were promised, during the course of the negotiations, sufficient supplies of food and boats to carry them to Allahabad, which was now once more in the possession of England. The relief was unspeakable for the survivors of that weary defence. The women, the children, the wounded, the sick, the dying, welcomed any terms of release. Not the faintest suspicion crossed any mind of the treachery that was awaiting them. How, indeed, could there be any such suspicion ? Not for years and years had even Oriental warfare given example of such practice as that which Nana Sahib and the graceful and civilised Azimoolah Khan had now in preparation.

The time for the evacuation of the garrison came. The boats were in readiness on the Ganges. The long procession of men, women, and children passed slowly down ; very slowly in some instances, because of the number of sick and wounded by which its progress was encumbered. Some of the chief among the Nana's counsellors took their stand in a little temple on the margin of the river, to superintend the embarkation and the work that was to follow it. Nana Sahib himself was not there. It is understood that he purposely kept away ; he preferred to hear of the deed when it was done. His faithful lieutenant, Tantia Topee, had given orders, it seems, that when a trumpet sounded, some work, for which he had arranged, should begin. The wounded and the women were got into the boats in the first instance. The officers and men were scrambling in afterwards. Suddenly the blast of a trumpet was heard. The boats were of the kind common on the rivers of India, covered with roofs of straw, and looking, as some accounts describe them, not unlike floating haystacks. The moment the bugle sounded, the straw of the boat-roofs blazed up, and the native rowers began to make precipitately for the shore. They had set fire to the thatch, and were now escaping from the flames they had purposely lighted up. At the same moment there came from both shores of the river thick showers of grapeshot and musketry. The banks of the Ganges seemed in an instant alive with shot ; a very rain of bullets poured in upon the devoted inmates of the boats. To add to the horrors of the moment, if, indeed, any addition were needed, nearly all the boats stuck fast in mudbanks, and the occupants became fixed targets for the fire of their enemies. Only three of the boats floated. Two of these drifted to the Oudh shore, and those on board them were killed at once. The third floated farther along with the stream, reserved for further adventures and horrors. The firing ceased when Tantia Topee and his confederates thought that enough had been done ; and the women and children who were still alive were brought ashore and carried in forlorn procession back again through the town where they had suffered so much, and which they had hoped that they were leaving for ever. They were about 125 in number, women and children. Some of them were wounded. There were a few well-disposed natives who saw them and were sorry for them ; who had perhaps served them, and experienced their kindness in other days, and who now had some grateful memory of it, which they dared not express by any open profession of sympathy. Certain of these afterwards described the English ladies as they saw them pass. They were bedraggled and dishevelled, these poor English women; their clothes were in tatters; some of them were wounded, and the blood was trickling from their feet and legs. They were carried to a place called the Savada House, a large building, once a charitable institution bearing the name of Salvador, which had been softened into Savada by Asiatic pronunciation. On board the one boat which had floated with the stream were more than a hundred persons. The boat was attacked by a constant fire from both banks as it drifted along. At length a party of some twelve men, or thereabouts, landed with the bold object of attacking their assailants and driving them back. In their absence the boat was captured by some of the rebel gangs, and the women and the wounded were brought back to Cawnpore. Some sixty men, twenty-five women, and four children were thus recaptured. The men were immediately shot. It may be said at once, that of the gallant little party who went ashore to attack the enemy, hand to hand, four finally escaped, after adventures so perilous and so extraordinary that a professional story-teller would hardly venture to make them part of a fictitious narrative.

The Nana had now a considerable number of English women in his hands. They were removed, after a while, from their first prison-house to a small building north of the canal, and between the native city and the Ganges. Here they were cooped up in the closest manner, except when some of them were taken out in the evening and set to the work of grinding corn for the use of their captors. Cholera and dysentery set in among these unhappy sufferers, and some eighteen women and seven children died. Let it be said for the credit of womanhood, that the royal widows, the relicts of the Nana's father by adoption, made many efforts to protect the captive Englishwomen, and even declared that they would throw themselves and their children from the palace windows if any harm were done to the prisoners. We have only to repeat here, that as a matter of fact no indignities, other than that of the compulsory corn-grinding, were put upon the English ladies. They were doomed, one and all, to suffer death, but they were not, as at one time was believed in England, made to long for death as an escape from shame. Meanwhile the prospects of the Nana and his rebellion were growing darker and darker. He must have begun to know by this time that he had no chance of establishing himself as a ruler anywhere in India. The English had not been swept out of the country with a rush. The first flood of the Mutiny had broken on their defences, and already the tide was falling. The Nana well knew it never would rise again to the same height in his day. The English were coming on. Neill had recaptured Allahabad, and cleared the country all round it of any traces of rebellion. Havelock was now moving forward from Allahabad towards Cawnpore, with six cannon and about a thousand English soldiers. Very small in point of numbers was that force when compared with that which Nana Sahib could even still rally round him ; but no one in India now knew better than Nana Sahib what extraordinary odds the English could afford to give with the certainty of winning. Havelock's march was a series of victories, although he was often in such difficulties that the slightest display of real generalship or even soldiership on the part of his opponents might have stopped his advance. He had one encounter with the lieutenant of the Nana, who had under his command nearly four thousand men and twelve guns, and Havelock won a complete victory in about ten minutes. He defeated in the same off-hand way various other chiefs of the Mutiny. He was almost at the gates of Cawnpore.

Then it appears to have occurred to the Nana, or to have been suggested to him, that it would be inconvenient to have his English captives recaptured by the enemy, their countrymen. It may be that in the utter failure of all his plans and hopes he was anxious to secure some satisfaction, to satiate his hatred in some way. It was intimated to the prisoners that they were to die. Among them were three or four men. These were called out and shot. Then some Sepoys were sent to the house where the women still were, and ordered to fire volleys through the windows. This they did, but apparently without doing much harm. Some persons are of opinion, from such evidence as can be got, that the men purposely fired high above the level of the floor, to avoid killing any of the women and children. In the evening five men, two Hindoo peasants, two Mohammedan butchers, and one Mohammedan wearing the red uniform of the Nana's body-guard, were sent up to the house, and entered it. Incessant shrieks were heard to come from that fearful house. The Mohammedan soldier came out to the door holding in his hand a sword-hilt from which the blade had been broken off, and he exchanged this now useless instrument for a weapon in proper condition. Not once but twice this performance took place. Evidently the task imposed on these men was hard work for the sword-blades. After a while the five men came out of the now quiet house and locked the doors behind them. During that time they had killed nearly all the English women and children. They had slaughtered them like beasts in the shambles. In the morning the five men came again with several attendants to clear out the house of the captives. Their task was to tumble all the bodies into a dry well beyond some trees that grew near. Any of the bodies that had clothes worth taking were carefully stripped before being consigned to this open grave. When Cawnpore was afterwards taken by the English those who had to look down into that well saw a sight the like of which no man in modern days had ever seen elsewhere. No attempt shall be made to describe it here. When the house of the massacre itself was entered, its floors and its walls told with terrible plainness of the scene they had witnessed. The plaster of the walls was scored and seamed with sword-slashes low down and in the corners, as if the poor women had crouched down in their mortal fright with some wild hope of escaping the blows. The floor was strewn with scraps of dresses, women's faded ragged finery, frilling, underclothing, broken combs, shoes, and tresses of hair. There were some small and neatly severed curls of hair too which had fallen on the ground, but evidently had never been cut off by the rude weapon of a professional butcher. These doubtless were keepsakes that had been treasured to the last, parted with only when life and all were going. One or two scraps of paper were found which recorded deaths and such like interruptions of the monotony of imprisonment; but nothing more. The well of horrors has since been filled up, and a memorial chapel surrounded by a garden built upon the spot.

Something, however, has still to be told of the Nana and his fortunes. He made one last stand against the victorious English in front of Cawnpore, and was completely defeated. He galloped into the city on a bleeding and exhausted horse; he fled thence to Bithoor, his residence. He had just time left, it is said, to order the murder of a separate captive, a woman who had previously been overlooked or purposely left behind. Then he took flight in the direction of the Nepaulese marches; and he soon disappears from history. Nothing of his fate was ever known. Many years afterwards England

and India were treated to a momentary sensation by a story
of the capture of Nana Sahib. But the man who was arrested
proved to be an entirely different person ; and indeed from the
moment of his arrest few believed him to be the long-lost
murderer of the English women. In days more superstitious
than our own, popular faith would have found an easy explanation of the mystery which surrounded the close of Nana
Sahib's career. He had done, it would have been said, the
work of a fiend ; and he had disappeared as a fiend would do
when his task was accomplished.

The capture of Delhi was effected on September 20. Brigadier-General Nicholson led the storming columns, and paid
for his bravery and success the price of a gallant life. Nicholson
was one of the bravest and most capable officers whom the war
produced. It is worthy of record as an evidence of the temper
aroused even in men from whom better things might have been
expected, that Nicholson strongly urged the passing of a law
to authorise flaying alive, impalement, or burning of the murderers of the women and children in Delhi. He urged this
view again and again, and deliberately argued it on grounds
alike of policy and principle. The fact is recorded here not
in mere disparagement of a brave soldier, but as an illustration of the manner in which the old elementary passions of
man's untamed condition can return upon him in his pride
of civilisation and culture, and make him their slave again.
The taking of Delhi was followed by an act of unpardonable
bloodshed. A young officer, Hodson, the leader of the little
force known as Hodson's Horse, was acting as chief of the In-
telligence Department. He was especially distinguished by an
extraordinary blending of cool, calculating craft and reckless
daring. By the help of native spies Hodson discovered that
when Delhi was taken the king and his family had sought refuge
in the tomb of the Emperor Hoomayoon, a structure which,
with the buildings surrounding and belonging to it, constituted
a sort of suburb in itself. Hodson went boldly to this place
with a few of his troopers and captured the three royal princes
of Delhi. He tried them as rebels taken red-handed, and borrowing a carbine from one of his troopers, he shot them dead
with his own hand. Their corpses, half-naked, were exposed
for some days at one of the gates of Delhi. Hodson was killed
not long after ; we might well wish to be free to allow him to
rest without censure in his untimely grave. He was a brave
and clever soldier, but one who unfortunately allowed a fierce

temper to overrule the better instincts of his nature and the guidance of a cool judgment.

General Havelock made his way to the relief of Lucknow. Sir James Outram, who had returned from Persia, had been sent to Oudh with complete civil and military authority. He would in the natural order of things have superseded Havelock, but he refused to rob a brave and successful comrade of the fruits of his toil and peril, and he accompanied Havelock as a volunteer. Havelock was enabled to continue his victorious march, and on September 25 he was able to relieve the besieged English at Lucknow. His coming, it can hardly be doubted, saved the women and children from such a massacre as that of Cawnpore ; but Havelock had not the force that might have driven the rebels out of the field, and if England had not been prepared to make greater efforts for the rescue of her imperilled people, it is but too probable that the troops whom Havelock brought to the relief of Lucknow would only have swelled the number of the victims. But in the meantime the stout soldier, Sir Colin Campbell, whom we have already heard of in the Crimean campaign, had been appointed Commander-in-Chief of the Indian forces, and had arrived in India. He set out for Lucknow. He had under his command only some 5,000 men, a force miserably inferior in number to that of the enemy ; but in those days an English officer thought himself in good condition to attack if the foe did not outnumber him by more than four or five to one. A series of actions was fought by Sir Colin Campbell and his little force attacking the enemy on one side, who were attacked at the same time by the besieged garrison of the residency. On the morning of November 17, by the combined efforts of both forces, the enemy was dislodged. Sir Colin Campbell resolved, however, that the residency must be evacuated ; and accordingly on the 19th heavy batteries were opened against the enemy's position, as if for the purpose of assault, and under cover of this operation the women, the sick, and the wounded were quietly removed to the Dilkoosha, a small palace in a park about five miles from the residency, which had been captured by Sir Colin Campbell on his way to attack the city. By midnight of the 22nd the whole garrison, without the loss of a single man, had left the residency. Two or three days more saw the troops established at Alumbagh, some four miles from the residency, in another direction from that of the Dilkoosha.

Alumbagh is an isolated cluster of buildings, with grounds

315

and enclosure to the south of Lucknow. The name of this place is memorable for ever in the history of the war. It was there that Havelock closed his glorious career. He was attacked with dysentery, and died on November 24. The Queen created him a baronet, or rather affixed that honour to his name on the 27th of the same month, not knowing then that the soldier's time for struggle and for honour was over. The title was transferred to his son, the present Sir Henry Havelock, who had fought gallantly under his father's eyes. The fame of Havelock's exploits reached England only a little in advance of the news of his death. So many brilliant deeds had seldom in the history of our wars been crowded into days so few. All the fame of that glorious career was the work of some strenuous splendid weeks. Havelock's promotion had been slow. He had not much for which to thank the favour of his superiors. No family influence, no powerful patrons or friends had made his slow progress more easy. He was more than sixty when the mutiny broke out. He was born in April 1795 ; he was educated at the Charterhouse, London, where his grave, studious ways procured for him the nickname of ' Old Phlos '—the schoolboy's ' short ' for ' old philosopher.' He went out to India in 1823, and served in the Burmese war of 1824, and the Sikh war of 1845. He was a man of grave and earnest character, a Baptist by religion, and strongly penetrated with a conviction that the religious spirit ought to pervade and inform all the duties of military as well as civil life. By his earnestness and his example he succeeded in animating those whom he led with similar feelings ; and ' Havelock's saints ' were well known through India by this distinctive appropriate title. ' Havelock's saints ' showed, whenever they had an opportunity, that they could fight as desperately as the most reckless sinners ; and their commander found the fame flung in his way, across the path of his duty, which he never would have swerved one inch from that path to seek. Amid all the excitement, of hope and fear, passion and panic, in England, there was time for the whole heart of the nation to feel pride in Havelock's career and sorrow for his untimely death. Untimely ? Was it after all untimely ? Since when has it not been held the crown of a great career that the hero dies at the moment of accomplished victory ?

Sir Colin Campbell left General Outram in charge of Alumbagh, and himself hastened towards Cawnpore. A large hostile force, composed chiefly of the revolted army of Scindia,

o

the ruler of Gwalior, had marched upon Cawnpore. General Windham, who held the command there, had gone out to attack them. He was compelled to retreat, not without severe loss, to his entrenchments at Cawnpore, and the enemy occupied the city itself. Sir Colin Campbell attacked the rebels at one place; Sir Hope Grant attacked them at another, and Cawnpore was retaken. Sir Colin Campbell then turned his attention to reconquering the entire city of Lucknow. It was not until March 19, 1858, that Lucknow fell completely into the hands of the English. Our operations had been almost entirely by artillery, and had been conducted with consummate prudence as well as boldness, and our loss was therefore very small, while the enemy suffered most severely. Among our wounded was the gallant leader of the naval brigade, Sir William Peel, son of the great statesman. Sir William Peel died at Cawnpore shortly after, of small-pox, his death remarked and lamented even amid all the noble deaths of that eventful time. One name must not be forgotten among those who endured the siege of Lucknow. It is that of Dr. Brydon, whom we last saw as he appeared under the walls of Jellalabad, the one survivor come back to tell the tale of the disastrous retreat from Cabul.

Practically, the reconquest of Lucknow was the final blow in the suppression of the great Bengal mutiny. Some episodes of the war, however, were still worthy of notice. For example, the rebels seized Gwalior, the capital of the Maharajah Scindia, who escaped to Agra. The English had to attack the rebels, retake Gwalior, and restore Scindia. The Maharajah Scindia of Gwalior had deserved well of the English Government. Under every temptation, every threat, and many profound perils from the rebellion, he had remained firm to his friendship. So, too, had Holkar, the Maharajah of the Indore territory. The country owes much to those two princes, for the part they took at her hour of need; and she has not, we are glad to think, proved herself ungrateful. One of those who fought to the last on the rebels' side was the Ranee, or Princess, of Jhansi, whose territory, as we have already seen, had been one of our annexations. For months after the fall of Delhi she contrived to baffle Sir Hugh Rose and the English. She led squadrons in the field. She fought with her own hand. She was engaged against us in the battle for the possession of Gwalior. In the uniform of a cavalry officer she led charge after charge, and she was killed among those who resisted to the last. Her body was found upon the field, scarred with wounds enough in the front to have done credit to any hero. Sir Hugh Rose paid her the well-deserved tribute which a generous conqueror is always glad to be able to offer. He said, in his general order, that 'the best man upon the side of the enemy was the woman found dead, the Ranee of Jhansi.'

It is not necessary to describe, with any minuteness of detail, the final spasms of the rebellion. Tantia Topee, the lieutenant of Nana Sahib, was taken prisoner in April 1859, was tried for his share in the Cawnpore massacre, and was hanged like any vulgar criminal. The old King of Delhi was also put on trial, and being found guilty, was sentenced to transportation. He was sent to the Cape of Good Hope, but the colonists there refused to receive him, and this last of the line of the Grand Moguls had to go begging for a prison. He was finally carried to Rangoon, in British Burmah. On December 20, 1858, Lord Clyde, who had been Sir Colin Campbell, announced to the Governor-General that the rebellion was at an end, and on May 1, 1859, there was a public thanksgiving in England for the pacification of India.

ROUND THE EMPIRE

FOR THE USE OF SCHOOLS

BY

GEORGE R. PARKIN, C.M.G., LL.D.

WITH A PREFACE BY

THE RIGHT HON. THE EARL OF ROSEBERY, K.G.

NEW AND REVISED EDITION

173rd THOUSAND

CASSELL AND COMPANY, LIMITED
LONDON, NEW YORK, TORONTO AND MELBOURNE

The Sepoy Mutiny.

We have seen how India was conquered for us largely by the help of natives troops, or Sepoys. These same Sepoys proved, however, to be a great danger as well as a great assistance. In 1857 occurred the Sepoy Mutiny, when great numbers of the men whom we had drilled and armed so carefully rose in rebellion against our rule. There were frightful massacres of our people. For a short time it seemed probable that British power in India would be overthrown. Had the whole of the people of India joined in the rebellion, this would no doubt have taken place. But they did not do so, and of the Sepoys themselves many regiments remained faithful, and helped us to fight the mutineers. The **Sikhs** of the Punjaub, whom we had conquered shortly before, fought valiantly upon the British side, and rendered great assistance, as did also the princes and people of some of the feudatory native States. The common people of the country went on as usual rendering us those services which are almost necessary for the existence of Europeans in the hot climate of India. Never perhaps did British soldiers display greater courage and endurance than during the Sepoy Mutiny. But it was put down by native aid as well as by the exertions of our own troops.

The Mutiny proved that India was not, and probably never will be, a country which can be united to oppose our rule.

The Empress of India.

The Mutiny of 1857 was followed by the important change in the method of government to which reference has been made.   Our people had gradually made up their minds that the East India Company, wonderful as was the work which it had done in building up our Indian Empire, was not a body suited for carrying on its government.   By a Bill passed through Parliament in 1858, the government of India was transferred from the Company to the Sovereign, as the representative of the people of this country.   In 1877 Queen Victoria took the title of **Empress of India**.   Our present King has the corresponding title of Emperor of India.   Since 1858 the English people have been entirely responsible, through the Sovereign and Parliament, for the good government of our fellow-subjects in India.   How this work is carried on we shall briefly explain in another place.

A SHORT
HISTORY OF ENGLAND

FROM THE EARLIEST TIMES TO THE DEATH OF KING EDWARD VII

BY

CYRIL RANSOME, M.A.

Merton College, Oxford

Sometime Professor of Modern History and English Literature, Yorkshire College
Victoria University

With Maps and Plans

NEW EDITION

LONGMANS, GREEN, AND CO.
39 PATERNOSTER ROW, LONDON
NEW YORK, BOMBAY, AND CALCUTTA
1910

Victoria.

Before the war with China had gone far, the country was startled by the news of a mutiny among the Bengal sepoys in India. The **Causes of the Indian mutiny.** causes of the outbreak were numerous. Much excitement had been caused by Lord Dalhousie's annexation of Oudh, from which many of the Bengal sepoys came. There was a widespread but unfounded fear among the natives that the British intended to introduce Christianity by force and to put an end to their cherished practices and superstitions. There was a prophecy that the British rule should only last for one hundred years, and that time had now elapsed since the battle of Plassey. Lastly, the authorities had served out rifle cartridges, the bullets of which were wrapped in greased rags. This grease was said by the natives to be made of cow's fat and hog's lard, and as the Hindoos reverenced the cow, while the Mohammedans detested the hog, the result of the mixture was to irritate both the Hindoos and the Mohammedans.

Accordingly, the Bengal sepoys broke into revolt, murdered their officers, seized Delhi, where they set up as leader the descendant **Outbreak of the mutiny.** of the Great Mogul, and tried to raise a national rebellion. Ths British army, however, at once besieged Delhi, which prevented the mutiny from spreading, while other parties held out at Lucknow, the capital of Oudh, and at

Cawnpore on the Ganges. Lower down the river the British never lost the upper hand. Unfortunately, Cawnpore was taken before relief came, and a terrible massacre followed. Lucknow held out till General Havelock forced his way in and reinforced the garrison. After great exertions Delhi was captured, mainly owing to the fidelity of the recently conquered Sikhs, which enabled Sir John Lawrence, the commissioner of the Punjab, whose admirable rule had in four years completely won over the Sikhs, to send large reinforcements to the besiegers of Delhi. This success broke the neck of the mutiny. Soon Sir Colin Campbell arrived from England with reinforcements, and though very severe fighting followed, especially at the final relief of Lucknow, the country was at length reduced to quiet.

THE BUILDING

OF THE

BRITISH EMPIRE

A READING BOOK FOR SCHOOLS

BY

E. M. RICHARDSON, B.A., F.R.Hist.S.

LONDON
G. BELL AND SONS LTD.
1924

5. The Great Mutiny (1857)

Some years of peaceful progress and reform followed, under the energetic governorship of Lord Dalhousie. The reforms were sometimes carried out with too little regard for the prejudices and racial customs of the Hindus themselves, and several times Lord Dalhousie offended them very much. He annexed, for example, several small states where there was no direct heir to the throne. Now, by Hindu law, a man who had no son might adopt one, and the adopted son could succeed to the throne, but Lord Dalhousie paid no attention to this custom, if he thought the State was badly managed and would be better off under English rule.

Further, Lord Dalhousie made railways, and introduced the telegraph and the use of postage stamps. The rapid changes upset the natives, and there were murmurings here and there. A prophecy was current that the rule of the white race would come to an end in one hundred years, and it was just a hundred years since the battle of Plassy was fought. Then in 1856 Lord Dalhousie annexed Oudh, because it was badly governed. The rulers of Oudh had always been faithful to the English, and the annexation disturbed the Indian princes, who could no longer feel safe in the possession of their states. Lastly, he refused to give the pension, which had been granted to the deposed Peishwa, to his adopted son, Nana Sahib, and he told the Mogul Emperor, who still exercised the shadow of authority at Delhi, that the title would be abolished when he died, and that his successor might not succeed to his dignity.

Viscount Canning became Governor-General in 1856. The discontent was rapidly growing, and the native troops, or sepoys, now began to grow disaffected. They were annoyed because the English had wished to send them to serve across the sea, and in regions far from their own homes. They feared that they were all to be forced to become Christians, and a story went about that the dust of human bones was mixed with the corn sold to them. Then came the rumour that the cartridges to fit the new rifles which had been lately given to them were greased with the fat of pigs and cows. The first animal was unclean to the Mohammedans, and the second was sacred to the Hindus. The religious feelings of both were outraged. Panic spread. One native regiment refused to receive the hateful cartridges; several others had to be disbanded. There were very few English regiments in the country, for they had been withdrawn to fight in the Crimean War, which was just over. But even with all these signs of discontent the majority of the English would see no danger.

The revolt first broke out violently at Meerut, forty miles from Delhi. Here eighty-five troopers in a native regiment refused to receive the cartridges. They were tried by court-martial and sentenced to terms of imprisonment. This was on Saturday, 9th May 1857. On the Sunday evening following, their companions rushed to the gaol, broke it open, set free their companions, and then, rushing to the European quarter, they murdered all they met, men, women, and children, and burnt down their houses.

The mutineers then set out for Delhi, which they entered the next morning. The same scenes of murder were repeated at Delhi; some of the English were slain at once, while others, less fortunate, were captured and taken to the palace, where they were butchered.

The revolt now spread rapidly, though many of the provinces remained faithful to the English. The governor-general telegraphed for troops, and brought over the soldiers who were in Burmah and Ceylon, while Sir George Grey, on hearing of the rebellion, sent some troops, which stopped at Cape Town on their way home, back to India. As many troops as could be spared were sent to lay siege to Delhi, but at first they were so few in number that they had hard work to maintain their position against the attacks of the rebels in the city.

At Cawnpur Nana Sahib led the mutineers. The English there, in number nearly nine hundred, had entrenched themselves in a field near the barracks. It was enclosed by a low mud wall, and there were a few bungalows inside. Here they were besieged by some thousands of natives, and held out heroically for three weeks, women as well as men taking part in the defence. But they were obliged to yield at last, and Nana Sahib agreed to send them safely down the river to Allahabad. But as they were embarking on the boats sent for them, Nana's troops fired on them, and many of them were killed. The rest were brought back to Cawnpur, the men were shot at once, and the women and children were imprisoned, until the news came that an English force was approaching. On this, Nana Sahib sent some ruffians among them, who slaughtered them and threw their bodies, " the dying with the dead," into a well.

At Lucknow the English were also hard beset by the rebels. Sir Henry Lawrence, the British Resident there, had foreseen the danger of a native rising, and had fortified the Residency. The Europeans took refuge within it, and here they held out for eighty-seven days. Sir Henry Lawrence was mortally wounded two days after the siege was begun, but his successor valiantly continued the defence. The rebels were able to fire into the Residency enclosure from the roofs of the

houses around. The little garrison soon had to face
hunger and disease. Meantime, a small force of soldiers,
led by Havelock, was marching to their relief. They
reached Cawnpur in July, only to find that they were
too late. Then, in spite of exhaustion and the ravages of
cholera and dysentery, they struggled on, fighting almost
the whole way to Lucknow. In September Havelock
was joined by Sir James Outram with reinforcements,
and after two days of hard fighting they forced their
way into Lucknow; and though they were unable to
fight their way out of the city, and had to remain there
for nearly two months longer, yet the worst part of the
siege was over, and they were well able to hold their
own against the rebels, until the city was captured by
Sir Colin Campbell.

Meantime, General Nicholson had brought some of
the Punjab forces, who remained faithful to the British,
to the relief of Delhi, and the city was carried by assault
in September. Nicholson was shot in attempting to
capture the gate called the Lahore Gate. The capture
of Delhi was the turning point in the war, though
there was much fighting to be done before the country
was pacified. Nana Sahib escaped, and is thought to have
died of fever in the jungle, though there is some reason
to believe that he escaped, and lived in concealment in
Nepal. The most vigorous resistance was made by the
Ranee of Jhansi in the west of the Mahratta country
of Bundelkhand. She had been enraged because the
British had put aside her husband's adopted son, and
had annexed the province. She now declared that she
was the ruler of the province, and stirred her people to
rebellion. When the fortress of Jhansi was captured by
the British, the Ranee rode away to join Nana Sahib's
former minister, Tantia Topi, who commanded an army of

22,000 mutineers. She persuaded him to seize Gwalior, and to proclaim Nana Sahib Peishwa. When the British appeared an engagement was fought, in which the young Mahratta princess was killed. Soon after, Tantia Topi

CALCUTTA.

was driven away from Gwalior, captured, and hanged for his share in the Cawnpur massacre. This put an end to the war. Measures were now taken to restore the Government. The East India Company was put aside in 1858, and the Queen became Empress of India, though the actual title was taken later. She promised that her viceroy should rule for her, that she would respect the rights, dignities, and honours of the native chiefs, and maintain full religious toleration.

6. India since the Mutiny

India has been extended since the Mutiny by the addition of the old kingdom of Ava in Burmah in 1885, while her frontier reaches as far as the Pamirs, and she holds part of Baluchistan, including Quetta and the Bolan Pass.   The British have promised Afghanistan and Baluchistan not to interfere with their independence, and to pay their rulers subsidies, provided they enter into no relations with foreign powers other than India.

Meanwhile, increased education and prosperity led to a certain amount of political unrest.   A section among the native Indians began to demand some share in the government of the country, and the Indian Councils Act of 1909 made some concessions, providing that elected representatives of India might be sent to the Legislative Council which had existed for a long time, though it consisted merely of the members of the Viceroy's Executive Council, with a few other members nominated by the Viceroy. · In 1919, a further important step was taken.   The Legislative Council was divided into two chambers, a Council of State and a Legislative Assembly, the latter being largely an elected body.   Some advance towards giving Responsible Government was made, and a Budget statement is laid annually before both Chambers of the new Legislature.   In 1921 a Chamber of Princes was established to discuss matters relating to treaties and affairs of Imperial concern.

THE
GREAT VICTORIAN AGE

FOR CHILDREN

BY

M. B. SYNGE, F.R.Hist.S.

AUTHOR OF "A SHORT HISTORY OF SOCIAL LIFE IN ENGLAND," "THE STORY
OF THE WORLD," "THE WORLD'S CHILDHOOD," ETC.

HODDER AND STOUGHTON
LONDON MCMVIII

XXI

THE INDIAN MUTINY

"Handful of men as we were, we were English in heart and in limb,
Strong with the strength of the race to command, to obey, to
endure."—TENNYSON.

BUT while the Queen was presenting the Victoria
Cross on that summer day of 1857 to those of
her brave soldiers who had distinguished themselves
in the Crimea, alarming news was reaching England
of a native revolt in another part of her Dominions,
a revolt known to history as the Indian Mutiny.

"There are times in the history of every nation
when she must either fight or go down."

Such a time had come now. Swiftly, silently the
blow fell, and heroically, alone, without an ally,
against odds too great to be counted, England in the
face of the world set to work to re-conquer India.

Discontent had long been simmering throughout
the country; Lord Dalhousie, one of the most
famous Governor-Generals India has ever seen, had
brought province after province under British rule.
He had added Satara in 1848, the first year of his
residence, and the Punjab in the following year.
Later, the Rajah of Nagpur died without heirs and
that Principality was likewise added to the British
Dominions, being known to-day as the Central
Provinces. After this the kingdom of Oudh was

111

annexed—a country as large as Belgium and Holland —until Lord Dalhousie had increased England's possessions in India by more than a third. A colossal worker, he sought to bind together the scattered parts by telegraph and railway. To this same end, he made the largest of Indian canals, he carried the Grand Trunk road through the Punjab, and only returned home to die, when his physical strength failed to bear the burden.

Utterly worn out with his efforts on behalf of the British Empire, he "tottered on crutches down the banks of the Hugli (Calcutta) to embark for England, predicting that troubles were ahead for India. England had increased her land, but there was no increase of English men to hold it.

This was because every one, both in India and at home, believed in the loyalty of the native soldiers, or Sepoys as they were called. When the Mutiny broke out, there were just five times as many Sepoys as British soldiers in India. At the death of Queen Victoria there was a large proportion of English soldiers, so that a repetition of this terrible catastrophe in English history is impossible.

But in 1857 there was a growing feeling among the natives that the old state of things was passing away; they thought the English wanted to make them Christians, and they believed the native prophecy that a hundred years after Plassey, English rule should cease. The anniversary fell on June 23, 1857, and but for the grand courage of Havelock, the fierce energy of Nicholson, the unsleeping toil and forethought of Lawrence, this prophecy would have come true.

Matters reached a climax at last.

Up to this time the Sepoys had been armed with a

334

MUTINY AT DELHI 113

musket popularly known as "Brown Bess." In 1857
an improved rifle, known as the Enfield, was substituted. It was rumoured that the new rifles required greased cartridges, and that they were
greased with hog's lard, forbidden to Mohammedans.
A panic of religious fear ran from regiment to
regiment, from village to village.

Early in May some cartridges were served out to
a native regiment at Meerut, near Delhi. They were
refused by eighty-five Sepoys, who were tried,
disarmed, publicly paraded, and marched in chains
to the local prison, which was guarded by native
officials.

The following day was Sunday. The weather
was fiercely hot, but as evening wore on, the little
English community made ready for church. They
little thought that the church bells were to mark
the beginning of the great Indian Mutiny. It was
the arranged signal for the Sepoys to revolt.

They burst open the prison, released the eighty-five
martyrs, and then proceeded to fire on their officers.
Some thirty English against two thousand angry
mutineers had little chance, and soon the dusky
natives were marching forth in full battle array for
Delhi, some thirty-eight miles distant.

Delhi, one of the oldest and stateliest towns in the
newly acquired Punjab, on the sacred Jumna, was
surrounded by a wall pierced by seven gates, about
a mile distant one from the other. In the centre
stood the Imperial Palace, where lived the last
King of Delhi—the descendant of the Great Mogul.
The mutineers arrived early on the morning of
May 11th, shouting defiantly and slaying any English
they met. Delhi was entirely held by Sepoys
officered by Englishmen.

Victorian Age   9

These Englishmen with their wives and children were now butchered without mercy or pity, and in a few days the mutineers had possession of the whole city, which they held till September, besieged by a mere handful of British. On June the 7th an English officer named Willoughby, in "heroic despair," blew up the powder-magazine to save it from falling into the hands of the enemy.

It has been said that "nothing in British history is a more kindling tale of endurance and valour than the story of how for months a handful of British clung to the Ridge outside Delhi, fighting daily with foes ten times more numerous than themselves," besieging the great city, which was the heart of the whole Mutiny, till at the last John Nicholson bought it with his life.

Meanwhile the Mutiny was breaking out in other parts of India. Cawnpore, on the banks of the Ganges, was 270 miles from Delhi, an important military station with vast magazines and a rich treasury. It was held only by Sepoys and a mere handful of British soldiers. An old man of seventy-five, Sir Hugh Wheeler, was in command.

On June 4th the Sepoys revolted, secretly roused by Nana Sahib, a powerful Hindu, who pretended to be on friendly terms with the English, while playing the villain's part of a traitor. The little white population entrenched themselves as best they might behind low mud walls and here for three long and dreary weeks a few Englishmen defended themselves, their wives, and children against the onslaught of the enemy. By the third day all shelter had been destroyed and the hot Indian sun beat pitilessly down on the sick and wounded.

"The annals of warfare contain no episode so

painful as the story of this siege," says Sir George
Trevelyan. "The sun never before looked on such
a sight as a crowd of women and children cooped
within a small space and exposed, during twenty
days and nights, to the concentrated fire of thousands
of muskets and a score of heavy cannon."

The days passed heavily by, each with its deeds
of heroism, its acts of self-sacrifice, its pitiful record
of wasted life. In three weeks no less than 250
had died from hunger, thirst, and wounds. On June
23rd—the anniversary of Plassey—a determined
assault was made by the enemy, but in vain. The
following day found the little garrison in despair.
"The British spirit alone remains," wrote the old
General, "but it cannot last for ever." This was true,
and when, on the twenty-first day, Nana Sahib
offered a safe passage to Allahabad to those willing
to surrender, he felt obliged to accept for the sake
of the women and children.

Slowly the feeble remnant of the besieged, "speech-
less and motionless as spectres" tottered from their
forlorn shelter, to make their way to the banks of
the Ganges, for them "the Valley of the Shadow of
Death." They had not reached the boats, when
suddenly a bugle rang through the silent air and
from the banks of the river a murderous fire was
poured into the hapless crowd. Sir Hugh Wheeler
was among the first to perish. Happy were those
whose sufferings were not prolonged.

Some hundred and twenty survivors were dragged
back to Cawnpore, where a yet more terrible fate
awaited them. Here they were crowded into a small
building with two rooms, no bedding, and no fur-
niture; the English ladies were made to grind corn
for the traitor Nana, who had already murdered all

the men, their husbands, brothers, and sons. Sickness and death thinned their ranks day by day. They did not know of the help even now approaching. General Havelock, a little iron-grey man, no longer young, with the "tiniest force that ever set forth to the task of saving an empire" was marching hard from Allahabad to the relief of Cawnpore. "If India is ever in danger," it had been said, "let Havelock be put in command of an army and it will be saved."

These words were ringing true now. On July 7th he began his march at the head of 1,500 men in a gallant if vain attempt to save the English women and children imprisoned at Cawnpore. The ground over which they marched was swampy with the first furious rains of summer, the skies were white with the glare of an Indian sun in July; but Havelock inspired his men with his own scorn of ease, his strong sense of duty, and deep earnestness, and "Havelock's Saints" as they have been called, never wavered in their allotted task.

They were resting at Futtehpore after five days of hard marching, when, with wild shouts, a huge mass of native cavalry rushed upon them. Fiercely and swiftly the little English band advanced; in ten minutes they had captured the rebel guns and the Nana's troops were in full flight. It was not till the 17th that, having marched 126 miles and fought four battles, Havelock reached the outskirts of Cawnpore.

But he was too late. A grim and awful massacre of the women and children had just taken place, by orders of Nana Sahib, from which not one soul had escaped alive, and all the bodies had been thrown into a well in the courtyard hard by. When

Havelock and his men entered the room where their fellow-countrywomen had been butchered so lately, the scene was both horrible and pitiful. The floor was strewn with relics: there were pinafores, little shoes and hats, the fly-leaf of a Bible, and some children's curls—all speaking of a time of anguish unspeakable.

To-day over the well at Cawnpore where the poor bodies were thrown stands a white marble angel by Marochetti with clasped hands and outspread wings—a memorial of those sufferings, which are part of the price of Empire.

XXII

LUCKNOW AND DELHI

"And ever aloft on the palace roof the old banner of England blew."—TENNYSON.

BUT there was no rest for Havelock and his brave little force. A few days later found him crossing the now swollen Ganges for the 45 miles' "march of fire" to Lucknow, a march that was to take him nine weeks to accomplish.

On May 20, 1857, Sir Henry Lawrence had arrived at Lucknow, the capital of the newly acquired provinces of Oudh, as Chief Commissioner. Though barely fifty, he looked like an old man after years of toil under the Indian sun; his thin cheeks were deeply lined and a long ragged beard added to his look of age. He was worn with deep anxiety, for he realised as no other Indian official how deep-seated was the discontent of the Sepoys. He foresaw a native rising of some sort and prepared for it. Quietly and simply he cleared a space round the Residency for the defence of Europeans in the town, laid in great supplies of grain, powder, and arms, and while others slept he disguised himself and visited the native town to learn the true progress of events for himself.

The summer wore on. It was the last day of June

when, about sunset, the Sepoys rose and swarmed angrily and defiantly into the town. Under a deadly fire the British withdrew to the Residency—some nine hundred Englishmen, with their wives and children—to be surrounded by fifteen thousand armed mutineers. One of their first acts was to put up the Union Jack.

" Banner of England, not for a season, O banner of Britain, hast thou
    Floated in conquering battle or flapt to the battle-cry!
    Never with mightier glory than when we had rear'd thee on high,
    Flying at top of the roofs in the ghastly siege of Lucknow—
    Shot thro' the staff or the halyard, but ever we raised thee anew,
    And ever upon the topmost roof our banner of England blew."

So dawned the first night of the famous siege of Lucknow, the story of which still thrills us though more than fifty years have passed away. "My God, my God! and I have brought them to this," moaned the brave Commissioner, as he took up his quarters in an upper room from which he could observe all that went on. But the room was exposed to the shot of the enemy, and the second day of the siege a shell crashed through the wall and burst—a sheet of flame lit the room and Sir Henry Lawrence was fatally injured.

"Sir Henry, are you hurt?" cried a friend who was with him.

There was a moment's silence.

"I am killed," answered the wounded man firmly.

He was right; the wound was fatal. He had but thirty-six hours to live. His one thought was how best to defend the Residency.

"Let every man die at his post—never make terms— God help the poor women and children!" he said in

120   DEATH OF SIR HENRY LAWRENCE

broken snatches to those around him as he lay dying. Then, speaking rather to himself than to others, he murmured the now historic words, "Here lies Henry Lawrence, who tried to do his duty," words which were carved on his tombstone and may be seen to this day at Lucknow. Tennyson has put this last day of Lawrence's life into verse :—

" Frail were the works that defended the hold that we held with
    our lives—
Women and children among us, God help them, our children
    and wives !
Hold it we might—and for fifteen days or for twenty at most.
' Never surrender, I charge you, but every man die at his post!'
Voice of the dead whom we loved, our Lawrence, the best of
    the brave:
Cold was his brow when we kiss'd him—we laid him that
    night in his grave."

Lawrence had thought that the relieving army under Havelock might arrive in fifteen days. He little realised the dangers to be encountered on the way. When he died, on July 4th, Havelock had not reached Cawnpore. He did not reach it for another fortnight and then was unable to leave for another week.

Furious rains had swollen the Ganges and it took four days to transport the little force across the waste of waters. In the face of obstacles, however, he made his way forward; during the first fifteen miles he had to fight two battles, in which he lost 250 men out of his small band of heroes. It was impossible to reach Lucknow till reinforcements arrived.

Meanwhile, as the month of July wore away pitiful indeed grew the state of the Residency. Sickness was increasing, mines had exploded within, weakening the defences and killing many of the brave defenders; wounded men lay in hospital, women and white-faced children lived from day to day in peril of their lives. August wore on and September came and still the flag was kept flying from the top of the Residency.

It was not till September 16th that Sir James Outram with fresh troops arrived at Cawnpore. He was senior to Havelock and in command of the relief expedition; but with unbounded chivalry—worthy of the olden days—he renounced the glory of relieving the besieged city to Havelock, who had struggled so hard with his tiny force for the past three months. It was one of the finest acts of self-sacrifice in England's history.

On September 25th the troops under Havelock and Outram fought their way to Lucknow. Joyfully they detected the tattered banner, riddled with shot but still flying from the roof of the Residency. They were not too late to save the little garrison.

With renewed hope, headed by Havelock and Outram, the troops fought the great rebel host that had gathered around Lucknow, till at last they gained the narrow streets by the city, and in the dusk of that famous September evening they were greeted with a very shout of joy, in which even the sick crawled from their beds to join.

" Big, rough, bearded rescuers caught up the little half-starved and terrified children and kissed them with tears running down their cheeks, thanking God they were in time to save them from the terrible fate of the little ones in Cawnpore."

"All on a sudden the garrison utter a jubilant shout,
Havelock's glorious Highlanders answer with conquering cheers,
Sick from the hospital echo them, women and children come out,
Blessing the wholesome white faces of Havelock's good fusileers.
Kissing the war-harden'd hand of the Highlander wet with their
      tears !

Dance to the pibroch!—saved! we are saved!—is it you? is it
    you?
Saved by the valour of Havelock, saved by the blessing of
    Heaven!
'Hold it for fifteen days!' we have held it for eighty-seven!
And ever aloft on the palace roof the old banner of England
    blew."

But it was not till November 17th, that Sir Colin
Campbell with fresh English troops carried the place
by storm, and safely withdrew the women and
children after their five months' agonised siege within
the walls of Lucknow. Touching indeed was the
death of Havelock, a few days after Sir Colin's arrival.
His son, who had won the Victoria Cross, watched
with him to the end, and one by one his faithful
comrades came to bid him goodbye.

"I have for forty years so ruled my life, that when
death came I might face it without fear," he said
to Sir James Outram, who was with him to the end.
They laid him "hard by the vast city, the scene alike
of his toil, his triumph, and his death."

Meanwhile desperate had grown the siege of Delhi,
which had lasted since June 4th. For three weary
months the besieging force of English stood their
ground, but they had not the strength to take the
city, which was only relieved five days before Lucknow. The gallant commander, who had held the
Ridge above the city for the first month, had died
of cholera.

His successor was already a broken-down man
and matters were growing desperate, when John
Nicholson appeared on the scene and hope once
more revived. He soon put fresh heart into the
weary men and enthused them with his own
youthful courage.

"If there is a desperate deed to be done in India, John Nicholson is the man to do it," men had said.

A "desperate deed" now awaited him. To look at him alone must have restored confidence. He was a man cast in a giant mould, of "commanding presence and with the heart of a lion" and almost superhuman strength. He soon showed that he had not come to wait, but to act and "the inspiration of his example on the Ridge was worth ten thousand men."

Delhi must be taken from the rebels and taken at once. This was decided, and it was arranged that five thousand men should make a last desperate attempt to wrest the city from its fifty thousand Sepoy defenders. John Nicholson himself, in command of the assault, was to lead the first company of a thousand men to the attack of the Cashmere Gate, while four others were to assault different points.

It was three o'clock in the early morning and the stars were still shining, when the men collected on that September day for one of the most daring exploits in history.

Nicholson stood out in front of his column, then he gave a signal, a fierce shout rent the air, and in the face of almost certain death, the men rushed forward. The great assault of Delhi had begun.

The breach was soon carried, the enemy fell back, and Nicholson forced his way into the city. Men were falling to right and left of him, but the "Lion of the Punjab" strode on unhurt. His troops were growing tired and began to drag behind. But he turned and, waving his sword above his head, pointed onwards to the foe in front, entreating them to follow on at once. His tall, straight figure was an easy mark for the enemy. A Sepoy aimed straight and John Nicholson fell, mortally wounded. The fighting went on, each column was successful, and the English made their way inch by inch into the city.

Through the next long days and nights Nicholson lay dying. His fall at the head of his men had made a deep impression on them.

"To lose Nicholson seemed at that moment to lose everything," said young Lieutenant Roberts,* who was having his first experience of active service at Delhi. The hero of Delhi just lived to hear that the city was in the hands of the English, that his life had not been given in vain. He was only thirty-seven when he died, a splendid specimen of an Irish soldier, and a grand example of lion-hearted courage.

With the capture of Delhi and Lucknow the Mutiny came to an end. It was arranged that the East India Company, which had governed India up to this time, should now cease to exist, and a better system of government should be established. An English Viceroy was appointed to serve under the Queen, who twenty years later, was proclaimed " Empress of India " † amid scenes of the greatest enthusiasm.

* Afterwards Earl Roberts of Kandahar.
† See page 158.

THE
GROUNDWORK OF
BRITISH HISTORY

BY

GEORGE TOWNSEND WARNER, M.A.

Sometime Fellow of Jesus College, Cambridge
Master of the Modern Side in Harrow School

AND

C. H. K. MARTEN, M.A.

Balliol College, Oxford
Assistant Master at Eton College

Part II

*From the Union of the Crowns
to the Present Day*

BY

C. H. K. MARTEN, M.A.

BLACKIE & SON, LTD., 50 OLD BAILEY, LONDON
GLASGOW AND BOMBAY

ment of *Oudh* by its rulers had been so scandalous that the East India Company sent orders for its annexation, which Dalhousie carried out in 1856. Moreover, Lord Dalhousie himself was strongly of opinion that the direct rule of the British was much superior to native rule; and he consequently refused, in certain cases, to sanction the old custom by which Hindoo princes who had no children of their own might adopt heirs to succeed them. Thus, when the rulers of *Nagpur* and of *Jhansi*, in Central India, died without direct heirs, their territories "lapsed" to the Company.

So far we have been concerned with the extension of the British control in India, but it must not be supposed that the **Social** efforts of British rulers were not directed to bettering **progress,** the lot of their subjects. On the contrary, especially **1823-56.** during the governorship of *Lord William Bentinck* (1828–35) and *Lord Dalhousie* (1848–56), great reforms were made. The former abolished *suttee*, as the compulsory suicide of Hindoo widows on the death of their husbands was called;[1] suppressed the *thugs*, bands of hereditary assassins who roamed about India strangling travellers; encouraged educated natives to take a share in the government; made important financial reforms; and initiated a measure for giving liberty of the press. The latter reorganized the internal administration of India; developed canals; introduced the telegraph, the railway, and cheap postage; and encouraged education. Indeed Lord Dalhousie must be regarded, whether as empire builder or reformer, as one of the greatest of our proconsuls.

Lord Dalhousie's policy, however, was one cause of the Indian Mutiny in 1857. Western reforms mystified and unsettled the **Causes of** Eastern mind, and natives thought that the world was **Mutiny** being turned upside down. To many natives the tele-**of 1857.** graph was magic, whilst the railway threatened the caste system because people of different castes had to travel together in the same carriage. It was even thought that all British projects of reform had but one design—the destruction of the Hindoo religion. Again, the annexation policy of Lord Dalhousie, though undertaken with the best intentions, had aroused distrust. It was unfortunate, moreover, that *Lord Canning*, Lord Dalhousie's

---

[1] During one year in Bengal alone no less than eight hundred widows were burnt to death.

successor, was not made aware of the peculiar conditions of land tenure in Oudh, and that his subordinates aroused the hostility of the great landowners in that province by a settlement of the land which did the landed aristocracy grievous injustice. Consequently, in the Mutiny, the landowners of Oudh were against the British.

But there were other causes of the Mutiny. It was primarily a mutiny of the Sepoys, and the causes were largely military. The native troops outnumbered the British by eight to one; they thought that the success of the British was due to them, and their opinion of British invincibility had been shaken by the Afghan and subsequently by the Crimean War. Moreover, an old prophecy that the rule of the British would end one hundred years after the Battle of Plassey was not without its effect. The occasion for the Mutiny arose, however, when the Enfield rifle was substituted for "Brown Bess." In those days the soldier had to bite the cartridge with his teeth, and the report spread like wildfire that the cartridges for the new rifle were smeared with the fat of cows and the lard of pigs. The cow was sacred to the Hindoos, whilst the pig was an abomination to the Mohammedans. The story may have had some slight foundation of truth in it.[1] At all events the Sepoys believed it, and the agitators against British rule thus found a ready illustration of the deceitful designs of the British upon the sacred religions of the Indian peoples, and a cry which united the Hindoo and the Mohammedan in a common opposition.

On Sunday afternoon, May 10, 1857, the Mutiny broke out at *Meerut*, where the Sepoys shot their officers and murdered what Europeans they could capture. From Meerut the mutineers streamed to *Delhi*, some 40 miles away, persuaded the native regiments stationed there to join in the rising, and proclaimed the descendant of the old Mogul Emperor, who still lived in the palace at Delhi, as ruler of India. About three weeks later, the Mutiny spread to the garrisons in Oudh and in the Ganges valley. The British position then

Outbreak of Mutiny, May, 1857.

---

[1] The cartridges had to be greased in order to fit into the groove of the barrel. Though the evidence is conflicting, it is probable that some of these cartridges—though they were almost immediately recalled—were smeared, by some mistake, with the ingredients to which objection was taken.

appeared desperate.   The districts affected by the Mutiny equalled in area France, Austria, and Prussia put together, and were inhabited by some ninety-four millions of people.   The British soldiers in all India numbered only thirty-nine thousand men, and at the opening of the Mutiny there were but three British regiments between Calcutta and Meerut.   The revolting Sepoys were in possession of the old capital of Delhi, and had secured a figurehead in the Mogul king; they had shut up one British garrison at Cawnpore and another at Lucknow, the capital of Oudh; and to these three centres the mutineers were flocking from the other garrisons of northern India.

The Indian Mutiny is, perhaps, the most tragic episode in our history.   British officers were so confident in the loyalty of their own native regiments that they refused to take precautions, and were pitilessly shot by their men.   Many white women and children were barbarously murdered, and the sufferings of the men and women besieged during the intense heat of that Indian midsummer were more fearful than can be imagined.   But all

The massacre of Cawnpore, July, 1857. else pales before the horrors of *Cawnpore*.   The Europeans there, numbering some two hundred and fifty fighting men, and more than double that number of women, children, and invalids, took refuge in an open plain, defended by small earthworks.   For eighteen days in the scorching heat they were exposed to attacks made by thousands of rebels.   At the end of that time their position was hopeless, and they accepted the offer of a safe-conduct by boat down the river made by *Nana Sahib*, a prince who had joined the rebels because he had not received from the British Government a pension to which he thought he was entitled.   The garrison marched to the river.   But when they had embarked, a murderous fire was opened upon them; many were killed or drowned, and of the survivors the men were pursued and butchered save four, who managed to escape, whilst the women and children were captured and imprisoned.   A fortnight later Nana Sahib gave orders for the slaughter of these prisoners, two hundred and ten in number; the horrible work was done, and the bodies, the dead with the dying, were thrown down a well (July 15).

Never, however, did the British race display more heroic qualities than at this crisis in its history. When the mutineers, at the opening of the Mutiny, reached Delhi, *Lieutenant Willoughby*, with a little garrison of eight men, defended the great **British** magazine of Delhi against hundreds of assailants, and **heroism.** then blew it up so that the mutineers should not gain possession of it. In the Punjab, *John Lawrence*, aided by *Edwardes*, *Chamberlain*, and *John Nicholson*, stamped out with stern and untiring energy the beginnings of mutiny amongst the regiments stationed in that province. A British force of barely four thousand men advanced upon Delhi, won a battle against overwhelming numbers, occupied the famous *Ridge*, which stretched to within three-quarters of a mile of the city walls, and held it against the desperate sorties of the thirty thousand Sepoys who defended the city. *Havelock* and one thousand five hundred men, in an attempt to save Cawnpore, marched in nine days, in an Indian July, one hundred and twenty-six miles, and fought four actions. The garrison in the Residency grounds of Lucknow—its gallant commander, Henry Lawrence, was killed on the second day of the siege—consisted of only a thousand British fighting men and seven hundred loyal Sepoys. It had to defend an enclosure a mile in circumference, made up of detached buildings and gardens connected by palisades and ditches, against an enemy which could bring up artillery within one hundred and fifty yards, and occupy houses within fifteen yards of its defences. Yet for eighty-seven days it successfully held this position against all attempts at storming, and the still greater dangers of mining, made by hugely superior forces.

Yet the heroism of British soldiers must not lead us to forget the services of those natives who were loyal. The native armies of Bombay and Madras remained unaffected by the **Native loyalty.** revolting Sepoys. The native princes, for the most part, held aloof from the Mutiny; and some gave the British active assistance, such as the chief of Patiala, who protected the great road running from the Punjab to Delhi. Sepoys fought bravely for us in the Residency at Lucknow, and on the "Ridge" at Delhi. The Guides, for instance, horse and foot, started for Delhi at six hours' notice, and marched "at the hottest season of the year through the hottest region on earth" for twenty-one days at an average of twenty-seven miles a day.   Their bravery in the operations at Delhi, when they lost half their men, and all their British officers were either killed or wounded, was only equalled by that of the Gurkhas.   Moreover, even some of the revolting regiments protected their officers and aided them to escape, whilst touching stories are told of the fidelity shown by native servants towards the British women and children.

By the end of *September* the critical period of the Mutiny was over.   In the previous month the "Ridge" had been reinforced by a column from the Punjab under John Nicholson.   Owing largely to Nicholson's heroism and energy, Delhi was finally stormed on the 14th September, though Nicholson himself was mortally wounded.   Five days of street fighting followed before the rebels were completely expelled from the city.   Havelock, through no fault of his own, had arrived too late to save Cawnpore, but he and Outram, "the Bayard of India", were able to fight their way to Lucknow and to relieve the garrison (September 25), though they were in turn besieged when they got there.   Reinforcements then began to pour in from Great Britain. In *November*, Colin Campbell was able to make a further advance upon Lucknow, and the Residency was again relieved and the troops withdrawn.

Storming of Delhi (Sept.) and relief of Lucknow (Sept. and Nov.), 1857.

It took some time, however, before the Mutiny was finally suppressed.   The city of Lucknow was not finally captured till 1858.   In the same year a brilliant campaign was carried out by Sir Hugh Rose in Central India, where the Mutiny had spread, and not till the spring of 1859 were hostilities completely at an end.   Stern punishment was meted out to those who deserved it, as the tragedies of the Mutiny, and especially of Cawnpore, made it impossible for the British to be altogether merciful. That considerable severity should be shown in revenge was inevitable, but the governor-general, Lord Canning, successfully exerted his influence on behalf of clemency.[1]

---

[1] He was called "Clemency Canning"—a nickname which was first given in impatience and anger, but remained to be an honour.

AN OUTLINE HISTORY

OF

THE BRITISH EMPIRE.

FROM 1500 TO 1920

BY

WILLIAM HARRISON WOODWARD

CHRIST CHURCH, OXFORD,
FORMERLY PRINCIPAL OF THE UNIVERSITY TRAINING
COLLEGE, LIVERPOOL.

CAMBRIDGE:
AT THE UNIVERSITY PRESS
1921

§ 347. Lord Canning, 1856–1862. The Mutiny, 1857: its symptoms.   We have now reached the period of the Sepoy Mutiny, the causes and nature of which it is important to understand. Early in 1857 warnings were received by Lord Canning, the new Governor-General, of impending trouble. There were circulated, and superstitiously believed, certain predictions of the downfall of the ruling Power on the completion of its century of rule (*i.e.* since Plassey, 1757) in Bengal. Calumnies of most extraordinary nature were spread and accepted with credulity. Behind all this there was much intrigue at work in Native Courts and amongst discontented politicians, initiated by the Moghul princes still keeping state at Delhi.

§ 348. Its causes.   Little effect, however, would have been produced but for other and more serious causes. It is undoubtedly true that the very passion for honest government which animated Lord Dalhousie had stirred up discontent amongst those who benefited most by his policy. He had not allowed—as Lawrence did in the Punjab—for the intense conservatism of Oriental races, to whom oppression from their own kin is preferable sometimes to freedom at the hand of foreigners. The interference with the right of adoption roused grave suspicion when it was

seen that it resulted in the aggrandisement of British
dominion.   Lord Canning was careful to confirm this right
when the day of pacification came in 1859.   The violent
changes in Oudh, well-meant from the English standpoint
but injudicious in their suddenness, had been ill received.
Moreover, it had been unwise to leave the Moghul as
nominal sovereign in the ancient capital, Delhi, where his
enormous wealth and the prestige of his name enabled his
household to create a network of anti-British intrigue.
Insignificant as he now was in a military or political sense,
the Moghul had not been forgotten: he stood for legitimate
and traditional supremacy in India.   There were, too, other
dispossessed rulers or their representatives : the Nawab of
Oudh, the Raja of Mysore, and Nana Sahib, the adopted
son of the last Peshwa : and these were all ready to take a
hand in treachery.   At the same time the English regiments
were just at the moment unduly weak, and their com-
plement of officers had been reduced by the needs of the
various new administrations in the Central Provinces,
Punjab and Oudh.   Perhaps Indian society had been
passing too quickly through a period of change; the British
temper was restless and pushing ; steam, electricity, education, newspapers, betokened a future still more disturbed.

§ 349.   **The Outbreak at Meerut, May 10, 1857.**
About January, 1857, it was rumoured in the barracks that
the new rifle cartridges had been greased with the fat of
pigs and cows to contaminate the religious purity of the
Sepoys.   During March and April, in certain regiments,
insubordination became frequent.   On May 10th the native
troops at Meerut broke out into open mutiny.   Their first
step was to march to Delhi, some 40 miles distant, to place
themselves under the authority of the Moghul.   The outbreak was probably premature, a concerted rising having
been arranged for a somewhat later date.   But the news
spread, and the Mutiny had begun.

§ 350. Characteristics of the Mutiny. The rising was mainly confined to the army; only at Delhi, in Oudh and in Rohilkhand was the populace seriously affected. In the next place, the Mutiny did not spread beyond the line of garrisons stationed from Benares up the Ganges valley, and on to Peshawar. The Sikh regiments remained loyal. In the Central Provinces the trouble was limited to the Ganges plain. Bombay, Madras, and Lower Bengal itself were untouched by it. The Nizam, under the influence of a sagacious prime minister, did not move. Rajputana was quiet.

§ 351. The danger at an end, Dec. 1857. The East India Company dissolved, 1858. The new Government of India. Further, the crisis was sharp and short. The 10th of May was the date of the first outbreak. Within a month the area of disaffection was fairly well revealed. The Cawnpore murders took place on June 27: on Sept. 20 Delhi was recovered, and the Moghul a prisoner. Lucknow was relieved on Nov. 16. Before the end of the year all danger was over, though Sir Colin Campbell and Sir Hugh Rose had still work to do in stamping out the last embers of revolt. There is no space to treat of the heroic incidents and personalities of the struggle, which left England more firmly established in her Indian empire than before.

One immediate effect of the Mutiny was the decision to terminate once for all the dual control of the Crown and the East India Company in Indian government. By an Act of 1858—under which India is still administered—the Company was brought to an end. The administration was now directly assumed by the Crown, acting through a Principal Secretary of State, a member of the Ministry, and responsible to the Queen and country for the general policy of Indian government. The Secretary for India is assisted by a Council of expert advisers sitting in London. The

Governor-General, with the new title of Viceroy, acts under the instructions and subject to the approval of the Secretary of State. He is assisted by a double Council; the Executive Council, a direct descendant of the old Council of Calcutta, as Hastings knew it, consisting of officials, and the Legislative Council, which includes in addition a certain number of non-official members, European and Native. The former body corresponds in a sense to the Cabinet of a constitutional country : the latter to the Legislative Council of a Crown Colony. The old Presidencies of Madras and Bombay were left with many marks of their historic equality with Bengal. Codes of Law, in which British, Anglo-Indian, and Native elements all find a place, were carefully drawn up and enforced in 1860–61. The Civil Service gained in status by the changes of 1858. It is through the strong, upright, and experienced men who from one end of India to the other, hold in their hands the local administration of justice, order, revenue, and public works, that the influence of British rule most makes itself felt.

References

Aarts, Jan 2005 "Corpus analysis." In Jan-Ola Östman and Jef Verschueren (eds.), *Handbook of Pragmatics* (9th annual installment). Amsterdam/Philadelphia: John Benjamins (also available online www.benjamins.nl/online).

Ahearn, Laura M. 2010 "Agency and language." In Jan-Ola Östman and Jef Verschueren (eds.), *Handbook of Pragmatics* (14th annual installment). Amsterdam/Philadelphia: John Benjamins (also available online www.benjamins.nl/online).

Aijmer, Karin and Anne-Marie Simon-Vandenbergen 2009 "Pragmatic markers." In Jan-Ola Östman and Jef Verschueren (eds.), *Handbook of Pragmatics* (13th annual installment). Amsterdam/Philadelphia: John Benjamins (also available online www.benjamins.nl/online).

Alavi, Seema 2007 "Jihadi Muslims and Hindu sepoys." *Biblio: A Review of Books* XII:3/4.10–12.

Allport, Gordon W. 1979 *The Nature of Prejudice*, 25th anniversary edn. New York: Addison Wesley.

Althusser, L. 1971a *Lenin and Philosophy*. London: Monthly Review.
1971b *Essays on Ideology*. London: Verso.

Ames, Mary Frances 1899 *An ABC for Baby Patriots*. London: Dean & Son.

Angermüller, Johannes 2011 "Fixing meanings: The many voices of the post-liberal hegemony in Russia." *Journal of Language and Politics*

Anscombe, Elizabeth 1957 *Intention*. Ithaca: Cornell University Press.

Antaki, Charles 1988b "Explanations, communication, and social cognition." In Antaki (ed.) 1988a, pp. 1–14.
(ed.) 1988a *Analysing Everyday Explanation: A Casebook of Methods*. London: Sage.

Arborio, Anne-Marie, Yves Cohen, Pierre Fournier, Nicolas Hatzfeld, Cédric Lomba and Séverin Muller 2008 *Observer le travail: Histoire, ethnographie, approches combinées*. Paris: La Découverte.

Auer, Peter (ed.) 1998 *Codeswitching in conversation*. London: Routledge.

Auer, Peter and Carol Eastman 2010 "Codeswitching." In Jan-Ola Östman and Jef Verschueren (eds.), *Handbook of Pragmatics* (14th annual installment). Amsterdam/Philadelphia: John Benjamins (also available online www.benjamins.nl/online).

Baker, Charlotte 1975 "This is just a first approximation, but …" *Papers from the 11th Regional Meeting, Chicago Linguistic Society*, 37–47.

Bakhtin, M. M. 1986 *Speech Genres and Other Late Essays*. Austin: University of Texas Press.

Ball, Terence and Richard Dagger 2001 *Political Ideologies and the Democratic Ideal*. London: Longman.

2004 *Ideas and Ideologies: A Reader*. New York: Pearson Education.

Baradat, Leon P. 1999 *Political Ideologies: Their Origins and Impact*. New York: Prentice-Hall.

Barnes, Harry Elmer 1962 *A History of Historical Writing*. New York: Dover Publications [First edition, 1937].

Barth, Hans 1961 *Wahrheit und Ideologie*. Zürich: Rentsch.

Baudemont, Suzanne 1980 *L'histoire et la légende dans l'école élémentaire victorienne (1962–1901)*. Paris: Klincksieck.

Bauman, Richard and Charles L. Briggs 1992 "Genre, intertextuality and social power." *Journal of Linguistic Anthropology* 2.131–172.

2003 *Voices of Modernity: Language Ideologies and the Politics of Inequality*. Cambridge: Cambridge University Press.

Bell, Daniel 1960 *The End of Ideology: On the Exhaustion of Political Ideas in the Fifties*. Cambridge, MA: Harvard University Press.

Bénabou, Roland 2008 "Ideology." *National Bureau of Economic Research Working Paper* 13907 (www.nber.org/papers/w13907).

Bentley, Michael (ed.) 1997 *Companion to Historiography*. London: Routledge.

Berger, Peter L. and Thomas Luckmann 1966 *The Social Construction of Reality: A Treatise in the Sociology of Knowledge*. New York: Doubleday.

Bertuccelli Papi, Marcella 1997 "Implicitness." In Jan-Ola Östman and Jef Verschueren (eds.), *Handbook of Pragmatics* (3rd annual installment). Amsterdam/Philadelphia: John Benjamins (also available online www.benjamins.nl/online).

Billig, Michael 1982 *Ideology and Social Psychology: Extremism, Moderation, and Contradiction*. Oxford: Basil Blackwell.

1988 "Methodology and scholarship in understanding ideological explanation." In Antaki (ed.) 1988a, pp. 199–215.

1991 *Ideology and Opinions: Studies in Rhetorical Psychology*. London: Sage.

1995 *Banal Nationalism*. London: Sage.

Blakemore, Diane 1995 "Relevance theory." In Jef Verschueren, Jan-Ola Östman and Jan Blommaert (eds.), *Handbook of Pragmatics: Manual*. Amsterdam/Philadelphia: John Benjamins (also available online www.benjamins.com/online).

Blommaert, Jan 1999a "Investigating narrative inequality: 'Home narratives' of African asylum seekers in Belgium." *Working Papers on Language, Power & Identity* 1.

(ed.) 1999b *Language Ideological Debates*. Berlin: Mouton de Gruyter.

2004 *Workshopping: Professional Vision, Practices and Critique in Discourse Analysis*. Ghent: Academia Press.

2008 *Grassroots Literacy: Writing, Identity, and Voice in Central Africa.* London: Routledge.

Blommaert, Jan and Jef Verschueren (eds.) 1991a *The Pragmatics of Intercultural and International Communication: Selected Papers of the International Pragmatics Conference, Antwerp, August 17–22, 1987 (Volume III), and the Ghent Symposium on Intercultural Communication.* Amsterdam/Philadelphia: John Benjamins.

1991b "The pragmatics of minority politics in Belgium." *Language in Society* 20:4.503–531.

1992 "The role of language in European nationalist ideologies." *Pragmatics* 2:3.355–375. Reprinted in Christina Schäffner and Anita Wenden (eds.) 1995, *Language and Peace*, Aldershot: Dartmouth, pp. 137–160, and in Schieffelin, Woolard and Kroskrity (eds.) (1998), pp. 189–210.

1993 "The rhetoric of tolerance, or: What police officers are taught about migrants." *Journal of Intercultural Studies* 14:1.49–63.

1994 "The Belgian migrant debate." *New Community* 20:2.227–251.

1996 "European concepts of nation building." In Ed Wilmsen and Patrick McAllister (eds.), *The Politics of Difference: Ethnic Premises in a World of Power*, Chicago: University of Chicago Press, pp. 104–123.

1998 *Debating Diversity: Analysing the Discourse of Tolerance.* London: Routledge.

Bosma, Ulbe 2009 "European colonial soldiers in the nineteenth century: Their role in white global migration and patterns of colonial settlement." *Journal of Global History* 4:2.317–336.

Boudon, Raymond 1986 *L'idéologie: Ou l'origine des idées reçues.* Paris: Librairie Arthème Fayard.

Bourdieu, Pierre 1991 *Language and Symbolic Power.* Cambridge: Polity Press.

Briggs, Charles L. 1986 *Learning How to Ask: A Sociolinguistic Appraisal of the Role of the Interview in Social Science Research.* Cambridge: Cambridge University Press.

Bublitz, Wolfram 1998 "Cohesion and coherence." In Jan-Ola Östman and Jef Verschueren (eds.), *Handbook of Pragmatics* (4th annual installment). Amsterdam/Philadelphia: John Benjamins (also available online www.benjamins.nl/online).

Cap, Piotr 2002 *Explorations in Political Discourse: Methodological and Critical Perspectives.* Frankfurt am Main: Peter Lang.

Carbó, Teresa 2001 "Regarding reading: On a methodological approach." *Discourse & Society* 12:1.59–89.

[Cassell's] 1903 *Cassell's Concise History of England – Being the Growth and Expansion of the British Empire from the Roman Invasion to the Diamond Jubilee.* Melbourne: Cassell & Company.

Chaudhuri, S. B. 1957 *Civil Rebellion in the Indian Mutinies (1857–1859).* Calcutta: World Press.

Chilton, Paul 2002 "Manipulation." In Jan-Ola Östman and Jef Verschueren (eds.), *Handbook of Pragmatics* (8th annual installment). Amsterdam/Philadelphia: John Benjamins (also available online www.benjamins.nl/online).

    2004 *Analysing Political Discourse: Theory and Practice*. London: Routledge.

    2005 "Missing links in mainstream CDA: Modules, blends and the critical instinct." In Ruth Wodak and Paul Chilton (eds.), *A New Agenda in (Critical) Discourse Analysis: Theory, Methodology, and Interdisciplinarity*, Amsterdam: John Benjamins, pp. 19–52.

Clayton, R. H. 1931 *A History of Britain and Her Empire*. Sydney: Angus & Robertson.

    1941 *Britain's First and Second Empires*. Sydney: Angus & Robertson.

    1958 *From Colonies to Commonwealth: The Story of the British Empire*. Melbourne: Robertson & Mullens.

Clift, Rebecca, Paul Drew and Ian Hutchby 2006 "Conversation analysis." In Jan-Ola Östman and J. Verschueren (eds.), *Handbook of Pragmatics* (10th annual installment). Amsterdam/Philadelphia: John Benjamins (also available online: www.benjamins.com/online).

Collier, William Francis 1875 *History of the British Empire*. London: T. Nelson and Sons.

Comaroff, John and Jean Comaroff 1992 *Ethnography and the Historical Imagination*. Oxford: Westview Press.

Currey, C. H. 1943 *The Growth of Australia and A Commonwealth of Nations*. Sydney/Melbourne: Whitcombe & Tombs.

Dalrymple, William 2006 *The Last Mughal: The Fall of a Dynasty, Delhi, 1857*. New Delhi: Penguin Viking Books.

    2007 "In defence of faith: Religious rhetoric in the Delhi uprising of 1857." *Biblio: A Review of Books* 12:3/4.6–9.

Davidson, Donald 1986 "A nice derangement of epitaphs." In Ernest LePore (ed.), *Truth and Interpretation: Perspectives on the Philosophy of Donald Davidson*. Oxford: Blackwell.

    2001 *Inquiries into Truth and Interpretation*. Oxford: Oxford University Press.

Decker, James M. 2004 *Ideology*. London: Palgrave Macmillan.

Delogu, Francesca 2007 "Presupposition." In Jan-Ola Östman and Jef Verschueren (eds.), *Handbook of Pragmatics* (11th annual installment). Amsterdam/Philadelphia: John Benjamins (also available online www.benjamins.nl/online).

Dendale, Patrick and Liliane Tasmowski-De Ryck (eds.) 2001 *On evidentiality*. Special issue *Journal of Pragmatics* 33:3.

Destutt de Tracy, Antoine 1803 *Éléments d'idéologie*. Paris: Courcier.

D'hondt, Sigurd, Jan Blommaert and Jef Verschueren 1995 "Constructing ethnicity in discourse: A view from below." In Marco Martiniello (ed.) (1995),

Migration, Citizenship and Ethno-National Identities in the European Union. Aldershot: Avebury, pp. 105–119.

D'hondt, Sigurd, Jan-Ola Östman and Jef Verschueren (eds.) 2009 *The Pragmatics of Interaction*. Amsterdam: John Benjamins.

Dupret, Baudouin 2011 *Practices of Truth*. Amsterdam: John Benjamins.

Eagleton, Terry (ed.) 1994 *Ideology*. London: Longman.

2007 *Ideology: An Introduction*, new and updated edition. London/New York: Verso.

Edwards, Jane A. and Martin D. Lampert (eds.) 1993 *Talking Data: Transcription and Coding in Discourse Research*. Hillsdale, NJ: Lawrence Erlbaum.

Eelen, Gino 2001 *A Critique of Politeness Theories*. Manchester: St. Jerome Publishing.

Embree, Ainslee 1987 *India in 1857: The Revolt Against Foreign Rule*. Delhi: Chanakya Publications.

Epstein, Steven A. 2001 *Speaking of Slavery: Color, Ethnicity, and Human Bondage in Italy*. Ithaca: Cornell University Press.

Fairclough, Norman 1992 *Discourse and Social Change*. Cambridge: Polity Press.

Farooqui, Mahmood 2007 "A million mutinies: The *Ghadar* in Delhi, gleaned from the Mutiny Papers." *Biblio: A Review of Books* 12:3/4.14–15.

Fauconnier, Gilles 1985 *Mental Spaces*. Cambridge, MA: MIT Press.

Fearenside, C. S. 1922 *Matriculation Modern History – Being English History from 1485 to 1901, with Some Reference to the Contemporary History of Europe and Colonial Developments*, 2nd edn. London: University Tutorial Press [1st edition 1902].

Feldman, Ronen and James Sanger 2006 *The Text Mining Handbook: Advanced Approaches in Analyzing Unstructured Data*. Cambridge: Cambridge University Press.

Ferro, Marc 1981 *Comment on raconte l'histoire aux enfants à travers le monde entier*. Paris: Payot.

Flyvbjerg, Bent 2001 *Making Social Science Matter: Why Social Inquiry Fails and How It Can Succeed Again*. Cambridge: Cambridge University Press.

Foolen, Ad 1996 "Pragmatic particles." In Jan-Ola Östman and Jef Verschueren (eds.), *Handbook of Pragmatics* (2nd annual installment). Amsterdam/Philadelphia: John Benjamins (also available online www.benjamins.nl/online).

Foucault, Michel 1972 *The Archaeology of Knowledge*. London: Routledge.

Fukuyama, Francis 1992 *The End of History and the Last Man*. London: Hamish Hamilton.

Gal, Susan 2005 "Language ideologies compared: Metaphors of public/private." *Journal of Linguistic Anthropology* 15:1.23–37.

Gal, Susan and Kathryn Woolard (eds.) 2001 *Languages and Publics: The Making of Authority*. Manchester: St. Jerome Press. (First published as a special issue of *Pragmatics* 5:2, 1995.)

Garfinkel, Harold 1967 *Studies in Ethnomethodology.* Englewood Cliffs: Prentice-Hall.

Georgakopoulou, Alexandra 2005 "Computer-mediated communication." In Jan-Ola Östman and Jef Verschueren (eds.), *Handbook of Pragmatics* (9th annual installment). Amsterdam/Philadelphia: John Benjamins (also available online www.benjamins.nl/online).

Ginzburg, Carlo 1982 *The Cheese and the Worms: The Cosmos of a Sixteenth-Century Miller.* New York: Penguin Books.

Glynos, Jason and David Howarth 2007 *Logics of Critical Explanation in Social and Political Theory.* London: Routledge.

Goffman, Erving 1979 "Footing." *Semiotica* 25.1–29.
   1981 *Forms of Talk.* Oxford: Blackwell.

Goldstrom, J. M. 1972 *Education: Elementary Education, 1780–1900.* Newton Abbot: David and Charles.

Goodwin, Charles 1994 "Professional vision." *American Anthropologist* 96:3.606–633.

Gramsci, Antonio 1971 *Selections from the Prison Notebooks.* London: Lawrence and Wishart.
   1985 *Selections from Cultural Writings.* London: Lawrence and Wishart.

Grice, H. Paul 1989 *Studies in the Way of Words.* Cambridge, MA: Harvard University Press.

Gundel, Jeanette K. and Thorstein Fretheim 2002 "Information structure." In Jan-Ola Östman and Jef Verschueren (eds.), *Handbook of Pragmatics* (7th annual installment). Amsterdam/Philadelphia: John Benjamins (also available online www.benjamins.nl/online).

Gundel, Jeanette K., Nancy Hedberg, and Ron Zacharski 1993 "Cognitive status and the form of referring expressions in discourse." *Language* 69:2.274–307

Gupta, Partha Sarathi and Anirudh Deshpande (eds.) 2002 *The British Raj and Its Indian Armed Forces 1857–1939.* Oxford: Oxford University Press.

Habermas, Jürgen 1979 *Communication and the Evolution of Society.* Boston: Beacon Press.

Hammersley, Martyn and Paul Atkinson 1995 *Ethnography: Principles and Practices*, 2nd edn. London: Routledge.

Hanks, William F. 1996 *Language and Communicative Practices.* Boulder, CO: Westview Press.

Harp, Stephen L. 1998 *Learning to be Loyal: Primary Schooling as Nation Building in Alsace and Lorraine, 1850–1940.* DeKalb, IL: Northern Illinois University Press.

Hawkes, David 2003 *Ideology*, 2nd edn. London: Routledge.

Hearnshaw, F.J.C. 1930 *A First Book of English History – with Epilogue AD 1913–1927.* London: Macmillan & Co. [1st edition 1914].

Heywood, Andrew 2007 *Political Ideologies: An Introduction*, 4th edn. London: Macmillan.

Hibbert, Christopher 1978 *The Great Mutiny: India 1857*. Harmondsworth: Penguin Books.

Hobsbawm, Eric J. 1987 *The Age of Empire, 1875–1914*. London: Abacus.

1995 *Age of Extremes: The Short Twentieth Century, 1914–1991*. London: Abacus.

1997 *On History*. London: Abacus.

Hobson, J. A. 1902 *Imperialism: A Study*. London: James Nisbet & Co.

Holt, Elizabeth 2009 "Reported speech." In Jan-Ola Östman and Jef Verschueren (eds.), *Handbook of Pragmatics* (13th annual installment). Amsterdam/ Philadelphia: John Benjamins (also available online www.benjamins.nl/ online).

Horn, Laurence 1989 *A Natural History of Negation*. Chicago: University of Chicago Press.

Huang, Yan 2007 *Pragmatics*. Oxford: Oxford University Press.

Hurt, John S. 1979 *Elementary Schooling and the Working Classes 1860–1918*. London: Routledge and Kegan Paul.

Iggers, Georg G. 1975 *New Directions in European Historiography*. Middletown, CT: Wesleyan University Press.

Innes, Arthur D. 1927 *History of England*, Part III, *1689–1918*. Cambridge: Cambridge University Press [1st edition 1907; with additions 1921].

Jalbert, Paul L. (ed.) 1999 *Media Studies: Ethnomethodological Approaches*. Lanham, MD: University Press of America.

Jaspers, Jürgen 2005a "Linguistic sabotage in a context of monolingualism and standardization." *Language and Communication* 25:3.279–297.

2005b *Tegenwerken, belachelijk doen: Talige sabotage van Marokkaanse jongens op een Antwerpse middelbare school*. Brussels: VUB Press.

2006 "Stylizing standard Dutch by Moroccan boys in Antwerp." *Linguistics and Education* 17:2.131–156.

2008 "Problematizing ethnolects: Naming linguistic practices in an Antwerp secondary school." *International Journal of Bilingualism* 12:1/2.85–103.

Jewitt, Carey (ed.) 2009 *The Routledge Handbook of Multimodal Analysis*. London: Routledge.

Joshi, P. C. (ed.) 1957 *Rebellion 1857: A Symposium*. New Delhi: People's Publishing House.

Kasper, Gabriele 1996 "Politeness." In Jan-Ola Östman and Jef Verschueren (eds.), *Handbook of Pragmatics* (2nd annual installment). Amsterdam/Philadelphia: John Benjamins (also available online www.benjamins.nl/online).

Kerr, P. H. and A. C. Kerr 1927 *The Growth of the British Empire*. London: Longmans, Green & Co. [1st edition 1911; revised 1921].

Khan, Syed Ahmed 2000 *The Causes of the Indian Revolt*. Karachi: Oxford University Press.

Kiefer, Ferenc 1998 "Modality." In Jan-Ola Östman and Jef Verschueren (eds.), *Handbook of Pragmatics* (4th annual installment). Amsterdam/Philadelphia: John Benjamins (also available online www.benjamins.nl/online).

Kienpointner, Manfred 2005 "Figures of speech." In Jan-Ola Östman and Jef Verschueren (eds.), *Handbook of Pragmatics* (9th annual installment). Amsterdam/Philadelphia: John Benjamins (also available online www.benjamins.nl/online).

Klemperer, Victor 1975 *LTI [Lingua tertii imperii]: Notizbuch einer Philologen,* (8th edn.) Leipzig: Philipp Reclam.

Kress, Gunther and Robert Hodge 1979 *Language as Ideology.* London: Routledge & Kegan Paul.

Kroskrity, Paul (ed.) 2000 *Regimes of Language: Ideologies, Polities, and Identities.* Santa Fe, NM: School of American Research.

　　2010 "Language ideologies: Evolving perspectives." In Jan-Ola Östman and Jef Verschueren (eds.), *Handbook of Pragmatics* (14th annual installment). Amsterdam/Philadelphia: John Benjamins (also available online www.benjamins.nl/online).

Kuhn, Thomas S. 1962 *The Structure of Scientific Revolutions.* Chicago: University of Chicago Press.

Laclau, Ernesto and Chantal Mouffe 2001 *Hegemony and Socialist Strategy: Towards a Radical Democratic Politics,* 2nd edn. London: Verso.

Lähdesmäki, Salla and Anna Solin 2000 "Linguistic analysis, social analysis and CDA." *Pragmatics, Ideology, and Contacts Bulletin* 5.15–27.

Lakoff, George 1996 *Moral Politics: What Conservatives Know that Liberals Don't.* Chicago: University of Chicago Press.

Lakoff, Robin Tolmach 1995 "Conversational implicature." In Jan-Ola Östman and Jef Verschueren (eds.), *Handbook of Pragmatics* (1st annual installment). Amsterdam/Philadelphia: John Benjamins (also available online www.benjamins.nl/online).

Larrain, Jorge 1994 *Ideology and Cultural Identity: Modernity and the Third World Presence.* Cambridge: Polity Press.

Lavisse, Ernest 1902 *Histoire générale: Notions sommaires d'histoire ancienne, du Moyen Âge et des temps modernes,* 17th edn. Paris: Librairie Armand Colin [1st edition 1882].

Lenin, V. I. 1969 *What Is to Be Done? Burning Questions of Our Movement.* New York: International Publishers.

Lenk, Uta 1997 "Discourse markers." In Jan-Ola Östman and Jef Verschueren (eds.), *Handbook of Pragmatics* (3rd annual installment). Amsterdam/Philadelphia: John Benjamins (also available online www.benjamins.nl/online).

　　1999 "Notation systems in spoken language corpora." In Jan-Ola Östman and Jef Verschueren (eds.), *Handbook of Pragmatics* (5th annual installment). Amsterdam/Philadelphia: John Benjamins (also available online www.benjamins.nl/online).

Léon, Antoine 1967 *Histoire de l'enseignement en France.* Paris: Presses Universitaires de France.

Levinson, Stephen 1983 *Pragmatics.* Cambridge: Cambridge University Press.

Lévi-Strauss, Claude 1958 *Anthropologie structurale*. Paris: Librarie Plon.
    1963 *Structural Anthropology*. New York: Basic Books.
Liauzu, Claude 2005 "Une loi contre l'histoire." *Le Monde diplomatique* (April
    2005), p. 28.
Lloyd, T. O. 1996 *The British Empire 1558–1995*, 2nd edn. Oxford: Oxford
    University Press.
Low, Sidney and Lloyd C. Sanders 1910 *The History of England During the
    Reign of Victoria (1837–1901)* (part XII of *The Political History of England*,
    ed. by William Hunt and Reginald L. Poole). London: Longmans, Green &
    Co.
Lucy, John A. (ed.) 1993 *Reflexive Language*. Cambridge: Cambridge University
    Press.
Lukács, Georg 1971 *History and Class Consciousness: Studies in Marxist
    Dialectics*. London: Merlin Press.
Majumdar, R. C. 1957 *The Sepoy Mutiny and the Revolt of 1857*. Calcutta: Firma
    K. L. Mukhopadhyay.
Malinowski, Bronislaw 1923 "The problem of meaning in primitive languages."
    Supplement to C. K. Ogden and I. A. Richards, *The Meaning of Meaning*.
    London: Kegan Paul, pp. 296–336.
Mann, William C. and Sandra S. Thompson 1992 *Discourse Description: Diverse
    Linguistic Analyses of a Fund-Raising Text*. Amsterdam/Philadelphia: John
    Benjamins.
Mannheim, Karl 1936 *Ideology and Utopia: An Introduction to the Sociology of
    Knowledge*. London: Routledge & Kegan Paul.
Marcus, Ruth Barcan 1983 "Rationality and believing the impossible." *Journal
    of Philosophy* 80:6.321–338.
Marshall, P. J. (ed.) 1996 *The Cambridge Illustrated History of the British
    Empire*. Cambridge: Cambridge University Press.
Marx, Karl 1977 *Selected Writings*. Oxford: Oxford University Press.
Marx, Karl and Frederick Engels 1970 *The German Ideology*. London: Lawrence
    and Wishart.
McCarthy, Justin 1908 *A Short History of Our Own Times, from the Accession
    of Queen Victoria to the Accession of King Edward VII*. London: Chatto &
    Windus [1st edition, title ending in *[…] to the General Election of 1880*,
    published in 1888].
McLellan, David 1995 *Ideology*, 2nd edn. Buckingham: Open University Press.
Meeuwis, Michael 1993 "Nationalist ideology in news reporting on the Yugoslav
    crisis: A pragmatic analysis." *Journal of Pragmatics* 20:3.217–237.
    1997 *Constructing Sociolinguistic Consensus: A Linguistic Ethnography of
    the Zairian Community in Antwerp, Belgium*. University of Antwerp Ph.D.
    dissertation.
    1999 "Flemish nationalism in the Belgian Congo versus Zairian anti-
    imperialism: Continuity and discontinuity in language ideological debates."
    In Blommaert (ed.) 1999b, pp. 381–423.

Mellet, Sylvie and Dominique Longrée (eds.) 2009 *New Approaches in Text Linguistics*. Thematic issue, *Belgian Journal of Linguistics* 23.

Meyer, Renate E., Kerstin Sahlin, Marc J. Ventresca and Peter Walgenbach (eds.) 2009 *Institutions and Ideology*. Bingley, UK: Emerald.

Miestamo, Matti 2006 "Negation." In Jan-Ola Östman and Jef Verschueren (eds.), *Handbook of Pragmatics* (10th annual installment). Amsterdam/ Philadelphia: John Benjamins (also available online www.benjamins.nl/ online).

Mitchell, Sally 1996 *Daily Life in Victorian England*. London: Greenwood Press.

Mukharji, Projit B. 2007 "My once erect form is now bent with woe: The Indian Revolt in Scottish ballads." *Biblio: A Review of Books* 12:3/4.18–19.

Mukherjee, Rudrangshu 1984 *Awadh in Revolt 1857–1858: A Study in Popular Resistance*. New Delhi: Oxford University Press.

Muntigl, Peter and Helmut Gruber (eds.) 2005 *Approaches to Genre. Special issue of Folia Linguistica* 39:1–2.1–212.

Nayar, Pramod K. 2007 *The Great Uprising: India 1857*. New Delhi: Penguin Books.

Novick, Peter 1988 *That Noble Dream: The "Objectivity Question" and the American Historical Profession*. Cambridge: Cambridge University Press.

O'Connell, Daniel C. and Sabine Kowal 1995 "Transcription systems for spoken discourse." In Verschueren, Östman and Blommaert (eds.), 1995. (Also available online www.benjamins.com/online).

Östman, Jan-Ola and Anne-Marie Simon-Vandenbergen 1995 "Firthian linguistics." In Verschueren, Östman and Blommaert (eds.), 1995. (Also available online www.benjamins.com/online).

Parkin, George R. 1911 *Round the Empire*. London: Cassell & Company [1892, revisions in 1898, 1903 and 1911].

Payrató, Lluís 2006 "Non-verbal communication." In Jan-Ola Östman and Jef Verschueren (eds.), *Handbook of Pragmatics* (10th annual installment). Amsterdam/Philadelphia: John Benjamins (also available online www.benjamins.nl/online).

Pennycook, Alastair 1998 *English and the Discourses of Colonialism*. London: Routledge.

Pollak, Senja, Roel Coesemans, Walter Daelemans and Nada Lavrač in press."Text mining for pragmatic discourse analysis: Detecting contrast patterns in newspaper articles on Kenyan elections." *Pragmatics*.

Porter, Andrew (ed.) 1999 *The Oxford History of the British Empire, Vol. III, The Nineteenth Century*. Oxford: Oxford University Press.

Prothero, M. 1917 *The Development of the British Empire*. London: Macmillan and Co.

Quine, W. V. 1976 *The Ways of Paradox and Other Essays*. Cambridge, MA: Harvard University Press.

Ransome, Cyril 1910 *A Short History of England, from the Earliest Times to the Death of King Edward VII*. London: Longmans, Green & Co. [12 earlier editions, gradually expanded with the course of events; 1st edition, with title ending in *[...] to the Pesent Day (1890)*, published by Rivingtons in 1890].

Reddy, Michael J. 1979 "The conduit metaphor: A case of frame conflict in our language about language." In Andrew Ortony (ed.), *Metaphor and Thought*. Cambridge: Cambridge University Press, pp. 284–324.

Reetz, Marie 2010 *Le sujet pris dans l'idéologie: Un philologue face au Discours Nazi*. Mémoire, Université Pastis III.

Renkema, Jan (ed.) 2009 *Discourse, of Course: An Overview of Research in Discourse Studies*. Amsterdam: John Benjamins.

Richards, Lyn 2008 *Handling Qualitative Data: A Practical Guide*. London: Sage.

   2009 *Teach Yourself NVIVO 7: The Introductory Tutorials*. www.uk.sagepub.com/richards/.

Richardson, E. M. 1924 *The Building of the British Empire*. London: G. Bell & Sons [1913, revisions and enlargement 1921, corrections 1924].

Ricoeur, Paul 1981 *Hermeneutics and the Human Sciences: Essays on Language, Action and Interpretation*. Cambridge: Cambridge University Press.

Rosen, Michael 1996 *On Voluntary Servitude: False Consciousness and the Theory of Ideology*. Cambridge: Polity Press.

Roulet, Eddy 2003 "Polyphony." In Jan-Ola Östman and J. Verschueren (eds.), *Handbook of Pragmatics* (9th annual installment). Amsterdam/Philadelphia: John Benjamins (also available online: www.benjamins.com/online).

Rudzka-Ostyn, Brygida 1995 "Case and semantic roles." In Jan-Ola Östman and J. Verschueren (eds.), *Handbook of Pragmatics* (1st annual installment). Amsterdam/Philadelphia: John Benjamins. (also available online: www.benjamins.com/online).

Sahlins, Marshall 1992 *Historical Ethnography*. Chicago: University of Chicago Press.

Savarkar, V. D. 1947 *The Indian War of Independence 1857*. Bombay: Nandi Books.

Schieffelin, Bambi B., Kathryn Woolard and Paul V. Kroskrity (eds.) 1998 *Language Ideologies: Practice and Theory*. Oxford: Oxford University Press.

Schwartz, Regina M. 1997 *The Curse of Cain: The Violent Legacy of Monotheism*. Chicago: University of Chicago Press.

Scollon, Ron 2008 *Analyzing Public Discourse: Discourse Analysis in the Making of Public Policy*. London: Routledge.

Searle, John R. 1969 *Speech Acts: An Essay in the Philosophy of Language*. Cambridge: Cambridge University Press.

   2009 "Why should you believe it?" *New York Review of Books* 61:14.88–92.

Sen, Ronojoy 2007 "Tilting at windmills: Indian historians and the contestation over 1857." *Biblio: A Review of Books* 12:3/4.5–6.

Senft, Gunter 1997 "Bronislaw Kasper Malinowski." In Jan-Ola Östman and J. Verschueren (eds.), *Handbook of Pragmatics* (3rd annual installment).

Amsterdam/Philadelphia: John Benjamins (also available online: www. benjamins.com/online).

Senft, Gunter, Jan-Ola Östman and Jef Verschueren (eds.) 2009 *Culture and Language Use* (*Handbook of Pragmatics Highlights* 2). Amsterdam: John Benjamins.

Sidnell, Jack 2006a "Repair." In Jan-Ola Östman and J. Verschueren (eds.), *Handbook of Pragmatics* (10th annual installment). Amsterdam/Philadelphia: John Benjamins (also available online: www.benjamins.com/online).

2006b "Sequence." In Jan-Ola Östman and J. Verschueren (eds.), *Handbook of Pragmatics* (10th annual installment). Amsterdam/Philadelphia: John Benjamins (also available online: www.benjamins.com/online).

Silverstein, Michael 1979 "Language structure and linguistic ideology." In P. R. Clyne, W. F. Hanks and C. L. Hofbauer (eds), *The Elements: A Parasession on Linguistic Units and Levels*. Chicago: Chicago Linguistic Society, pp. 193–247.

Silverstein, Michael and Greg Urban (eds.) 1996 *Natural Histories of Discourse*. Chicago: University of Chicago Press.

Sinha, Nitin 2007 "Contest and communications: The geography of rebellion in Bihar." *Biblio: A Review of Books* 12:3/4.16–17.

Slembrouck, Stef 1995 "Channel." In Jan-Ola Östman and Jef Verschueren (eds.), *Handbook of Pragmatics* (1st annual installment). Amsterdam/Philadelphia: John Benjamins (also available online www.benjamins.nl/online).

Smith, Anthony 2001 *Nationalism: Theory, Ideology, History*. Cambridge: Polity Press.

Solin, Anna 2009 "Genre." In Jan-Ola Östman and J. Verschueren (eds.), *Handbook of Pragmatics* (13th annual installment). Amsterdam/Philadelphia: John Benjamins (also available online: www.benjamins.com/online).

Southgate, George W. 1947 *An Introduction to English History, Vol. III, From 1763 to the Present Time*. London: J. M. Dent & Sons.

Spear, Percival 1965 *A History of India, vol. II*. London: Penguin Books.

Spilsbury, Julian 2007 *The Indian Mutiny*. London: Weidenfeld & Nicolson.

Stokes, Eric 1986 *The Peasant Armed: The Indian Rebellion of 1857*. Oxford: Oxford University Press.

Sturt, Mary 1970 *The Education of the People: A History of Primary Education in England and Wales in the Nineteenth Century*. London: Routledge and Kegan Paul.

Susser, Bernard 1988 *The Grammar of Modern Ideology*. London: Routledge.

Synge, M. B. 1908 *The Great Victorian Age*. London: Hodder & Stoughton.

Talshir, Gayil, Mathew Humphrey and Michael Freeden (eds.) 2006 *Taking Ideology Seriously: 21st Century Reconfigurations*. London: Routledge.

Taylor, Graham 2010 *The New Political Sociology: Power, Ideology and Identity in an Age of Complexity*. New York: Palgrave Macmillan.

Thompson, John B. 1984 *Studies in the Theory of Ideology*. Cambridge: Polity Press.

1990 *Ideology and Modern Culture: Critical Social Theory in the Era of Mass Communication*. Cambridge: Polity Press.

1995 *The Media and Modernity: A Social Theory of the Media*. Stanford: Stanford University Press.

Titscher, Stefan, Ruth Wodak, Michael Meyer and Eva Vetter 1998 *Methoden der Textanalyse: Leitfaden und Überblick*. Opladen: Westdeutscher Verlag.

Unsworth, Len and Chris Cléirigh 2009 "Multimodality and reading: The construction of meaning through image-text interaction." In Jewitt (ed.) 2009, pp. 151–163.

van Dijk, Teun 2001 "Discourse, ideology and context." *Folia Linguistica* 35:1/2.11–40.

Van Ginderachter, Maarten and Marnix Beyen (eds.) in press. *Nationhood from Below: Continental Europe in the Long 19th Century*. London: Palgrave.

Verne, Jules 1880 *La maison à vapeur: Voyage à travers l'Inde septentrionale*. Paris: Collection Hetzel.

Verschueren, Jef 1980 *On Speech Act Verbs*. Amsterdam: John Benjamins.

1984 "Linguistics and crosscultural communication." *Language in Society* 13.489–509.

1985a *International News Reporting: Metapragmatic Metaphors and the U-2*. Amsterdam/Philadelphia: John Benjamins.

1985b *What People Say They Do with Words: Prolegomena to an Empirical-Conceptual Approach to Linguistic Action*. Norwood, NJ: Ablex.

1989 "English as object and medium of (mis)understanding." In Ofelia García and Ricardo Otheguy (eds), *English Across Cultures – Cultures Across English: A Reader in Cross-Cultural Communication*. Berlin: Mouton de Gruyter, pp. 31–53.

1995 "The pragmatic return to meaning: Notes on the dynamics of communication, degrees of salience, and communicative transparency." *Journal of Linguistic Anthropology* 5.127–156.

1996 "Contrastive ideology research: Aspects of a pragmatic methodology." *Language Sciences* 18:3/4.589–603.

(ed.) 1999a *Language and Ideology: Selected Papers from the 6th International Pragmatics Conference*, Vol. I. Antwerp: International Pragmatics Association.

1999b *Understanding Pragmatics*. London: Edward Arnold.

1999c "Whose Discipline? Some critical reflections on linguistic pragmatics." *Journal of Pragmatics* 31:7.869–879.

2000 "Notes on the role of metapragmatic awareness in language use." *Pragmatics* 10:4.439–456.

2001 "Predicaments of criticism." *Critique of Anthropology* 21:1.59–81.

2008 "Context and structure in a theory of pragmatics." *Studies in Pragmatics* 10.14–24.

Verschueren, Jef and Frank Brisard 2002 "Adaptability." In Jan-Ola Östman and Jef Verschueren (eds.), *Handbook of Pragmatics* (8th annual installment).

Amsterdam/Philadelphia: John Benjamins (also available online www.benjamins.nl/online).

Verschueren, Jef, Jan-Ola Östman, Jan Blommaert *et al.* (eds.) 1995ff. *Handbook of Pragmatics* (1995 bound *Manual* followed by annual loose-leaf installments). Amsterdam/Philadelphia: John Benjamins (also available online www.benjamins.com/online).

Verschueren, Jef, Jan-Ola Östman and Michael Meeuwis 2002 "The International Communication Monitor (ICM): The idea." In Jef Verschueren, Jan-Ola Östman and Michael Meeuwis (eds.), *International Communication Monitoring*. Brussels: KVAB, pp. 7–15.

Vygotsky, L. S. 1978 *Mind in Society: The Development of Higher Psychological Processes*. Cambridge, MA: Harvard University Press.

Waldinger, Renée, Philip Dawson and Isser Woloch (eds.) 1993 *The French Revolution and the Meaning of Citizenship*. London: Greenwood Press.

Warner, George Townsend and C.H.K. Marten 1912 *The Groundwork of British History, Part II, From the Union of the Crowns to the Present Day* (by C.H.K. Marten). London: Blackie & Son.

Wårvik, Brita 2006 "Grounding." In Jan-Ola Östman and Jef Verschueren (eds.), *Handbook of Pragmatics* (10th annual installment). Amsterdam/Philadelphia: John Benjamins (also available online www.benjamins.nl/online).

Watson, Rod 2009 *Analysing Practical and Professional Texts: A Naturalistic Approach*. Farnham, UK: Ashgate.

Watson, Rod and Jeff Coulter 2008 "The debate over cognitivism." *Theory, Culture & Society* 25:1.1–17.

Weber, Eugen 1977 *Peasants into Frenchmen: The Modernization of Rural France 1870–1914*. London: Chatto & Windus.

Willett, T. 1988 "A cross-linguistic survey of the grammaticalization of evidentiality." *Studies in Language* 12:1.51–97.

Williamson, James A. 1956 *The Foundation and Growth of the British Empire*. London: Macmillan & Co. [1916, revised and expanded editions in 1923, 1932, 1943, 1953].

Wilson, Deirdre 2010 "Relevance theory." In Louise Cummings (ed.), *The Pragmatics Encyclopedia*. London: Routledge, pp. 393–399.

Winch, Peter 1958 *The Idea of a Social Science and Its Relation to Philosophy*. London: Routledge & Kegan Paul.

Wittgenstein, Ludwig 1958 *Philosophical Investigations*. Oxford: Basil Blackwell.

Wodak, Ruth and Michael Meyer (eds.) 2009 *Methods of Critical Discourse Analysis*. London: Sage.

Woloch, Isser 1993 "The right to primary education in the French revolution: From theory to practice." In Waldinger, Dawson and Woloch (eds.) 1993, pp. 137–152.

Woodward, William Harrison 1921 *An Outline History of the British Empire from 1500 to 1920*. Cambridge: Cambridge University Press [1901, 2nd edn. 1912, 3rd edn. 1921].

Woolard, Kathryn A. and Bambi B. Schieffelin 1994 "Language ideology." *Annual Review of Anthropology* 23.55–82.

Yong, Tan Tai 2002 "Sepoys and the colonial state: Punjab and the military base of the Indian army 1849–1900." In Partha Sarathi Gupta and Anirudh Deshpande (eds.), *The British Raj and Its Indian Armed Forces 1857–1939*. Oxford: Oxford University Press, pp. 7–44.

Žižek, Slavoj (ed.) 1989 *The Sublime Object of Ideology*. London: Verso.

(ed.) 1994 *Mapping Ideology*. London: Verso.

2005 *Interrogating the Real*. London/New York: Continuum.

Index

Lightning Source UK Ltd.
Milton Keynes UK
UKOW02f1313050314

227594UK00005B/137/P